lonely planet

Amsterdam

Rob van Driesum
Nikki Hall

LONELY PLANET PUBLICATIONS
Melbourne • Oakland • London • Paris

Amsterdam
3rd edition – March 2002
First published – June 1997

Published by
Lonely Planet Publications Pty Ltd ABN 36 005 607 983
90 Maribyrnong St, Footscray, Victoria 3011, Australia

Lonely Planet offices
Australia Locked Bag 1, Footscray, Victoria 3011
USA 150 Linden St, Oakland, CA 94607
UK 10a Spring Place, London NW5 3BH
France 1 rue du Dahomey, 75011 Paris

Photographs
Many of the images in this guide are available for licensing from
Lonely Planet Images.
Web site: www.lonelyplanetimages.com

Front cover photograph
Busy street scene, Leidsestraat (Ed Pritchard, Getty Images)

ISBN 1 74059 092 9

Printed by The Bookmaker International Ltd
Printed in China

Although the authors and Lonely Planet try to make the information as accurate as possible, we accept no responsibility for any loss, injury or inconvenience sustained by anyone using this book.

Contents – Text

2 Contents – Text

Contents – Maps

The Authors

Rob van Driesum

Rob wrote the 1st edition of this book and coordinated the subsequent editions. This time he updated the front-end chapters, the Things to See & Do and Excursions chapters, and the new Architecture and Cycling Tours sections. He grew up in several Asian and African countries before moving to the Netherlands, where he finished school in The Hague and studied Modern History at the University of Amsterdam. He lived in a canal house on Reguliersgracht for 11 years, studying and working as a history teacher, bartender and freelance journalist to finance his motorcycle travels. A motorcycle journey around the world was cut short in Australia, where he worked as a labourer, flower salesman, truck driver, radio presenter and motorcycle magazine editor before joining Lonely Planet to help set up its range of Europe titles. He eventually became Lonely Planet's Associate Publisher in charge of guidebooks, but after 10 years behind a desk he decided it was time to move on. He now does a bit of authoring and freelance teaching. Though happily ensconced in Mt Macedon outside of Melbourne, which he considers an ideal place to live, he still thinks of Amsterdam as 'home' and an ideal place to visit.

Nikki Hall

Melbourne-based Nikki helped update the last two editions of this book, this time focusing on the Things to See & Do, Places to Stay & Eat, Entertainment and Shopping chapters. She whipped around Amsterdam's canalside streets at cyclonic speeds on her trusty, rusty second-hand bike – with only one major road splat to report. She loves Amsterdam's ever-changing moods, streetscapes and marvellous melange of high and low culture, from ultra-grungy coffeeshops to glitzy 17th-century theatres. Nikki has co-authored Lonely Planet's *Sydney Condensed* and *Amsterdam Condensed* guides and contributed to the Melbourne and Sydney *Out to Eat* restaurant guides. She also turns her hand to article writing for magazines and visual merchandising.

This Book

FROM THE PUBLISHER

Publication of this 3rd edition of *Amsterdam* was coordinated in Lonely Planet's Melbourne office by Shelley Muir (editorial) and Cris Gibcus (mapping and design). Nina Rousseau assisted with editing, and Emma Koch and Quentin Frayne compiled the language chapter. Jenny Jones designed the cover, illustrations were provided by Mick Weldon and Tamsin Wilson, and Mark Germanchis provided layout support. Photographs were supplied by Lonely Planet Images; thanks to Barbara Dombrowski and Brett Pascoe. Grateful thanks to the Amsterdams Historisch Museum and the Rijksmuseum for permission to reproduce artworks.

FROM THE AUTHORS

Rob van Driesum Many people helped with tips and advice, including dozens of readers of the previous edition who provided invaluable feedback – thank you all. Thanks also to the following people: Rommy Albers (for help with the Cinema section), Annemarie Berens (books and literature), Pauline Boomsma, Kees Brouwer and Michaëla Germing (economy and business), Peter van Brummelen (music), Erik van Driesum (last-minute checking), Reinier van den Hout (quirky advice and red herrings), Allard Jolles (urban planning), Doekes Lulofs (general advice and wine), Laura Martz (digital Amsterdam), Mylène van Noort (gay and lesbian Amsterdam), Han Quast (government and politics), Patrice Riemens (a great 'landlord' and source of contacts), Harry van Veenendaal (urban planning) and Els Wamsteeker (tourism and sights).

I'd also like to thank my editor, Shelley Muir, for putting up with this book yet again; my cartographer, Cris Gibcus (an Amsterdam native), for reorganising the maps; and my co-author, Nikki, for her usual enthusiasm and panache (I love her one-liners!). Last but by no means least, a very warm thanks to Liesbeth Blomberg for being so tolerant throughout it all.

Nikki Hall The wonderfully-wise-beyond-her-years Kelly McConville was the finest flatmate a girl could ask for; thanks for your home-cooked meals, helpful telephone translations and nightlife tips. Gallons of gratitude to good friends Alan Lazer (the Pijp's proudest and most pulchritudinous resident), the sweet and stylish Neil Finaughty and John Linseen and Borneo Island's most beautiful couple, Nick Kidman and Marre van Opdorp. My time in Amsterdam was made all the more enjoyable for meeting Mel Koster, Ruud van der Hedge, Daniel Wald, Kim Kornermann, Cathy and Roger Molenkamp. Once again, a special thank you to the super-smooth Roel de Boer, Amsterdam's A1 nightclub informant and always up-for-it club companion.

THANKS
Many thanks to the travellers who used the last edition and wrote to us with helpful hints, advice and interesting anecdotes. Your names appear in the back of this book.

...Y PLANET GUIDEBOOKS

... with a classic travel adventure: Tony and Maureen
.../2 journey across Europe and Asia to Australia. There was
... information about the overland trail then, so Tony and Maureen
p. ...ished the first Lonely Planet guidebook to meet a growing need.

From a kitchen table, Lonely Planet has grown to become the largest
independent travel publisher in the world, with offices in Melbourne
(Australia), Oakland (USA), London (UK) and Paris (France).

Today Lonely Planet guidebooks cover the globe. There is an ever-
growing list of books and information in a variety of media. Some things
haven't changed. The main aim is still to make it possible for adventurous
travellers to get out there – to explore and better understand the world.

At Lonely Planet we believe travellers can make a positive contribu-
tion to the countries they visit – if they respect their host communities
and spend their money wisely. Since 1986 a percentage of the income
from each book has been donated to aid projects and human rights
campaigns, and, more recently, to wildlife conservation.

> Although inclusion in a guidebook usually implies a recommen-dation we cannot list every good place. Exclusion does not necessarily imply criticism. In fact there are a number of reasons why we might exclude a place – sometimes it is simply inappropriate to encourage an influx of travellers.

UPDATES & READER FEEDBACK

Things change – prices go up, schedules change, good places go bad and bad places go bankrupt.
Nothing stays the same. So, if you find things better or worse, recently opened or long-since closed,
please tell us and help make the next edition even more accurate and useful.

Lonely Planet thoroughly updates each guidebook as often as possible – usually every two years,
although for some destinations the gap can be longer. Between editions, up-to-date information
is available in our free, quarterly *Planet Talk* newsletter and monthly email bulletin *Comet*. The
Upgrades section of our website (w www.lonelyplanet.com) is also regularly updated by Lonely
Planet authors, and the site's *Scoop* section covers news and current affairs relevant to travellers.
Lastly, the *Thorn Tree* bulletin board and *Postcards* section carry unverified, but fascinating,
reports from travellers.

Tell us about it! We genuinely value your feedback. A well-travelled team at Lonely Planet reads
and acknowledges every email and letter we receive and ensures that every morsel of information
finds its way to the relevant authors, editors and cartographers.

Everyone who writes to us will find their name listed in the next edition of the appropriate guidebook, and will receive the latest issue of *Comet* or *Planet Talk*. The very best contributions will be
rewarded with a free guidebook.

We may edit, reproduce and incorporate your comments in Lonely Planet products such as guidebooks, websites and digital products, so let us know if you don't want your comments reproduced
or your name acknowledged.

How to contact Lonely Planet:
Online: e talk2us@lonelyplanet.com.au, w www.lonelyplanet.com
Australia: Locked Bag 1, Footscray, Victoria 3011
UK: 10a Spring Place, London NW5 3BH
USA: 150 Linden St, Oakland, CA 94607

Introduction

Amsterdam is a work of art, a living monument with some of Europe's finest 17th- and 18th-century architecture. It's also at the cutting edge of social, cultural and economic developments thanks to its famed tolerance, which brings together people, ideas and products and allows them to flourish.

There's a lively arts scene, fantastic pubs and unrivalled nightlife. Gays and lesbians find the city a breath of fresh air. Affordable restaurants serve food from all corners of the globe. Street artists – musicians, acrobats, fire-eaters – provide ready entertainment. Open-air markets sell anything from food and flowers to funky clothes, disused furniture and 78rpm records, and myriad shops full of quirky items line side streets and alleyways.

Despite the ready availability of sex and drugs there's surprisingly little violent crime. Whoever made this whole affair work has done a great job.

Amsterdam has often been called the Venice of the north, and in many respects the comparison is apt. Venice occupies a lagoon, Amsterdam a marshland where river meets sea, and both have had to struggle with water in order to survive (Venice has 117 islands, 150 canals and 400 bridges; Amsterdam has 90 islands, 160 canals and 1281 bridges). Both were city-states that built far-flung maritime trading empires. Both had a ruling class with strongly republican sentiments, whose wealth rested on money created through commerce and finance, not on inherited land-holdings. Both left a world-class legacy in visual arts.

But there are marked differences: Venice has no road traffic – only pedestrians and a large fleet of busy water craft; Amsterdam has 550,000 bicycles, less road traffic than it used to, and little water transport apart from tourist boats. Venice is an architectural marvel full of tourists, but in the off season the place seems dead; Amsterdam is equally attractive and full of tourists, but in the off season it keeps powering along and shows no signs of slowing down. In short, Amsterdam is a thriving city that's alive in all respects; Venice is a museum with relatively little to sustain itself in the modern age.

The phrase 'cosmopolitan melting pot' is often used carelessly for cities around the world but it is appropriate for Amsterdam,

PAUL BERNSSEN

Amsterdam – a city of picturesque canals and bridges

which has always enticed migrants and non-conformists. Despite (or because of) this transient mix, people accept each other as they are and strive to be *gezellig*, a nigh-untranslatable term that means something like 'chummy' or 'convivial', a mood often experienced by people warmly chatting over a drink or two in a cosy 'brown' café.

The whole city is *gezellig* – buildings are attractive, intimate, very rarely imposing, and pleasantly balanced by tree-lined canals and scattered parks (Amsterdam is Europe's greenest capital city). Everything seems designed on a human scale. The city is compact and easily explored on foot, with frequent and efficient public transport to and from the central canal belt.

The rest of the country is compact too, and is serviced by an efficient train network. Within an hour you can walk along the beach and through magnificent dunes; explore old fishing villages along the IJsselmeer; visit small but proud cities such as Haarlem, Leiden or Delft; admire Europe's most beautiful sculpture garden in the forested Hoge Veluwe national park; shop along the refined streets of The Hague; tour the busiest harbour in the world at Rotterdam; or cycle through endless, brightly coloured fields of blossoming bulbs.

On these sorts of trips you'll realise that Amsterdam is unique even within the Netherlands, with a mix of old and new, moral rectitude and sleaze, and traditional and alternative cultures that visitors both Dutch and foreign find baffling and delightful.

This book provides background reading, advice and tips, but a lot of things happen in Amsterdam that guidebook researchers can't always know about. Go out and discover the place for yourself: few cities are more rewarding.

Facts about Amsterdam

HISTORY
Birth of the City

The oldest archaeological finds in Amsterdam date from Roman times, when the IJ (pronounced as the 'ey' in 'they'), an arm of the shallow Zuiderzee or 'Southern Sea', formed part of the northern borders of the Roman Empire. Coins and a few artefacts betray human presence but there is no evidence of settlement.

This is not surprising because most of the region that later became known as Holland (in the west of the present-day Netherlands) was a soggy land of constantly shifting lakes, swamps and spongy peat lying at or below sea level. Its contours kept changing with fierce autumn storms and floods. This was certainly the case where the Amstel River emptied into the IJ – the site of what was to become Amsterdam.

Isolated farming communities gradually tamed the marshlands with ditches and dikes. Between 1150 and 1300 the south bank of the IJ was diked from the Zuiderzee westwards all the way to Haarlem. Dams were built across the rivers flowing into the IJ, with locks to let water out and boats in. Around 1200 there was a fishing community known as 'Aemstelredamme' – the dam built across the Amstel, at what is now Dam Square.

The distant feudal authorities (the bishop of Utrecht and later the Holy Roman Emperor) cared little for these massive water-engineering feats and the ever-present threat of dike-bursts. So the local inhabitants, under the tutelage of the count of Holland, set up a network of work-and-maintenance groups and pooled their resources against the common foe. This tradition of local democracy and pioneering self-help fostered notions of local autonomy, and no doubt instilled a regard for individual opinions and contributions – precursor perhaps to today's 'polder model' of endless deliberations.

On 27 October 1275 the count of Holland granted toll freedom to those who lived around the Amstel dam, which meant they didn't have to pay tolls to sail through the locks and bridges of Holland. This event stands as the official founding of Amsterdam. The town had obviously become important in the count's power struggle with the bishop of Utrecht, and soon it received city rights – the right to self-government and taxation. Shortly after 1300, the count incorporated the surrounding areas into Holland, severing Amsterdam's ties with the bishopric of Utrecht for good.

Early Trade

The city grew rapidly. Agriculture in this marshland was difficult at the best of times so fishing remained important, but trade provided new growth opportunities. Powerful cities of the day, such as Dordrecht, Utrecht, Haarlem, Delft and Leiden, concentrated on overland trade to and from the burgeoning economies of Flanders and northern Italy. Amsterdam, however, focused on maritime trade in the North and Baltic Seas, which was dominated by the Hanseatic League.

Using cheap timber from Germany and the Baltic regions, Amsterdam's wharves churned out cogs – broad-beamed merchant ships with a capacity of 100 tonnes, five times that of their predecessors. They revolutionised maritime trade and enabled the city to play a key role in the transit trade between Hanseatic cities and southern Europe. The toll freedom helped, too.

Instead of joining the League, Amsterdam's freebooters (from the Dutch word *vrijbuiters*, 'booty-chasers') bypassed prominent Hanseatic cities such as Hamburg and Lübeck and sailed straight to the Baltic themselves, with cargoes of cloth and salt in return for grain and timber. Their efficient transport and acute business sense outclassed the intricate contracts and transport agreements of the Hanseatic merchants.

The Amsterdammers cooperated as their forebears had done when they built dikes, pooling resources into firms that financed ships and spread risk by dividing large and

FACTS ABOUT AMSTERDAM

St Andrew's Crosses & the Cog

Amsterdam's coat of arms consists of three St Andrew's crosses arranged vertically – a wonderfully simple design that is found on anything from VVV tourist brochures to the thousands of brown bollards or 'penises' (so-called *Amsterdammertjes*) that keep cars from parking on pavements. Its origins are unclear, though the St Andrew's Cross itself was a popular symbol in this part of the world before Amsterdam existed.

According to legend, Amsterdam came into being when a damaged boat carrying a Norwegian prince on the run with a Frisian fisherman and his dog was blown into the reeds along the IJ, where they founded Amsterdam. When the city began to engage in Baltic trade it did so with cogs, ships of a late-medieval design known around Europe. The clinker-built (or lapstrake) ves-

St Andrew's crosses, topped by the crown of Holy Roman Emperor Maximilian I

AMSTERDAMS HISTORISCH MUSEUM

sels had a single mast, a rounded bow and stern, fore and after castles and were very broad in the beam. They reduced the cost of transport to a fraction of what it had been with the smaller and less seaworthy ships used previously.

The city authorities gave thanks to the cog by promoting a coat of arms (see left) that consisted of a cog with two men (a soldier and a merchant) and a dog (symbolising loyalty). This survived for several centuries, often depicted together with the St Andrew's crosses, but the crosses proved more durable.

---

valuable cargoes among several ships, thus enabling them to undertake audacious ventures without fear of losing everything in a single shipwreck. This novel form of cooperation was spectacularly successful: by the late 1400s, 60% of ships sailing to and from the Baltic Sea were from Holland, and the vast majority had Amsterdam as their base.

The original harbour in the Damrak and Rokin had been extended into the IJ along what is now Centraal Station. Canals were cut to cater for growing numbers of merchant warehouses – in the 1380s the Oudezijds Voorburgwal and Oudezijds Achterburgwal, as well as the Nieuwezijds Voorburgwal and Nieuwezijds Achterburgwal (the present Spuistraat), then the Geldersekade and Kloveniersburgwal, and around 1500 the Singel (the 'girdle canal' or moat). By then the population numbered 10,000. A great fire in 1452 destroyed three-quarters of the city, including most of the wooden buildings, but it was soon rebuilt, with regulations stipulating the use of brick.

Amsterdam started life as a 'modern' city, a place where skippers, sailors, merchants, artisans and opportunists from the Low Countries (roughly the present-day Netherlands, Belgium and Luxembourg) gained their livelihood through contacts with the outside world. There was no tradition of stable feudal relationships sanctioned by the Church, no distinction between nobility and serfs, and little if any taxation by some far-away monarch. In time, of course, class distinctions did develop based on wealth, with the so-called patricians at the top of the pyramid, but it's fair to say that Amsterdam society was more individualistic and proto-capitalist than others in Europe – even the Italian city-states.

Ironically, Amsterdam was also a city of religious pilgrimage, a 'Canterbury of the Low Countries' thanks to a banal but profitable religious miracle: in 1345 a dying man regurgitated the Host, which was thrown in the fire where it refused to burn. A miracle was proclaimed and soon the city crammed no fewer than 20 monasteries into its confined space, and Holy Roman Emperors such as Maximilian I and Charles V visited to pay their religious respects. In 1489 Maximilian recovered from an illness here and showed his gratitude by allowing the city to use the imperial crown on its documents, buildings and ships.

The Reformation put an end to all this but Amsterdam never became as staunchly Protestant as Holland's other cities – after all, diversity and tolerance were good for trade.

Independent Republic

The northern European Protestant reform movement known as the Reformation was more than just a religious affair: it was a struggle for power between the emerging class of merchants and artisans in the cities on the one hand, and the aristocratic order sanctioned by the established – the 'universal', or 'Catholic' – Church on the other; between 'new money' earned through trade and manufacturing, and 'old money' rooted in land ownership.

The form of Protestantism that took hold in the Low Countries was Calvinism, the most radically moralistic stream. It stressed the might of God as revealed in the Bible and treated humans as sinful creatures whose duty in life was sobriety and hard work. It scorned Church hierarchy and based religious experience on local communities led by lay elders, similar to Presbyterianism in Scotland.

Calvinism was integral to the struggle for independence from the fanatically Catholic Philip II of Spain, who, thanks to the inheritance politics of the day, had acquired the 17 provinces that made up the Low Countries and ruled them as if they were a South American colony. The trouble began in 1566 when a coalition of Catholic and Calvinist nobles petitioned Philip not to introduce the Spanish Inquisition in the Low Countries. Philip refused and the resulting war of independence lasted more than 80 years.

Fanatical Calvinist brigands, who wore the disparaging nickname *geuzen* (beggars)

The Anabaptists

The city authorities promoted tolerance and diversity in the name of trade but ruthlessly persecuted the Anabaptists, a revolutionary Protestant sect of the early 16th century that was strong in Germany and the Low Countries. Anabaptists, influenced by the teachings of Ulrich Zwingli in Zürich, believed that people shouldn't be baptised until they knew the difference between right and wrong; they also believed in a form of communism that included polygamy, and sometimes walked around naked because everyone was equal that way. Martin Luther was appalled and advised his followers to join even with Catholics to suppress the movement.

Many Anabaptists fled from Germany to Amsterdam, where their ideas appealed to the city's artisans in a time of rising prices and stagnating incomes. Their political agenda (a communist state, ruled by the faithful) was fleetingly carried out in the German town of Münster in 1534–35 under the dictatorship of a Dutch tailor, John of Leyden, but the expected world revolution failed to materialise. In Amsterdam a group of Anabaptists occupied the city hall but

John of Leyden

were defeated by the city watch. The survivors had their hearts ripped out and thrown in their faces – uncharacteristically harsh treatment in a city that punished other heretics (eg, Lutherans) by making them take part in Catholic processions. But Anabaptists advocated the abolition of property and called for the overthrow of the state, and this was too much even for the tolerant Amsterdam authorities.

An Anabaptist was last burned at the stake on Dam Square in 1576, the symbolic end of Protestantism's radical fringe. The more moderate Baptists retained the principle of mature baptism but not the Anabaptists' revolutionary politics.

as a badge of honour, roamed from city to city, murdering priests, nuns and Catholic sympathisers and smashing 'papist idolatry' in the churches. Some took to the water as *watergeuzen* and harassed Spanish and other Catholic ships. Amsterdam was caught in the middle: its ruling merchants were pragmatic Catholics, but the merchants who weren't in power adopted Calvinism along with most of the population, who resented the heavy Spanish taxation imposed from Brussels. In 1578 the geuzen captured Amsterdam in a bloodless coup, the so-called Alteration.

With mighty Amsterdam now on their side, the seven northern provinces, led by Holland and Zeeland, formed the Union of Utrecht the following year and declared themselves an independent republic. The union was led by a stadholder (chief magistrate), a role played by William the Silent of the House of Orange, the forefather of today's royal family (dubbed 'the Silent' because he wisely refused to enter into religious debate). The provinces were represented in a parliament, the Estates General, that sat in The Hague. The Seven United Provinces (the republic's official name) became known to the outside world as the Dutch Republic – or simply 'Holland' because of that province's dominance. Within Holland, Amsterdam towered over the other cities put together.

Golden Age (1580–1700)

Amsterdam's fortunes continued to rise when its major trading rival in the Low Countries, the Protestant city of Antwerp, was retaken by the Spaniards. In retaliation, watergeuzen from Zeeland closed off the Scheldt River, which was Antwerp's access to the sea and its trade lifeline. Half the population fled, including the merchants, skippers and artisans who flocked to Amsterdam with trade contacts and silk and printing industries – the world's first regular newspaper, full of trade news from around Europe, was printed in Amsterdam in 1618.

Amsterdam also welcomed persecuted Jews from Portugal and Spain (some via Antwerp) who knew about trade routes to the West and East Indies. They also introduced the diamond industry (fed by Brazilian diamonds) and made Amsterdam a tobacco centre. In later years came Germans who provided a ready source of sailors and labourers; a new wave of Jews from Central and Eastern Europe; and many persecuted Calvinists from France, the enterprising Huguenots. Amsterdam had become a cosmopolitan city where money and pragmatism combined to pioneer new developments in the world economy.

The Bank of Amsterdam

European money in the 16th century was in a mess. There were hundreds of different coins minted by states, cities and even individuals who sometimes tampered with the silver or gold content. Having founded the world's first stock exchange in 1602 to trade in East India Company shares, the Amsterdam authorities realised that a stable, reliable currency was vital if trade was to flourish, and founded the Bank of Amsterdam in the city hall's cellars in 1609.

The bank accepted coins in any currency from anyone, assessed their gold or silver content, and allowed the depositor to withdraw the equivalent amount in gold florins minted by the bank. A *gulden florijn* – hence *gulden*, or guilder, and the abbreviation *f* or *fl* – was of fixed weight and purity, and was soon sought as 'real' money throughout Europe and parts of Asia, Africa and the Americas.

Depositors could also draw cheques against their accounts, which were guaranteed by the government, and take out loans at regulated interest rates. Amsterdam thus attracted capital far and wide, and remained the financial centre of Europe until Napoleon ruined the show and London took over.

The stable *gulden florijn*, or gold florin, became a currency of choice throughout Europe and beyond.

Money reigned supreme and Amsterdam was not averse to trading with the enemy. Spanish armies were paid with money borrowed from Amsterdam banks and fed on Baltic grain imported through Amsterdam; wrecked Spanish fleets including the Armada were rebuilt with timber supplied by Amsterdam merchants. Amsterdam shrewdly avoided land battles and was never raided by Spanish troops like so many other Dutch cities were.

Meanwhile the city kept growing – in 1600 the population numbered 50,000, by 1650 it was 150,000 and from 1700 it stabilised at around 220,000. In the 1580s land was reclaimed from the IJ and Amstel to the east (the current Nieuwmarkt neighbourhood). Two decades later, work began on the famous canal belt that more than tripled the area of the city.

By 1600, Dutch ships dominated seaborne trade between (and often along) England, France, Spain and the Baltic, and had a virtual monopoly on North Sea fishing and Arctic whaling.

Meanwhile, Portugal and Spain built trading empires beyond Europe. Some of this trade flowed to Amsterdam through the port of Lisbon until Spain conquered Portugal in 1580 and closed Lisbon to Dutch ships. Thanks to Jewish refugees, however, Dutch mariners learned something about distant trade routes and soon they plied the world's oceans, acquiring navigational intelligence of their own.

They searched in vain for an Arctic route to the Pacific and rounded the tip of South America instead, naming it Cape Horn after the city of Hoorn north of Amsterdam. In 1619, Dutch traders expelled the Portuguese from the Moluccas (the so-called Spice Islands) in what is now Indonesia, and established the town of Batavia (Latin for Holland, now Jakarta) as administrative centre for what was to become the Dutch East Indies. Five years later they founded a trading post on Manhattan Island called New Amsterdam, the future New York. They set up posts along the west coast of Africa, established plantations in South America and the Caribbean, and took a keen interest in the slave trade.

Merchants & Burgomasters

The city government during Amsterdam's Golden Age was headed by four burgomasters *(burgemeesters)*, or mayors, who were elected for a one-year period. Their power was almost unlimited, although judicial matters were handled by a *schout* (sheriff) and nine *schepenen* (magistrates) who were also elected for one-year periods. The electing was done by a *vroedschap* (council) of 36 *burgers* (citizens) who had to be consulted on important matters.

These officials and 'citizens' almost always came from the wealthiest merchant families, the so-called patrician class, who made sure they stayed in control through co-optation and nepotism and so cultivated a new aristocracy in all but name. Nevertheless, the division of power and the annual elections meant that a lot of politicking went on, with constantly shifting coalitions and factions, and government was probably as democratic as it could get in those days. It was also remarkably efficient and competent, at least until about 1700 when self-serving lethargy took over.

Order was upheld by several *schutterijen* (citizen militias) that were also dominated by patricians. Rembrandt's famous *Nightwatch* (a name later given to the painting because it had become so dirty) shows one of these militias in full regalia.

The Dutch competed with the Spaniards for control of Formosa (Taiwan) and gained the upper hand there in 1641. That year Japan expelled all foreigners except the Dutch, who received sole trading rights on an island at Nagasaki because their aims were clearly commercial rather than territorial or religious. In 1652 they captured the Cape of Good Hope from the Portuguese, a crucial staging post in trade with the East Indies. There they established one of the few colonies to attract Dutch settlers in significant numbers (the East Indies overtook it in later years), and the only colony apart from Suriname and the Antilles where Dutch language and culture persist to this day. They booted the Portuguese out of Ceylon (Sri Lanka) soon after. They also explored the coastlines of New

Zealand (named after the province of Zeeland) and New Holland (known as Australia since the 1850s) but found nothing of value there and focused their resources elsewhere.

The Dutch were traders first and foremost and didn't have the population reserves for the settler-type colonisation pursued by other European powers. They were often welcomed by local rulers who had suffered the missionary and imperial zeal of earlier colonists. Dutch traders consolidated their settlements with divide-and-rule tactics, bribery, gunship diplomacy and, where necessary, local mercenary forces. They also engaged in piracy, especially against the Spaniards, with whom they were theoretically at war until the Peace of Münster, one of the treaties comprising the Peace of Westphalia in 1648.

These overseas ventures were financed by merchants and other investors who pooled their resources in trading companies: the United East India Company (Vereenigde Oostindische Compagnie, or VOC) founded in 1602, which pursued trade in India and the Far East; and the West India Company (WIC, 1621), which ran plantations in the Americas and soon controlled half the world's slave trade.

Despite the glamour of these expeditions and the exotic products that became commodities back home (coffee, tea, spices, tobacco, cotton, silk, porcelain), most of Amsterdam's wealth was still generated by the mundane fishing industry and European trade. In the 1590s Amsterdam's shipwrights introduced the flûte (from the Dutch *fluyt*), a small supply vessel that could be sailed by 10 people instead of the 30 required for ships of similar size – perfect for coastal freight. Around 1650 the Dutch had more seagoing merchant vessels than England and France combined, and half of all ships sailing between Europe and Asia were Dutch.

It still seems a bit of a mystery why tiny Amsterdam played such a prominent role on the world stage (Venice at the height of its power was an overture by comparison) but several factors helped. Both England and France were beset by internal troubles, and Spain was far too busy managing its overstretched colonial empire. Meanwhile, Dutch freight was unrivalled in terms of cost and efficiency thanks to a combination of cheap Baltic hemp and timber, Europe's largest shipbuilding industry, abundant investment capital supplied by thousands of

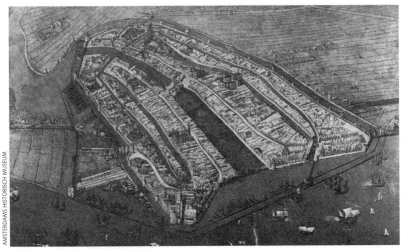

AMSTERDAMS HISTORISCH MUSEUM

Bird's-eye view of Amsterdam, looking southwards, painted in 1538 by Cornelis Anthonisz. This is the oldest surviving 'map' of the city.

The First Multinationals

The United East India Company (VOC) and West India Company (WIC) were the world's first multinationals. Their trading posts around the globe operated with a great degree of autonomy. They were authorised to negotiate with local rulers on behalf of the Dutch Republic, to pursue trade opportunities as they saw fit, to build forts and to raise local militias. More than 1000 shareholders back home – not only merchants but also artisans, clergy, shopkeepers and even servants – contributed capital for ships and trade ventures, thus spreading risk and reaping rewards through generous annual dividends when risks paid off.

The VOC was founded to coordinate the often competing trade efforts of cities in Holland and Zeeland. It consisted of six 'chambers' representing Amsterdam, Middelburg, Delft, Rotterdam, Hoorn and Enkhuizen, and was supervised by 17 directors (the Heeren XVII, or '17 Gentlemen') on behalf of the shareholders. Because of the high degree of risk and long turnaround times in trade with the East, the VOC's shareholders tended to be people with money to spare – usually wealthy merchants based in Amsterdam, who owned more than half the VOC's shares.

The WIC consisted of five 'chambers' supervised by 19 directors. Trade in the Atlantic was less risky and had shorter turnaround times but offered a lower rate of return. The WIC attracted small investors, particularly in Zeeland. Competition from Spain and Portugal (and later Britain and France) was fierce, and the WIC's expenditures often outstripped income. The company relied on state subsidies to conquer and defend its sugar plantations and slave ports, and was thus more truly colonial than the VOC. As with the VOC, more than half the WIC's shares were owned in Amsterdam, but there was more internal bickering and jealousy between Holland and Zeeland.

---

shareholders, and low wages for sailors, many of whom had small farming plots north of Amsterdam.

England, however, began to flex its muscle and in 1651 passed the first of several Navigation Acts: goods shipped to England and its colonies had to be carried in English ships, or ships of the country where the goods originated. This posed a serious threat to the Dutch transit trade, and the two countries fought several naval wars that were generally inconclusive, though the Dutch lost New Amsterdam. Louis XIV of France took the opportunity to march into the Low Countries, where he occupied the Spanish provinces in the south and three of the seven republican provinces in the north during what was known as the 'Disaster Year' of 1672.

The Dutch rallied behind their stadholder, William III of Orange, who repelled the French with the help of Austria, Spain and Brandenburg (Prussia). A consummate politician, William then supported the Protestant factions in England against their Catholic King James II, who was to all intents and purposes in Louis XIV's employ. In 1688

William invaded England, where he and his wife, Mary Stuart (James II's Protestant daughter – the plot thickens), were proclaimed king and queen.

After this, England played a key role in checking France's expansion on the Continent. It is ironic that the military leader of the Dutch Republic, denied a throne at home because of Amsterdam's opposition, became king of a foreign country and thus ensured the Republic's survival.

Wealthy Decline (1700–1814)

The dramatic events in the second half of the 17th century stretched the Republic's resources to the limit, and its naval heroism made way for peace at all costs – a combination of neutrality and bribery. The Republic didn't have the human resources to keep meeting France and England head-on but at least it had Amsterdam's money to hold them off and ensure freedom of the seas. Money became more important than trade as merchants began to invest their fortunes more securely, often in the form of loans to foreign governments.

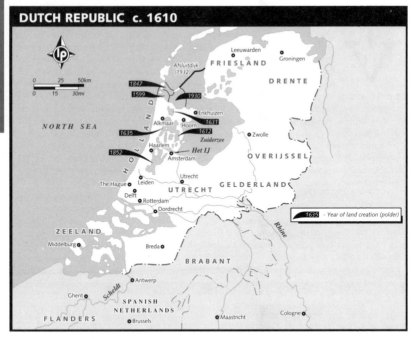

DUTCH REPUBLIC c. 1610

1635 - Year of land creation (polder)

The result in the 18th century was stagnation. Gone were the heady days of daring sea voyages to unknown lands, of new trading posts and naval expeditions against the Spaniards, of monumental achievements in art, science and technology, of pioneering forms of government and finance. The cosmopolitan melting pot of Amsterdam, where everything was possible if it turned a profit, became a lethargic place where wealth creation was a matter of interest rates. It was still the wealthiest city in Europe and Dutch freight was still the cheapest, but the 17th-century ambition to conquer the world was gone. Harbours such as London and Hamburg became powerful rivals.

The decline in trade brought poverty to those without money in the bank, among them many Jews who had escaped pogroms in Germany and Poland – between 1700 and 1800, the proportion of Jews in Amsterdam's population increased from 3% to 10%. To compound matters, the 18th century brought

a mini ice age over Europe, with exceptionally cold winters that made for colourful paintings of skating scenes but also hampered transport and led to serious food shortages. The winters of 1740 and 1763 were so severe that some Amsterdam residents froze to death and many suffered thirst – the canals doubled as sewers and clean water supplies from elsewhere had come to a halt.

The ruling patrician class became ever more corrupt and self-centred, and there was intense political bickering between patricians, Orangists (monarchists) and a new-generation middle class with enlightened ideals, the so-called Patriots.

Amsterdam's rulers naively supported the American War of Independence, resulting in a British blockade of the Dutch coast followed by British conquests of Dutch trading posts around the world. The West India Company folded in 1791, and the mighty East India Company, which once controlled European trade with Asia, went bankrupt in 1800.

Majestic Centraal Station, the transport hub of the city, designed by Pierre Cuypers

Reflections in canals

Opulent mansion along Singelgracht

Magna Plaza shopping centre, formerly the GPO

Nationaal Monument on Dam Square

Royal Palace on Dam Square, the historic heart of the city

Amsterdam's patricians eventually allied themselves with Orangists against the Patriots, who had become emboldened by the American example and were ever more vocal in their democratic demands. A Patriot coup in Amsterdam in 1787 was put down by Prussian troops who had come to the aid of William V of Orange. By now, Amsterdam's leadership of the Dutch Republic was over.

In 1794, French revolutionary troops invaded the Low Countries, and marched straight across frozen rivers that should have formed a natural barrier. They were accompanied by exiled Patriots who helped the French install a Batavian Republic, transforming the fragmented 'united provinces' into a centralised state with Amsterdam as its capital.

In 1806 this republic became a monarchy when Napoleon nominated his brother Louis Napoleon as king. In 1808 the city prostrated itself by offering the grand city hall on Dam Square, symbol of the wealth and power of the merchant Republic, as a palace to the new king. Two years later Napoleon dismissed his uncooperative brother and annexed the Netherlands into the French Empire.

Britain responded to Napoleon's conquests by blockading the Continent and occupying the Dutch colonies on behalf of William V. In turn, Napoleon prohibited all trade with Britain and tried to make the Continent self-sufficient with France as its hub – the so-called Continental System. Amsterdam's trade, already in decline, came to a complete halt along with its important fishing industry. Dutch society turned to agriculture and Amsterdam became a local market town.

Republicans & Monarchists

Contrary to the European trend, the Netherlands began life as a republic and regressed to a monarchy. The Dutch Republic was a loose federation of autonomous provinces dominated by cities, with almighty Amsterdam determining foreign policy and influencing most other things the weak central government did. Amsterdam's role was similar to that played by Athens among the ancient Greek city-states, except that there was no Sparta to act as a counterweight. There was, however, the stadholder, the chief magistrate of the Republic and the military leader of the revolt against Spain. After William the Silent's assassination the mantle passed to his son, who in turn passed it on to his, thus laying the foundations for a monarchy under the House of Orange. This was not to the liking of the patricians of Amsterdam who had established their own oligarchy based on trade wealth and were not about to have this taxed by some monarch.

William the Silent

Dutch politics between 1580 and 1800 seesawed between the republican (and 'pacifist', pro-business) sentiments of Amsterdam's ruling elite and the monarchistic, 'militaristic' aspirations of the House of Orange. The latter faction was often supported by the poorest classes of society and the many cities who were keen to keep 'arrogant' Amsterdam in its place. In 1673, in the midst of war against France, the provinces (with the sole exception of Holland) voted to make the office of stadholder hereditary in the House of Orange, but Amsterdam's influence was strong enough to keep the state a republic until Napoleon installed his brother as king in 1806.

Under French occupation the provinces became a unitary state with Amsterdam as its capital. In 1813 the French left, and in 1814 William VI of Orange was proclaimed King William I of the Netherlands in Amsterdam's Nieuwe Kerk.

After Napoleon's defeat at Leipzig in 1813, the French troops left Amsterdam peacefully. William V had died in exile, but his son returned to Holland and was crowned King of the Netherlands in the Nieuwe Kerk in 1814. The city hall became the new king's palace and has remained with the House of Orange ever since. The Britons returned the Dutch East Indies but kept the Cape of Good Hope and Ceylon. Amsterdam's seaborne economy recovered only slowly from Napoleon's disastrous Continental System and Britain now dominated the seas.

New Infrastructure (1814–1918)

The new kingdom included present-day Belgium which fought for its independence in 1831. Apart from this incident, Amsterdam in the first half of the 19th century was a sleepy place. Its harbour had been neglected, and the sand banks in the IJ, which were always an obstacle in the past, proved too great a barrier for modern ships. Rotterdam was set to become the country's premier port.

Things began to look up again as the rail system took shape – the country's first railway, between Amsterdam and Haarlem, opened in 1839. Major infrastructure projects were funded by the notorious 'culture system' in the East Indies – forced, large-scale production of tropical crops for export, overseen by the VOC and WIC's successor, the Netherlands Trading Society. Trade with the East Indies was now the backbone of Amsterdam's economy. The North Sea Canal between Amsterdam and IJmuiden, built between 1865 and 1876, and later the Merwede Canal to the Rhine (expanded into the Amsterdam-Rhine Canal after WWII) also allowed the city to benefit from the industrial revolution at home and in Germany.

The harbour was expanded to the east. The diamond industry boomed after the discovery of diamonds in South Africa. Amsterdam again attracted immigrants and its population, which had declined in the Napoleonic era, doubled in the second half of the 19th century, passing the half-million mark by 1900. Speculators hastily erected new housing estates beyond the canal belt – dreary, shoddily built tenement blocks with minimal facilities.

In 1889 the city was literally cut off from its harbour by the massive Centraal Station, built on a series of artificial islands in the IJ. Commentators at the time saw this as the symbolic severing of Amsterdam's ties with the sea. An open waterfront was no longer considered vital to the city's survival, and in the closing years of the 19th century some of its major waterways (Damrak, Rokin, Nieuwezijds Voorburgwal) and smaller canals were filled in, both for hygienic reasons (after several cholera epidemics) and to allow for increased road traffic. Plans to fill in more canals were shelved amid mounting criticism of 'ostentatious boulevards'.

The Netherlands remained neutral in WWI but Amsterdam's trade with the East Indies suffered from naval blockades. There were riots over food shortages, exacerbated by refugees from Belgium, but on the whole things could have been worse. There was even an attempt to extend the socialist revolutions in Russia and Germany to the Netherlands but this was quickly put down by loyalist troops.

Boom & Depression (1918–40)

After the war Amsterdam remained the country's industrial centre, with a wide range of enterprises that fed each other. Its shipbuilding industry was no longer the world leader, but the Dutch Shipbuilding Company still operated the world's second-largest wharf and helped carry an extensive steel and diesel-motor industry. The harbour handled tropical produce that was finished locally (tobacco into cigars, copra into margarine, cocoa into chocolate – Amsterdam is still the world's main distribution centre for cocoa).

In 1920 the KLM (Koninklijke Luchtvaart Maatschappij – Royal Aviation Company) began the world's first regular air service, between Amsterdam and London, from an airstrip south of the city and bought many of its planes from Anthony Fokker's aircraft factory north of the IJ. There were two huge breweries, a sizable clothing industry, and even a local car factory that produced the venerable Spijker. The 1920s were boom years for Amsterdam, crowned by the Olympic Games hosted in 1928.

The population kept growing until it reached 700,000 in the mid-1920s, still the figure today. The city had already begun expanding north of the IJ, with housing projects for harbour workers and dockers in the new suburb of Amsterdam North. Then it expanded southwards, filling in the area between the Amstel and what was to become the Olympic Stadium.

Unfortunately the world depression in the 1930s hit Amsterdam hard. Unemployment rose to 25% and would have risen further if the East Indies hadn't borne the brunt of the misery. Labour party members, who dominated the city council, resigned in protest at public-service salary cuts, and the conservative, spend-nothing national government of Hendrik Colijn (the Herbert Hoover of the Netherlands) had free reign.

Public-works projects such as the Amsterdamse Bos (a recreational area south-west of the city) did little to defuse mounting tensions between socialists, communists and the small but vocal party of Dutch fascists. The fascists' influence on national politics was negligible, but they gained a few seats in the Amsterdam council elections of 1939 and had strong support among colonists in the East Indies. The city received some 25,000 Jewish refugees from Germany, although a shamefully large number were turned back at the border because of the Netherlands' neutrality policy.

WWII (1940–45)

The Netherlands tried to stay neutral in WWII but Germany had other plans and invaded in May 1940. For the first time in almost 400 years the population of Amsterdam experienced the grim realities of war first-hand. Few wanted to believe that things would turn nasty, and when the German occupiers began to introduce anti-Jewish measures they did so in a series of carefully staged small steps. In February 1941 Amsterdam's working class finally came out in force to support their Jewish compatriots in a general strike led by dockworkers, but the strike was soon put down and by then it was already too late.

At the start of the war Amsterdam had 90,000 Jews, more than half the Jews in the country. Only one in seven Dutch Jews survived the war, but in Amsterdam the survivors numbered only one in 16. It was the highest proportion of Jews murdered anywhere in Western Europe, though this sad fact was effectively whitewashed after the war by Anne Frank's diary which created the impression that Amsterdam hid its Jews.

Historians are still grappling for an explanation because anti-Semitic feeling was not particularly strong among the Dutch and they didn't care much for fascism. Yet the occupiers could count on the cooperation of local police and public servants, efficient as ever and armed with Europe's most sophisticated population register. Perhaps the ingrained – some would say Calvinist – ethos of order and propriety told them to shun the futile grand gesture, to retreat within their homes and mind their own business in order to survive. Even the Jewish Council cooperated.

The Germans cultivated such compliance by treating the country relatively leniently at first, strengthening people's hopes that things would be all right if they avoided trouble. The resistance movement, set up by an unlikely alliance of Calvinists and Communists, only became large-scale when the increasingly desperate Germans began to round up able-bodied men to work in Germany, shattering the sanctity of home and family.

The severe winter of 1944–45 was the Hunger Winter. The Allies had liberated the south of the country but were checked at Arnhem and decided to concentrate on their push into Germany, thus isolating the north-west and Amsterdam. Coal shipments from the south ceased, men aged between 17 and 50 had gone into hiding or worked in Germany if they had no dispensation, public utilities ground to a halt, and the Germans began to plunder anything that could help their war effort. Dark, freezing Amsterdam suffered severe famine and thousands died. In May 1945, at the very end of the war in Europe, Canadian troops finally liberated the city.

Postwar Growth (1945–62)

The city's growth resumed after the war, with US aid (through the Marshall Plan) and newly discovered fields of natural gas compensating for the loss of the East Indies, which became independent Indonesia after a four-year fight. The focus of the harbour moved westwards, towards the widened North Sea Canal that had provided access to the sea since the 1932 completion of the Afsluitdijk – the 30km-long barrier dam between North Holland and Friesland that closed off the Zuiderzee and turned it into the IJsselmeer (IJssel Lake). The long-awaited Amsterdam-Rhine Canal opened in 1952.

Massive apartment blocks arose in areas annexed to the west of the city – Bos en Lommer, Osdorp, Geuzenveld, Slotermeer and Slotervaart – to meet the continued demand for housing, made ever more acute by the demographic shift away from extended families. The massive Bijlmermeer housing project (now called the Bijlmer) south-east of the city, begun in the mid-1960s and finished in the 1970s, was built in a similar vein.

Cultural Revolution (1962–82)

In the early 1960s Amsterdam began to undergo a cultural revolution that lasted 20 years and was at the cutting edge of similar developments abroad. It was fuelled by interaction between a conservative established order that was tolerant of (but didn't necessarily like) alternative views, and the tradition of incorporating such views into the structure of society.

Over the previous 80 years Dutch society had become characterised by *verzuiling* ('pillarisation'), a social order sanctioned by the 1917 'Pacification' compromise in which each religion and/or political persuasion achieved the right to do its own thing, with its own schools, political parties, trade unions, cultural institutions, sports clubs etc. Each persuasion represented a pillar that supported the status quo in a general 'agreement to disagree'. This elegant solution for a divided society in the 19th and early 20th centuries, however, was overtaken by a society where the old divisions were increasingly irrelevant. In the 1960s people began to question the status quo and the pillars came tumbling down.

Provos & the 'Magic Centre' The first group to rattle the structure were the Provos, successors to the local beatniks, whose core consisted of a small group of anarchic individuals. They staged 'happenings' – creative, playful provocations (hence, Provos) that elicited senseless and disproportionately harsh police reprisals. These polarised public opinion and led even the older generation to wonder whether this was what they had stood for during the war. See the boxed text for further details on them.

The Provos won a seat in the municipal elections of 1966, much to the horror of some of the creative anarchists at the heart of the movement. In the summer of 1967, they buried Provo in the Vondelpark with a ceremony involving a coffin. However, their representative in the city council, Roel van Duijn, kept alive their concerns about urban congestion and pollution.

As society broke out of its prewar framework, Amsterdam became Europe's 'Magic Centre', an exciting place where anything was possible. The late 1960s saw an influx of hippies smoking dope at the Nationaal Monument on Dam Square, unrolling sleeping bags in the Vondelpark, and tripping in the nightlife hot spots of Paradiso, Fantasia and the Melkweg.

It was also a time of upheaval in the universities, with students demanding a greater say and, in 1969, occupying the Maagdenhuis on Spui Square, the administrative centre of the University of Amsterdam. The women's movement took hold: the Dolle Minas ('Mad Minas', after the radical late-19th-century Dutch feminist Wilhelmina Drucker) began a *Baas in eigen Buik* ('Boss in own Belly') campaign that fuelled the abortion debate throughout the 1970s.

Kabouters The Provos' successors called themselves kabouters (gnomes), after the helpful, bearded gnomes of Dutch folklore. In 1970 they proclaimed an Orange Free State on Dam Square, an alternative city populated by caring people preoccupied with the environment. In the elections that year they won five seats in the Amsterdam city council and several more in other cities. Kabouter idealism soon fell victim to the grim realities of urban politics, but many of their ideals – such as banning cars from the city centre to foster

The Protesting Provos

The *Lieverdje* (Little Darling) on Spui Square, an appropriate focus for campaigns by the Provos against addictive consumerism

The Provos awoke Dutch society from its slumber in the 1960s with their street 'happenings'. In 1962 a self-professed window cleaner and sorcerer, Robert Jasper Grootveld, began to deface cigarette billboards with a huge letter 'K' (for *kanker*, cancer) in order to expose the role of advertising in addictive consumerism by the *klootjesvolk* ('narrow-minded populace'). He held get-togethers in his garage – dressed as a medicine man and chanting antismoking mantras under the influence of pot – which attracted other bizarre types, such as the poet Johnny van Doorn, aka Johnny the Selfkicker, who bombarded his audience with frenzied, stream-of-consciousness recitals; Bart Huges, who drilled a hole in his forehead – a so-called 'third eye' – to relieve pressure on his brain and attain permanently expanded consciousness; and Rob Stolk, a rebellious, working-class printer, whose streetwise tactics came to the fore when the get-togethers moved to the streets.

In the summer of 1965 the venue of choice was the rather appropriate *Lieverdje* ('Little Darling') on Spui Square, the endearing statuette of an Amsterdam street-brat donated to the city by a cigarette company. The police, unsure of how to deal with 'public obstructions' by excited young folk chanting unintelligible (and indeed often meaningless) slogans around 'medicine man' Grootveld, responded the only way they knew: with the baton and arbitrary arrests.

The pub terraces lining the square were a favourite haunt of journalists, resulting in eyewitness accounts of senseless police brutality against kids having fun. Soon it seemed the whole country was engaged in heated debate for and against the authorities. The generation gap was only part of it: many of the older generation, uneasy about how little had changed after the war, came out in favour of the Provos and could not understand why the authorities had so completely lost the plot.

Throughout 1965 and 1966 the Provos maintained the initiative with a series of White Plans to protect the environment, including the famous White Bicycle Plan to tackle the city's traffic congestion with a fleet of free white bicycles. They symbolically donated a white bicycle that was promptly confiscated by the police.

Provos were at the centre of public protests against the wedding on 10 March 1966 of Princess Beatrix and the congenial German diplomat Claus von Amsberg, who had served in Hitler's army. The princess insisted on getting married in Amsterdam, against the advice of the mayor. In spite of massive security precautions a live chicken was hurled at the royal coach, smoke bombs ignited as the procession made its way along Raadhuisstraat, and bystanders chanted 'my bicycle back' – a reference to the many bikes commandeered by German soldiers in the final months of the war. Scuffles and police charges were beamed out live on TV.

The following June, Provos supported construction workers in a violent strike in which one of the workers died of a heart attack. The resulting political fallout led to the dismissal by the national government in The Hague of Amsterdam's chief of police and later the mayor himself.

an inner city where people could live, work and shop – became widely accepted.

In the early 1970s, while city planners were still preoccupied with vast apartment blocks in the suburbs populated by commuters who worked in offices in the city centre, the public mood was shifting. A projected motorway from the south-east to the IJ-Tunnel and Centraal Station – the wide Weesperstraat and Wibautstraat are ugly reminders – was stopped by public protests from intruding any farther into the city.

Metro & Nieuwmarkt The fiercest conflict between arrogant planners and disaffected Amsterdammers involved the metro line through the Nieuwmarkt neighbourhood. The original plans for the huge Bijlmermeer housing project south-east of the city called for a four-line metro network, though this was eventually whittled down to a single line between the Bijlmermeer and Centraal Station. The available technology did not yet allow tunnelling through swampy ground, and a large portion of the derelict Nieuwmarkt had to be razed so caissons could be lowered. The inhabitants, many of them former Provos and kabouters who had settled there as *krakers* (squatters), refused to leave and turned the area into a fortress. The Nieuwmarkt was eventually cleared with much violence on 'Blue Monday', 24 March 1975. Some 30 people were injured, most of them policemen, and it was surprising that no-one was killed.

The Nieuwmarkt episode was a watershed: in the following years the council set about renovating inner-city neighbourhoods and providing new housing there. Nieuwmarkt itself was rebuilt, not with the planned office complexes and luxury apartments but with affordable council houses. The metro opened in 1980, with wall paintings in Nieuwmarkt station commemorating the events five years earlier.

Squatters Meanwhile families still deserted the city and the demographic balance continued to shift towards the elderly and the young – small households with modest incomes whose housing needs outstripped the council's efforts to meet them. The housing shortage fuelled a speculative trend, particularly within the desirable canal belt, which pushed free-market rents – let alone the cost of buying a house – out of reach of the average citizen. The waiting period for a council apartment was anything up to five years.

Many young people saw squatting as the only solution, and buildings left empty by speculators (or assumed speculators) provided an appropriate target. Existing legislation made eviction difficult, giving rise to the phenomenon of *knokploegen*, or 'fighting groups' of tracksuited heavies sent by owners to evict squatters by force. The squatters of the late 1970s, however, were of a new generation, less ideologically or politically motivated than their predecessors and more prepared to defend personal needs with barricades and a well-organised support network.

In February 1980 police evicted squatters from an empty office at Vondelstraat 72. Hundreds of squatters retook the building and erected street barricades that were eventually cleared by tanks fitted with bulldozer blades. A few months later, on 30 April, Queen Beatrix was crowned in the Nieuwe Kerk and the squatting movement vented its anger with a large demonstration that soon got out of hand. Literally everyone who was out on the streets that day had tears in their eyes – not for joy over the coronation but from tear gas that hung thick in the air. The term 'proletarian shopping', a euphemism for looting, entered the national lexicon. Never before or since has Amsterdam experienced rioting on such a scale.

In the following months and years several famous squats made world headlines, but the movement was weakened by internal power struggles and became more and more isolated. 'Ordinary' Amsterdammers, initially sympathetic towards exposure of the housing shortage, became fed up with violent riots, such as the three-day rampage (complete with burning tram) that followed the clearing of the 'Lucky Luyk' villa in the Jan Luyckenstraat in October 1982.

Law-abiding citizens who waited years for council accommodation watched squatters jump the queue and grab choice living space. Squatters often reached rental agreements with the owners or were bribed to leave peacefully. Sometimes the council bought the building so the squatters could stay with subsidised rents. By the mid-1980s the movement had little or no outside support and was all but dead. Squatting still takes place now, but the rules of the game are clear and the mood is far less confrontational.

New Consensus (1982–2000)

Twenty years after the first Provo 'happenings' on Spui Square, Amsterdam's cultural revolution had run its course. Gone were the days of unbridled growth for growth's sake, of autocratic government, of arrogant planners and grandiose housing schemes in distant suburbs, of motorways and parking garages in the heart of the city, of demolition of old neighbourhoods.

A new consensus had arrived, epitomised by the amiable mayor of the time, Ed van Thijn. The ideals were decentralised government through neighbourhood councils; a livable city integrating work, schools and shops within walking distance (or at least cycling distance); a city no longer strangled by cars; renovation rather than demolition; friendly neighbourhood police on hybrid bikes; a practical, non-moralistic approach towards drugs; and legal recognition of homosexual couples. The 1980s saw an unprecedented peak in the construction of social housing, with 40,000 affordable apartments easing the plight of 100,000 house-hunters.

Thanks to this new consensus, the opening of the combined city hall and opera house in 1986 passed relatively peacefully, although opposition had been anything but peaceful when it was planned and built. This monstrosity, dominating the Amstel waterfront at what used to be the heart of the Jewish quarter on Waterlooplein, had attracted much criticism for its size and hybrid design. Opponents dubbed it the Stopera – pronounced 'stowpera', a contraction of *stadhuis* (city hall) and opera, and of 'Stop the Opera' – and the name has stuck. But it proved to be the last project to arouse such passions.

Amsterdam had changed as it entered the calm 1990s. Families and small manufacturing industries, which dominated inner-city neighbourhoods in the early 1960s, had been replaced by tertiary-sector professionals and a service industry of pubs, 'coffeeshops', restaurants and hotels. The ethnic make-up had changed too: Surinamese, Moroccans, Turks and Antillians, once a small minority, now comprised 25% of the population, and including other non-Dutch nationalities it was 45%. Meanwhile, the city's success in attracting large foreign businesses (see the later Economy section) was resulting in a large influx of higher-income expatriates.

The Power of Money (2000–)

Partly as a result of these shifts, it seems that money is back in favour in 21st-century Amsterdam and anything is possible, so long as it's 'sensibly' planned and all stakeholders are consulted.

The harbour has a new lease of life with petrochemical industries and container transshipment, and is moving ever farther westwards. Schiphol airport is booming and running out of space to expand. The same applies to Amsterdam in general and the new catch phrase is *inbreiding*, 'inspansion' – turning old industrial complexes and docklands into (often very expensive) housing estates. The eastern harbour areas have rapidly been transformed in this way, and the same has begun to happen in the old western harbour districts. New land has been reclaimed in the IJmeer out to the east, a major focus for development in the coming decade.

New office towers are arising to the southeast, south and west of the city around the completed ring freeway, including the largest office complex in the country, the new ABN-AMRO head office in the southern section which defies architectural convention by being wider at the upper floors than at ground level. Amsterdam's first baby skyscraper, the 165m Rembrandttoren (Rembrandt Tower), owned by the Nedlloyd insurance company, arose along the Amstel next to Amstelstation in the late 1990s. Its 'lighthouse' spire topped by a bright light bulb can be seen from almost anywhere and no-one seems to mind its presence – quite astonishing, considering what public attitudes would have been if this had been tried 20 years ago. The neighbouring Mondriaantoren and Breitnertoren were completed in 2001 – the latter houses the new Philips head office, decamped from Eindhoven in the south of the country.

The metro network is back on the agenda, with new technology allowing tunnelling through swampy ground. A line from Amsterdam North through the city to the World Trade Centre in the south should open in 2009.

Tourists keep flocking to the city – only London, Paris and Rome attract more of them in Europe. But in spite of all the frantic building activity of the past 20 years, the lack of affordable tourist accommodation shows that the housing shortage remains Amsterdam's most pressing problem.

GEOGRAPHY

Much of the land around Amsterdam is *polder*, land that used to be at the bottom of lakes or the sea. It was reclaimed by building dikes across sea inlets or across rivers feeding lakes, and pumping the water out with windmills (later with steam and diesel pumps). Polders were created on a massive scale: in this century for instance, huge portions of the former Zuiderzee (now the IJsselmeer, a lake closed off from the sea by the Afsluitdijk) were surrounded by dikes and the water was pumped out to create vast swathes of flat and fertile agricultural land – the complete province of Flevoland, northeast of Amsterdam, was reclaimed from the sea. For more on water management, see Cleaning the Canals in the following Ecology & Environment section.

Peat & Piles

Amsterdam, that big city, is built on piles/And if that city were to fall over, who would pay for it?
Dutch nursery rhyme

Amsterdam sits on a mixture of spongy peat and clay resting on a stable layer of sand more than 12m down. The first wooden houses were simply placed on top of the peat and occasionally had to be raised as they sank. When heavier brick and stone replaced wood, engineers perfected the art of driving wooden piles down to the sand layer, sawing off the protruding ends to equal height and erecting buildings on top of the stable foundation – there are 13,659 piles under the palace on Dam Square alone!

So long as the piles were completely submerged in ground water and air couldn't get to them, they wouldn't rot, but ground-water levels varied a bit and problems were unavoidable. Also, less scrupulous builders didn't always use enough piles, drive them deeply enough or worry about piles that snapped in the process, and many old buildings show signs of unequal subsidence – very expensive to fix. Since WWII, concrete piles have been used: they cannot rot and can be driven deeper – 20m, into the second sand layer, or even 60m, into the third.

CLIMATE

Amsterdam has a temperate maritime climate with cool winters and mild summers. Precipitation is spread rather evenly over the year, often in the form of endless drizzle, though in the spring months of March to

Sea Level & NAP

It is said that most of Amsterdam (and indeed more than half the country) lies a couple of metres below sea level, but what is sea level? This varies around the globe, and even the average level of the former Zuiderzee, in the lee of Holland, was slightly lower than that of the North Sea along Holland's exposed west coast. A display in the Stopera, in the arcade between the Muziektheater and City Hall (near the Waterlooplein metro exit), shows the ins and outs of NAP (Normaal Amsterdams Peil – 'Normal Amsterdam Level' or Amsterdam Ordnance Datum), established in the 17th century as the average high-water mark of the Zuiderzee. This still forms the zero reference for elevation anywhere in the country and is also used in Germany and several other European countries.

Water in the canals is kept at 40cm below NAP and many parts of the city lie lower still. Touch the bronze knob as you walk down the stairs in the Stopera display and you'll realise the importance of all those dikes. Three water columns represent the sea levels at IJmuiden and Flushing (Vlissingen), and the highest level reached in the disastrous floods in 1953 (4.55m above NAP) that led to the extensive Delta Works in the province of Zeeland. Pamphlets in Dutch, English, French, German, Italian and Spanish explain the details.

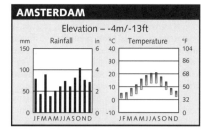

AMSTERDAM

Elevation – -4m/-13ft

May it tends to fall in short, sharp bursts. May is a pleasant time to visit: the elms along the canals are in bloom and everything is nice and fresh.

The sunniest months are May to August and the warmest are June to September. Summer can be humid and uncomfortable for some people, exacerbated by swarms of annoying mosquitoes. Indian summers are common in September and even into early October, which is usually an excellent time to visit. Blustery autumn storms occur in October and November.

December to February are the coldest months with occasional slushy snow and temperatures around freezing point. Frosts usually aren't severe enough to allow skating on the canals, but when they are, the city comes alive with colourfully clad skaters. When snow adds a serene white setting, you couldn't wish for better photo material.

ECOLOGY & ENVIRONMENT

Foreign visitors in the past commented on residents obsessively scrubbing stoops and cleaning windows. The spotless houses stood in stark contrast to smelly, filthy canal water and foul air thick with smoke from coal and peat fires.

Today's young residents are less obsessed with cleaning their houses than with sorting their rubbish – the environment is cherished in a country with so little of it. The canals are cleaner than they've ever been (see the following section) and environmentally friendly natural gas has cleared the air. Industrial pollution is kept firmly in check with some of the strictest regulations in the world. Even the visual pollution of thousands of TV antennas disappeared in the 1980s when everyone

got hooked up to cable TV. The inner city is a pleasant place for pedestrians thanks to the council's *autoluw* (car-abatement) policies. The number of parking spaces is strongly curtailed and cars are actively discouraged. Amsterdam is very much a residential city, and cars and highways have a very limited role to play.

One environmental problem persists, however: Amsterdam is still the dog-shit capital of the world, even though owners are compelled to steer pooch to the gutter and have to carry a spade and bag on their daily walk. Amsterdammers love dogs, which is nothing new: Japanese artists used to depict Dutchmen with dogs. They keep them in great numbers, cooped up in 3rd-floor apartments, and will stand up for their mutt's right to do whatever it damn well likes on its daily sniff around the block. Dogs are welcome in many pubs and shops, some hotels, and on trains and local transport, but generally not in restaurants.

Greenpeace supporters will be interested to know that the international head office (☎ 523 62 22) is at Keizersgracht 176; the Dutch branch (☎ 626 18 77, information on ☎ 422 33 44) is in the same complex at Keizersgracht 174.

Cleaning the Canals

Until the 1980s the canals doubled as sewers and had to be flushed daily. Before the 17th century this was relatively straightforward: the water level in the canals was regulated by locks leading into the IJ, and sea water was allowed into the canals at rising tide and back out again as the tide dropped. This made the canal water brackish and led to a backup of filth in the Amstel. From 1674 the Amstelsluizen in front of today's Carré Theatre allowed flushing to occur with fresh water from the Amstel, a vast improvement. Maids protested that they would lose their jobs because they wouldn't have to clean windows and stoops as often.

With the opening of the North Sea Canal in the 19th century and the completion of locks at Schellingwoude at the mouth of the IJ, the IJ was cut off from tidal influences. The solution, used to this day, was to pump water from the Zuiderzee (later IJsselmeer) into the canals, since WWII by means of a huge pumping station on the artificial island of Zeeburg opposite Schellingwoude. Locks on the west side of the city were left open so water could flow out into the North Sea Canal, taking canal filth with it. This was released into the North Sea at low tide (or pumped out if necessary), completing the hydraulic system.

Until the mid-1980s the Zeeburg station pumped 600,000 cubic metres of water each night, the equivalent of 300 swimming pools. Now that all households are connected to sewerage pipes (the 2500 houseboats are in the process of being connected), the pumps are turned on twice a week in winter and four times a week in summer. When the Amstel is in flood, or westerly storms increase water levels in the North Sea Canal, the pumps at Zeeburg are reversed and water is pumped out of the canals into the IJsselmeer.

The canal water is relatively clean these days, despite its dirty appearance and occasional algal blooms. Oxygen levels are healthy and many fish species have returned, though you still wouldn't want to drink it.

The water in the canals is about 3m deep but residents reckon you can deduct 1m for sludge and another metre for discarded objects – anything from unwanted bikes (about 10,000 a year) and bits of driftwood to old fridges, dolls and handbags. People have indeed received nasty cuts from falling into the water. The council employs seven boats to collect flotsam, while three dredges slowly work their way around the 100km of canals, completing the circuit every 10 years. The polluted sludge they dredge up is processed in special facilities in the Jan van Riebeeckhaven.

FLORA

An aerial photo of Amsterdam creates the impression of a huge park because it includes the many gardens rarely visible from the street. Indeed, the centre of Amsterdam has more trees per square kilometre than any other capital city in Europe. The canals used to be lined with linden trees but these were replaced with elms in the 18th century, chosen for their light leaf cover that allows daylight to filter into the houses. Dutch elm disease is so named because local arborists did much research into this beetle-induced fungus that first entered the country in the 1920s.

The city has many pleasant parks with an amazing variety of species. The Hortus Botanicus at Plantage Middenlaan is justly famous, but the Vondelpark, Artis zoo and the Amsterdamse Bos also hold much of interest, as do smaller local parks such as the Sarphatipark and Oosterpark. And when it comes to flowers, where do you start? Try March or April, when bulbs (tulips, hyacinths and daffodils) burst into bloom everywhere.

FAUNA

There are some 35 mammal species in the city, including the mole and the wood mouse, found in parks, along with rabbits and hares a bit farther out; bats, especially the dwarf bat that you can hear squeaking on summer nights (sounding a bit like a cricket); rats, including the water vole and brown rat; and the house mouse.

Sparrows, thrushes, swifts and crows are common here, as elsewhere in Europe, but in some parts of the city you might wonder whether any other birds exist besides feral pigeons. The canals are favoured by mallards, coots and the occasional heron, swan or grebe, and in water areas around the city you'll see herons, cormorants and coots. Black-headed gulls (with white heads in winter) seem to be everywhere, supremely adapted to this windswept, coastal habitat. The Vondelpark is now home to a large colony of screeching roseringed parrots, escaped pets that have thrived in this lush environment. They survive the coldest winter days by congregating around the ventilation shafts of large buildings.

The common toad and both brown and green frogs are prevalent, while about 60 fish species exist in Amsterdam waters. The habitat varies from fresh (the canals) to salt (the deeper parts of the North Sea Canal, the western harbour area and parts of the IJ), with transitional, brackish zones. Many sea fish enter the North Sea Canal through the huge sluices at IJmuiden. The eel, which survives in both fresh and salt water (and hails from the Sargasso Sea off Bermuda!), is common in the city's canals, as is bream – outnumbered only by the roach. White bream, rudd, pike, perch, stickleback and carp also enjoy the canal environment.

Crustacean species in the waters in and around Amsterdam include the common shrimp and the epidemic import, the Chinese mitten crab.

GOVERNMENT & POLITICS

The Greater Amsterdam area (population 1.2 million) consists of the City of Amsterdam (population 731,000), Amstelveen, Haarlemmermeer (Schiphol), Purmerend, Zaanstad and 11 other municipalities. They established formal administrative cooperation in 1992, though the anticipated full integration under a single council has been put on hold.

The City of Amsterdam's city council and municipal executive (consisting of the mayor and eight aldermen) oversee the city's 14 districts – each with their own district council and executive committee – and run the western harbour area. The 45 members of the council are elected every four years by all residents over 18 years of age, including foreigners who have been resident for at least five years. Council members elect the aldermen from their midst, but the mayor is appointed by the Crown (the queen plus the national government) for six years.

District councils serve residents in their daily lives. Water, sewerage, water management, health and public transport are handled by the central city administration, while electricity and gas are privatised.

Amsterdam has been a left-wing city ever since its residents achieved the vote. At the last council elections (1998) the labour party (PvdA) won 15 seats, followed by the conservative liberals (VVD) with nine, environmental socialists (Green Left) with seven, progressive liberals (D66) with four, the Christian Democrats, radical socialists (SP) and Greens with three each, and Mokum Mobiel 99 (pro-car lobbyists) with one. The current municipal executive, which includes the appointed mayor (traditionally labour), is a coalition of four labour, two conservative liberal, one progressive liberal and until recently two environmental socialists. The current mayor is Job Cohen, successor to the ailing Schelto Patijn who couldn't complete his term; both are held in high regard by most parties.

City politics are lively, with plenty of media coverage. Amsterdammers have strong opinions about their city and aren't afraid to voice them, though only 40% bother to vote. Burning issues are the persistent housing shortage with 50,000 house-hunters and the attendant development of new residential areas; the commercial construction boom; infrastructural concerns including traffic and parking policies; and the future of Schiphol airport. The more sensationalist press tends to focus on crime, ethnic minorities and 'overly permissive' social policies.

Land & Housing Policies

About 80% of land in the city is government-owned and is leased to private owners under 50-year leasehold arrangements (also 100-year leaseholds since 1991). Most land within the canal belt, however, is freehold (ie, owned privately in perpetuity), but any freehold land acquired by the government is converted to leasehold. A leasehold is only granted when a property developer has an end user lined up,

Living on the Water

There are about 2500 houseboats, accommodating 6000 people, moored along the canals. These converted barges began proliferating with the first acute housing shortage in the 1950s, but rules have been tightened and the only way you can live on a boat these days is to buy an existing one (though new quayside 'plots' are being sold on IJburg in the Eastern Harbour). Few are rented. An average boat in the older parts of Amsterdam costs around €180,000, which includes the rights to the spot. Owners pay €450 to €900 a year in tax, as well as fees for garbage service and connections to gas, electricity and water. It might seem romantic to live on a boat, but it can get cold and damp in winter if there's no central heating, and maintenance bills are high.

which keeps speculation in check and ensures that supply meets demand.

A mere 15% of city real estate is owner-occupied, the rest being rented out. Rents are strictly controlled, unless the property is so upmarket that it jumps the hurdle into the free-market category. There are also strict controls on the number of rooms a household may occupy, regardless of whether the dwelling is rented or owner-occupied.

The cost of real estate has skyrocketed in the past decade, and buying an apartment is out of reach for most Amsterdammers. The going rate within the canal belt is €4500 per square metre, which puts a modest one-bedroom apartment at €250,000-plus; a two-bedroom apartment in the suburbs starts at €200,000.

ECONOMY

Until about 25 years ago Amsterdam was the industrial centre of the Netherlands, a role it had played since the industrial revolution of the mid-19th century. In the 1960s and 1970s, however, the city's worsening congestion and environmental constraints forced many industries to move to parts of the country where industrial conditions were more relaxed. Meanwhile, low-wage competitors in Asia killed off the huge shipbuilding industry and its many support industries. These developments caused great hardship among employees who were too old to relocate or reskill, but the city bounced back as it reinvented its historical role as a centre of trade, finance and services.

The main economic activities in the Greater Amsterdam area can now be divided into four categories employing roughly equal numbers of people: manufacturing and crafts; commerce, tourism and finance; administration; and science and arts. Tourism generates a turnover of €900m a year and employs 6% of the workforce.

The harbour is still the fifth-largest in Europe and Schiphol airport is the fastest growing – the third-largest in terms of freight and fourth-largest in terms of passengers. Less well known is the fact that the Dutch control about 45% of European road freight and many of these trucking companies are based in Amsterdam. The government has stimulated public and private investments in office complexes to the west, south and south-east of the city. This, coupled with a highly skilled, multilingual workforce and easy-going tax laws, has prompted many multinationals to establish their European headquarters and distribution centres here to take advantage of the single European market.

The city remains the undisputed financial capital of the country and a major money centre in Europe. It holds the headquarters of the mighty ABN-AMRO banking group, the ING (Postbank) and the Nederlandsche Bank (the central bank), along with several other private banks and the offices of some 70 foreign banks. The European Options Exchange and the national stock exchange, which merged into Amsterdam Exchanges (the 'AEX') and in turn merged with the Paris and Brussels stock exchanges to form Euronext, add to the city's financial clout – 15% of the working population is employed in finance and related sectors.

Industry remains important in the corridor between Amsterdam and IJmuiden, particularly chemicals, petrochemicals, food and steel. Other important industries include cars and trucks, engine-building, clothing, paper and of course diamonds (industrial-grade). It is also one of the world centres for the development of digital media.

The Amsterdam region has the strongest economy in the country (5% growth in 2000) and a solid base in the service economies of the future, but its economy is under continual strain from generous social security provisions. These include the blanket public pension scheme in a greying population, but more specifically welfare cheques of €680 a month guaranteed to every resident aged between 21 and 65 who cannot find employment. This problem exists in the national economy too, but Amsterdam is particularly hard hit because so much of its population is aged between 20 and 40 and unemployed.

The unemployment rate in Amsterdam is assumed to be 10%, more than three times the national average, though only 6% are registered as unemployed. Some people claim that the real rate is more like 35% but is masked by the high proportion of part-time jobs and workers who have been declared medically unfit – and these categories aren't considered unemployed.

A survey by *The Economist* newspaper found that the incidence of part-time work in the country is well over 30% of employees (76% of whom are women) and rising, by far the highest percentage in the developed world; in the USA, part-timers form 13% of the working population, and in Britain, 23%. Only 11% of Dutch men and less than 5% of women work more than 40 hours a week, the lowest percentage in the developed world; in the USA, those figures are 80% for men and 60% for women, and in the Czech Republic they're over 90% for men and 80% for women.

Why is this so? Good social security plays a role, coupled with woeful child-care services, but the Dutch proudly proclaim that the process is driven by the fact that they're pioneers in the flexible working arrangements of the future.

POPULATION & PEOPLE

Amsterdam has an official population of 731,000 plus an estimated 20,000 unregistered ('illegal') residents. About 40% of the population is aged between 20 and 40; children, middle-aged and elderly people are underrepresented compared with other Dutch cities. All in all, 55% of households are single and that figure is rising. Couples without children far outnumber those with.

Ethnic minorities make up about 45% of the population, and 60% of primary school kids now have a non-Dutch background. In the mid-1970s, the granting of independence to the Dutch colony of Suriname in South America saw a large influx of Surinamese, who now number 72,000 and form the bulk of the city's 10% black population. In the 1960s, 'guest labourers' from Morocco and Turkey performed jobs spurned by the Dutch; they and their descendants now number 54,000 and 34,000 respectively. There are about 24,000 people from Indonesia, 19,000 Germans and 11,000 migrants from the Netherlands Antilles. Next in line are the Brits, with 7500. About 3700 Americans and

1000 Aussies also call Amsterdam home – officially, that is. Thousands of (temporary) expatriates are not included in these figures.

ARTS

Amsterdam has always been an international centre of the arts thanks to its tolerant and cosmopolitan spirit. It lacked a powerful court and wealthy Church – the usual art patrons elsewhere in Europe – but more than compensated for this with a large middle class that didn't mind spending a bit of money on art. Amsterdam achieved international renown in painting and architecture (see the separate Amsterdam Architecture section), and the current music scene is second to none. Unfortunately the city's impressive literary and theatrical traditions are less accessible to foreigners.

Painting

The distinction between Dutch and Flemish painting dates from the late 16th century, when the newly Protestant northern provinces of the Low Countries kicked out the Spaniards but couldn't dislodge them from the provinces in the south. Until then, most paintings in the Low Countries originated in the southern, 'Flemish' centres of Ghent, Bruges and Antwerp, and dealt with the biblical and allegorical subject matter popular with patrons of the day (the Church, the court and to a lesser extent the nobility).

Famous names include **Jan van Eyck** (d. 1441), the founder of the Flemish School who perfected the technique of oil painting; **Rogier van der Weyden** (1400–64), whose religious portraits showed the personalities of his subjects; **Hieronymus (Jeroen) Bosch** (1450–1516), with macabre allegorical paintings full of religious topics; and **Pieter Breugel the Elder** (1525–69), who used Flemish landscapes and peasant life in his allegorical scenes.

In the northern Low Countries, meanwhile, artists began to develop a style of their own. In Haarlem, painters were using freer, more dynamic arrangements in which people came to life. **Jan Mostaert** (1475–1555), **Lucas van Leyden** (1494–1533) and **Jan van Scorel** (1494–1562) brought realism into their works, modifying the mannerist ideal of exaggerated beauty. Around 1600 the art teacher Karel van Mander proclaimed that Haarlem was creating a distinctively Dutch style of painting.

In Utrecht, however, followers of the Italian master Caravaggio, such as **Hendrick ter Bruggen** (1588–1629) and **Gerrit van Honthorst** (1590–1656), made a much more fundamental break with mannerism. They opted for realism altogether and played with light and shadow, with night scenes where a single source of light created dramatic contrasts – the *chiaroscuro* (clear-obscure) approach used to such dramatic effect by Caravaggio in Rome.

Golden Age (17th Century) Both these schools influenced the Golden Age of Dutch painting in the 17th century with its stars like Rembrandt, Vermeer and Frans Hals. Unlike earlier painters or some contemporaries, none of this trio made the almost obligatory pilgrimage to Italy to study the masters. Their work showed that they no longer followed but led – much like the young Republic that seemed to burst out of nowhere.

Artists suddenly had to survive in a free market. Gone was the patronage of Church and court. In its place was a new, bourgeois society of merchants, artisans and shopkeepers who didn't mind spending 'reasonable' money to brighten up their houses and workplaces with pictures they could understand. Painters rose to the occasion by becoming entrepreneurs themselves, churning out banal works, copies and masterpieces in studios run like factories. Paintings became mass products that were sold at markets among the furniture and chickens. Soon the wealthiest households were covered in paintings from top to bottom like wallpaper. Foreign visitors commented that everyone seemed to have a painting or two on the wall, even bakeries and butcher shops.

Artists specialised in different categories. There was still a market for religious art but it had to be 'historically correct' rather than mannerist, in line with the Calvinist emphasis on 'true' events as described in the Bible. Greek or Roman historical scenes were an extension of this category. Portraiture, in which Flemish and Dutch painters had already begun to excel, was a smash hit in this society of middle-class upstarts brimming with confidence, though group portraits cost less per head and suited a republic run by committees and clubs. Maritime scenes and cityscapes sold well to the government, and landscapes, winter scenes and still lifes (especially of priceless, exotic flowers and delicious meals) were found in many living rooms. Another favourite in households was genre painting, which depicted domestic life or daily life outside.

These different categories may help visitors to the Rijksmuseum understand what they're looking at, but some painters defy such easy classification. **Rembrandt van Rijn** (1606–69), the greatest and most versatile of 17th-century artists, excelled in all these categories and pioneered new directions in each. Sometimes he was centuries ahead of his time, as with the emotive brush strokes of his later works. See the boxed text for further details of his life.

Another great painter of this period, **Frans Hals** (1581/85–1666), was born in Antwerp but lived in Haarlem. He devoted most of his career to portraits, dabbling in occasional genre scenes with dramatic chiaroscuro. His ability to render the expressions of his subjects was equal to that of Rembrandt though he didn't explore their characters as much. Both masters used the same expressive, unpolished brush strokes, and seemed to develop from a bright exuberance in their early careers to a darker, more solemn approach later on.

A good example of Hals' 'unpolished' technique is *The Merry Drinker* (1630) in the Rijksmuseum, which could almost have been painted by one of the 19th-century impressionists who so admired his work. His famous children's portraits are similar. Hals was also an expert of beautiful group portraits in which the groups almost looked natural, unlike the rigid lineups produced by lesser contemporaries – though he wasn't as cavalier as Rembrandt in subordinating faces to the composition. A good example is the pair of paintings known collectively as *The*

Rembrandt: From Wealth to Bankruptcy

The 17th century's greatest artist, Rembrandt van Rijn, grew up in Leiden as the son of a miller and was already an accomplished chiaroscuro painter when he came to Amsterdam in 1631 to run Hendrick van Uylenburgh's painting studio. Portraits were the most profitable line and Rembrandt and his staff (or 'pupils') churned out scores of them, including group portraits such as *The Anatomy Lesson of Dr Tulp* (1632). In 1634 he married Van Uylenburgh's Frisian niece Saskia, who often modelled for him.

Rembrandt fell out with his boss, but his wife's capital helped him buy the sumptuous house (the current Rembrandthuis) next door to Van Uylenburgh's studio, where he set up his own studio, with staff who worked in a warehouse in the Jordaan. These were happy years: his paintings were a success and his studio became the largest in Holland, though his gruff manners and open agnosticism didn't win him dinner-party invitations from the elite.

MARTIN MOOS

See how the master lived and worked in the Rembrandthuis Museum.

Rembrandt became one of the city's main art collectors and often sketched and painted for himself, urging staff to do likewise. Residents of the surrounding Jewish quarter provided perfect material for his dramatic biblical scenes.

In 1642, a year after the birth of their son Titus, Saskia died and business went downhill. Rembrandt's majestic group portrait, *The Nightwatch* (1642), was considered innovative by the art critics of the day (it's now the Rijksmuseum's prize exhibit), but the people in the painting had each paid 100 guilders and some were unhappy that they were pushed to the background. Rembrandt told them where to push the painting and suddenly he received far fewer orders. He began an affair with his son's governess but kicked her out a few years later when he fell for the new maid, Hendrickje Stoffels, who bore him a daughter, Cornelia. The public didn't take kindly to the man's lifestyle and his spiralling debts, and in 1656 he went bankrupt. His house and rich art collection were sold and he moved to the Rozengracht in the Jordaan.

No longer the darling of the wealthy, he continued to paint, draw and etch – his etchings on display in the Rembrandthuis are some of the finest ever produced in this medium – and received the occasional commission. His pupil Govert Flinck was asked to decorate the new city hall, and when Flinck died Rembrandt scored part of the job and painted the monumental *Conspiracy of Claudius Civilis* (1661). The authorities disliked it and soon had it removed. In 1662 he completed the *Staalmeesters* (the 'Syndics') for the drapers' guild and ensured that everybody remained clearly visible, but it was the last group portrait he did.

The works of his later period show that Rembrandt lost none of his touch. No longer constrained by the wishes of wealthy clients, he enjoyed a new-found freedom and his works became more unconventional while showing an even stronger empathy with their subject matter, for instance in *A Couple: The Jewish Bride* (1665). The many portraits of Titus and Hendrickje, and his ever gloomier self-portraits, are among the most stirring in the history of art.

A plague epidemic in 1663–64 killed one in seven Amsterdammers, among them Rembrandt's faithful companion Hendrickje. Titus died in 1668, aged 27 and just married, and Rembrandt died a year later, a broken man.

Regents & the Regentesses of the Old Men's Alms House (1664) in the Frans Hals Museum in Haarlem, which he painted near the end of his long life (he lived in the almshouse which is now the museum).

The grand trio of 17th-century masters is completed by **Jan Vermeer** (1632–75) of Delft. He produced only 35 meticulously crafted paintings in his career and died a poor man with 10 children – his baker accepted two paintings from his wife as payment for a debt of more than 600 guilders. His work is devoted mainly to genre painting, which he mastered like no other. Other paintings include a few historical/biblical scenes in his earlier career, his famous *View of Delft* (1661) in the Mauritshuis in The Hague, and some tender portraits of unknown women, such as the stunningly beautiful *Girl with a Pearl Earring* (1666), also in the Mauritshuis. His Catholicism and lingering mannerism help explain the emphasis on beauty rather than the personalities of the people he portrayed.

The Little Street (1658) in the Rijksmuseum is Vermeer's only street scene; the others are set indoors, bathed in serene light pouring through tall windows. The calm, spiritual effect is enhanced by dark blues, deep reds and warm yellows, and by supremely balanced compositions that adhere to the rules of perspective. Good examples include the Rijksmuseum's *The Kitchen Maid* (also known as *The Milkmaid*, 1658) and *Woman in Blue Reading a Letter* (1664), or, for his use of perspective, *The Love Letter* (1670). In Woman in Blue, note the map on the wall, a backdrop he used in several other works, as did many other artists of the period. Maps were appreciated as valuable works of art in 17th-century Dutch society just like paintings, which might say something about Dutch appreciation for spatial relationships (something to do with the flat country and ongoing land reclamation perhaps?).

Around the middle of the century the atmospheric unity in Dutch paintings, with their stern focus on mood and the subtle play of light, began to make way for the splendour of the baroque. **Jacob van Ruysdael** went for dramatic skies and **Albert Cuyp** for Italianate landscapes, while Ruysdael's pupil **Meindert Hobbema** preferred less heroic and more playful bucolic scenes full of pretty detail.

This almost frivolous aspect of baroque also announces itself in the genre paintings of **Jan Steen** (1626–79), the tavern-keeper whose depictions of domestic chaos led to the Dutch expression 'a Jan Steen household' for a disorderly household. A good example is the animated revelry of *The Merry Family* (1668) in the Rijksmuseum. It shows adults having a good time around the dinner table, oblivious to the children in the foreground pouring themselves a drink. There's a lot going on in this painting, and it's very busy as baroque art so often is, but it all comes together well.

18th & 19th Centuries The Golden Age of Dutch painting ended almost as suddenly as it began, when the French invaded the Low Countries in the 'Disaster Year' of 1672. The economy collapsed and with it the market for paintings. A mood of caution replaced the carefree optimism of the years when the world lay at the Republic's feet. Painters who stayed in business did so with 'safe' works that repeated earlier successes, and in the 18th century they copied French styles, pandering to the awe for anything French.

They produced many competent works but nothing ground-breaking. **Cornelis Troost** (1697–1750) was one of the best genre painters, sometimes compared to Hogarth for introducing quite un-Calvinistic humour into his pastels of domestic revelry reminiscent of Jan Steen.

Gerard de Lairesse (1640–1711) and **Jacob de Wit** (1695–1754) specialised in decorating the walls and ceilings of buildings – De Wit's trompe l'oeil decorations in the current Theatermuseum and Bijbels Museum are worth seeing.

The late 18th century and most of the 19th century produced little of note, though the landscapes and seascapes of **Johan Barthold Jongkind** (1819–91) and the gritty, almost photographic Amsterdam scenes of **George Hendrik Breitner** (1857–1923) were a bit of an exception. They appear to have inspired French impressionists, many of whom visited Amsterdam at the time.

These two painters reinvented 17th-century realism in their work and influenced the Hague School in the last decades of the 19th century, with painters such as **Hendrik Mesdag** (1831–1915), **Jozef Israels** (1824– 1911) and the three **Maris brothers** (Jacob, Matthijs and Willem). The landscapes, seascapes and genre works of this school are on display in the Mesdag Museum in The Hague, where the star attraction is the *Panorama Mesdag* (1881), a gigantic, 360-degree painting by the artist of the seaside town of Scheveningen viewed from a dune. It's quite impressive.

Without a doubt the greatest 19th-century Dutch painter was **Vincent van Gogh** (1853–90), whose convulsive patterns and furious colours were in a world of their own and still defy comfortable categorisation. A post-impressionist? A forerunner of expressionism? For more about his life and works, see the description of the Van Gogh Museum in the Things to See & Do chapter.

20th Century In his early career, **Piet Mondriaan** (1872–1944) – he dropped the second 'a' in his name when he moved to Paris in 1910 – painted in the Hague School tradition, but after discovering theosophy he began reducing form to its horizontal (female) and vertical (male) essentials. After flirting with Cubism he began painting in bold rectangular patterns, using only the three primary colours of yellow, blue and red set against the three neutrals (white, grey and black), a style known as 'neo-plasticism' – an undistorted expression of reality in pure form and pure colour. His *Composition in Red, Black, Blue, Yellow & Grey* (1920) in the Stedelijk Museum is an elaborate example of this. Mondriaan's later works were more stark (or 'pure') and became dynamic again when he moved to New York in 1940. The world's largest collection of his paintings resides in the Gemeentemuseum (Municipal Museum) of his native The Hague.

Mondriaan was one of the leading exponents of De Stijl (The Style), a Dutch design movement that aimed to harmonise all the arts by bringing artistic expressions back to their essence. Its advocate was the magazine of the same name, first published in 1917 by **Theo van Doesburg** (1883–1931). Van Doesburg produced works similar to Mondriaan's, though he dispensed with the thick, black lines and later tilted his rectangles at 45°, departures serious enough for Mondriaan to call off the friendship.

Throughout the 1920s and 1930s, De Stijl attracted not just painters but also sculptors, poets, architects and designers. One of these was **Gerrit Rietveld** (1888–1964), designer of the Van Gogh Museum and several other buildings but best known internationally for his furniture, such as the Mondriaanesque *Red Blue Chair* (1918) on display in the Stedelijk Museum, and his range of uncomfortable zigzag chairs that, viewed side-on, are simply a 'Z' with a backrest.

Other schools of the prewar period included the Bergen School, with the expressive realism of **Annie 'Charley' Toorop** (1891–1955), daughter of the symbolist painter Jan Toorop; and De Ploeg (The Plough), headed by **Jan Wiegers** (1893–1959) in Groningen, who were influenced by the works of Van Gogh and German expressionists. In her later works Charley Toorop also became one of the exponents of Dutch surrealism, more correctly known as Magic Realism, which expressed the magical interaction between humans and their environment. Leading Magic Realists included Carel Willink (1900–83) and the almost naive autodidact Pyke Koch (1901–91).

One of the most remarkable graphic artists of the 20th century was **Maurits Cornelis Escher** (1902–72). His drawings, lithos and woodcuts of blatantly impossible images continue to fascinate mathematicians. Strange loops defy the laws of Euclidean geometry: a waterfall feeds itself, people go up and down a staircase that ends where it starts, a pair of hands draw each other. He also possessed an uncanny knack for tessellation, or 'tiling' – the art of making complex, preferably 'organic' shapes fit into one another in recurring but subtly changing patterns. Though sometimes dismissed as novelties that belong in poster shops,

Escher's meticulously crafted works betray a highly talented artist who deserves credit for challenging our view of reality.

After WWII, artists rebelled against artistic conventions and vented their rage in abstract expressionism, the more furious the better. In Amsterdam, **Karel Appel** (1921–) and **Constant** (Constant Nieuwenhuis, 1920–) drew on styles pioneered by Paul Klee and Joan Miró, and exploited bright colours and 'uncorrupted' children's art to produce incredibly lively works that leapt off the canvas. In Paris in 1945, they met up with the Dane Asger Jorn (1914–73) and the Belgian Corneille (Cornelis van Beverloo, 1922–), and together with several other artists and writers formed a group known as CoBrA (Copenhagen, Brussels, Amsterdam).

Their first major exhibition, in the Stedelijk Museum in 1949, aroused a storm of protest with predictable comments along the lines of 'My child paints like that too'. Still, the CoBrA artists exerted a strong influence in their respective countries even after they disbanded in 1951. The Stedelijk Museum has a good collection of their works but the CoBrA Museum in Amstelveen displays the more complete range, including the most colourful ceramics you're ever likely to see.

It is probably too early to say much about the significance of Dutch art from the 1960s onwards – form your own opinions in the Stedelijk Museum. Works include the op art of Jan Schoonhoven, influenced by the Zero movement in Germany; the abstracts of Ad Dekkers and Edgar Fernhout; and the photographic collages of Jan Dibbets.

Music

The dour church elders of the past dismissed music as frivolous but began to allow organ music in churches in the 17th century, as it kept people out of pubs. With the possible exception of Jan Pieterszoon Sweelinck (1562–1621), an organ player in the Oude Kerk with an international reputation as a composer and a strong following in Germany, Amsterdam contributed relatively little to the world's music scene, which makes its vivid music scene today all the more remarkable.

The world's top acts are billed matter-of-factly, and local musicians excel in (modern) classical music, jazz and techno/dance. In July and August, free jazz, classical and world-music performances are staged in the Vondelpark, and free lunch-time concerts are held at various venues throughout the year. The Uitmarkt festival at the end of August (see Public Holidays & Special Events in the Facts for the Visitor chapter) also provides lots of free music. For more about music venues, see the Music section in the Entertainment chapter, and check the free entertainment paper *Uitkrant* for details.

Classical The country's best symphony orchestras and classical musicians perform in the Concertgebouw. You can't go wrong with tickets for the world-renowned, Riccardo Chailly-conducted Concertgebouw Orkest, which plays music by 'big' composers but also highlights modern and unknown works.

If pianist Ronald Brautigam is on the bill you'll be guaranteed a top-flight performance. He often collaborates with violinist Isabelle van Keulen. Cellists of note (so to speak) are Quirine Viersen and Pieter Wispelwey.

The pianist Wibi Soerjadi is one of the most successful classical musicians in the country. He specialises in romantic works, and elderly ladies swoon over this handsome youngster who looks like a Javanese prince and likes driving his Ferrari fast. Sopranos Charlotte Margiono and Miranda van Kralingen are worth catching too.

In 'old music', you can't go past the Combattimento Consort Amsterdam (Bach, Vivaldi and Händel), or the Amsterdam Baroque Orchestra conducted by Ton Koopman. He also heads the Radio Chamber Orchestra, along with Frans Brüggen, best known for his work with The 18th Century Orchestra. Performances by the Radio Philharmonic Orchestra, conducted by the Sydney Symphony's Edo de Waart (usually in the Concertgebouw), are often recorded for radio and TV.

The Nederlandse Opera is based in the Stopera (officially called the Muziektheater), where it stages world-class performances, though not everyone will appreciate the sometimes experimental approach.

Modern Classical & Experimental The IJsbreker is the usual venue for this type of music, which seems to thrive in Amsterdam. Dutch modern composers include Louis Andriessen, Theo Loevendie, Klaas de Vries and the late Ton de Leeuw. Worthwhile performers include The Trio, Asko Ensemble, Nieuw Ensemble and, last but not least, the Reinbert de Leeuw-conducted Schönberg Ensemble.

Jazz The distinction between modern classical and improvised music can be vague. Jazz band leaders such as Willem Breuker and Willem van Manen of the Contraband have a decades-long reputation for straddling the two genres.

More recently, the Dutch jazz scene has become more mainstream with gifted young chanteuses such as Fleurine and especially Suriname-born Denise Jannah, widely recognised as the country's best jazz singer. The latter is the first singer from Suriname to be signed to the legendary Blue Note label. Her repertory consists of American standards but she adds elements of Surinamese music on stage.

Astrid Seriese and Carmen Gomez operate in the crossover field, where jazz verges on, or blends with, pop. Father and daughter Hans and Candy Dulfer, tenor and alto saxophonists respectively, are a bit more daring. Dad in particular constantly extends his musical boundaries by experimenting with sampling techniques drawn from the hip-hop genre. Daughter is better known internationally, thanks to her performances with Prince, Van Morrison, Dave Stewart, Pink Floyd and Maceo Parker, among others.

Trumpeter Saskia Laroo mixes jazz with dance but is also respected in more traditional circles. In instrumental jazz, you can't go past pianist and Thelonius Monk Award-winning Michiel Borstlap and bass player Hein van de Geyn. Borstlap has also plunged into dance music – his recent (triple) CD, *Gramercy Park*, features house-DJ Ronald Molendijk along with traditional jazz tracks and even classical music.

The city's most important jazz venue is the Bimhuis on Oude Schans – others come and go but the Bimhuis remains an institu-tion. It will move to a new venue in the eastern docklands (west of the ship-passenger terminal) in 2003.

Pop & Dance Amsterdam may have been a 'Magic Centre' in the 1960s but its pop scene was slow to develop (the country's pop centre in those days was The Hague, with bands like Shocking Blue and Golden Earring who both hit No 1 in the USA). Famous Amsterdam bands in the 1960s were the Outsiders – a wild band whose lead singer, Wally Tax, was reputed to be the man with the longest hair in the country – and the Hunters, an instrumental guitar group that included Jan Akkerman, who later achieved international fame in the progressive rock band Focus and was proclaimed the best guitarist in the world in a 1973 magazine poll.

In the late 1970s the squatter movement provided fertile ground for a lively punk music scene, followed by synthesizer-dominated New Wave. In the mid-1980s Amsterdam was a centre for guitar-driven rock bands, such as garage rockers Claw Boys Claw.

It then evolved into a capital of the dance genre, from house to techno to R&B. Perhaps the best-known Dutch dance variant internationally was the so-called 'gabber', a style in which the number of beats per minute and the noise of buzzing synthesizers went beyond belief, though the genre – along with the shaved heads and tracksuits – has now passed into history. Amsterdam also boasts a vital hip-hop scene, spearheaded by the Osdorp Posse who rap in their mother tongue.

Rave parties are organised in the Amsterdam dance clubs, such as Mazzo, iT and especially Escape with its Saturday Chemistry evenings. The Westergasfabriek, along with other venues in Amsterdam and elsewhere, host Speedfreax evenings, where fashionable hipsters sip champagne while undergoing mostly English speed garage and 2-step.

Worthwhile DJs who do the club rounds include the Belgian grandmaster and Amsterdam resident Eddy de Clerq, as well as Dimitri, Marcello and 100% Isis.

Alternative rockers Claw Boys Claw, 1960s pop legend Wally Tax and the Dutch-language rockers The Scene, De Dijk and

Tröckener Kecks have survived everything new (though the latter finally disbanded in December 2001), but rock bands are making a comeback and promising new bands are surfacing – check the bills at Paradiso, Melkweg and Arena, or mingle with Amsterdam's rock musicians at music café De Koe. The Excelsior Records label is home to Daryll Ann and upstarts such as Caesar, Johan, Benjamin B and Scram C Baby.

Experimental pop's heyday is over and it seems to have gone underground again. The guitar group Betty Serveert ('Betty Serves', after a book about Dutch tennis legend Betty Stöve) toured the American underground circuit for a while but returned home after terminating its contract with Matador Records. Its former drummer set up the Bauer project, a cross between Kraftwerk and the Beach Boys. Another band worth mentioning is Solex, with sampling music published by Matador Records.

Experimental pop music that's perhaps best known internationally right now is produced by Arling & Cameron, whose creations have made their way into movies, TV series and commercials. Their interesting CD *Music for Imaginary Films* is just that: sound tracks for nonexistent movies, with accompanying posters designed by leading Dutch graphic designers.

World Music Cosmopolitan Amsterdam offers a wealth of world music. Suriname-born Ronald Snijders, a top jazz flautist, often participates in world-music projects. Another jazz flautist heading towards 'world' is the eternal Chris Hinze, for instance with his album *Tibet Impressions*, though most of his repertoire falls in the New Age category.

Fra-Fra-Sound plays 'paramaribop', a unique mixture of traditional Surinamese kaseko and jazz (the moniker is a contraction of Paramaribo, the capital of Suriname, and bebop), but the bulk of world repertoire from Amsterdam is Latin, ranging from Cuban salsa to Dominican merengue and Argentinian tango. Try the following bands to get a taste of the local world scene: Nueva Manteca (salsa), Sexteto Canyengue (tango) and Eric Vaarzon Morel (flamenco).

An interesting 'Amsterdam-Brazilian' band is Zuco 103, which combines bossa nova and samba with dance. It has strong ties with the equally eclectic New Cool Collective, a 22-member big band that blends jazz with drum'n'bass.

For more information about these artists and gigs at Melkweg (especially), Paradiso, Akhnaton and Latin bars, see the excellent monthly salsa magazine *Oye Listen*. It's published in Dutch and Spanish, costs €3.25, and is available in shops that sell world music such as Concerto (☎ 623 52 28), Utrechtsestraat 52-60. Look for CDs by the above-mentioned bands on the Lucho, Munich and M&W labels.

The Roots Music Festival of world music is organised at different locations every year in June – check with the Uitburo or the VVV, or W̄ www.amsterdamroots.nl. The theatre of the Tropenmuseum (Museum for the Tropics) often hosts non-Western music concerts – ring ☎ 568 85 00 for details.

Literature

Dutch literature has been neglected by the English-speaking world, which is a shame. The lack of English translations is partly to blame. While Flemish authorities are happy to subsidise translations of their authors, Dutch authorities are less inclined to do so.

The Dutch Shakespeare, Joost van den Vondel, is heavy going in his tragedy *Gijsbrecht van Aemstel* (1637), which is available in translation. It describes the agony of the local count who went into exile after losing out to the count of Holland and his toll privileges. Vondel's best tragedy, *Lucifer* (1654), has also been translated. Other big authors of this period, Bredero (comedies) and Hooft (poems, plays, history, philosophy), have yet to appear in English.

The most interesting 19th-century author was Eduard Douwes Dekker, a colonial administrator and Amsterdam native who wrote under the pseudonym Multatuli (Latin for 'I have suffered greatly'). His *Max Havelaar: or the Coffee Auctions of the Dutch Trading Company* (1860) exposed colonial narrow-mindedness in the dealings of a self-righteous coffee merchant. It shocked Dutch society and led to a review of the 'culture system' in the East Indies (the forced production of tropical crops for export). The Hague author Louis Couperus (*The Hidden Force*, 1900) explored the mystery of the East Indies from the colonialist's perspective.

The WWII occupation was a traumatic period that spawned many insightful works. *The Diary of Anne Frank* is a moving account of a Jewish girl's thoughts and yearnings while hiding in an Amsterdam annexe to avoid deportation by the Germans. The poignancy is enhanced by the knowledge that she was killed in the end. Etty Hillesum's *Etty: An Interrupted Life* is in a similar vein but more mature. Marga Minco (*The Fall, An Empty House, Bitter Herbs*) explores the war years from the perspective of a Jewish woman who survived. A brilliant, more recent novel that deals with the war years is Tessa de Loo's *The Twins* (1993, English translation 2001), about separated twins who grow up on different sides of the fence.

Amsterdam author Harry Mulisch focuses on Dutch apathy during WWII (*The Last Call* and *The Assault*, which was made into an Oscar-winning film), but he has written much else that doesn't involve the war. His more recent work, often translated, has had its ups and downs but he remains one of the Great Authors of Dutch literature.

Jan Wolkers shocked Dutch readers in the 1960s with his provocatively misogynist but powerful *Turkish Delight*, made into a (Dutch) film by Paul Verhoeven starring Rutger Hauer. Xaviera Hollander (Vera de Vries) shocked the USA with an account of her callgirl experiences in *The Happy Hooker*.

Simon Carmiggelt (*A Dutchman's Slight Adventures, I'm Just Kidding*) wrote amusing vignettes of Pijp neighbourhood life in his column in the newspaper *Het Parool*. Nicolas Freeling (*A Long Silence, Love in Amsterdam, Because of the Cats*) created the BBC's Van der Valk detective series. Jan-Willem van der Wetering (*Hard Rain*) is another author of off-beat detective stories.

Cees Nooteboom (*A Song of Truth and Semblance, In the Dutch Mountains*) is accessible and amusing. For more substance, read *The Virtuoso* by Margriet de Moor, a novel about a mother, daughter and piano (*not* set in New Zealand); or *A Heart of Stone* by Renate Dorrestein, the Dutch Fay Weldon. *In Babylon* by Marcel Möring is the perfect novel, a sort of *Arabian Nights* where people tell each other stories. Arthur Japin's *The Two Hearts of Kwasi Boachi* is a true account of two African princes who were dragged off to Holland in 1837 to please the king, who soon lost interest. One of them died and the other ended up in the East Indies.

Lieve Joris, a Flemish author who lives in Amsterdam, writes about cultures in transition in Africa, the Middle East and Eastern Europe. Her *Gates of Damascus*, about daily life in Syria, has been published in the Lonely Planet Journeys series, as has *Mali Blues*, an account of her quest to get to know a Mali musician. Another book in this series is *The Rainbird: A Central African Journey* by Jan Brokken, a highly regarded novelist, travel narrator and literary journalist. It's a fascinating account of white explorers, missionaries, slavers and adventurers who traipsed through the jungles of Gabon.

For more about books and where to buy them, see the Bookshops and Markets sections in the Shopping chapter. See also Books in the Facts for the Visitor chapter for nonfiction works about Amsterdam and the Netherlands. The third week in March is the national Boekenweek, when buyers who spend more than a certain amount in a bookshop receive a free (Dutch) book.

Cinema

Dutch films haven't exactly set the world on fire, though this has more to do with the language barrier and funding problems in a modest distribution area than with lack of talent.

One of the most important Dutch directors of all time was Joris Ivens (1898–1989), who was influenced by Russian film-makers but added his own impressionistic lyricism. He made award-winning documentaries about social and political issues – the Spanish Civil War, impoverished Belgian miners, Vietnam – but was also an accomplished visual artist in his own right; for instance in *Rain* (1929), a 15-minute impression of a rain shower in Amsterdam that took four months to shoot.

Directors, actors and camera operators who made the jump to English have often done quite well for themselves. Paul Verhoeven *(Robocop, Total Recall, Basic Instinct, Starship Troopers)* is perhaps the best-known director abroad, though his reputation has suffered from his disastrous *Showgirls*. George Sluizer *(The Vanishing)*, Dick Maas *(Flodder in Amerika, Amsterdamned)*, Fons Rademakers *(The Assault)* and Marleen Gorris *(Antonia's Line,* which won the Oscar for best foreign film in 1996) have also made a name internationally, if not always among the general public. Ms Gorris' follow-up was an English-language adaptation of Virginia Woolf's *Mrs Dalloway*, starring Vanessa Redgrave. Dick Maas wrote and directed *Down* (2001), a gripping horror film about a feral elevator.

Jan de Bont, who won accolades for his camera work in *Jewel of the Nile* and *Black Rain*, directed the box-office hits *Speed* and *Twister*.

Rutger Hauer began his acting career at home as the lead in Paul Verhoeven's *Turks Fruit* (Turkish Delight, an Oscar nominee for best foreign film in the early 1970s), but has since gained glory in Hollywood with convincing bad-guy performances in disturbing films such as *The Hitcher* and *Blade Runner*. Jeroen Krabbé also became a well-paid Hollywood actor *(The Fugitive, The Living Daylights, Prince of Tides)* and has now turned to directing, including *Left Luggage* starring Isabella Rosselini.

Mike van Diem is a new-generation director with success abroad – his *Karakter* won the Oscar for best foreign film in 1998. His cameraman, Rogier Stoffers, went on to make a name for himself in Hollywood.

One of the most hilarious films featuring Amsterdam is French director Jacques Tati's classic *Traffic* (1971), which follows Monsieur Hulot as he bumbles his way through the car show in the RAI exhibition buildings. Bert Haanstra, a leading Dutch documentary-maker, co-directed the Amsterdam scenes.

The Filmmuseum in the Vondelpark is the national museum on this subject – it's not a museum with regular displays but it screens interesting films from its huge archive. See Cinemas in the Entertainment chapter for more about films.

Theatre

The city has a rich theatrical tradition dating back to medieval times. In the Golden Age, when Dutch was the language of trade, local companies toured the theatres of Europe with Vondel's tragedies, Bredero's comedies and Hooft's verses. They're still performed locally in more modern renditions.

Theatre was immensely popular with all levels of society, perhaps because the city lacked a decent theatre building and plays were often performed outdoors. Gradually, however, the patrician class and their pre-occupation with French culture turned theatre into a more elitist affair, and towards the end of the 19th century it had become snobbish, with little room for development.

This attitude persisted until the late 1960s, when disgruntled actors began to throw tomatoes at their older colleagues and engaged the audience in discussion about the essence of theatre. Avant-garde theatre companies such as Mickery and Shaffy made Amsterdam a centre for experimental theatre, and many smaller companies sprang up in the 1970s and 1980s.

Most of these have now merged or disappeared as a result of cutbacks in government subsidies, while musicals and cabaret are enjoying a revival. But survivors and newcomers are still forging ahead with excellent productions – visual feasts with striking sets, lighting and creative costumes – and the Dutch produce some of the best youth theatre in the world. The language barrier is of course an issue with Dutch productions, though with some of them it's hardly relevant.

English-language companies often visit Amsterdam, especially in summer – check the *Uitkrant* or ask at the AUB Uitburo. For more about theatre venues, see Theatre in the Entertainment chapter. The Holland Festival in June and the Uitmarkt on the last weekend in August are big theatre events (see Public Holidays & Special Events in the Facts for the Visitor chapter). Also worth catching is the International Theatre School Festival at the end of June, which is held in the theatres around Nes (Frascati, Brakke Grond etc).

SOCIETY & CONDUCT
Stereotypes

The Netherlands in general and Amsterdam in particular can be 15 years ahead of the rest of the world on some moral and social issues (drugs, abortion, euthanasia, homosexuality). But sometimes they step 15 years sideways, for instance in preaching to the rest of the world about right and wrong. Perhaps the only other preachers with similar drive are the Americans.

Critics attribute this to the 'minister's mentality' of moral rectitude epitomised by the Calvinist minister scowling from the pulpit. Indeed, an acute sense of moral right and wrong comes through in the earnest insistence that it hardly matters *how* you say something, it's *what* you say that counts, which gives the Dutch a bit of a reputation for bluntness. And they do get carried away, hence the English term 'Dutch uncle' for someone who criticises frankly and severely.

It also gives them a reputation for lack of humour, yet they have an unusual ability to laugh at themselves and will cut down people who take themselves too seriously. 'Act normal, that's crazy enough', goes the saying.

Amsterdammers have little nationalist pride except on the soccer field. They love to complain about their city and their 'irrelevant' country, and are keen to learn new things foreign. English words in daily speech and print almost betray a national inferiority complex. Similarly, the city has few monumental buildings or projects. Most attempts at grandeur have traditionally been criticised, ridiculed and sabotaged, though Calvinist frugality has played a role too. Every separate house or building shines in its own individual way; grandeur is considered gross. It's almost as if people are proud of not being proud, except in their opinions.

It is said that the Calvinist Dutch, like the Presbyterian Scots, are careful with money, and they certainly have proven to be astute traders. It's worth remembering that the Netherlands and especially Amsterdam have always had a money culture: there was little

or no traditional aristocracy with large landholdings. The people who dominated society built their own wealth and did so entirely on money – if they squandered it, they had nothing to fall back on. Money determined prosperity and thus virtue.

The earlier History section discussed the phenomenon of 'pillarisation' (verzuiling), which allowed different ideologies their place in society so long as they maintained the status quo by compromise – important in an overpopulated country where opinions are taken so seriously. Verzuiling's social and cultural segmentation is considered outdated now, but it has left a strong legacy in a culture of tolerance and willing acceptance of an endless string of petty rules and regulations to make things work fairly. The Dutch will deliberate endlessly before they issue a planning permit or form a government – the so-called 'polder model' of involving everybody who may have a legitimate say. Everyone is expected to have an opinion and to voice it, but meddling in others' affairs is 'not done' – at least not without following the proper procedures.

For instance, many foreigners have commented that thick cigarette smoke not just in pubs seems at odds with the high level of ecological concern. But it flows out of the Dutch commandment to be 'reasonable', to allow everyone their place and let them live their own life even if this puts some burdens on society. Public smoking is slowly being pushed back but these things take time. Can't get more Dutch than that.

Dos & Don'ts

The accepted greeting is a handshake – firm but not bone-crushing. Cheek-kissing (three pecks) is common between men and women (and between women) who know one another socially.

The typically pragmatic convention for queuing is to take a numbered ticket from a dispenser and await your turn. Always check whether there's a dispenser if you're in a post office, government office, bakery, at a delicatessen counter in a supermarket etc.

If you're invited home for dinner, bring something for the host: a bunch of flowers or a plant, a bottle of wine, or some good cake or pastries. It's polite to arrive five to 15 minutes late (never early) but business meetings start on time.

Dress standards are casual (most concerts, most restaurants) or smart casual (theatre, opera, upmarket restaurants and some business dealings); and slightly formal (most business dealings) or quite formal (bankers).

A special note for drug tourists: it is 'not done' to smoke dope in public. At 'coffee-shops' it's OK and in some other situations too, but even the hippest locals detest foreigners who think they can just toke anywhere. The same applies to drinking out on the street: the fact that you can do it in a decreasing number of places doesn't mean it's accepted.

RELIGION

Amsterdam began as a Catholic city without being fervently anti-Protestant – after all, the money machine dictated tolerance. Even after the Alteration of 1578, when Amsterdam went over to the Protestant camp and Calvinism became the leading faith in the northern Netherlands, the city authorities still promoted religious tolerance (though not freedom), even towards those who didn't belong to any church. Civil marriages (sanctioned by public officials rather than clergy) were legally recognised as early as the 17th century, a first in Europe.

The Protestant Hervormde Kerk (Dutch Reformed Church) was also fairly tolerant of dissenting views among its members, but in the late 19th century a growing minority of low-income strugglers disagreed with such tolerance and broke off to form the Gereformeerde Kerk ('Re-reformed' Church) in pursuit of orthodox-Calvinist doctrine. The schism persists to this day though it affects an ever smaller number of people.

Agnosticism and atheism reign supreme: almost 60% of Amsterdammers say they have no religious affiliation. Catholics are the largest religious grouping with 19% of the population against a national average of 32% – the term 'Catholic' should be used in preference to 'Roman Catholic' because many Catholics locally and nationally disagree with the pope on church hierarchy, contraception and abortion. The next largest religious grouping is Muslim at 8.3% (the national average is 3.7%), followed by Hervormd at 5.5% (15%), Gereformeerd at 3% (7%) and other religions (mainly Hindu and Buddhist) at 5.2% (3%).

LANGUAGE

Almost every Amsterdammer from age eight onwards seems to speak English, often very well and better than you're ever likely to learn Dutch. So why bother trying to communicate in the local language? That's a good question because you'll rarely get the opportunity to practise: your Dutch acquaintances will launch into English, maybe to show off but also because they're probably avid travellers, familiar with foreigners, and know what it's like to struggle in situations like these. Nevertheless, a few words in Dutch are always appreciated, especially the phrase *Spreekt u Engels?* (Do you speak English?) with elderly people. You might even begin to understand a bit more of what's going on around you.

For a brief guide to Dutch and some useful words and phrases, see the language chapter at the back of this book. For more extensive coverage of the language, pick up Lonely Planet's *Western Europe phrasebook*.

Amsterdam Architecture

msterdam is an architectural marvel with no fewer than 7000 registered historical buildings, though there are no grand structures and only a few buildings that impress with size. Its beauty, especially within the canal belt, lies in the countless private dwellings with distinguishing features that make each one stand out in its own particular way. No other city in Europe has such a wealth of residential architecture. Amsterdam was built by citizens and businesses, not by government.

This is not to say the government's role has been negligible. It has traditionally provided land for building purposes, determined maximum and minimum sizes for housing plots, and enforced often stringent building standards. But even today, the authorities tend to give architects and their principals more leeway than they're used to in other parts of the world, ensuring that Amsterdam remains at the architectural cutting edge – especially when it comes to architecture on a 'human' scale that makes the best use of limited space.

Information Sources

A great Web site for Amsterdam architecture, especially the older, listed buildings, is run by the city's conservation office (Bureau Monumentenzorg) at **w** www.bmz.amsterdam.nl.

Many aspects of current urban planning are on permanent display in the Zuiderkerk (see Zuiderkerk in the Nieuwmarkt Neighbourhood section in the Things to See & Do chapter). The Architectuur Centrum Amsterdam (Arcam; Map 2; ☎ 620 48 78), Waterlooplein 213, organises temporary displays about architectural themes.

There are countless books on Amsterdam architecture, many of them in English – the Arcam can advise you. For practical architecture and engineering, see *Building Amsterdam* by Herman Janse (De Brink, 1994), with clear drawings showing how it was done in the past, from houses and churches to bridges and locks. Unfortunately, the most beautifully produced book about canal-belt architecture, *Het Grachtenboek* (1993) by Paul Spies and others, is out of print – try the antiquarian bookshops. It catalogues every building along the canals with a wealth of historical photos and illustrations. Part 1, which was available in English, deals with the major canals and Part 2 with the medieval city.

Architecture students should get hold of Paul Groenendijk & Piet Vollaard's *Guide to Modern Architecture in Amsterdam* (010 Publishers, 1996), along with the companion *Guide to Modern Architecture in the Netherlands*. Maristella Casciato's *The Amsterdam School* (1996) by the same publisher is one of the better books on this unique urban-planning movement.

Previous page: Detail of het Schip housing estate, an example of the Amsterdam School style (photo by Doekes Lulofs)

MIDDLE AGES

The oldest surviving building is the Gothic Oude Kerk (Old Church), which dates from the early 14th century. The second-oldest is the late-Gothic Nieuwe Kerk from the early 15th century. In both these churches, note the timber vaulting (the marshy ground precluded the use of heavy stone) and the use of brick rather than stone in the walls. Stone was not only heavy but also scarce; there was plenty of clay and sand to produce bricks. Also note how the interior focus has shifted from the (Catholic) choir and altar to the (Protestant) pulpit. The pulpit takes centre stage in churches built after the Protestant takeover in 1578; a good example is the Noorderkerk in the Jordaan.

The earliest houses were made of timber and clay with thatched roofs. In the 15th century, timber side walls made way for brick in a process of natural selection brought about by fires, and in the 16th century the thatched roofs were replaced by tiles. Timber was still used for facades and gables into the 17th century but eventually brick and sandstone triumphed here too. Only two houses have survived with timber facades: Begijnhof 34 (mid-15th century) and Zeedijk 1 (mid-16th century). Timber, however, remained an essential building material for floor beams and roof frames.

DUTCH RENAISSANCE

From about the middle of the 16th century the Italian Renaissance began to filter through to the Netherlands, where architects developed a unique style with rich ornamentation that merged classical and traditional elements. In the facades they used mock columns, so-called pilasters, and they replaced the traditional spout gables with step gables richly decorated with sculptures, columns and obelisks. The playful interaction of red (or rather, orange) brick and horizontal bands of white or yellow sandstone was based on strict mathematical formulas that pleased the eye.

Right: The Nieuwe Kerk, a late-Gothic basilica

EDWARD AM SNIJDERS

The city carpenter Hendrick Staets (who planned the canal belt), the city bricklayer Cornelis Danckerts and the city sculptor **Hendrick de Keyser** (1565–1621) were jointly responsible for municipal buildings. Utrecht-born De Keyser's artistic contributions were the most visible and it was he who perfected Dutch-Renaissance architecture. His Bartolotti House at Herengracht 170–172 is one of the finest examples of his work. He also designed the Zuiderkerk and the Westerkerk in which he retained Gothic elements, but he set a new direction in Dutch Protestant church-building with the Noorderkerk, laid out like a Greek cross with the pulpit in the centre.

DUTCH CLASSICISM

During the Golden Age of the 17th century, architects such as **Jacob van Campen** (1595–1657) and **Philips Vingboons** (1607–78) and his brother **Justus** adhered more strictly to Greek and Roman classical design and dropped many of De Keyser's playful decorations. Influenced by Italian architects such as Palladio and Scamozzi, they made facades resemble temples. The pilasters looked more like columns, with pedestals and pediments. In order to accentuate the vertical lines, the step gable changed to a neck gable with decorative scrolls, topped by a triangular or rounded fronton to imitate a temple roof. Soft red brick was made more durable with brown paint. Van Campen's city hall (now Royal Palace) on Dam Square is the most impressive example of this style.

The Vingboons brothers specialised in residential architecture and their work can be found throughout the western canal belt, such as the current Bijbels Museum at Herengracht 364–370 and the White House (now Theatermuseum) next to the Bartolotti House, or the fine example at Keizersgracht 319.

Classical elements became more restrained later in the 17th century. Make-believe columns became less ornamental or disappeared altogether as external decorations made way for sumptuous interiors. This was the period of the southern canal belt, when wealthy Amsterdammers often bought two adjoining plots and built houses five windows wide instead of the usual three. Justus Vingboons' Trippenhuis at Kloveniersburgwal 29 is a good example.

This austere classicism is best seen, however, in the works of **Adriaan Dortsman** (1625–82), whose designs include the Round Lutheran Church and the current Museum Van Loon at Keizersgracht 672–674. A mathematician by training, he favoured a stark, geometrical simplicity – preferably with flat, sandstone facades – that enhanced the grandeur of his buildings.

18TH-CENTURY 'LOUIS STYLES'

The wealthy class now began to enjoy the fortunes amassed by their merchant predecessors. Many turned to banking and finance and conducted their business from the comfort of opulent homes. Those who still engaged actively in trade no longer stored goods in the attic but in warehouses elsewhere.

Gables and Hoists

A gable not only hid the roof from public view but also helped to identify the house until the French-led government introduced house numbers in 1795 (though the current system of odd and even numbers dates from 1875). The more ornate the gable, the easier it was to recognise. Other distinguishing features included facade decorations, signs or wall tablets (cartouches).

There are four main types of gables. The simple **spout gable** with semicircular windows or shutters, a copy of the earliest wooden gables, was used mainly for warehouses from the 1580s to the early 1700s. The **step gable** was a late-Gothic design favoured by Dutch-Renaissance architects from 1580 to 1660. The **neck gable**, also known as the bottle gable because it resembled a bottle spout, was introduced in the 1640s and proved most durable, featuring occasionally in designs of the early 19th century. Some neck gables incorporated a step. The **bell gable** first appeared in the 1660s and became popular in the 18th century.

Many houses built from the 18th century onwards no longer had gables but straight, horizontal cornices that were richly decorated, often with pseudo-balustrades. These cornices could be quite long if the roofline ran parallel to the street; if it ran perpendicular, the cornice often incorporated a 'bulge' for the hoist in the attic (see below).

Many canal houses have a slight forward lean. This has nothing to do with subsidence but everything to do with hoisting goods into the attic and furniture into the (removable) windows without them bumping into the house. A few houses have huge hoist-wheels in the attic with a rope and hook that run through the hoist beam. Almost all others, even those built today, have a beam with a hook for a hoist block. The forward lean also allows the facade and gable to be admired from the street – a fortunate coincidence.

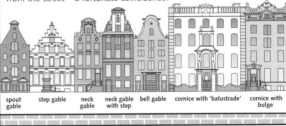

spout gable step gable neck gable neck gable with step bell gable cornice with 'balustrade' cornice with bulge

The preoccupation with all things French provided fertile ground for Huguenot refugees, such as **Daniel Marot** (1661–1752) and his assistants **Jean** and **Anthony Coulon**, who introduced French interior design with matching exteriors. Interiors were bathed in light thanks to stuccoed ceilings and tall sash windows (a French innovation), and everything from staircases to furniture was designed in harmony. Elegant bell gables, introduced around 1660, became commonplace, though many architects did away with gables altogether in favour of richly decorated horizontal cornices.

KIM GRANT

The Louis XIV style dominated until about 1750, with its dignified symmetry and facades decorated with statuary and leaves. Around 1740 the Louis XV style brought asymmetrical rococo shapes resembling rocks and waves. Pilasters or pillars made a comeback around 1770 with Louis XVI designs that showed a renewed interest in classical motifs. An extreme example of this is the Felix Meritis building at Keizersgracht 324 designed by **Jacob Otten Husly** (1738–97), with enormous Corinthian half-columns that seem to carry the structure. The Maagdenhuis on Spui Square, designed by city architect **Abraham van der Hart** (1747–1820), is a much more sober interpretation of the new classicism.

19TH-CENTURY NEO-STYLES

Architecture stagnated in the first half of the 19th century as Amsterdam struggled to recover from the economic disasters of the Napoleonic era. Safe neoclassicism held sway until the 1860s when architects here and elsewhere in Europe began to rediscover other styles of the past.

The main Amsterdam styles in the latter half of the century were neo-Gothic, harking back to the grand Gothic cathedrals in which no

Left: Detail of a neck gable

design element was superfluous; and neo-Renaissance, which brought De Keyser's Dutch-Renaissance architecture back into the limelight. The former suited the boom in Catholic church-building now that Catholics were free to build new churches in Protestant parts of the country; the latter appealed to local architects because houses in this style were being demolished at a rapid rate.

One of the leading architects of this period was **Pierre Cuypers** (1827–1921), who built several neo-Gothic churches but often merged the two styles, as can be seen in his Centraal Station and Rijksmuseum which have Gothic structures and Dutch-Renaissance brickwork. Another fine example of this mixture is CH Peters' general post office (now Magna Plaza) at Nieuwezijds Voorburgwal 182. Alfred Tepe's Krijtberg church at Singel 448 is more clearly Gothic (but note the use of brick), while the milk factory at Prinsengracht 739–741 designed by Eduard Cuypers (Pierre's nephew) sits firmly in the Dutch-Renaissance tradition.

Other architects were more eclectic and also incorporated medieval Dutch and German designs in a very personal way. Good examples are Isaac Gosschalk's houses at Reguliersgracht 57–59 and 63, and AC Bleijs' PC Hooft store on the corner of Keizersgracht and Leidsestraat. AL van Gendt's Concertgebouw is obviously neoclassical but its interplay of red brick and white sandstone is Dutch Renaissance.

A popular European style around the turn of the century was Art Nouveau. In Amsterdam, Art Nouveau's abundant use of steel and glass with curvilinear designs resembling plants showed up mainly in shop fronts but in little else (The Hague has far more Art Nouveau architecture). There are, however, a handful of fine examples, such as the current Greenpeace headquarters at Keizersgracht 174–176, the American Hotel at Leidseplein, and the riotous Tuschinskitheater at Reguliersbreestraat 26–28.

Right: Detail of the Rijksmuseum's facade

MARTIN MOOS

AMSTERDAM ARCHITECTURE

BERLAGE & THE AMSTERDAM SCHOOL

The neo-styles and their reliance on the past were strongly criticised by **Hendrik Petrus Berlage** (1856–1934), the father of modern Dutch architecture. Instead of expensive construction and excessive decoration, he favoured simplicity and a rational use of materials. His Beurs (Bourse, or Stock Exchange) on the Damrak displayed his ideals to the full. He cooperated with sculptors, painters and tilers to ensure that ornamentation was integrated into the overall design in a supportive role, rather than being tacked on as an embellishment to hide the structure.

Berlage's residential architecture approached a block of buildings as a whole, not as a collection of individual houses. In this he influenced the young architects of what became known as the Amsterdam School, though they rejected his stark rationalism and preferred more creative designs. Leading exponents of this style were **Michel de Klerk** (1884–1923), **Piet Kramer** (1881–1961) and **Johan van der Mey** (1878–1949). The latter heralded the Amsterdam School in his Scheepvaarthuis at Prins Hendrikkade.

These architects built in brick and treated housing blocks as sculptures, with curved corners, oddly placed windows and ornamental, rocket-shaped towers. Their housing estates, such as De Klerk's 'Schip' in the Oostzaanstraat and Kramer's Cooperatiehof in the Pijp neighbourhood, have been described as fairy-tale fortresses rendered in a Dutch version of Art Deco. Their preference for form over function meant that their designs were interesting to look at but not always fantastic to live in, with small windows and inefficient use of space. A typically Dutch, somewhat patronising benevolence played a role too: kitchens were tiny because residents weren't supposed to eat in the kitchen but in a proper dining room; windows were set high because residents weren't supposed to look out, they were supposed to read a book; and so forth.

MARTIN MOOS

Left: Patterned brickwork of the ABN-AMRO bank building, completed in 1923

Top Left: Architecture of the peaceful Begijnhof, a former convent

Top Right: Gothic-style Oude Kerk (Old Church), built in the early 14th century

Middle: A variety of decorative gables

Bottom Left: Dutch Renaissance gable of the Bartolotti House on Herengracht, designed by Hendrik de Keyser

Bottom Right: Detail of the Royal Palace on Dam Square, designed by Jacob van Campen in Dutch Classicist style

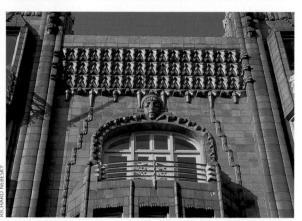

Top Left: The neo-Gothic Krijtberg church

Top Right: Magna Plaza, a mixture of Dutch Renaissance and Gothic

Middle: The riotous Tuschinskitheater, one of the few buildings in Art Nouveau style

Bottom: Detail of 'Het Schip' housing estate, a fine example of the Amsterdam School

Many architects of this school worked for the city council and designed the buildings of the ambitious 'Plan South'. This was a large-scale expansion of good-quality housing, wide boulevards and cosy squares between the Amstel and what was to become the Olympic Stadium. It was mapped out by Berlage and instigated by the labour party alderman FM Wibaut, though Berlage didn't get much of a chance to design the buildings, with council architects pushing their own designs. Subsidised housing corporations provided the funding here and elsewhere in the 1920s, a period of frantic residential building activity beyond the canal belt. This close cooperation between housing corporations, city planners and council architects made the Amsterdam School more than just an architectural movement: it was a complete philosophy of city planning.

See the New South section in the Things to see & Do chapter for details about the Housing Act of 1901 and its enormous impact on residential construction in the first decades of the 20th century.

FUNCTIONALISM

While Amsterdam School-type buildings were being erected all over the city, a new generation of architects began to rebel against the school's impractical (not to mention expensive) structures. Influenced by the Bauhaus School in Germany, Frank Lloyd Wright in the USA and Le Corbusier in France, they formed a group called de 8 (the 8) in 1927.

Architects such as **Ben Merkelbach** and **Gerrit Rietveld** believed that form should follow function and sang the praises of steel, glass and concrete. Buildings should be spacious, practical structures with plenty of sunlight, not masses of brick treated as works of art to glorify architects.

The all-important Committee of Aesthetics Control didn't agree with this, however, and kept the functionalists out of the canal belt, relegating them to the new housing estates on the outskirts of the city

Right: The controversial Pentagon housing estate, designed by Theo Bosch

DOEKES LULOFS

– although Rietveld did build his glass gallery on top of the Metz department store at Keizersgracht 455.

Functionalism finally came to the fore after WWII and put its stamp on new suburbs west and south of the city, thanks to the General Extension Plan that had been adopted in 1935 but interrupted by the war. The acute housing shortage meant that these suburbs were built on a larger scale than originally planned, yet they still weren't sufficient and the Bijlmermeer south-east of the city was added in the 1960s and 1970s. By this time, however, there was increasing resistance to such large-scale housing estates.

In the inner city, the emphasis shifted towards urban renewal with innovative designs on a scale appropriate to their surroundings. Architects followed examples set by **Aldo van Eyck** and his student **Theo Bosch**. Van Eyck's designs included the Moederhuis at Plantage Middenlaan 33; Bosch's included the Pentagon housing complex on the corner of St Antoniesbreestraat and Zwanenburgwal. Opinions are still mixed, however, with critics dismissing such designs as 'parasite architecture' – modern housing projects that look a bit out of place, with huge windows so residents can stare out of their aquarium onto wonderful 17th- and 18th-century surroundings.

Suburbs have been built on a more human scale since the 1970s, with low and medium-rise apartments integrated with shops, schools and offices. The eastern docklands in the harbour are a good example of current developments. Strict functionalism has also made way for more imaginative designs, such as A Alberts and M van Huut's ING Bank (1987) in the Bijlmermeer: built on anthroposophical principles, this S-shaped complex of linked towers has few right angles.

For more about current architecture and the accompanying issues, see The Power of Money at the end of the History section in the Facts about Amsterdam chapter, and the Eastern Harbour District section in the Things to See & Do chapter. The latter includes a cycling tour of the major architectural sights there.

Facts for the Visitor

WHEN TO GO

Any time can be the best time to visit. The summer months, June to August, are wonderful as the whole city seems to live outdoors and things happen everywhere. It's also the peak tourist season: accommodation is hard to find and prices are high, especially in August. Bear in mind that many Amsterdammers go on holidays in summer and some businesses close down or adapt their activities (eg, museums, orchestras).

From mid-October to mid-March the climate is miserable but there are fewer tourists. Accommodation is cheaper (except around New Year) though some hotels might be closed. You'll mingle with 'real' Amsterdammers in cosy pubs and be able to enjoy the city's cultural life at its most authentic. The shoulder seasons, roughly from mid-March to late May and late August to mid-October, can offer the best of both worlds, though you might want to avoid Easter with its hordes of tourists and expensive hotels. If you could pick one month of the year, choose September and hope for an Indian summer.

A festival or special event can enhance your visit – see Public Holidays & Special Events later in this chapter – but it won't be a secret and you may have trouble finding accommodation during the more popular ones. August is the top month for special events. If weather's a major concern, see Climate in the Facts about Amsterdam chapter.

ORIENTATION

Most of Amsterdam lies south of the IJ, an arm of what was once the Zuiderzee (an extension of the North Sea) but is now a vast lake, the IJsselmeer. The modern city sprawls in all directions and is several times larger than it was 50 years ago.

The old city is contained within the ring of concentric canals *(grachten)*, dating from the 17th century, that form the crescent-shaped canal belt *(grachtengordel)* bordered by the Singelgracht. Most areas beyond this tidy structure have been added since the second half of the 19th century.

The Amstel River cuts through the old city, which arose around Dam Square. East of this is the Old Side (Oude Zijde) and west is the New Side (Nieuwe Zijde). This medieval *binnenstad* (inner city) is enclosed by the Singel (moat, not to be confused with the Singelgracht) to the west and south, and by the Kloveniersburgwal/Geldersekade to the east.

Centraal Station – the central train station – lies on the south bank of the IJ at what used to be the mouth of the Amstel River, but the 'centre of town' is Dam Square a little to the south. It's the city's largest square and major road arteries radiate out from it, though there are several other 'centres' where everything seems to happen: Leidseplein, with much of the city's cultural life and nightlife, Rembrandtplein (nightlife), Spui ('intellectual' life), Muntplein (the city's busiest intersection), Stationsplein in front of Centraal Station (the main transport hub), Nieuwmarkt Square (daily life in general), Waterlooplein with the Stopera (market life behind a landmark on the Amstel), the large Museumplein (culture), and other, smaller focal points that make the city such a joy to explore.

Finding your way around the canal belt can be confusing, though it's a breeze compared with Venice. Think of it as the bottom half of a bicycle wheel: the medieval city is the hub, and several main roads and minor canals (and the Amstel itself) function as spokes. The major canals, in a series of semicircles, connect the spokes. Orientation becomes easier once you know the sequence of the main canals (from the centre outwards: Singel, Herengracht, Keizersgracht, Prinsengracht and Singelgracht) and the names of some of the major 'spokes' (anticlockwise: Haarlemmerstraat/Haarlemmerdijk, Brouwersgracht, Raadhuisstraat/Rozengracht, Leidsestraat, Vijzelstraat, Utrechtsestraat, Amstel, Weesperstraat and Plantage Middenlaan).

House numbers along the main canals start at the north-western end, at Brouwersgracht, with odd numbers along the inner quays (the 'city-centre' sides). Elsewhere, numbers start at the end of the street closest to the city centre.

MAPS

The maps in this book will probably suffice in most cases. Lonely Planet's handy *Amsterdam City Map* has a street index that covers the more popular parts of town in detail – and is plastic-coated to make it rainproof. The VVV tourist offices also have a map but it's not free.

If you need something that shows every street in the whole city including the outer suburbs, then newsagencies and many other outlets sell the Dutch-produced Cito Plan or the German Falkplan. They're both good but the Cito is probably the clearest, though it has to be tilted clockwise a bit to get north facing up. The Swiss Hallwag sheet map is also good and clear but the smallest streets aren't labelled. The Michelin sheet map has the meticulous linework expected from this renowned map maker; unfortunately its long turnaround time means that even the 'updated' version is out of date and doesn't show as much detail in the new parts of the city as the Cito does.

A beautiful souvenir map to hang on the wall when you get home is the lovingly drawn bird's-eye view produced by Bollmann, a German map publisher specialising in this type of product. It can be hard to find, but geographical bookshop Jacob van Wijngaarden (Map 4; ☎ 612 19 01) at Overtoom 97 should have it.

TOURIST OFFICES
Local Tourist Offices

Within the Netherlands, tourist information is supplied by the VVV (Vereniging voor Vreemdelingenverkeer – Society for Foreigner Traffic; pronounced 'vay vay vay'), which has four offices in Amsterdam and a fifth, called Holland Tourist Information, at the airport. All its publications cost money and it charges high commissions for services (€11.35 per booking to find a room,

€1.82 to €2.73 on theatre tickets etc). The offices are often very busy but it's worth queuing to get an Amsterdam Pass (see Other Documents & Cards in the following Documents section).

The GWK office (official exchange bureau, see Exchanging Money in the later Money section) inside Centraal Station also books rooms, for €4.54 per person (maximum of €9.08).

The VVV information number, ☎ 0900-400 40 40, operates 9am to 5pm weekdays and costs a hefty €0.48 a minute; people ringing from abroad could try ☎ 551 25 25 (free apart from normal phone costs). Web sites are **W** www.visitamsterdam.nl and **W** www.amsterdamtourist.nl. Office details are as follows:

VVV (Map 2) Stationsplein 10 in front of Centraal Station. The main VVV office, open 9am to 5pm daily; expect long queues and variable service.
VVV, inside Centraal Station, along track 2A (spoor 2A). Open 8am to 7.45pm Monday to Saturday, 9am to 5pm Sunday; often busy but sometimes not.
VVV (Map 4) Leidseplein 1 on the corner of Leidsestraat. Open 9am to 7pm Monday to Friday, to 5pm weekends; shares premises with a GWK-affiliated exchange office that offers reasonable rates.
VVV (Map 1) Argonautenstraat 98 at Stadionplein. Open 9am to 5pm daily; useful if you're arriving by car from the south (A10 exit 's108') and usually much quieter than the other offices.
Holland Tourist Information (VVV), Schiphol Plaza in the airport. Open 7am to 10pm daily.

Tourist Offices Abroad

The Nederlands Bureau voor Toerisme (NBT, **W** www.holland.com) handles tourism inquiries outside the country:

Belgium & Luxembourg (☎ 02-543 08 00) NBT, Louizalaan 89, Postbus 136, 1050 Brussels
Canada (☎ 416-363 15 77) Netherlands Board of Tourism, 25 Adelaide St East, Suite 710, Toronto, Ont, M5C 1Y2
France (☎ 1 43 12 34 27) Office Néerlandais du Tourisme, 9 rue Scribe, 75009 Paris
Germany (☎ 0221-9257 1721) Niederländisches Büro für Tourismus, Friesenplatz 1, Postfach 270580, 50511 Cologne

Japan (☎ 03-32 22 11 12) Netherlands Board of Tourism, NK Shinwa Building 5F, 5-1 Koijmachi, Chiyoda-ku, Tokyo 102-0083
Sweden, Denmark, Norway & Finland (☎ 08-5560 0750) Holländska Turistbyrån, Högbergsgatan 50-1tr, 118 26 Stockholm
UK & Ireland (☎ 020-7539 7950) Netherlands Board of Tourism, 15–19 Kingsway, 7th Floor, Imperial House, London WC2B 6UN
USA (☎ 888-GOHOLLAND) Netherlands Board of Tourism, 355 Lexington Ave, 19th Floor, New York 10017

There are smaller offices in several other countries – check the Web site – but none in Australia (the embassy in Canberra or consulate in Sydney might be able to help).

Other Information Sources
The VVV is all right for mainstream tourist information but other places might serve you better. If you're interested in the arts (theatres, concerts, films, museums etc), the Amsterdam Uitburo Ticketshop, or AUB (Map 4; ☎ 0900-01 91, €0.40 per minute), Leidseplein 26, has lots of free magazines and brochures, and sells tickets for a €1.82 markup. The staff are friendlier and more helpful than at the VVV. The office is open 10am to 6pm daily, to 9pm Thursday. The telephone number, called the Uitlijn (Out-Line), operates 9am to 9pm daily for information and ticket sales. For further information, see Ⓦ www.uitlijn.nl or Ⓦ www.aub.nl (unfortunately, both Dutch-only).

The Dutch automobile association ANWB (Map 4; ☎ 673 08 44), Museumplein 5, has free or discounted maps and brochures and provides a wide range of useful information and assistance if you're travelling with any type of vehicle (car, bicycle, motorcycle, yacht etc). The material on Amsterdam itself is limited but there's plenty about the Netherlands and Europe. You'll probably have to show proof of membership of your automobile club (see Driving Licence & Permits in the following section).

If you plan to stay in Amsterdam for a while, the city hall information centre (Map 2; ☎ 624 11 11), Amstel 1 (near the Waterlooplein Metro exit), has pamphlets and booklets on almost every aspect of living in

the city, some in English. It's open 8.30am to 5pm Monday to Friday. The staff are quite helpful and, as almost everywhere else, speak good English. Their computerised database can track down addresses and phone numbers of relevant organisations.

See also the Digital Resources section later in this chapter for useful Web sites on Amsterdam.

DOCUMENTS
Visas
Tourists from Australia, Canada, Israel, Japan, Korea (south), New Zealand, Singapore, the USA and most of Europe need only a valid passport – no visa – for a stay of up to three months. EU nationals can enter for three months with just their national identity card or a passport expired less than five years.

Nationals of most other countries need a so-called Schengen Visa valid for 90 days, named after the Schengen Agreement that abolished passport controls between the EU member states (except the UK and Ireland) plus Norway and Iceland. A visa for any of these countries should, in theory, be valid throughout the area, but it pays to double-check with the embassy or consulate of each country you intend to visit because the agreement is not yet fully implemented – some countries impose additional restrictions on some nationalities. Residency status in any of the Schengen countries negates the need for a visa, regardless of your nationality.

Schengen visas are issued by Dutch embassies or consulates and can take a while to process (up to three months, if you're unlucky), so don't leave it till the last moment. You'll need a valid passport (valid till at least three months after your visit) and 'sufficient' funds to finance your stay. Fees vary depending on your nationality – the embassy or consulate can tell you more.

Visas for study purposes are complicated – check with a Dutch embassy or consulate. For work visas, see Work later in this chapter.

Visa Extensions The Netherlands is the most densely populated country in Europe and voters support the government crackdown on people who don't 'belong'. Tourist visas can be extended for another three months maximum, but you'll need a very good reason and the extension will only be valid for the Netherlands, Belgium and Luxembourg, not the Schengen area. You can't turn a tourist visa into a residence permit without returning to your home country and (re)applying from there.

Visa extensions and residence permits are handled by the Vreemdelingenpolitie (Aliens' Police; Map 1; ☎ 559 63 00), Johan Huizingalaan 757 out in the south-western suburbs, open 8am to 5pm Monday to Friday. A visa extension shouldn't take long if you make an appointment – if you just turn up you may have to wait a couple of hours. Residence permits are handled by appointment only.

Travel Insurance

Medical or dental costs might already be covered through reciprocal health-care arrangements (see Health later in this chapter) but you'll still need cover for theft or loss, and for unexpected changes to travel arrangements (ticket cancellation etc). Check what's already covered by your local insurance policies or credit card: you might not need separate travel insurance. In most cases, though, this secondary type of cover is very limited with lots of tricky small print. For peace of mind, nothing beats straight travel insurance at the highest level you can afford.

Driving Licence & Permits

Naturally you'll need to show a valid driving licence when hiring a car. Visitors from outside the EU should also consider getting an international driving permit (IDP), to be used in conjunction with your original licence. Car-rental firms will rarely ask for one but the police might do so if they pull you up and can't make sense of your home-country licensing codes. An IDP can be obtained for a small fee from your local automobile association – bring along a valid licence and a passport photo – and is only valid for a year.

Automobile Association If you're travelling with any type of vehicle, the Dutch automobile association ANWB (Map 4; ☎ 673 08 44), Museumplein 5, will provide a wide range of services free of charge if you can show proof of membership of the equivalent association at home, preferably in the form of a letter of introduction such as the yellow Entraide Touring Internationale document. Your automobile club should be able to provide this (if the staff have never heard of it, ask for someone who knows their stuff).

Hostel Cards

A Hostelling International card is useful at the official youth hostels – nonmembers are welcome but pay €3 more per night. Other hostels may give small discounts. If you don't get an HI card before leaving home you can buy one at youth hostels in the Netherlands.

Student & Youth Cards

An International Student Identity Card (ISIC) won't give many admission discounts but it might pay for itself through discounted air and ferry tickets, and the GWK exchange offices will charge 25% less commission when exchanging cash. The same (but not the 25% GWK discount) applies to hostel cards, as well as the IYTC (International Youth Travel Card) for people aged under 26 who aren't students, issued by the International Student Travel Confederation (ISTC), through student unions or student travel agencies.

The Cultureel Jongeren Paspoort (CJP, Cultural Youth Passport) is a national institution that gives people aged under 27 whopping discounts to museums and cultural events around the country – any young person with a particular interest in the arts is well advised to get one. It costs €11 a year and is available at VVV offices or the Amsterdam Uitburo (see Other Information Sources earlier in this chapter). You don't have to be Dutch but you do need decent ID.

Other Documents & Cards

If you plan to visit several of Amsterdam's excellent but expensive museums, invest in a Museumjaarkaart (Museum Year Card), which gives free admission to most of the city's museums – see the boxed text 'A Medley of Museums' in the Things to See & Do chapter.

Teachers, professional artists, museum conservators and certain categories of students may sometimes get discounts at a few museums or even be admitted free. Bring proof of affiliation, eg, an International Teacher Identity Card (ITIC).

The VVV offices and some large hotels sell the Amsterdam Pass. This contains 32 vouchers that give free public transport anywhere in the city for three days, free entry or substantial discounts to the most important museums, a free canal cruise, and discounts on other water transport, some tours and restaurants. The pass represents a total value of €90 and sells for €29 – a wise investment especially if you use a lot of public transport.

Seniors get discounts on a wide range of services (see Senior Travellers later in this chapter).

Copies

All important documents (passport data page and visa page, credit cards, travel insurance policy, air/bus/train ticket, driving licence etc) should be photocopied before you leave home. Leave one copy with someone at home and keep another with you, separate from the originals.

It's also a good idea to store details of your vital travel documents in Lonely Planet's free online Travel Vault in case you lose the photocopies. Your password-protected Travel Vault is accessible online anywhere in the world – create it at W www .ekno.lonelyplanet.com.

EMBASSIES & CONSULATES
Dutch Embassies & Consulates
Dutch embassies abroad include:

Australia (☎ 02-6273 3111) 120 Empire Circuit, Yarralumla, ACT 2600
Belgium (☎ 02-679 17 11) Herrmann Debroux-laan 48, 1160 Brussels
Canada (☎ 613-237 5030) Suite 2020, 350 Albert St, Ottawa, Ont K1R 1A4
France (☎ 01 40 62 33 00) 7–9 Rue Eblé, 75007 Paris

Germany (☎ 030-20 95 60) 20th & 21st Floor, Friedrichstrasse 95, 10117 Berlin
Ireland (☎ 01-269 3444) 160 Merrion Rd, Dublin 4
Luxembourg (☎ 22 75 70) 5 rue CM Spoo, L2546 Luxembourg
New Zealand (☎ 04-471 6390) Investment House, Cnr Featherston & Ballance Sts, Wellington
UK (☎ 020-7590 3200) 38 Hyde Park Gate, London SW7 5DP
USA (☎ 202-244 5300) 4200 Linnean Ave, NW Washington, DC 20008

Consulates in Amsterdam
Amsterdam is the country's capital but the government and ministries are based in The Hague, so that's where all the embassies are located. The Hague is a 45-minute train ride away, costing €14.07 return.

There are, however, 36 consulates in Amsterdam, listed under 'Consulaat' in the phone book. These include:

Denmark (☎ 682 99 91) Radarweg 503
France (Map 4; ☎ 530 69 69) Vijzelgracht 2; open 9am to noon weekdays
Germany (Map 4; ☎ 673 62 45) De Lairesse-straat 172
Italy (Map 4; ☎ 550 20 50) Herengracht 581
Japan (Map 4; ☎ 691 69 21) Vijzelgracht 50
Luxembourg (☎ 301 56 22) Reimersbeek 2
Norway (Map 4; ☎ 624 23 31) Keizersgracht 534-I
Spain (Map 4; ☎ 620 38 11) Frederiksplein 34; open 9am to 11am weekdays, 2pm to 4pm Wednesday
Thailand (☎ 465 15 32) Amstelplein 1
UK (Map 1; ☎ 676 43 43) Koningslaan 44 near the Vondelpark; open 9am to noon and 2pm to 3.30pm weekdays
USA (Map 4; ☎ 575 53 09) Museumplein 19 near the Concertgebouw; open 8.30am to noon and 1.30pm to 3.30pm weekdays

Embassies in The Hague
Australia (☎ 070-310 82 00) Carnegielaan 4
Belgium (☎ 070-312 34 56) Lange Vijverberg 12
Canada (☎ 070-311 16 00) Sophialaan 7
Finland (☎ 070-346 97 54) Groot Hertoginne-laan 16
Ireland (☎ 070-363 09 93) Dr Kuijperstraat 9
Korea (south) (☎ 070-358 60 76) Verlengde Tolweg 8
New Zealand (☎ 070-346 93 24) Carnegielaan 10-IV

FACTS FOR THE VISITOR

South Africa (☎ 070-392 45 01) Wassenaarse-weg 40
Sweden (☎ 070-412 02 00) Van Karnebeeklaan 6A

Your Own Embassy

It's important to realise what your own embassy – the embassy of the country of which you are a citizen – can and can't do if you get into trouble. Generally speaking, it won't be much help in emergencies if the trouble is remotely your own fault. Remember that you are bound by the laws of the country you are in. Your embassy will not be sympathetic if you end up in jail after committing a crime locally, even if such actions are legal in your own country.

In genuine emergencies you might get some assistance, but only if other channels have been exhausted. For example, if you need to get home urgently, a free ticket home is exceedingly unlikely – the embassy would expect you to have insurance. If you have all your money and documents stolen, it might assist with getting a new passport, but a loan for onward travel is out of the question.

CUSTOMS

Visitors from EU countries can bring virtually anything they like – up to 110L of beer, 90L of wine, 20L of liquor less than 22% alcohol by volume (A/V) and 10L of liquor more than 22% A/V – provided it's for personal use and they bought it in an EU country where the appropriate local tax was levied. Duty-free allowances no longer exist within the EU. The staff at duty-free shops will ask to see your ticket and will tell you in no uncertain terms how much (or rather, little) they're willing to sell you.

Visitors arriving from a country outside the EU can import goods and gifts valued up to €175 (bought tax-free) as well as 200 cigarettes (or 50 cigars or 250g of tobacco), 1L of liquor more than 22% A/V or 2L less than 22% A/V, plus 2L of wine, 50g of perfume and 250ml of eau de toilette. Tobacco and alcohol may only be brought in by people aged 17 and over.

The Netherlands has no quarantine for foreign pets (but check the policy of the country you're returning to). Most can enter with a health certificate under 10 days old, plus a certificate of rabies vaccination between 30 days and nine months old; both must be issued by a certified vet and include specific details. For more information, contact the Amsterdam District of Dutch Customs (☎ 586 75 11), a KLM office, or a Dutch consulate.

MONEY
Currency

On 1 January 2002 the Netherlands adopted the euro, along with 11 other EU countries – Austria, Belgium, Finland, France, Germany, Greece, Ireland, Italy, Luxembourg, Portugal and Spain (Denmark, Sweden and the UK opted out for the time being). The Dutch weren't ecstatic about the euro but accepted it as inevitable, and there was little resistance.

The venerable guilder, Europe's first 'hard' currency in modern times (in use since 1609), has been consigned to the history books and is no longer legal tender (unlike some other euro countries that use two sets of currencies until July 2002). People still holding guilder coins and notes can exchange them for euros at any bank until 1 January 2003, at the official rate of 2.20371 guilders to the euro; a commission may be charged. After that date, the Nederlandsche Bank (the central bank) will exchange coins free of charge until 1 January 2007, and notes until 1 January 2023. In principle, other euro-zone former currencies can only be exchanged for euros in the relevant countries.

There are €5, €10, €20, €50, €100, €200 and €500 notes, and €0.01, €0.02, €0.05, €0.10, €0.20, €0.50, €1 and €2 coins (amounts under €1 are called cents). Euro notes are the same in all participating countries; coins have a 'European' side and a 'national' side (in the Netherlands, with an image of Queen Beatrix) but, like the notes, are legal tender throughout the euro area.

If you're on the sort of budget where you would receive a €500 note from the bank, ask to have it broken down into €100 or preferably €50 and €20 notes because many places refuse the largest denominations.

For more information about the euro, check Ⓦ europa.eu.int/euro.

Euro Pricing

Prices are always subject to change, but the introduction of the euro brings a new factor into play. As the new currency settles in and people become used to comparing prices across several countries, some things will probably become slightly less expensive and others will become more expensive. This period of readjustment could take up to a year.

Research for this book took place before the euro big bang, and although businesses were supposed to sort out their euro pricing months before the switch, very few of them had done so. Wherever possible we obtained the quoted euro price but often we had to do our own conversion from guilders. Readers therefore might find slight differences in the prices we give and the actual prices in euros.

Exchange Rates

Exchange rates at the time of printing were:

Australia	A$1	=	€0.58
Canada	C$1	=	€0.72
Denmark	Dkr1	=	€0.13
Japan	¥100	=	€0.91
New Zealand	NZ$1	=	€0.46
Sweden	Skr1	=	€0.11
Switzerland	Sfr1	=	€0.68
UK	UK£1	=	€1.60
USA	US$1	=	€1.12

Exchanging Money

Avoid the private exchange booths dotted around the tourist areas: they're convenient and open late hours but rates and/or commissions are lousy, though competition is fierce and you may do reasonably well if you hunt around. Banks (such as ABN-AMRO and Fortis) and post offices (every post office is an agent for the ING Postbank) stick to official exchange rates and charge a fair commission, as do the Grenswisselkantoren (GWK, Border Exchange Offices; ☎ 0800-05 66, free information service). For ease of use and low transaction costs, however, nothing beats ATMs (see the ATMs section below). Reliable exchange centres include:

GWK (☎ 627 27 31) Centraal Station at the west end of the station in the west tunnel. Open 7am to 10.45pm daily; charges various commissions on cash and travellers cheques (with a student card there's 25% less commission on cash). Usually very busy. Also has a hotel-booking service (to 10pm) daily. There's a GWK-affiliated office with slightly worse rates next to the VVV office in Leidsestraat, on the corner of Leidseplein.

GWK (☎ 653 51 21) Schiphol airport. Open 24hrs.

American Express (Map 2; ☎ 504 87 70, central number ☎ 504 87 77) Damrak 66. Open 9am to 5pm weekdays, to noon Saturday; no commission on AmEx cheques.

Thomas Cook (Map 2; ☎ 625 09 22) Dam 23–25, with other offices at Damrak 1–5 at the beginning of Damrak opposite Centraal Station (Map 2), and at Leidseplein 31A (Map 4). Open 9.15am to 6.15pm daily; no commission on Thomas Cook cheques; report lost or stolen cheques to ☎ 0800-022 86 30.

Cash This is still very much a cash-based society and nothing beats cash for convenience – or risk of theft/loss. Plan to pay cash for most daily expenses, though staff at upmarket hotels might cast a dubious glance if you pay a huge bill with small-denomination notes rather than a credit card, and car-rental agencies will probably refuse to do business if you only have cash. Keep about €50 separate from the rest of your money as an emergency stash.

Travellers Cheques & Eurocheques
Banks charge a commission to cash travellers cheques (with ID such as a passport). American Express and Thomas Cook don't charge commission on their own cheques but their rates might be less favourable. Shops, restaurants and hotels always prefer cash; a few might accept travellers cheques but their rates will be anybody's guess.

Eurocheques (with guarantee card) – not to be confused with the new currency – are much more widely accepted, and because you write the amount in euros there's no confusion about exchange rates; they get charged to your account at the more favourable interbank rate.

ATMs Automated teller machines are definitely the way to go and can be found outside most banks, though in some cases you might have to swipe your card through a slot to gain entry to a secure area. There are ATMs around the airport halls as well, and a couple with horrendous queues in the main hall of Centraal Station (diagonally to the left as you enter through the main entrance). Visa and MasterCard/Eurocard are widely accepted, as well as cash cards that access the major international networks (Cirrus, Maestro etc). Logos on ATMs show what they accept. Your card issuer will probably charge a fee for accessing a foreign ATM, though this is likely to be lower than the commission at an exchange office. ATM exchange rates are usually calculated at the interbank rate. Beware that if you're limited to a maximum withdrawal per day, the 'day' will be in your home country's hours, so take time differences into account.

Credit Cards All the major international cards are recognised, but Amsterdam is still strongly cash-based and many restaurants and hotels (even some of the more upmarket ones) may refuse payment by card. Check first. Shops often levy a cheeky 5% surcharge (sometimes more) on credit cards to offset the commissions charged by card providers.

Report lost or stolen cards to the following 24-hour numbers:

American Express (☎ 504 80 00, 9am to 6pm weekdays; ☎ 504 86 66 other times; for cheques ☎ 0800-022 01 00)
Diners Club (☎ 654 55 11)
Eurocard and **MasterCard** have a number in Utrecht (☎ 030-283 55 55) but foreigners are advised to ring the emergency number in their home country to speed things up.
Visa (foreigners ☎ 0800-022 31 10; locals ☎ 660 06 11)

International Transfers Transferring money from your home bank will be easier if you've authorised somebody back home to access your account. In Amsterdam, find a large bank and ask for the international division. A commission is charged on telegraphic transfers, which can take up to a week but usually less if you're well prepared; by mail, allow two weeks.

Large post offices and GWK offices are agents for Western Union and money is transferred within 15 minutes of lodgment at the other end. The person lodging the transfer pays a commission that varies from country to country. Money can also be transferred via American Express and Thomas Cook.

Costs
The sky's the limit in Amsterdam: you can easily throw hundreds of euros down the drain each day with little to show for it (a good time maybe, but only maybe). Accommodation is likely to be your biggest daily expense. At rock-bottom, if you stay at a camp site or hostel and eat cheaply, you might get away with €25 to €30 a day. A (very) cheap hotel, pub meals and the occasional beer and sundries will set you back €50 to €60. Things become a bit more comfortable on €75 a day. If you speak Dutch or know someone who does, check ⓦ www.kortingsbon.nl for hundreds of worthwhile discount coupons on museums, attractions, hotels, trips, McDonald's etc.

Tipping & Bargaining
Tipping is not compulsory, but if you're pleased with the service by all means 'round up' the bill by 5% to 10% – many people do so in taxis and restaurants. A tip of 10% is considered generous. In pubs with pavement or table service it's common practice (but not compulsory) to leave the small change. Service is hardly ever formal and often quite indifferent, which unfortunately is just the way it is; shouting or 'talking down' to staff will ensure they ignore you. Toilet attendants should be tipped €0.15 to €0.20, though in some clubs they demand €0.50.

Ironically for a city with such a rich trading history, there's very little bargaining – it's definitely not done in shops. People do bargain at flea markets, though you'll have to be pretty good at this if your Dutch isn't fluent. Prices at food markets are generally set but become more negotiable later in the day.

The so-called Dutch auction, where the auctioneer keeps lowering the price until somebody takes the item, is still practised at flower and plant auctions such as the huge flower market in Aalsmeer and the Monday plant market on Amstelveld.

Taxes & Refunds

Value-added tax (Belasting Toegevoegde Waarde, or BTW) is calculated at 19% for most goods except consumer items like food, medicines and books, which attract 6% (intended harmonisation of rates across the EU still has a long way to go). The usual high excise *(accijns)* is levied on petrol, cigarettes and alcohol – petrol here is among the most expensive in Europe. The price for a packet of cigarettes is indicated on an excise sticker, and it will cost the same whether you buy it in the Amstel Hotel or the corner tobacco shop, separately or by the carton.

Hotel accommodation is subject to a 5% 'city hotel tax' that's usually included in the quoted price except at the more expensive hotels.

Travellers from non-EU countries can have the BTW refunded on goods over €175 if they're bought from one shop on one day and are exported out of the EU within three months. To claim the tax back, ask the shop owner to provide an export certificate when you make the purchase. When you leave for a non-EU country, get the form endorsed by a Dutch customs official, who will send the certificate to the supplier, who in turn refunds you the tax by cheque or money order. If you want the tax as you leave the country, it's best to buy from shops displaying a 'Tax Free for Tourists' sign, though you'll lose about 5% of the refund in commissions. In this case the shopkeeper gives you a stamped cheque that can be cashed when you leave the country.

Buying with a credit card is the best system as you won't pay tax so long as you get customs to stamp the receipt the shop owner gave you and you send the receipt back to the shop – but check whether the shop is willing to do this.

POST & COMMUNICATIONS
Post

Post offices are open 9am to 5pm weekdays, more or less. The main post office at Singel 250 (Map 2) is open 9am to 6pm weekdays (to 8pm Thursday) and 10am to 1.30pm Saturday. The poste restante section is to the left of the main entrance as you face the building, downstairs in the postbox area. The district post office near Centraal Station, Oosterdokskade 3 (Map 6), a few hundred metres east of the station, alongside the huge boat hotel, is open 9am to 9pm weekdays and to noon Saturday. The large post office in the Stopera, the city hall/opera complex at Waterlooplein (Map 2), is open 9am to 6pm weekdays, and 10am to 1.30pm Saturday.

For queries about postal services, ring ☎ 0800-04 17 (free) 8am to 8pm weekdays, 9am to 1pm Saturday – wait for the messages to finish and you'll eventually be helped by a human.

Mail is delivered locally six days a week. Unless you're sending mail within the Amsterdam region, the slot to use in the rectangular, red letterboxes is *Overige Postcodes* (Other Postal Codes).

Rates Letters within Europe up to 20g cost €0.54 (air mail, or 'priority') or €0.50 (standard); beyond Europe they cost €0.75 (priority) or €0.65 (standard). Postcards (only priority) cost €0.54 to anywhere outside the country. An aerogram *(priorityblad)* costs €0.54. Within the country, letters (up to 20g) or postcards cost €0.39. For parcel post outside the country you can choose between Worldpack Basic up to 2kg, Worldpack Special from 2kg to 20kg (with free registration and insurance), and Books from 2kg to 5kg (special low rate) – inquire at the post office.

Standard mail is not much cheaper than priority and takes about twice as long to reach the destination. For instance, priority mail to the UK takes two to three days whereas standard takes five to seven; to the USA, it's four to six days as opposed to eight to 12.

Addresses The postal code (four numbers followed by two letters) comes in front of the city or town name, eg, 1017 LS Amsterdam (Amsterdam postal codes start with 10). The telephone book gives the appropriate postal code for each address. No two streets in the city have the same name, so if you don't know the code but you've got the address right your mail should still arrive with a few days' delay.

There are a few peculiarities with street numbers. Sometimes they're followed by a letter or number (often in Roman numerals). Letters (eg, No 34A or 34a) usually indicate the appropriate front door when two or more share the same number, whereas numbers (34-2, 34² or 34-II) indicate the appropriate floor. In modern dwellings, letters often indicate the appropriate apartment irrespective of the floor. The suffix 'hs' (34hs) stands for *huis* (house) and means the dwelling is on the ground floor, which may be half a floor above street level (in which case it's sometimes called *beletage*, the floor behind the door bell). The suffix 'bg' (34bg) stands for *begane grond* (ground floor). The suffix 'sous' (34sous) stands for *souterrain* and means the dwelling is in the basement (or rather, a basement that's half under street level; it can't be much deeper because of groundwater).

Telephone

The Dutch phone network is efficient and prices are reasonable by European standards, though not quite down there with the UK or USA. Unfortunately there's no official telephone centre but there are plenty of public telephones and you can always call from a post office.

For local directory information, call ☎ 118 (€0.40 per number), though this computerised system doesn't cope well with odd pronunciation. It's easier to call a directory operator on ☎ 0900-80 08 (€0.90 for up to six numbers). International directory inquiries are on ☎ 0900-84 18 (€1.14 for up to two numbers). To place a collect call *(collect gesprek)* within the Netherlands, ring ☎ 0800-01 01 (free call); for international collect calls, ☎ 0800-04 10 (free call). For other operator-assisted calls, ring ☎ 0800-04 10 (free call, though you'll be charged a hefty €3.50 service fee if you could have rung the country direct).

Dialling Tones Tones are similar to those used throughout most of Continental Europe:

an even dialling tone at fairly lengthy intervals means the number is ringing; a similar tone at shorter intervals means the number is engaged; a three-step tone means the number isn't in use or has been disconnected.

Costs Calls within the metropolitan area are time-based, and the official, KPN-Telecom public phone boxes cost €0.03 connection fee plus a flat €0.03 a minute regardless of when you ring (public phones in cafés, supermarkets and hotel lobbies often charge more). Calls from private phones cost €0.03 connection fee plus €0.03 a minute 8am to 7pm weekdays, €0.015 a minute 7pm to midnight, and €0.01 a minute midnight to 8am and all Saturday and Sunday. For calls outside the metropolitan area, KPN's public phones charge €0.045 connection fee plus €0.045 a minute regardless of when you ring, whereas private phones cost €0.045 connection fee plus €0.044 a minute 8am to 7pm weekdays and €0.02 at other times.

The cost of international calls varies with the destination and changes frequently due to competition. At the time of writing, Britain and the USA cost €0.045 connection fee plus €0.06 to €0.07 a minute (Australia €0.17 a minute) – but add €0.03 a minute to these rates when ringing from a KPN phone box.

As always, using the phone in your hotel room is much more expensive than any other type of phone.

Phonecards There's a wide range of local and international phonecards. Lonely Planet's eKno Communication Card works from private as well as public phones and is aimed specifically at independent travellers. It provides budget international calls (for local calls you're better off with a local card), a range of messaging services, free email and travel information. You can join online at Ⓦ www.ekno.lonelyplanet.com, or by phone from Amsterdam on ☎ 0800-023 39 71 (free call).

Most public telephones in Amsterdam are cardphones and there may be queues at the remaining coin phones. KPN-Telecom cards are available at post offices, train station counters, tobacco shops and VVV and

GWK offices for €4.54 and €9.08, and calls cost the same regardless of the value of the card (ie, no discount). Note that railway stations have Telfort phone booths that accept coins or a Telfort card (available at GWK offices or ticket counters), though there should be KPN booths outside.

0800, 0900 & 06 Numbers Many information services, either recorded or live, use phone numbers beginning with ☎ 0800 (free) or ☎ 0900 (which cost between €0.10 and €0.48 a minute depending on the number). To avoid running up big phone bills, care should be taken whenever dialling ☎ 0900. Businesses that quote an ☎ 0900 number are required by law to state what it costs, but costs can vary depending on where you ring from so this isn't always clear.

Numbers beginning with ☎ 06-2 or ☎ 06-5 are mobile (cellphone) numbers, and those beginning with ☎ 06-5 or ☎ 06-6 are pagers. Beware: the cost of ringing a mobile number is two to three times that of a fixed phone.

Using Phone Books Identical surnames are listed alphabetically by address and not by initials, because local research has shown that people recall an address more readily than someone's initials. Confusingly, Dutch dictionaries and most other listings put the contracted vowel 'ij' after the 'i' but phone books treat it as a 'y'. Note that surnames beginning with 'van', 'de' etc are listed under the root name, eg, 'V van Gogh' would be listed as 'Gogh, V van' (unless it's written as one word, eg, Vandamme). For women who use their husbands' names, the maiden name traditionally comes after the name of the husband.

The phone book lists postal codes for each entry and fax numbers where relevant. The pink pages at the front are business pages but business names are copied in the white pages as well. The Web version is at W www .detelefoongids.nl; it's in Dutch but you only have to fill in the name of the person or business and then the place of residence.

The area code for Schiphol is the same as for Amsterdam but numbers are listed separately at the end of the phone book, just be-

Phone Codes

Greater Amsterdam area code	☎ 020
(drop the leading 0 if calling from another country)	
Netherlands country code	☎ 31
International access code	☎ 00

To ring abroad, dial the international access code followed by the country code for your target country, the area code (drop the leading 0 if there is one) and the subscriber number.

Other area codes include:

Alkmaar	☎ 072
Delft	☎ 015
Haarlem	☎ 023
IJmuiden	☎ 0255
Leiden	☎ 071
Rotterdam	☎ 010
The Hague	☎ 070
Utrecht	☎ 030
Zaandam	☎ 075

fore the ☎ 0800/0900 listings. The southern suburb of Amstelveen is not included in the Amsterdam phone book, nor is the eastern suburb of Diemen, though they share the ☎ 020 area code.

Home Country Direct Instead of placing a collect call through the local operator you could dial directly to your home country operator and then reverse charges, charge the call to a phone company credit card or perform other credit feats. This is possible to many (not all) countries and costs a fair bit – check with your home phone company before you leave though you might not get the full cost story. The following is a selection (with the relevant country codes in brackets for reference); ring international directory inquiries if your country isn't listed or the number appears to have changed:

Australia (61)	☎ 0800-022 00 61 (Telstra)
	☎ 0800-022 55 61 (Optus)
Belgium (32)	☎ 0800-022 11 32
Canada (1)	☎ 0800-022 91 16
Denmark (45)	☎ 0800-022 00 45
Finland (358)	☎ 0800-022 53 81
France (33)	☎ 0800-022 20 33

Germany (49)	☎ 0800-022 00 49
Hong Kong (852)	☎ 0800-022 08 52
Ireland (353)	☎ 0800-022 03 53
Israel (972)	☎ 0800-022 09 72
Italy (39)	☎ 0800-022 60 39
Japan (81)	☎ 0800-022 00 81
Korea (south) (82)	☎ 0800-022 00 82
Luxembourg (352)	☎ 0800-022 03 52
New Zealand (64)	☎ 0800-022 44 64
Norway (47)	☎ 0800-022 00 47
Singapore (65)	☎ 0800-022 88 65
South Africa (27)	☎ 0800-022 02 27
Spain (34)	☎ 0800-022 00 34
Sweden (46)	☎ 0800-022 00 46 (Telia)
	☎ 0800-022 46 07 (Tele2)
Taiwan (886)	☎ 0800-022 08 86
Thailand (66)	☎ 0800-022 01 66
UK (44)	☎ 0800-022 99 44 (BT)
	☎ 0800-022 44 05 (Mercury)
USA (1)	☎ 0800-022 91 11 (AT&T)
	☎ 0800-022 02 24
	(IDB Worldcom)
	☎ 0800-022 91 22 (MCI)
	☎ 0800-022 91 19 (Sprint)

Mobile Phones (Cellphones) The Netherlands uses GSM 900/1800, which is compatible with the rest of Europe and Australia but not with the North American GSM 1900 or the totally different system in Japan (though some North Americans have GSM 1900/900 phones that do work here). Check with your service provider about using your phone in the Netherlands, and beware of calls being routed internationally (very expensive for a 'local' call). You can rent a mobile at the KPN-Telecom Rent Centre (☎ 653 09 99) at Schiphol airport (diagonally left from the central customs exit at Schiphol Plaza) for €11.35/43.10 a day/week; you can't use your existing number, however.

'Prepaid' mobile phones, which run on chips that store calling credit, are available at mobile shops (which are clustered along the Rokin) from about €70. Some foreign GSMs without simlocks may accept these chips too – bring the phone in to check.

Fax

It's difficult to send or receive faxes as a visitor. Some of the more upmarket hotels are happy to help if you announce your requirements in advance, and most hotels with fax (some of the cheaper hotels don't have one) will at least let you receive the occasional message. (Business travellers take note: this might convince the boss that you need to stay at something a bit more upmarket.) Copy shops will send faxes, but in order to receive one you have to be on good terms with the proprietor. Kinko's (Map 4; ☎ 589 09 10, fax 589 09 20), Overtoom 62 near Leidseplein, open 24 hours, will send faxes for €1.59/2.04 a page within/outside Europe and receive them for €0.45 a page.

You can send (but not receive) faxes from post offices but only to a private machine (no 'fax telegrams' via another post office). Within the Netherlands and Europe, this costs a basic charge of €2.27 plus €0.45 a page; outside Europe, the basic charge is €4.54 plus €0.90 a page. Depending on the number of pages, this can work out (far) cheaper than a copy shop.

The Netherlands no longer has a telegram service.

Email & Internet Access

If you packed your laptop, note that the Netherlands use a four-pin phone plug similar to a US, French or Australian-style jack at the laptop end but not a six-pin UK one. Adapters are cheaply picked up at the airport and the usual retail outlets. You can rent a laptop for €43.10/128.85 a day/week at the KPN-Telecom Rent Centre (see the earlier Mobile Phones section).

KPN's public outdoor Net terminals are a thing of the past, replaced by coin-op stations at many hotels, hostels and tourist-zone coffeeshops. The really hard-up can get free Net access at any public library *(openbare bibliotheek)* or some hostels, but there'll probably be a wait.

Some big international ISPs have Amsterdam dial-up numbers for their subscribers, so you can log in the same as at home. Before you leave home, however, ask about extra charges and how to adjust your settings. Setting up an account with a local ISP in Amsterdam isn't worth it for the short term because of connection fees and minimums, but free CD-ROMs available at Shell service stations get you a free account

Silicon Polder

As other silicon centres ached from the dot-com hangover at the dawn of the new millennium, Amsterdam got off relatively easily.

It's always been an important hub on the Internet backbone. A pipe sending a goodly portion of European online traffic to and from North America disappears into the ground in the east of the city, and a thriving science park (in Watergraafsmeer) and cyber-complex (the Matrix buildings) grew up around this important telecoms node.

Amsterdam's medium-rise 'Silicon Polder' suburbs currently boast more than 1700 IT companies employing 15,000 people. The recent labour crunch notwithstanding, foreign techies are happy to move here, though the relatively low Dutch salaries (certainly in comparison to California) cause friction. Indeed, Amsterdam claims to be the most popular city in Europe among (mostly young, often male) IT employees. Why would that be?

There was no big dot-bomb here, mainly because the Dutch were too smart to blow a big bubble in the first place. Still, scores of companies, mostly jump-on-the-bandwagon startups, have gone bankrupt. Others are panicking as the venture capitalists snap shut their purses (the e-business club First Tuesday Amsterdam held a 'pink-slip party' for the laid-off). And companies eager to establish a presence in Amsterdam faced a six-month waiting list as the power grid filled to bursting with connectivity-intensive business customers.

More regrettably, a significant flush of Amsterdam-style social idealism has cooled since the 1990s. In 1999, xs4all, the country's first ISP, which battled for privacy and free speech in court and online, sold out to former state telecom company KPN, which vaguely promised to keep carrying the political torch. The same KPN quietly removed its own outdoor, phonecard-operated Net terminals, much admired by the foreign press but otherwise neglected except by vandals, by summer 2001. Around the same time, DDS, the grassroots nonprofit organisation that gave local residents free Net access and online meeting spaces, went commercial. Access for all, e-democracy, a wired world? Maybe not. Half of Amsterdam was online by 2001, but nonwhites and the elderly lagged behind.

These days, the Net is what the Dutch call *ingeburgerd* – naturalised, established, part of the landscape. Presentations of digital art are common now at places like Montevideo, De Balie and De Waag. The state is still doing forward-looking things like spending €450m to wire 20,000 households in Eindhoven into a high-speed-connectivity testbed, to see what happens to business and social relations. And with a typically Dutch attention to social responsibility, it's given casinos permission to serve online gamblers, as long as they donate some of the loot to charity and look out for users who go overboard.

But the activists are hanging in where the carpetbaggers have dropped away. HAL2001, the most recent in a series of big Dutch hacker gatherings, tried to guide geek politics into the future, urging 'script kiddies' to turn their talents to socially responsible, pro-privacy ends. And a group of e-activists set up Vereniging Open Domein (Association Open Domain) as a putative replacement for DDS. Hardercore activists have set up the Netherlands' own Independent Media Center, after the Seattle example.

The starry-eyed Learyites may have drifted off, but the chattering classes continue to talk about social change in an online context. Amsterdam remains Amsterdam, and happily, online as off, it keeps pushing the envelope.

Oh, and did you know? *Wired* magazine began life as an Amsterdam-based bimonthly called *Electric World*.

---

with the AOL-style portal 12move (W www .12move.nl – in Dutch only), if you have Windows 95/98 or NT4.0. There are a few other, similar services but how long they'll last is anyone's guess.

Internet Cafés Bars and coffeeshops offering Internet access are commonly available around the areas where tourists congregate. Indeed, for travellers from prohibitionist countries, there's a bit of a frisson in sitting down and beginning your emails: 'Hi, I'm sitting here with a fat joint in my mouth.' Many of these places come and go, and the following is just a snapshot of what was available at the time of research. Unless stated otherwise, they charge €1.14 to €2.73 per half-hour. (Several coffeeshops in Warmoesstraat also have coin-op terminals – just look for 'Internet' in the windows.)

ASCII This free, leftist Net café that welcomes activists but not yuppies was squatting in the basement below underground bookshop Fort van Sjakoo in Jodenbreestraat at the time of writing. But the owner has increased the rent tenfold, so check **W** www.squat.net/ascii for updates and events.

Boek 'n Serve (☎ 664 34 46) Ferdinand Bolstraat 151–153, open 9.30am to 7pm weekdays (from noon Monday and to 9pm Thursday), 9am to 6pm Saturday. A charming (mostly Dutch) magazine and bookshop, in the south of the city (tram No 25), that also sells CD-ROMs, coffee and ice cream. While the relaxing music tinkles away downstairs, enjoy smokefree Web surfing upstairs on five PCs for €1.36 per 15 minutes.

easyEverything (**W** www.easyeverything.com) Reguliersbreestraat near Rembrandtplein (as well as a 200-machine branch at Damrak 33 near Centraal Station). This cybercafé, hyped as the world's biggest, has turned out to be too big for this wired little city. Its 650-terminal fleet and 24-hour access are set to be cut back, but for now you'll have no trouble finding a free terminal (nor the mammoth storefront). It also has Net phone, chat and Microsoft applications. Prices go down at night.

Freeworld (☎ 620 09 02) Korte Nieuwendijkstraat 30, **Internet Coffeeshop Tops** (☎ 638 41 08/627 34 36) Prinsengracht 480, and **Get Down** (☎ 420 15 12) Korte Leidsedwarsstraat 77 are all fairly standard smoking venues with Net access, the latter being a dingy basement with a permanent heavy rock soundtrack and emailing and printing from seven PCs.

Internet Café (☎ 627 10 52) Martelaarsgracht 11, open 9am to 1am daily (to 3am Friday and Saturday). Just 50m from Centraal Station, this offers a free email address and about 20 PCs, and 20 minutes free with a drink.

Kabul (☎ 623 71 58) Warmoesstraat 42. For that backpacker vibe, log in at this youth hotel, which has 25 PCs available 24 hours and has the shortest minimum time: seven minutes for €0.46.

La Bastille (☎ 623 56 04, **W** www.labastille.nl) Lijnbaansgracht 246, open 10am-11pm daily.

With brick walls, chandeliers, a few dozen workstations with flat screens, and a full bar, this spiffy little place has purportedly appeared in TV shows and photo shoots.

Mad Processor (☎ 421 14 82, **W** www.madprocessor.com) Bloemgracht 82, open 2pm to midnight Tuesday to Saturday. Aims to be a sort of 'Kinko's for the masses' on the ground floor of a Jordaan canal house. It offers 22 PCs connected to the Net, office facilities, networked games like Quake and Counterstrike (€3.40 an hour), laminating, DTP etc.

Siberië (☎ 623 59 09) Brouwersgracht 11, open 11am to 11pm daily (to midnight Friday and Saturday). One of the liveliest coffeeshops in central Amsterdam, and though it has just one PC, it's free as long as you consume something (20 minutes max).

The Site (☎ 520 60 80) Nieuwezijds Voorburgwal 323, open noon to 8pm Tuesday to Saturday. An 'info-theque' for Amsterdam youth (aged 15 to 20) with free Net access, advice, talks, workshops and even a job centre. Foreigners can use the facilities for the usual fee.

In De Waag (☎ 422 77 72) Nieuwmarkt, open 10am to midnight daily. Catch it while you can: this restaurant-bar in the old weigh house in the middle of Nieuwmarkt Square offered statesubsidised free surfing for customers in the late 1990s, but by mid-2001 all but one of the halfdozen screens were broken and there were no plans to fix the others.

Zoëzo (☎ 330 67 67) Vijzelgracht 63, open 10am to midnight Monday to Friday, noon to midnight Saturday and Sunday. A small, cheerful place with snacks and a bar, located near the Heineken Museum.

DIGITAL RESOURCES

The Web is a rich resource for travellers and there's no better place to start than the Lonely Planet Web site (**W** www.lonelyplanet.com). Here you'll find succinct summaries on travelling to most places on earth, postcards from other travellers and the Thorn Tree bulletin board, where you can ask questions before you go or dispense advice when you get back. You can also find travel news and updates to many of our most popular guidebooks, and the subWWWay section links you to useful travel resources elsewhere on the Web.

In the Netherlands, URLs for most organisations and events tend to be wonderfully straightforward: www.(name).nl. The definitive Web reference for anything to do

Photogenic intersection of Keizersgracht and Reguliersgracht

't Smalle, a charming brown café in the Jordaan

Afternoon stroll in the Vondelpark

Many canal bridges are lit up at night – a pretty sight.

ELLIOT DANIEL

Care for some cannabis with your coffee?

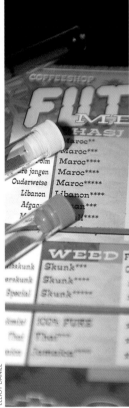

ELLIOT DANIEL

Coffeeshop menu

MARTIN MOOS

Not your usual shop window

MARTIN MOOS

Unmistakably the red-light district

with Amsterdam, for instance, is Ⓦ www .amsterdam.nl, with more information and links than you'll ever need, plus a very useful map-finder function. You could also try Ⓦ www.visitamsterdam.nl, run by the Netherlands Board of Tourism, or its parent site Ⓦ www.visitholland.com. An enjoyable, interactive site that allows you to walk through the city and shows what you'll see (or have missed) is Ⓦ www.channels.nl.

Expatica Netherlands, Ⓦ www.expatica .com/index.asp, updated daily, provides the English-speaking population with news and features on living in Holland. The biweekly underground events zine, *Shark*, is online at Ⓦ www.underwateramsterdam.com and has a searchable database. A quirky site run by students, with some interesting features and links, is Ⓦ www.amsterdambackdoor.com.

Homesick Aussies who want to keep up to date with the footy or the latest furphies in Canberra should check Ⓦ www.firststep .com.au/gday (the authors of this book live in Australia, after all!).

CitySync Amsterdam is Lonely Planet's digital city guide for Palm OS hand-held devices. With CitySync you can quickly search, sort and bookmark hundreds of Amsterdam's restaurants, hotels, attractions, clubs and more – all pinpointed on scrollable street maps. Sections on activities, transport and local events mean you get the big picture plus the details. Purchase or try it at Ⓦ www.citysync.com.

BOOKS

For literature by Amsterdam authors, see the Arts section in the Facts about Amsterdam chapter.

Guidebooks

There are more guidebooks to Amsterdam than you can shake a bicycle spoke at, and we'll only touch on a few here.

If you plan to settle in Amsterdam for a while, get hold of *Live & Work in Belgium, The Netherlands and Luxembourg* from Vacation Work Publications, with detailed explanations of the necessary paperwork and more. *Living & Working in the Netherlands* by Pat Rush (How To Books) isn't

bad either. *Ethnic Amsterdam* (Vassallucci, 2001) by Patricia Gosling & Fitzroy Nation lets you experience the city's ethnic mix to the full.

History

CR Boxer's *The Dutch Seaborne Empire 1600–1800*, first published in 1965, remains one of the most readable academic textbooks on how this small corner of Europe dominated world trade. PJAN Rietbergen's *A Short History of the Netherlands* (1995) casts its net wider and is a good general introduction. Simon Schama's *The Embarrassment of Riches: An Interpretation of Dutch Culture in the Golden Age* (1987) deals astutely with the tensions between vast wealth and Calvinist sobriety, and much more.

Amsterdam, A Short History (1994) by Richter Roegholt provides a good, concise summary but few insights. You'll find plenty of these, along with potted dramas, in Geert Mak's *Amsterdam – a Brief Life of the City* (2001), which we can recommend highly. It includes a perceptive analysis of the cultural revolution that swept the city from the mid-1960s to mid-1980s – Mak calls it the '20-Year Civil War'.

Serious students should track down Pieter Geyl's *The Revolt of the Netherlands, 1555–1609* (1958) and *The Netherlands in the 17th Century, 1609–1648* (1961/64). Johan Huizinga's *The Waning of the Middle Ages: A Study of the Forms of Life, Thought, and Art in France and the Netherlands in the 14th and 15th Centuries* (1924) is justly famous, as much a literary work as a study.

General

See the Amsterdam Architecture special section for books about architecture.

The UnDutchables (1989) by Colin White & Laurie Boucke claims to take a humorous look at Dutch life, and sometimes is spot-on but often so wide of the mark it's cheap slapstick. More realistic (and genuinely humorous) appraisals of Dutch customs, attitudes and idiosyncrasies are found in Rodney Bolt's excellent *Xenophobe's Guide to the Dutch*; Hunt Janin's very readable *Culture Shock! Netherlands* (1998); or the rather serious but knowledgeable *Dealing with the Dutch* by Jacob Vossestein, who runs the Royal Tropical Institute's 'Understanding the Dutch' training programs for business-people and expatriates.

Looking for a reliable book on current Dutch cooking? There isn't one. Heleen Halverhout's *Dutch Cooking* (1972) has 'real traditional' dishes but even in that respect it's getting ancient. Gillian Riley's *The Dutch Table – Gastronomy in the Golden Age of the Netherlands* is a beautifully illustrated book that re-creates some of the dishes depicted on 17th-century Dutch paintings – including the liberal use of herbs and exotic spices that masked decaying ingredients and made Dutch cooking so much tastier than it is today.

Henry James described the Amsterdam canals as 'perfect prose' and 'perfect bourgeois' in *Transatlantic Sketches* (1875).

Dutch Painting (1978) by RH Fuchs is a good introduction to the subject, though it's out of print – try second-hand shops.

Most books are published in different editions by different publishers in different countries. As a result, a book might be a hardcover rarity in one country while it's readily available in paperback in another. Your local bookshop or library can advise you on the availability of the above recommendations.

NEWSPAPERS & MAGAZINES

The European editions of *The Economist* and *Time* are printed here, and most of the major international newspapers and magazines (and many obscure ones) are readily available. Newsagents at the airport and Centraal Station stock a wide selection, as do the Athenaeum newsagency on Spui Square and Waterstone's in the Kalverstraat.

By far the largest national newspaper is the Amsterdam-based *De Telegraaf*, a right-wing daily with sensationalist news but good coverage of finance. Its Wednesday edition lists rental accommodation. Also based in Amsterdam are *De Volkskrant*, a one-time Catholic daily with leftist leanings, and *Het Parool*, an evening paper full of Amsterdam politics and *the* paper to read if you want to know what's happening in the

city (especially the daily supplement, *PS*, or better still, the weekly what's-on listing in the Saturday *PS*). The highly regarded *NRC Handelsblad* sets the country's journalistic standards. *Het Financieele Dagblad* focuses on business and finance, with an English-language section at the back.

Useful Publications

The free *Uitkrant* is the definitive publication for art and entertainment – if it's not listed here it's not happening. It's published 11 times a year, unfortunately all in Dutch but you can usually decipher enough to make a phone call to the relevant establishment for more information. Pick up a copy at the Amsterdam Uitburo or anywhere with free publications, such as Centraal Station, the Stopera, book and magazine outlets, shopping centres and many museums.

The VVV's English-language *Day by Day* is published monthly and costs €1.14. It has entertainment schedules and an address listing but is far less comprehensive than the *Uitkrant*. It's available from the VVV, large book and magazine outlets and many hotels.

Other publications in English come and go, but a handful have established themselves over the last few years. The most underground of the bunch, the photocopied events zinelet *Shark*, is also the most enjoyable. *Expats Magazine* serves lifestyle, arts and how-to content to the foreign business community. *Roundabout* has very mainstream events listings, covering Amsterdam and other nearby cities.

Via Via, a paper with reams of classified ads, is published Tuesday and Thursday (in Dutch) and lists everything from apartments to starter motors.

RADIO & TV

The BBC broadcasts on 648kHz medium wave, loud and clear on any AM radio. Most of the programs are in English. Dutch TV sends insomniacs to sleep, though the large proportion of ad-free, English-language sitcoms and films with Dutch subtitles is a plus. Fortunately the Netherlands have the highest density cable TV network in the world, and in Amsterdam nearly 100% of households are hooked up to cable. Cable means access not just to Dutch and Belgian channels but many channels from Britain, France, Germany, Italy and Spain, and all sorts of other so-called Euro-channels with sport and music clips, as well as Turkish and Moroccan stuff and, of course, CNN.

Teletext, a wonderful information service that hides behind many TV channels, offers hundreds of pages of up-to-date information. English-language versions are available on BBC and CNN.

PHOTOGRAPHY & VIDEO

Film is widely available, and a 36-exposure slide film costs about €5.80 to €9. High-speed film (200 ASA or higher) is sensible because the sky is often overcast, and even if it's not, buildings and trees tend to cast shadows. If there's a blanket of snow with sunshine (a rare combination but a fantastic photo opportunity) you might want slower film. Film developing is quick and costs about €2.25 plus about €0.22 per print. A 90-minute, 8mm cassette for a video camera costs between €5.50 and €10. Shop around because there's a fair bit of competition.

Home video cassette recorders here use the PAL image-registration system, the same as most of Europe and Australia, which is incompatible with the NTSC system used in North America and Japan or the SECAM system used in France. If you buy a pre-recorded video tape here check that it's compatible with your home unit (many modern units have a PAL/NTSC switch). Shops might stock NTSC versions but very few have tapes in SECAM.

TIME

The Netherlands are on Central European time, GMT/UTC plus one hour. Noon in Amsterdam is 3am in San Francisco, 6am in New York and Toronto, 11am in London, 9pm in Sydney and 11pm in Auckland, and then there's daylight-saving time. Clocks are put forward one hour at 2am on the last Sunday in March and back again at 3am on the last Sunday in October.

When telling the time, beware that Dutch uses *half* to indicate 'half before' the hour.

If you say 'half eight' (8.30 in many forms of English), a Dutch person will take this to mean 7.30. Dutch also uses constructions like *tien voor half acht* (7.20) and *tien over half acht* (7.40), and less surprisingly, *kwart voor acht* (7.45) and *kwart over acht* (8.15).

ELECTRICITY

Electricity is 220V, 50Hz and plugs are of the Continental two-round-pin variety. If you need an adapter, get it before you leave home because most of the ones available in the Netherlands are for locals going abroad.

WEIGHTS & MEASURES

Napoleon introduced the metric system which has been used here ever since (before then it was a local version of feet, inches and pounds). In shops, 100g is an *ons* and 500g is a *pond* (sound familiar?). EU directives prohibit the use of *ons* in pricing and labelling but the term is ingrained. Like other Continental Europeans, the Dutch indicate decimals with commas and thousands with points.

If you need help with metric measures, see the conversion chart in the back of this book.

LAUNDRY

A self-service laundry is called a *wasserette* or a *wassalon* and Amsterdam could do with more of them. They normally cost about €5 to wash 5kg; add a few coins for the dryer. You can also get the staff to wash, dry and fold a load (a full garbage bag) for around €7.50 – drop it off in the morning, pick it up in the afternoon. Upmarket hotels will of course do your laundry too, but at a price. The following are a small selection – look under *Wasserette* in the phone book:

The Clean Brothers (Map 4; ☎ 622 02 73) Kerkstraat 56 off Leidsestraat. Costs €3.65 to wash up to 6kg plus €0.60 to dry, or leave it with them for €7. Open 7am to 9pm daily.

Happy Inn (Map 2; ☎ 624 84 64) Warmoesstraat 30 near Centraal Station. Costs €7.50 to wash, dry and fold up to 6kg. Open 9am to 6pm Monday to Saturday.

Wasserette Rozengracht (Map 3; ☎ 638 59 75) Rozengracht 59 in the Jordaan. Costs €7.50 to wash, dry and fold 5kg. Open 9am to 9pm daily.

Wasserette Van den Broek (Map 2; ☎ 624 17 00) Oude Doelenstraat 12 (eastern extension of Damstraat). Full service (€7.94/9.53 to wash, dry and fold up to 5/7kg) or cheaper self-service. Open 8.30am to 7pm weekdays, 10am to 4pm Saturday.

TOILETS

Public toilets are scarce, though men can use the open, green-coloured urinals placed throughout the city (the enclosed, steel urinals are gradually being removed). Otherwise there are plenty of bars or other establishments you can pop into. Their toilets aren't always the cleanest – those in department stores are more hygienic. Toilet attendants (of which there are a lot) should be tipped €0.15 to €0.20 (up to €0.50 in clubs).

LEFT LUGGAGE

For details of left-luggage facilities at the airport, see the Airport section of the Getting Around chapter. Luggage lockers at Centraal Station can be rented up to a maximum of 72 hours.

HEALTH

The Netherlands have reciprocal health arrangements with other EU countries and Australia – check with your public health insurer which form to include in your luggage (E111 for British and Irish residents, available at post offices). You still might have to pay on the spot but you'll be able to claim back home. Citizens of other countries are advised to take out travel insurance: medical or dental treatment is less expensive than in North America but still costs enough.

There are no compulsory vaccinations but if you've just travelled through a yellow fever area you could be asked for proof that you're covered. Up-to-date tetanus, polio and diphtheria immunisations are always recommended whether you're travelling or not.

For minor health concerns, pop into a local *drogist* (chemist) or *apotheek* (pharmacy, to fill prescriptions). For more serious problems, go to the casualty ward of a *ziekenhuis* (hospital) or ring the Centrale Doktersdienst (☎ 0900-503 20 42), the 24-hour central medical service that will refer you to an appropriate doctor, dentist or pharmacy.

In a life-threatening emergency, the national telephone number for ambulance, police and fire brigade is ☎ 112.

Forget about buying flu tablets and antacids at supermarkets: for anything more medicinal than toothpaste you'll have to go to a drogist or apotheek.

The following hospitals have 24-hour emergency facilities:

Onze Lieve Vrouwe Gasthuis (Map 5; ☎ 599 91 11) Eerste Oosterparkstraat 1 at Oosterpark near the Tropenmuseum. The closest public hospital to the centre of town.
Sint Lucas Ziekenhuis (Map 1; ☎ 510 89 11) Jan Tooropstraat 164, in the western suburbs
Slotervaart Ziekenhuis (Map 1; ☎ 512 41 13) Louwesweg 6, in the south-western suburbs
Academisch Ziekenhuis der VU (Map 1; ☎ 444 36 36) De Boelelaan 1117, Amsterdam Buitenveldert. Hospital of the VU (Vrije Universiteit, Free University).
Academisch Medisch Centrum (☎ 566 91 11) Meibergdreef 9, Bijlmer. Hospital of the Universiteit van Amsterdam.
Boven-IJ Ziekenhuis (☎ 634 63 46) Statenjachtstraat 1, Amsterdam North; bus No 34 from Centraal Station

STDs & HIV/AIDS

Free testing for sexually transmitted diseases is available at the Municipal Medical & Health Service (GG&GD; Map 2; ☎ 555 58 22), Groenburgwal 44 in the old town. It's open 8am to 10.30am and 1.30pm to 3.30pm weekdays (also 7pm to 8.30pm Thursday) but you must arrive in the morning to be tested that day. Bring a book or magazine as you'll probably have to wait a couple of hours. If a problem is diagnosed they'll provide free treatment immediately, but blood test results take a week (they'll give you the results over the phone if you aren't returning to Amsterdam). This excellent service is available to all and it's not necessary to give an address or show identification (English is spoken). There's also a gay STD and HIV clinic (tests etc) 7pm to 9pm Friday, but you have to make an appointment between 9am and 12.30pm or 1.30pm and 5.30pm weekdays.

HIV/AIDS is a problem in the Netherlands but it has been contained to some extent by practical education campaigns and free needle-exchange programs. Telephone help lines include:

AIDS Information Line (☎ 0800-022 22 20, free call) Questions about HIV and AIDS answered 2pm to 10pm weekdays; discretion guaranteed.

AIDS-HIVpluslijn (☎ 685 00 55) Telephone support line for people with HIV who want to talk to others with similar problems; 8pm to 10pm Tuesday, 2pm to 4pm Wednesday and Friday; alternatively, a service point and help desk (☎ 689 25 77) operates 2pm to 10pm weekdays.

WOMEN TRAVELLERS

Dutch women attained the right to vote in 1919, and in the late 1960s and '70s the Dolle Minas (Mad Minas – see the History section) made sure that abortion on demand was more or less accepted and paid for by the national health service. There is some way to go before it can be said that women are fully emancipated (their participation rate in the labour force, for instance, is one of the lowest in Europe, with the highest proportion of part-time work), but Dutch women on the whole are a rather confident lot. On a social level, equality of the sexes is taken for granted and women are almost as likely as men to initiate contact with the opposite sex. There's little street harassment and Amsterdam is probably as safe as it gets in the major cities of Europe. Just take care in the red-light district, where it's best to walk with a friend to minimise unwelcome attention.

The feminist movement is less politicised than elsewhere, more laid-back and focused on practical solutions such as cultural centres and archives, bicycle repair shops run by and for women, or support systems to help women set up businesses.

Organisations

For more information, contact the following organisations:

Het Vrouwenhuis (The Women's House; Map 6; ☎ 625 20 66) Nieuwe Herengracht 95, near the Botanical Garden. A centre for several women's organisations and magazines, with workshops and exhibitions; there's also a bar and a library.

IIAV (International Information Centre & Archives of the Women's Movement; Map 1; ☎ 665 08 20, W www.iiav.nl) Obiplein 4, east of Muiderpoortstation. Centre for feminist studies; extensive collection of clippings, magazines, books.

De Eerste Lijn (The First Line; ☎ 613 02 45) For victims of sexual violence.

Aletta Jacobshuis (Map 4; ☎ 616 62 22) Overtoom 323. Clinic offering information and help with sexual problems and birth control, including morning-after pills.

Vrouwengezondheidscentrum Isis (Women's Health Centre; Map 1; ☎ 693 43 58) Obiplein 4. For advice, support and self-help groups.

GAY & LESBIAN TRAVELLERS

Partisan estimates put the proportion of gay and lesbian people in Amsterdam at 20% to 30%. This is probably an exaggeration, but there's no doubt that Amsterdam is the gay and lesbian capital of Europe – although the lesbian scene, as always, is less developed than the gay one. Mainstream attitudes have always been reasonably tolerant but it wasn't until the early 1970s that the age of consent for gay sex was lowered to 16, in line with hetero sex, and in 1993 it became illegal to discriminate against jobseekers on the basis of sexual orientation.

The fact that Christian parties are in opposition for the first time since 1917 has finally made it possible to tackle issues relating to family law. Same-sex marriage has been recognised, though the attendant right to adopt children could take a bit longer to be sorted out. The government has long subsidised the national organisation COC – one of the world's largest organisations for gay and lesbian rights – but now trade unions are busy researching the lot of homosexual employees, police advertise in the gay media for new applicants, and the acceptance of homosexuality in the army is greater than ever.

One attractive feature of gay and lesbian venues in the city is their openness and welcoming attitude to anyone who wants to come in (and 'out'). There's no lack of places to go to, with more than 100 bars and nightclubs, gay hotels, bookshops, sport clubs, choirs, archives etc, and a wide range of support organisations. See the listings here and in the Places to Stay, Places to Eat, Shopping and Entertainment chapters for further details.

FACTS FOR THE VISITOR

Homomonument

Amsterdam's Homomonument, the first such monument in the world, was designed by Karin Daan and unveiled under the shadow of the Westerkerk in 1987. It consists of three triangles of pink granite: one points to the Amsterdam office of the COC, the second to the Anne Frankhuis and the third to the water. It commemorates those who were persecuted for their homosexuality by the Nazis. From May to the end of August, gay and lesbian visitors can consult an information kiosk here from noon to 6pm called the Pink Point of Presence, or PPP (a play on the official tourist information office, VVV). It sells souvenirs too.

Information

One of the best guidebooks is the *Spartacus Guide for Amsterdam* by Bruno Gmünder Verlag. An 'in the know' guide for lesbians, in Dutch with English translations, is *Dykes Below Sealevel* published by Xantippe. *Friends the Gaymap Amsterdam* published by Friends the Gaymap and *Gay Map Amsterdam* published by Gay News Amsterdam both give the lowdown on gay locations. They are available for free at gay venues and can also be ordered online at W http://guide .gayamsterdam.com.

Three formerly free tabloids, all partly in English, now come at a reasonable price: *Gay News* (W www.gaynews.nl), *Gay and Night* and *Culture & Camp*, available at gay venues and bookshops. A biweekly free publication in English with excellent queer listings is *Shark*, also available online at W www .underwateramsterdam.nl. Gay and lesbian bookshops (see the Shopping chapter) sell most of the major foreign publications, and many newsagencies also have extensive selections. Athenaeum Nieuwscentrum at Spui stocks quirky, limited-edition publications like *Butt* and the hip *RE* magazine.

A good English-language lifestyle site is W www.gayamsterdam.com. The Web site of the volunteer-run Gay & Lesbian Switchboard is also a good starting point: W www .switchboard.nl (click on 'English'). A selection of the Switchboard info is available on

Teletext at TV3, page 447. Information on current lesbian events and the rapidly changing lesbian club and bar scene is best accessed through W www.wild4women.nl, W www.technodyke.com or the aforementioned *Shark* brochure.

The local gay radio station MVS broadcasts 6pm to 8pm Monday to Thursday, 6pm to 9pm Friday and 6pm to 7pm Saturday and Sunday on 106.8 FM (cable 88.1 FM), with an English program on Sunday.

Organisations

The following organisations may be useful:

Gay & Lesbian Switchboard (☎ 623 65 65, W www.switchboard.nl) The best first source for gay and lesbian information, addresses, what's on etc, 10am to 10pm daily.

COC Amsterdam (Map 3; ☎ 623 40 79, W www .cocamsterdam.nl) Rozenstraat 14. Amsterdam branch of the national gay and lesbian organisation. There's a mixed nightclub Friday and women's nightclub Saturday, both open 10pm to 4am – the women's is the only one in Amsterdam to have survived for years. A coffee shop is open 1pm to 5pm and from 8pm Saturday.

Schorer Foundation (Map 4; Helpdesk ☎ 662 42 06) PC Hooftstraat 5. NGO offering lesbian and gay health-care services; HIV prevention, buddy care. Open 10am to 5pm Monday to Thursday.

Schorer Poli/GG&GD STD Clinic (Map 2; ☎ 555 58 22, W www.schorer.nl) Groenburgwal 44. A gay STD clinic provided by the Schorer Foundation 7pm to 9pm Friday (make a telephone appointment between 9am and 11.30pm or 1.30pm and 5.30pm weekdays).

HIV Vereniging (Map 4; ☎ 616 01 60) Eerste Helmersstraat 17. National organisation for those who are HIV positive; provides personal assistance; also operates the AIDS-HIVpluslijn (see the earlier Health section).

AIDS Information Line – see Health

IHLIA (Internationaal Homo/Lesbisch Informatiecentrum & Archief) (Map 3; ☎ 606 07 12, W www.homodok-laa.nl) Nieuwpoortkade 2A. The largest international gay/lesbian library collection in the Netherlands, open 10am to 4pm Monday to Friday; telephone inquiries 9am to 5pm weekdays; e info@homodok.nl (gay) or e laa@dds.nl (lesbian).

Safe Sex

The Dutch government and organisations such as the COC, Schorer Foundation and

HIV Vereniging all do their bit to prevent the spread of STDs and HIV. Virtually all bars, bookshops and saunas that cater for gays provide safe-sex leaflets. Many also sell condoms suitable for anal sex.

Special Events

A Canal Parade takes place on the first Saturday in August, the only water-borne gay-pride parade in the world. Sport and culture programs are organised in the week leading up to this, inspired by the 1998 Amsterdam Gay Games. The Gay & Lesbian Switchboard can tell you more.

The biggest party in Amsterdam each year is Koninginnedag (Queen's Day) which celebrates the Queen Mother's birthday on 30 April. Queen Beatrix and Princess Máxima, the Argentine wife of future king Willem-Alexander, are very popular among the gay community and this day is celebrated with great enthusiasm, causing some confusion among foreigners about the 'queen' everyone is celebrating. On this day a big gay and lesbian party called the Roze Wester (Pink Wester) is held at the Homomonument, with bands and street dancing; the Reguliersdwarsstraat and Amstel also get very lively. It helps if you like beer because you can hardly get anything else.

Dangers & Annoyances

Gays and lesbians can generally move freely in Amsterdam but violent crime is a distinct possibility when cruising – don't carry too much money and certainly no cards or passport, and an emergency whistle is worth considering. Always report antigay or antilesbian violence to the police. Most police stations have staff members who are trained to treat your case with respect.

DISABLED TRAVELLERS

Travellers with a mobility problem will find Amsterdam only moderately well equipped to meet their needs, or fairly well considering the natural limitations of many of the older buildings. A large number of government offices and museums have lifts (elevators) and/or ramps. Many hotels, however, are in old buildings with steep stairs and no

lifts; restaurants tend to be on ground floors, though 'ground' sometimes includes a few steps. The metro stations have lifts, many trains have wheelchair access, and most train stations and public buildings have toilets for the disabled.

People with a disability get discounts on public transport and, with some limitations, can park in the city free of charge (see the sections on Public Transport and Car & Motorcycle in the Getting Around chapter). Train timetables are published in Braille.

Residents can use the *stadsmobiel* (city-mobile), a fabulous taxi service for people with limited mobility, but foreigners have to use one of the commercial wheelchair-taxi services: Garskamp (☎ 633 39 43, 7am to midnight daily) or Connexxion Jonkcars (☎ 606 22 00, 6am to 6pm daily). Ring a couple of days in advance to ensure a booking at a time that suits you. One-way trips within Amsterdam cost €16 to €50 depending on the destination.

If you're flying into Amsterdam, let your airline know of any special requirements so it can ensure the proper reception at Schiphol, or you can ring IHD Schiphol Service on ☎ 316 14 15/07. See also Car Rental in the Getting Around chapter for information about a car offered by Budget that's specially adapted for wheelchairs.

Organisations

While many Dutch organisations work with and for people with disabilities, there's no central information service. But the helpful Nederlands Instituut voor Zorg & Welzijn NIZW (☎ 030-230 66 03, e infolijn@nizw.nl), Postbus 19152, 3501 DD Utrecht, has extensive information and can refer you to other organisations for more specific requests.

The Amsterdam Uitburo (see Other Information Sources under the earlier Tourist Offices section) has information about accessible entertainment venues and museums, as does the VVV. Travel and Tourism for All maintains an accessibility guide to Amsterdam at W www.ttfa.nl, but it's rather limited and impossible to keep up to date.

Britain's Royal Association for Disability & Rehabilitation (RADAR; ☎ 020-7250

3222, W www.radar.org.uk), 12 City Forum, 250 City Rd, London EC1V 8AF, is a good place to start – its Web site contains many useful links. Holiday Care (☎ 01293-774 535, W www.holidaycare.org.uk), 2nd Floor, Imperial Buildings, Victoria Rd, Horley, Surrey RH6 7PZ, has information and advice on all aspects of holidays for disabled people.

In the USA, the Society for Accessible Travel and Hospitality (SATH; ☎ 212-447 7284, W www.sath.org), 347 Fifth Ave, Suite 610, New York, NY 10016, has information sheets on a wide range of destinations or will research your specific requirements. Membership is $45 a year ($30 for seniors and students). Mobility International (☎ 541-343 1284, W www.miusa .org), PO Box 10767, Eugene, OR 97440, offers international educational exchanges but will also answer questions and help travellers with special needs.

An interesting site for travellers in wheelchairs, with tips mainly from other travellers, is W www.geocities.com/Paris/1502. Finally, it's well worth checking some of the many links at W www.access-able.com, a great information service for mature and disabled travellers.

SENIOR TRAVELLERS

The minimum age for senior discounts is 65 (60 for the male or female partner) and they apply to public transport, museum entry fees, theatres, concerts and more. You could try flashing your home-country senior card but you might have to show your passport to be eligible.

Senior travellers who are concerned about personal safety can perhaps take heart from the fact that people under 24 years of age are six times more likely to become a victim of crime in Amsterdam than those aged over 65.

Organisations

An organisation worth knowing about is Gilde Amsterdam (☎ 625 13 90, 1pm to 4pm Monday to Friday). This is a group of volunteers aged 50 and over who share their experience in a variety of ways. Gilde

members with a keen knowledge of Amsterdam organise walks for small groups of locals and visitors (maximum of eight people per guide) – a wonderful way to discover the city with mature-aged people and to see and learn things that professional tours ignore. It helps if you're reasonably mobile because the walks last an hour or two. It's all very informal; every guide does it differently and you might even take the tram. There are four walks to choose from – City Centre, Jordaan, Maritime History and 'Roving' – and the cost per person is €2.50, which gets you 50% off entry fees to the Amsterdams Historisch Museum (city history) and the Museum Willet-Holthuysen ('classical' canal house), as well as a 25% discount on pancakes at the end of the walk.

Stichting Wijzer (☎ 668 40 92; 10am to noon Monday to Friday) organises a range of activities – film nights, music programs, summer excursions etc – aimed at Amsterdammers aged over 50 but foreigners are welcome too.

AMSTERDAM FOR CHILDREN

There is much to keep kids occupied in Amsterdam, but be careful of all the open water (Dutch kids all learn to swim at school). Lonely Planet's *Travel with Children* is worth reading; much of the advice is valid in Amsterdam.

Attitudes to children are very positive, apart from some hotels with a no-children policy – check when you book. Most restaurants have high chairs and children's menus. Facilities for changing nappies (diapers), however, are limited to the big department stores and Centraal Station and you have to pay to use them.

Amsterdam's children are surprisingly spontaneous and confident, a reflection of the relaxed approach to parenting. They're allowed in pubs (but aren't supposed to buy beer till they're 16) and the age of consent is 12, though parents can intervene if the partner is over 16.

Baby-sitters charge between €4.50 and €5.70 an hour depending on the time of day, sometimes with weekend and/or hotel supplements, and you might have to pay for their taxi home if it gets late. Agencies use male and female students and you may not always be able to specify which sex; they get busy on weekends so book ahead. Try Oppascentrale Kriterion (☎ 624 58 48; 5pm to 8pm daily, or 9am to 11am Monday and Wednesday), Valckenierstraat 45hs, which has been in business for a long time and seems to be consistently reliable. Oppascentrale De Peuterette (☎ 679 67 93; 2.30pm to 4pm Monday and Thursday), Roelof Hartplein 2A, also gets good reports.

Some hotels offer a baby-sitting service and others may be able to advise.

Many special events and activities aimed at children take place throughout the year. Check the *Uitkrant* (under 'Agenda Jeugd') or contact the Amsterdam Uitburo. Or try the following options, most of which are described in more detail elsewhere in this book:

- the Vondelpark (Maps 1 & 4) – for picnics, children's playground, ducks etc
- Amsterdamse Bos (Map 1) – huge recreational area with animal enclosure, children's farm etc
- Tram Museum Amsterdam (Map 1) – ride in a historic tram past the Amsterdamse Bos
- Tropenmuseum (Map 5) – separate children's section with activities focusing on exotic locations
- climb a church tower – if that doesn't exhaust them, nothing will
- Artis zoo (Map 5)
- the beach at Zandvoort – only a short train ride away
- hire a canal bike
- harbour cruise
- swimming pool – especially the high-tech Mirandabad (Map 1)
- circus – in Theater Carré (Map 5); from mid-December to early January
- Koninginnedag (Queen's Day) on 30 April – a wonderful party for kids as much as grown-ups
- NEMO science and technology centre (Map 6)
- hire a bike for a day out in the country
- ice skating at the Jaap Edenbaan (Map 1)

Kids love the **Madame Tussaud Scenerama** (Map 2; ☎ 522 10 10, recorded message), Dam 20 on the corner of Dam Square and Rokin, open 10am to 5.30pm (to 7.30pm from 15 July to 31 August). Admission costs a hefty €11.35, children up to 15 pay €8.17 (free for those under five), and family and group rates are available. Some characters on display won't mean much to foreigners.

The national aviation museum, **Aviodome** (☎ 406 80 00, W www.aviodome.nl), Westelijke Randweg 201, at the airport (take the train to Station Schiphol and then it's a 1km walk), is also a hit with kids, who can play in old planes and sit in a cockpit. Adults will also enjoy the displays, comprising 25 aeroplanes including the Wright Flyer (which made the first motorised flight in 1903), several Fokker aircraft including a 1911 Fokker Spin (Spider) and Baron von Richthofen's WWI triplane, a Spitfire and of course a Dakota. The museum is open 10am to 5pm daily (from October to April it's closed Monday and opens at noon on weekends) and costs €6.80 (children between four and 12 pay €5.67).

LIBRARIES

Many museums and institutes have private libraries, mentioned throughout this book. To borrow books from a public library *(openbare bibliotheek)* you need to be a resident, but everyone's free to browse or read.

The main public library, the Centrale Bibliotheek (Map 3; ☎ 523 09 00), is at Prinsengracht 587 and is open 1pm to 9pm Monday, 10am to 9pm Tuesday to Thursday, 10am to 5pm Friday and Saturday, and 1pm to 5pm Sunday. It has a wide range of English-language newspapers and magazines, a coffee bar and a useful notice board. For other public libraries, look in the phone book under *Bibliotheken, Openbare*.

UNIVERSITIES

Amsterdam has two universities and over 40,000 students. About 27,000 attend the Universiteit van Amsterdam (UvA), which has existed in various guises since 1632. Its buildings are spread throughout the city. For information about international education programs in English, contact Universiteit van Amsterdam, Service & Informatiecentrum (☎ 525 33 33, fax 525 29 21, W www.uva.nl), Binnengasthuisstraat 9, 1012 ZA Amsterdam. Tuition fees begin at €1360 (for regular study programs in Dutch) and go up to €9500 per academic year.

Another 13,500 students attend the Vrije Universiteit (VU, Free University; Map 1) established by orthodox Calvinists in 1880. It occupies a large campus along De Boelelaan in the southern suburb of Buitenveldert. Calvinism is no longer an issue but Philosophy is still a compulsory subject, so students think about the role of science in society. The Free University can be contacted at Onderwijsvoorlichting Vrije Universiteit (☎ 444 50 00, W www.vu.nl), De Boelelaan 1105, 1081 HV Amsterdam, 8.30am to 4.30pm Monday to Friday.

The Foreign Student Service (☎ 671 59 15), Oranje Nassaulaan 5, 1017 AH Amsterdam, is a support agency for foreign students. It provides information about study programs and intensive language courses, and helps with accommodation, insurance and personal problems. It's open 9am to 5.30pm weekdays.

CULTURAL CENTRES

There are many cultural centres and institutes besides the city's museums and theatres. These include:

British Council (☎ 550 60 60, W www.britishcouncil.org/netherlands) Keizersgracht 269. Educational and cultural exchanges. Education Centre (☎ 524 76 76), Nieuwezijds Voorburgwal 328K, open 1pm to 5pm Tuesday and Wednesday, to 6pm Thursday.
Cedla (☎ 525 34 98, library ☎ 525 32 48) Keizersgracht 395–397. Centre for Latin American studies and documentation, open 10am to 4pm weekdays.
De Balie (Map 4; ☎ 553 51 51, recording in Dutch and English) Kleine Gartmanplantsoen 10 at Leidseplein. Café, restaurant, theatre, seminars, political debates, lectures etc; hang-out of trendy intellectuals; open 9am to 5pm weekdays.
Goethe Institut (Map 4; ☎ 623 04 21) Herengracht 470. German cultural centre with lectures, films (some with English subtitles), plays and discussions, plus German language courses at all levels and Dutch courses for Germans; office hours 9am to 6pm weekdays (to 4.30pm Friday); library open 1pm to 6pm Wednesday, to 8pm Thursday.
Italian Cultural Institute (☎ 626 53 14) Keizersgracht 564. Open 10am to noon and 2pm to 4pm weekdays.

Jewish Cultural Centre (☎ 646 00 46) Van der Boechorststraat 26. Open by appointment only.
John Adams Institute (Map 2; ☎ 624 72 80, W www.john-adams.nl) Herenmarkt 97 in the Westindisch Huis. Dutch-US friendship society that organises lectures, readings and discussions on US culture and history led by heavyweights such as Saul Bellow, Gore Vidal, Annie Proulx and Seamus Heaney; the lectures (once a month or more) are often interesting and affordable, and provide a focus for the US and British expat community; definitely worth checking.
Maison Descartes (Map 4; ☎ 531 95 00, W www.ambafrance.nl) Vijzelgracht 2A, attached to the French Consulate. French cultural centre named after the philosopher who in Amsterdam found the intellectual freedom denied him at home; office open 9.30am to 4pm weekdays, library 1pm to 6pm (to 8pm Tuesday and Thursday); many activities are organised by the Alliance Française (☎ 627 92 71), Keizersgracht 635-II.
South African Institute (☎ 624 93 18, W www.zuidafrikahuis.nl) Keizersgracht 141. Information centre and library, open 10am to 4pm Tuesday to Friday, by appointment Monday and Saturday.
Vlaams Cultureel Centrum de Brakke Grond (Map 2; ☎ 622 90 14) Nes 45. Flemish cultural centre; very active (readings, plays, lectures, music, dance, exhibitions); includes a theatre, café and restaurant; open 10am to at least 6pm Monday to Saturday, 1pm to 5pm Sunday.

DANGERS & ANNOYANCES

Amsterdam is a small city by world standards but requires big-city street sense, though it's positively tame if you're used to New York or Johannesburg. Violent crime is unusual but theft, especially pickpocketing, is a real problem, and unfortunately tourists are much more likely to be a victim of crime than locals. Don't carry more money than you intend to spend – use a secondary wallet or purse and keep your main one safe. Don't walk around with conspicuous valuables, or give away that you're a tourist with map, camera or video. Walking purposefully helps.

A car with foreign registration is a popular target, and if it's parked along a canal it will probably get broken into. Don't leave things in the car: definitely remove registration and ID papers, and if possible the radio.

If something is stolen, by all means get a police report for insurance purposes but don't expect the police to retrieve your property or to apprehend the thief – put the matter down to experience. There's usually very little they can do. What they will do, however, is refer about 10% of cases to a voluntary support group in the police station at Nieuwezijds Voorburgwal, called Amsterdam Tourist Assistance Service, where traumatised victims receive the help they need to get back on their feet.

If you have trouble on the train to Amsterdam or at Centraal Station itself, contact the railway police *(spoorwegpolitie)* at the west end of track 2A. You can report violence or missing/stolen property here, and the staff can put you in touch with your consulate or other relevant support agencies. They'll also put through a station announcement if you're looking for someone. This office is more or less always open.

The red-light district is full of shady characters loitering on street corners. They seem harmless enough, but if you're accosted, simply say *Nee dank* (No thanks) and keep walking. Don't take photos of the prostitutes.

Mosquitoes can be another nuisance in summer. They breed in stagnant parts of the canals and in water under houses. In some parts of the city they're no problem, but one author of this book used to live in a canal house where the tenants slept under mosquito nets six months of the year!

Amsterdam is still the dog-shit capital of the world (see Ecology & Environment in the Facts about Amsterdam chapter) and you soon learn to look where you're walking. Also, North Americans and Australians should accept that nonsmokers have few rights here: tobacco smoke in pubs can be thick enough to deter all but the most committed smokers, and unfortunately the Dutch seem allergic to open windows.

EMERGENCIES

The national emergency number (police, ambulance, fire brigade) is ☎ 112. The Amsterdam police can also be contacted directly on ☎ 559 91 11 at the headquarters on Elandsgracht 117 (along Marnixstraat; Map 3). For 24-hour medical service, call the Centrale Doktersdienst (☎ 0900-503 20 42) to be referred to a doctor, dentist or pharmacy.

DRUGS

Contrary to what you may have heard, cannabis products are illegal. The confusion arises because the authorities have had the sense to distinguish between 'soft' drugs (cannabis) and addictive 'hard' drugs (heroin, crack, pills) when deciding where to focus their resources. Soft drugs for personal use (defined as up to 5g, down from 30g after table-thumping from France) are unofficially tolerated, but larger amounts put you in the persecuted 'dealer' category.

The key phrase is *gedogen* (sometimes translated as 'tolerating'), a wonderful Dutch term that means official condemnation but looking the other way when common sense dictates it. Hard drugs (including LSD) are treated just as seriously as anywhere else and can land you in big trouble, although the authorities tend to treat genuine, registered addicts as medical cases rather than as serial killers – Amsterdam was an early adopter of methadone and needle exchange programs and of safe injecting houses.

Neighbouring countries take a dim view of such tolerance now that border controls have been abolished in theory, and the government is under EU pressure to clamp down – never mind that most hashish reaches the Netherlands through France and Belgium and most heroin through Germany. In typical Dutch fashion this has led to some tightening of rules and regulations without losing sight of the common-sense approach.

One of the positive results of this approach has been to move cannabis out of the criminal circuit and into registered 'coffeeshops', driving a wedge between cannabis users and predatory street dealers who would rather sell the more profitable hard stuff. Since the late 1980s the number of heroin addicts in the Netherlands has stabilised at around 1.6 per 1000 inhabitants, slightly more than in Germany, Norway, Austria or Ireland; but in hardline France the proportion is 2.6 per 1000, and in Greece, Spain and Italy it's higher still. Dutch addicts have the best average survival rate in Europe and the lowest incidence of HIV infection – Rotterdam has even opened a retirement home for addicts.

These tolerant policies attract many drug tourists: drugs are cheaper and more readily available here than elsewhere, and generally of better quality. The country has become a major exporter of high-grade marihuana (grown locally) and is the European centre for the production of ecstasy. Much of Europe's cocaine passes through Rotterdam harbour.

For more about (soft) drugs, see the boxed text 'Cafés, Pubs & Coffeeshops' in the Entertainment chapter.

LEGAL MATTERS

The Amsterdam police *(politie)* are a pretty relaxed and helpful lot. If you do something wrong, they can hold you up to six hours for questioning (another six hours if they can't establish your identity, or 24 hours if they consider the matter serious) and do not have to grant a phone call, though they'll ring your consulate.

Since 1994 there's a 'limited' requirement for anyone aged over 12 to carry ID; typically, theory doesn't always match practice and everyone is confused, but it seems that foreigners should carry their passport. Then again, a photocopy of the relevant data pages should be OK unless there's reason to suspect you're an illegal immigrant. Logical, isn't it? A driving licence is not OK because it doesn't show your nationality.

The Bureau voor Rechtshulp (Office for Legal Help; Map 2; ☎ 520 51 00), Spuistraat 10 and other locations, is a nonprofit organisation of law students and lawyers who give free legal advice during business hours to those who can't afford it. They deal with a wide range of issues, including immigration and residency, but will refer you if they can't deal with the matter themselves or if they think you're wealthy enough.

BUSINESS HOURS

As a general rule, Amsterdam banks are open 9am to 4pm Monday to Friday, offices 8.30am to 5pm Monday to Friday, and shops 9am to 5.30pm Monday to Saturday. Now for the exceptions:

On Monday many shops don't open till noon but they stay open until 8pm or 9pm on Thursday. Department stores and supermarkets generally close around 6pm weekdays and at 5pm on Saturday but most supermarkets near the city centre stay open till 8pm – the big Albert Heijn supermarket behind the palace on Dam Square till 10pm Monday to Saturday, till 7pm Sunday. Most regular nontourist shops outside the canal belt close at 5pm or 6pm weekdays and at midday Saturday, depending on their line of trade, and almost all are closed on Sunday. Within the canal belt, however, most shops are open 9am (noon on Monday) to 5pm (9pm on Thursday) throughout the week including Saturday, and many are open noon to 5pm on Sunday (especially the first Sunday of the month).

Government offices, private institutions, monuments and even museums follow erratic and sometimes very limited opening hours to suit themselves; they're mentioned in this book where possible. Many museums are closed Monday.

PUBLIC HOLIDAYS & SPECIAL EVENTS

Public holidays are New Year's Day (Nieuwjaarsdag), Good Friday (Goede Vrijdag), Easter Sunday and Easter Monday (Eerste and Tweede Paasdag), Queen's Day (Koninginnedag) on 30 April, Ascension Day (Hemelvaartsdag), Whit Sunday (Pentecost) and Monday (Eerste and Tweede Pinksterdag), Christmas Day and Boxing Day (Eerste and Tweede Kerstdag). Dutch people take public holidays seriously and you won't get much done.

There are many festivals and special events throughout the year. Summer is a time of open-air concerts, theatre and other events

---

Warning

Never, *ever* buy drugs on the street: you'll get ripped off or mugged. And *don't* light up in view of the police, or in an establishment without checking that it's OK to do so. Locals detest drug tourists who think they can just smoke dope anywhere.

around the city, often free, and favoured venues include the Vondelpark and the Amsterdamse Bos. The queen mother's birthday on 30 April is celebrated with the biggest street party in the country, an unforgettable experience. Culture-lovers might aim for the Holland Festival in June or the Uitmarkt at the end of August, or the quirky Parade early in August. A few of the following events aren't in Amsterdam but are worth a day trip:

January

Elfstedentocht (Eleven Cities' Journey) Skating on the canals (frost permitting) is the only excitement in this seemingly never-ending month, with cold, dull, dark days. If it has been freezing hard enough for long enough, this gruelling skating marathon through the countryside of Friesland is organised, attracting thousands of participants and stopping the nation. It was last held in 1997 but years may pass before conditions are right.

February

Carnaval A southern (Catholic) tradition best enjoyed in Breda, Den Bosch or (especially) Maastricht, but Amsterdammers also know how to do such silly costumes and party. Information: Stichting Carnaval in Mokum (☎ 623 25 68), Herengracht 513, 1017 BV Amsterdam.

Commemoration of the February Strike 25 February, in memory of the anti-Nazi general strike in 1941; wreath-laying at the Dockworker monument in the former Jewish quarter.

March

Stille Omgang Silent Procession, Sunday closest to 15 March; Catholics walk along the Holy Way (the current Heiligeweg is a remnant) to St Nicolaaskerk to commemorate the Miracle of Amsterdam.

HISWA boat show The latest pleasure craft in the RAI exhibition grounds (☎ 549 12 12, fax 646 44 69, W www.rai.nl).

April

Floriade 2002 1 April to 15 October 2002; an international horticultural exhibition that's held every 10 years, drawing 3.3 million visitors last time. This fifth Floriade will take place in Hoofddorp just south-west of Amsterdam. Information: Stichting Floriade 2002 (☎ 023-562 20 02, W www.floriade.nl), Postbus 2002, 2130 GE Hoofddorp.

World Press Photo exhibition Mid-April to end May, in the Oude Kerk; information: Bureau World Press Photo (☎ 676 60 96, W www .worldpressphoto.nl), Jacob Obrechtstraat 26, 1071 KM Amsterdam.

National Museum Weekend Usually second weekend of April; free entry to all museums (extremely crowded). Information: Amsterdam Uitburo or Stichting Museumjaarkaart (☎ 0900-404 09 10).

Koninginnedag Queen's Day, 30 April, actually Queen Mother Juliana's birthday (Queen Beatrix's birthday is in January, far too cold for *the* party of the year); if you could visit Amsterdam at any time, this is it. There's a free market throughout the city (anyone can sell anything they like, kids love it), street parties, live music, dense crowds and lots of beer – a collective madhouse. The whole country under the age of 30 visits Amsterdam, while all of Amsterdam over the age of 30 escapes.

May

Remembrance Day 4 May, for the victims of WWII; Queen Beatrix lays a wreath at the Nationaal Monument on Dam Square and the city observes two minutes' silence at 8pm; making noise then is thoughtless in the extreme (Germans in particular should take care).

Liberation Day 5 May, end of German occupation in 1945; street parties, free market, live music. The Vondelpark is a good place to be.

Luilak 'Lazy-Bones', Saturday before Whit Sunday; children go around in the early hours ringing door bells, making noise and waking people up. Remnant of pre-Christian festival celebrating the awakening of spring.

National Cycling Day Second Saturday; family cycling trips along special routes. Information: VVV, ANWB or NBT.

National Windmill Day Second Saturday; windmills unfurl their sails and are open to the public. Information: Vereniging De Hollandsche Molen (☎ 623 87 03, Zeeburgerdijk 139, 1095 AA Amsterdam.

Drum Rhythm Festival Mid-month; avant-garde dance but also soul and funk on Java Eiland in the Eastern Harbour region. Information: Amsterdam Uitburo.

Open Garden Days Mid-month; see some of the beautiful private gardens behind canal houses. Information: VVV.

Pinkpop Around Pentecost (May/June); three-day outdoor rock festival near Landgraaf in the south-east of the country. Information: Buro Pinkpop (☎ 046-475 25 00, W (Dutch) www .pinkpop.nl).

Canal Run End of month or early June; event consisting of 5km, 9km and 18km runs along canals, organised by *De Echo*, a local weekly paper. Information: VVV or Echo Grachtenloop (☎ 585 92 22), Basisweg 30, 1043 AP Amsterdam.

June

Over het IJ Festival From June or July throughout summer months; big performing-arts events (dance, theatre, music) around the former NDSM shipyards north of the IJ, often exciting and always interesting. Information: W (Dutch) www.overhetij.nl, Amsterdam Uitburo or VVV.

RAI Arts Fair First week; exhibition of all facets of contemporary art in RAI exhibition grounds (☎ 549 12 12, fax 646 44 69, W www.rai.nl).

Holland Festival All month; the country's biggest music, drama and dance extravaganza, mainly in Amsterdam and The Hague. World premieres etc, often highbrow and pretentious but also many fringe events. Information: VVV, Amsterdam Uitburo, or Stichting Holland Festival (☎ 530 71 10, W www.holndfstvl.nl/festival), Kleine Gartmanplantsoen 21, 1017 RP Amsterdam.

Oerol Festival Mid-month; 10-day festival on the Wadden island of Terschelling. Open-air theatre and music acts, landscape arts etc, with visitors (45,000 during the 2001 event) cycling from act to act. Each year has a different theme. Information: W www.oerol.nl.

Roots Music Festival Mid-month; 10-day festival of world music and culture at various locations throughout the city. Information: Amsterdam Uitburo or W www.amsterdamroots.nl.

Dutch TT Assen Last Saturday; Dutch round of the world series motorcycle grands prix, held since 1925 near Assen in the north-east of the country. Many European championship events during 'Speedweek' leading up to the main event that attracts crowds in excess of 150,000. A unique experience even if you're not particularly interested in motorcycles; just turn up at the gate.

Parkpop Last Sunday; Europe's largest free rock festival, in the Zuiderpark in The Hague. In 2001 it drew a crowd of 400,000. Information: W www .parkpop.nl.

International Theatre School Festival End of month; Dutch and international theatre schools strut their stuff. Information: Amsterdam Uitburo or VVV.

July

North Sea Jazz Festival Mid-month; world's largest indoor jazz festival, in the Congresgebouw in The Hague. Many musicians take the opportunity to visit Amsterdam at this time. Information: W www.northseajazz.nl, Amsterdam Uitburo or VVV.

August

Canal Parade First Saturday; the only waterborne gay pride parade in the world. Information: Gay & Lesbian Switchboard.

Parade First two weeks; carnavalesque outdoor theatre festival held in the Martin Luther King Park. Unforgettable ambience. Information: VVV, Amsterdam Uitburo, or Mobilearts (☎ 033-465 45 77, W www.mobilearts.nl).

Grachtenfestival Canal Festival, second half of month; one-week music festival (mainly classical) at various locations in the canal belt. Main focus is the Prinsengracht Concert from barges in front of the Pulitzer Hotel. Information: W www .grachtenfestival.nl, Amsterdam Uitburo, VVV or Pulitzer Hotel (☎ 523 52 35), Prinsengracht 315–331, 1016 GZ Amsterdam.

Hartjesdag Zeedijk Third Monday and weekend leading up to it; theatre, parade and music along Zeedijk and Nieuwmarkt square celebrate this festival that dates back to medieval times. Information: VVV.

Lowlands Festival Last weekend; charming, three-day festival at Biddinghuizen, near Dronten east of Lelystad (Flevoland) with all sorts of alternative music on nine stages, from hip-hop and rock to world. It was a sell-out in 2001 with 57,000 visitors. Information: W www.lowlands.nl.

Uitmarkt Last weekend; local troupes and orchestras present their coming repertoires free of charge throughout the city. A bit like Koninginnedag but much more easy-going. Information: W (Dutch) www.uitmarkt.nl, Amsterdam Uitburo or VVV.

September

Bloemencorso Flower Parade, first Saturday; spectacular procession of floats wends its way from Aalsmeer in the morning to Dam Square and back again at night (illuminated). Information: VVV.

Jordaan Festival Second week; street festival with merriment and entertainment in a 'typically Amsterdam' neighbourhood. Information: VVV.

Monumentendag Second weekend; registered historical buildings have open days. Information: VVV or Bureau Monumentenzorg (☎ 552 48 88, W www.bmz.amsterdam.nl), Keizersgracht 123, 1015 CJ Amsterdam.

Chinatown Festival Mid-month; the Chinese community celebrates on Nieuwmarkt square. Information: VVV, or ☎ 642 23 99 (English) or ☎ 620 33 33 (Chinese).

Prinsjesdag Third Tuesday; opening of parliament in The Hague. Queen Beatrix arrives in Golden Coach and presents budget.

October

Jumping Amsterdam International indoor show-jumping at RAI exhibition grounds (☎ 665 48 35, fax 665 55 00, **W** (Dutch) www.jumpingamst erdam.nl).

Delta Lloyd Amsterdam Marathon Mid-month; 8000 runners and in-line skaters do a 21 km loop through the city twice, starting and finishing at the Olympic Stadium. Information: ☎ 663 07 81, **W** www.amsterdammarathon.nl.

November

Sinterklaas arrives Mid-month; the children's saint arrives by ship 'from Spain' (see December). The mayor presents the city key on Dam Square. Information: VVV.

Cannabis Cup Third week; marihuana festival hosted by *High Times* magazine. The cup itself goes to the best grass, other awards to the biggest spliff etc; also hemp expo and fashion show. Information: any 'coffeeshop' or **W** www .hightimes.com/Events.

Zeedijk Jazz & Blues Festival Last weekend; Amsterdam's biggest jazz festival, with hundreds of jazz and blues acts out on the street and in the pubs along Zeedijk, free of charge. Information: Amsterdam Uitburo or VVV.

December

Sinterklaas Officially 6 December but the main focus is gift-giving on the evening of the 5th, in honour of St Nicholas.

Christmas 25 and 26 December, but religious families traditionally celebrate Christmas Eve on the 24th, with Bible-readings and carols around the Christmas tree.

New Year's Eve Wild parties everywhere; drunken revelry with fireworks and injuries.

DOING BUSINESS

Amsterdam's authorities make much of the city's function as the gateway to Europe with its busy airport and harbour, its multilingual, highly educated and productive workforce, its easy-going tax laws, its international outlook and 'neutral' image, and its expertise in trade, transport, finance and communication. A growing number of companies have set up their European headquarters and distribution centres in Amsterdam, including IBM, Xerox, Sony, HP, Canon, Nissan, Cisco and Worldcom. The trade office at the Dutch embassy in your home

Sinterklaas

Every year on 6 December the Dutch celebrate Sinterklaas in honour of St Nicholas, historically the bishop of Myra in western Turkey around AD 345 and the patron saint of children, sailors, merchants and pawnbrokers (Klaas is a nickname for Nicholas, or Nicolaas in Dutch).

A few weeks beforehand, the white-bearded saint, dressed as a bishop with mitre and staff, arrives in Amsterdam by ship 'from Spain' (a legacy of Spanish colonial rule over the Netherlands) and enters the city on a grey or white horse to receive the city keys from the mayor. He is accompanied by a host of mischievous black servants called Black Peters *(Zwarte Pieten)* – or politically correct Blue and Green Peters – who throw sweets around and carry sacks in which to take naughty children away. Well-behaved children get presents in a shoe that they've placed by the fireplace with a carrot for the saint's horse (he stays on the roof while a Black Peter climbs down the chimney).

On the evening of 5 December people give one another anonymous and creatively wrapped gifts *(surprises)* accompanied by funny/perceptive poems about the recipient written by Sinterklaas. The gift itself matters less than the wrapping (the greater the surprise the better) and poetry (the more the person is put on the spot the better).

The commercialisation of Christmas has weakened the impact of this charming festival. Ironically, the American Santa Claus who dominates the commercial Christmas spirit these days evolved from the Sinterklaas celebrations at the Dutch settlement of New Amsterdam (New York).

country can provide initial information and help establish the necessary contacts, as can your embassy's trade office in The Hague. Also in The Hague, the Netherlands Foreign Investment Agency (fax 070-379 63 22) offers similar support.

Once you've decided to establish a base in Amsterdam, get in touch with the Amsterdam Foreign Investment Office (Map 5; ☎ 552 35 36, fax 552 28 60, e afio@ez.amsterdam.nl), PO Box 2133, 1000 CC Amsterdam (street address: Metropool Building, Weesperstraat 89), who can provide the know-how and know-who to get you started. For trade contacts, try the Amsterdam Chamber of Commerce & Industry (Map 2; ☎ 531 40 00, fax 531 47 99), De Ruijterkade 5, 1013 AA Amsterdam.

Businesswomen might find the Women's International Network useful, an association that offers business contacts, advice and support for professional women aged over 25 and employed for at least five years. Membership (€80 a year) is open to foreign women working in the Netherlands and Dutch women working for international companies or with experience of working abroad. Guests are welcome at monthly events. Contact the president (☎ 070-385 9085, w www.womensinternational.net) at Postbus 90291, 1006 BG Amsterdam.

Business Services

The luxury hotels – and of course Schiphol airport – all offer business services. Some have full-blown business centres that can be quite expensive. A cheaper option might be the first European branch of the Kinko's chain, at Overtoom 62 near Leidseplein (Map 4; ☎ 589 09 10, fax 589 09 20). Open 24 hours, it does video-conferencing. An Internet café such as easyEverything might suit your purposes as well – see Internet Cafés under Post & Communications earlier in this chapter.

If you want to start operating straight away without the headaches of establishing a base from scratch, the Euro Business Center (Map 2; ☎ 520 75 00, fax 520 75 10), Keizersgracht 62–64, can help with the paperwork and will supply an office with

furniture, phone, computer etc. Secretarial help and other services are also available. The market-leading Regus Business Centre (☎ 301 22 00), Strawinskylaan 3051, 1077 ZX Amsterdam (and two other locations) is similar and has an excellent reputation at the top end of the price range.

For difficult translations, contact Berlitz Globalnet (☎ 639 14 06, fax 620 39 59), Rokin 87, though they're not cheap. The aforementioned Amsterdam Foreign Investment Office may also be able to help with translators.

Exhibitions & Conferences

Amsterdam is a popular place for trade fairs and conferences – it hosts more than 100 international and many hundreds of national conventions each year.

The major luxury hotels, such as Grand Hotel Krasnapolsky on Dam Square, the Barbizon Palace opposite Centraal Station or the Okura Hotel in the southern suburbs, are often used for modest meetings and shows, and have facilities to handle groups of 25 to 2000 people.

Amsterdam RAI (Map 1; ☎ 549 12 12, fax 646 44 69), Europaplein 8, is the largest exhibition centre in the country (see the New South section in the Things to See & Do chapter). It's also a conference centre with 21 conference rooms and a main auditorium that seats 1750. If necessary, one of the 11 exhibition halls can be converted for even larger gatherings. Nearby is the World Trade Center (Map 1; ☎ 575 91 11, fax 662 72 55), Strawinskylaan 1, with conference rooms for four to 200 people, and a full range of facilities and support services including a branch office of the Chamber of Commerce & Industry.

WORK

Nationals from EU countries (as well as Iceland, Norway and Liechtenstein) may work in the Netherlands but they need a renewable residence permit, a tedious formality. There are very few legal openings for non-EU nationals and the government tries to keep immigrants out of this already over-populated country. You may be eligible if you are filling a job that no Dutch or EU national has the (trainable) skill to do, are aged between 18 and 45, and have suitable accommodation, but there will be a mountain of red tape. (Forget about teaching English: there's very little demand.) All this has to be set in motion before you arrive (with the exception of US nationals, who may look for work within three months after they arrive as a tourist).

As a rule, you need to apply for temporary residence before an employer can apply for a work permit in your name. If all goes well, you will be issued a residence permit for work purposes. The whole rigmarole should take about five weeks. Self-employed individuals are subject to other regulations but they must serve 'an essential Dutch interest'.

For more information, contact the Dutch embassy or consulate in your home country. Alternatively, for residence permits you can contact the Immigratie- en Naturalisatiedienst (☎ 070-370 31 24, fax 370 31 34), Postbus 30125, 2500 GC The Hague. For work permits and details of the Aliens Employment Act, contact the Landelijk Bureau Arbeidsvoorziening, Postbus 883, 2700 AW Zoetermeer.

Au pair work is easier to organise, provided you're aged between 18 and 25, hold medical insurance and your host family earns at least €1360 a month after tax. The maximum period is one year. Nationals of the EU, Australia, Canada, Japan, Monaco, New Zealand, Switzerland and the USA can organise the necessary residence permit with the Vreemdelingenpolitie (Aliens' Police – see Visa Extensions in the earlier Documents section) after arrival in the Netherlands; others must organise this with the Dutch embassy or consulate in their home country – but check with your embassy first because regulations change.

Nationals of Australia, Canada, Japan, New Zealand and maybe the USA can apply for a one-year working holiday visa if they're aged between 18 and 25 (though this can be stretched to 30), but the whole scheme is under review. Contact the Dutch embassy or consulate in your home country for further details.

Illegal jobs are pretty rare these days, with increased crackdowns on illegal immigrants working in restaurants, pubs and bulb fields. Some travellers' hotels in Amsterdam still employ touts to pounce on newly arrived backpackers; the pay isn't much but you may get free lodging.

If you're fortunate enough to find legal work, the minimum adult wage is €1154.46 a month before tax.

Getting There & Away

Amsterdam is an easy city to get to, and many travellers pass through. It's also an easy place to get away from – if you're looking for cheap deals, advice, shared rides or whatever, you're likely to find them in Amsterdam.

AIR

Many of the world's airlines fly directly to/from Amsterdam's Schiphol airport. As always, it pays to shop around but keep in mind that the best quote might not always be the cheapest: a package deal that includes hotel accommodation, for instance, could save you a small fortune on Amsterdam's notoriously expensive hotels.

Also consider the option of flying to other airports in the region, such as Frankfurt, Luxembourg, Brussels, Paris or London (one of the cheapest destinations from outside Europe). It doesn't cost much to take a train or bus from there to Amsterdam, and if you're flying from outside Europe, many airlines offer a free return flight within Europe anyway.

Warning

The information in this chapter is particularly vulnerable to change: Prices for international travel are volatile, routes are introduced and cancelled, schedules change, special deals come and go, and rules and visa requirements are amended. You should check directly with the airline or a travel agent to make sure you understand how a fare (and ticket you may buy) works, and be aware of the security requirements for international travel.

The upshot of this is that you should get opinions, quotes and advice from as many airlines and travel agents as possible before you part with your hard-earned cash. The details given in this chapter should be regarded as pointers and are not a substitute for your own careful, up-to-date research.

Amsterdam is a major European centre for discounted tickets to many destinations – see Travel Agents later in this chapter. For special deals, you should also check the Saturday travel sections of the *Volkskrant* or *Telegraaf* newspapers.

A useful Web site to refer to when researching (somewhat US-centric) flight options is W www.artoftravel.com – click the chapter called 'How to Get Cheap Airline Tickets'.

For information about Schiphol airport and transport to/from the city, see the start of the Getting Around chapter.

Departure Tax

A small airport tax is included in your flight ticket.

The UK & Ireland

There isn't really a low or high season for flights to Amsterdam: prices depend more on special offers and availability of seats.

By taking advantage of special offers (which usually involve booking in advance and staying a minimum number of nights), you should be able to fly London-Schiphol return for less than UK£100. Keep in mind that a regular, fully flexible and fully refundable ticket could cost as much as UK£320.

The flight takes just under an hour and then it's another 20 minutes by train into the centre of Amsterdam (by bus, train or car from London you'll spend five to 10 hours or more).

STA Travel (☎ 020-7361 6161, W www.statravel.co.uk) has some very worthwhile deals but these change all the time and the flights mentioned here are just an indication of what might be on offer. Also check the Sunday newspapers, the listings magazine *Time Out* or the *Evening Standard* for good-value benchmarks.

Discount airline easyJet (☎ 08706-000 000, W www.easyjet.com) has one-way flights between London and Amsterdam from

Air Travel Glossary

Alliances Many of the world's leading airlines are now intimately involved with each other, sharing everything from reservations systems and check-in to aircraft and frequent-flyer schemes. Opponents say that alliances restrict competition. Whatever the arguments, there is no doubt that big alliances are the way of the future.

Courier Fares Businesses often need to send urgent documents or freight securely and quickly. Courier companies hire people to accompany the package through customs and, in return, offer a discount ticket which is sometimes a bargain. However, you may have to surrender all your baggage allowance and take only carry-on luggage.

Fares Airlines traditionally offer 1st class (coded F), business class (coded J) and economy class (coded Y) tickets. These days there are so many promotional and discounted fares available that few passengers pay full fare.

Lost Tickets If you lose your airline ticket, an airline will usually treat it like a travellers cheque and, after inquiries, issue you with another one. Legally, however, an airline is entitled to treat it like cash and if you lose it then it's gone forever. Take very good care of your tickets.

Onward Tickets An entry requirement for many countries is that you have a ticket out of the country. If you're unsure of your next move, the easiest solution is to buy the cheapest onward ticket to a neighbouring country or a ticket from a reliable airline which can later be refunded if you do not use it.

Open-Jaw Tickets These are return tickets where you fly out to one place but return from another. If available, this can save you backtracking to your arrival point.

Overbooking Since every flight has some passengers who fail to show up, airlines often book more passengers than they have seats. Usually excess passengers make up for the no-shows, but occasionally somebody gets 'bumped' onto the next available flight. Guess who it is most likely to be? The passengers who check in late. If you do get 'bumped', you are normally offered some form of compensation.

Reconfirmation Some airlines require you to reconfirm your flight at least 72 hours prior to departure. Check your travel documents to see if this is the case

Restrictions Discounted tickets often have various restrictions on them – such as needing to be paid for in advance and incurring a penalty to be altered or cancelled. Others are restrictions on the minimum and maximum period you must be away.

Round-the-World Tickets RTW tickets give you a limited period (usually a year) in which to circumnavigate the globe. You can go anywhere the carrying airlines go, as long as you don't backtrack. The number of stopovers or total number of separate flights is decided before you set off and they usually cost a bit more than a basic return flight.

Ticketless Travel Airlines are gradually waking up to the realisation that paper tickets are unnecessary encumbrances. On simple one-way or return trips, reservations details can be held on computer and the passenger merely shows ID to claim their seat.

Transferred Tickets Airline tickets cannot be transferred from one person to another. Travellers sometimes try to sell the return half of their ticket, but officials can ask you to prove that you are the person named on the ticket. On an international flight, tickets are compared with passports.

as low as UK£14.50 (and even then there are specials!) but more realistically at around the UK£30 mark. Add UK£5 tax. Flights vary due to availability and are slightly cheaper booked online. Flights leave from Gatwick and Luton, with greater frequency from Luton (but at the expense of an additional UK£5.50 charge imposed by Luton).

KLM (or rather, KLM-UK; ☎ 08705-074 074, W www.klmuk.co.uk) flies from 14 UK airports. Heathrow-Schiphol return starts at UK£95 to UK£135 including airport taxes; from Edinburgh and Leeds-Bradford, fares start at UK£130 and UK£107 respectively. Advance-purchase specials can be had for about UK£20 less and occasionally there are even cheaper deals. Other airlines include BA (☎ 0845-773 3377, W www.britishairways.com) and British Midland (☎ 08706-070 555, W www.flybmi .com), and lively competition ensures that their prices are similar.

From Ireland, Aer Lingus (☎ 01-886 8888, W www.aerlingus.ie) offers returns from Dublin and Cork with fares starting at IR£175 and IR£125 respectively.

The USA

Tickets in the high season can cost almost twice as much as those in the low season. The high season lasts roughly from mid-June to mid or late September, with August at the peak; low is roughly from October to March. The few months on either side are the shoulder seasons.

Many US airlines fly direct to Amsterdam. United, Delta and Northwest offer decent fares but KLM offers the most frequent flights in conjunction with its partner, Northwest. Approximate fares are US$600/1200 return in the low/high season from San Francisco or US$430/900 from New York. Many flights from the west coast stop in one other US city along the way. Check with a travel agent or in your local Sunday newspaper for the best deals.

Council Travel (☎ 800-226 8624, W www .counciltravel.com) and STA Travel (☎ 800-777-0112, W www.statravel.com) are both agencies that specialise in discount tickets for students, teachers and under-26s. Even if

you don't fit any of these descriptions, it's worth giving them a try for general discount fares. Both companies have offices in major US cities.

If you are flexible in your travel dates and locations you might consider flying on stand-by or as a courier. For the former, try Whole Earth Travel (☎ 800-326 2009, 212-864 2000, W www.4standby.com) which offers one-way fares from $139 to $269 depending on your destination. For courier travel, one option is Now Voyager (☎ 212-431 1616, W www.nowvoyagertravel.com) where, for a US$50 annual membership fee, you can sign up to become a courier and gain access to sizable discounts. In this form of travel you can only bring carry-on luggage and there are restrictions regarding the length of your travel.

Icelandair operates a flight between JFK (New York) and Amsterdam for US$510/800 return in the low/high season, and there are flights as low as $298/590 (don't make the mistake of buying the high-season one-way ticket for US$1092!). Flights also leave from Baltimore, Boston, Minneapolis and for part of the year from Orlando. The flights go via Reykjavík, where you can stop over and visit Iceland (not many people can say they've done that). There's no extra charge but the accommodation cost is up to you.

Canada

Travel CUTS is a budget travel agency geared toward student travellers, with offices throughout Canada. The main office is in Toronto (☎ 416-614 2887) but you can also call ☎ 866-246 9762 or consult the Web site at W www.travelcuts.com. It doesn't list fares on its Web site but will give you quotes if you call or drop by. Flights from Montreal to Amsterdam cost around C$470 return in the low season, and from Vancouver around C$750; expect to pay double in the high season. Of course, the occasional low-season super saver is also available to diligent bargain-hunters.

FB On Board Courier Services in Montreal (☎ 514-631 7925) offers courier flights for C$875 to London year-round. Its services are restricted to Canadian citizens.

Australia & New Zealand

The high season for travel to Amsterdam is from June until late August and during the Christmas period. The changes between low and high-season fares are more sudden than they are on trans-Atlantic flights, where prices rise and fall gradually on either side of the high season. Book well ahead if you intend to fly close to the crossover dates. There are few high-season bargains, but at other times there are usually some good-value fares from Australia either directly to Amsterdam or to another European city, where you can connect to Amsterdam (maybe using your free return flight within Europe).

Return fares on discount airlines, such as Garuda Indonesia and Royal Jordanian Airlines, range from around A$1575 in the low season to A$2025 in the high season. For a bit more money (but offering more reliability), airlines including KLM (in conjunction with Malaysian Airlines via Kuala Lumpur to Amsterdam) and Qantas (via Singapore to London) have return fares starting from A$2069/2599 in the low/high season.

Two well-known agents for cheap fares are STA Travel (☎ 03-9349 2411, ☎ 131 776 Australia-wide, W www.statravel.com.au) and Flight Centre (☎ 131 600 Australia-wide, W www.flightcentre.com.au).

From New Zealand, airfares start at NZ$2199/2399 return in the low/high season. A round-the-world ticket could be cheaper still and this is sometimes also the case from Australia.

Well-known New Zealand agents are Flight Centre (☎ 09-309 6171, W www.flightcentre.co.nz) and STA Travel (☎ 09-309 0458, W www.statravel.co.nz).

Airline Offices

Airline offices in Amsterdam, listed under *Luchtvaartmaatschappijen* (Aviation Companies) in the pink pages of the phone book, include:

Aer Lingus (☎ 623 86 20) Heiligeweg 14
Aeroflot (☎ 625 40 49) Weteringschans 26-III
Air France (☎ 446 88 00) Evert van de Beekstraat 7, Schiphol
Air India (☎ 624 81 09) Papenbroekssteeg 2
Alitalia (☎ 648 68 67) Planetenweg 5, Hoofddorp

British Airways (☎ 346 95 59, call centre)
British Midland (☎ 346 92 11) Strawinskylaan 721
Cathay Pacific (☎ 653 20 10) Evert van der Beekstraat 18, Schiphol
China Airlines (☎ 646 10 01) De Boelelaan 7
Delta Air Lines (☎ 201 35 36) De Boelelaan 7
easyJet (☎ 023-568 48 80)
El Al (☎ 644 01 01) De Boelelaan 7-VI
Garuda Indonesia (☎ 627 26 26) Singel 540
Icelandair (☎ 627 01 36) Muntplein 2-III
Japan Airlines (☎ 305 00 60) Jozef Israelskade 48E
KLM (☎ 474 77 47) Amsterdamseweg 55, Amstelveen
Lufthansa (☎ 582 94 56) Wibautstraat 129
Malaysia Airlines (☎ 626 24 20) Weteringschans 24A
Northwest Airlines – see KLM
Olympic Airways (☎ 405 72 15) Schiphol Boulevard 223, Schiphol
Qantas (☎ 023-569 82 83, call centre)
Singapore Airlines (☎ 548 88 88) De Boelelaan 1067
South African Airways (☎ 023-554 22 88) Polarisavenue 49, Hoofddorp
Thai Airways (☎ 596 13 00) Wibautstraat 3
Transavia (☎ 406 04 06) Westelijke Randweg 3, Schiphol
United Airlines (☎ 504 05 55) Strawinskylaan 831-B8

BUS

Amsterdam is well connected to the rest of Europe, Scandinavia and North Africa by long-distance bus. For information about regional buses in the Netherlands, for instance to places not serviced by the extensive train network, call the costly transport information service on ☎ 0900-92 92 (€0.48 a minute). See also Getting Around the Country in the Excursions chapter.

Eurolines

The most extensive European bus network is maintained by Eurolines, a consortium of coach operators with offices all over Europe. Its Web site, W www.eurolines.com, has links to each national Eurolines Web site.

Eurolines UK (☎ 08705-143 219) has returns from London to Amsterdam from UK£39 for those aged under 26 or UK£44 for those 26 and over, and the journey takes 10 to 12 hours. The fares may rise or fall considerably depending on cut-throat competition among cross-Channel services, and there are often special deals from as little as UK£33. Some Eurolines buses cross the Channel via Calais in France, and travellers using this service should check whether they require a French visa.

In Amsterdam, tickets can be bought at most travel agencies. The main Eurolines office (☎ 560 87 87/88) is at Amstelstation, but the most convenient office (Map 2; ☎ 560 87 87/88) is at Rokin 10 near Dam Square. Free timetables with fare information are cheerfully supplied, and fares are consistently lower than the train. Buses leave from the bus station next to Amstelstation (Map 1), easily accessible by metro.

Cities like Bruges, Paris, Berlin, Copenhagen and Budapest are also easily accessible by Eurolines buses. The buses to Paris (eight hours) and London (10 to 12 hours) also travel overnight, allowing you to save a night's hotel bill coming and going.

Gullivers

Berlin-based Gullivers Reisen (Germany ☎ 030-3110 2110, W (German) www.gullivers.de) connects Berlin with Amsterdam Centraal Station (€50.50/91.30 one way/return or €40.30/76 for students and pensioners, nine hours).

TRAIN

Amsterdam's main train station is Centraal Station (Map 2), commonly known as CS, which has regular train connections to all neighbouring countries and to most corners of the Netherlands. Eurail, Inter-Rail, Europass and Flexipass tickets are valid on Dutch trains, which are run by the Nederlandse Spoorwegen (NS). See Getting Around the Country in the Excursions chapter for detailed information about trains within the country and a regional map.

Information

For international train information and reservations, use the NS international reservations office inside the station along track 2A (50m past the railway police office), open 6.30am to 10.30pm daily, but be prepared for number-taking and long waits. There's another international reservations office at Amstelstation, open 10am to 5pm daily, which is far less crowded though it's a bit out of the way. In peak periods it's wise to reserve international seats in advance. You can buy tickets to Belgium, Luxembourg and the western parts of Germany at the normal ticket counters.

For international train information, you can also ring the Teleservice NS Internationaal on ☎ 0900-92 96 (€0.23 a minute) but the information can be a bit dodgy.

For national trains, simply turn up at the station: you'll rarely have to wait more than an hour for a train to anywhere. See also Getting Around the Country in the Excursions chapter.

Main Lines & Fares

There are two main lines south from Amsterdam. One passes through The Hague and Rotterdam and on to Antwerp (€25.40, 2¼ hours, hourly) and Brussels (€28.13, three hours, hourly) and then on to either Paris (€59.89, six to eight hours, 10 per day) or Luxembourg City (€46.28, six hours). To/from Paris, however, you have to change trains a few times and the direct, high-speed *Thalys* is far preferable – and not much more expensive (see below).

The other line south goes via Utrecht and Maastricht to Luxembourg City (€40.84, six hours) and on to France and Switzerland, or branches at Utrecht and heads east via Arnhem to Cologne (€38.57 plus a €5.45 ICE or €3.63 EC supplement, 2½ hours, every one to two hours) and farther into Germany.

The main line east eventually branches off to the north-east of the country or continues east to Berlin, with a branch north to Hamburg. There's also a line north from Amsterdam to Den Helder in the northern tip of Holland.

All these fares are one way in 2nd class; people aged under 26 get a 25% discount. Weekend returns are 40% cheaper than during the week – eg, a weekend Amsterdam-Brussels return (departure all day Friday, and returning any time on Monday, or for travel any time in between) costs €34 compared to the normal €56.26.

The high-speed train, the *Thalys*, runs four times a day between Amsterdam and Antwerp (€29.49, two hours), Brussels (€34.94, 2½ hours) and Paris (€76.68, or €65.34 in the weekend, 4¼ hours). Under-26s and seniors can get substantial discounts, though these sell out quickly and you need to book well in advance.

A special weekend deal, a so-called Tourist Ticket, gets you a return on the *Thalys* to Paris for €73.05 or the EuroCity to Cologne for €40.83, but demand is high and you need to reserve at least two months (!) in advance.

The UK

Rail Europe (☎ 08705-848 848, Ⓦ www.raileurope.co.uk) will get you from London to Amsterdam using the highly civilised Eurostar passenger train service from Waterloo Station through the Channel Tunnel to Brussels, with an onward connection on the *Thalys* from there. This takes about six hours and starts from UK£80 return in 2nd class with special student deals, or UK£140 return as a normal, advance-purchase fare.

Train-boat-train combos are cheaper but take a fair bit longer. The ferry companies offer special deals in conjunction with ferry tickets – see Boat later in this chapter.

CAR & MOTORCYCLE

Freeways link Amsterdam to The Hague (A4/E19 and A44), Rotterdam (A4/E19) and Utrecht (A2/E35) in the south, and Amersfoort (A1/E231) and points farther east and north-east. The A10/E22 ring freeway encircles the city, with tunnel sections under the IJ. Amsterdam is about 480km (six hours' drive) from Paris, 840km from Munich, 680km from Berlin and 730km from Copenhagen.

The ferry port at Hook of Holland is about 80km away, while the one at IJmuiden is just up the road along the North Sea Canal – see the following Boat section for ferry details. Coming from the UK it's slightly cheaper to take the ferry rather than the shuttle through the Tunnel, though the

latter might save a few hours' travelling time; contact Eurotunnel (☎ 08705-353 535, Ⓦ www.eurotunnel.com) for the latest schedules and prices.

Vehicles, obviously, have to be roadworthy, registered and insured for the Netherlands. The standard European road rules and traffic signs apply. Traffic from the right has priority (including bicycles) but many through-roads are right-of-way roads (indicated with little priority signs on the road itself and big white 'shark's teeth' painted across entering roads). Traffic on roundabouts (traffic circles) has to give way to traffic entering from the right, though more and more roundabouts have right of way (clearly signposted). Trams always have priority coming from the left or right (unless you're on a right-of-way road) or turning across your path. Out on the highways, many cars drive with their lights on during the day, though this is not (yet) compulsory.

Speed limits are 50km/h in built-up areas, 80km/h in the country, 100km/h on major highways and 120km/h on freeways (sometimes 100km/h, clearly indicated). The blood-alcohol limit when driving is 0.05%. Petrol is very expensive.

For more information about driving (or rather, not driving) in Amsterdam and about rental cars, see Car & Motorcycle in the Getting Around chapter.

Documents

Anyone driving a car or riding a motorcycle in the Netherlands must be able to show a valid licence as well as the vehicle's registration papers on the spot. With rental cars the registration papers usually live in the dashboard compartment; take them with you whenever you park, to avoid theft. Foreign-registered vehicles must have proof of third-party insurance in the form of a Green Card.

The Dutch automobile association ANWB (Map 4; see under Tourist Offices in the Facts for the Visitor chapter) provides a wide range of information and services if you can show a letter of introduction from your own association.

BICYCLE

The Netherlands are extremely bike-friendly; once you're in the country you can pedal most of the way to/from Amsterdam on dedicated bicycle paths. Everything is wonderfully flat, but that also means powerful winds and they always seem to be headwinds. Beware: mopeds sometimes have to use bike paths too and might be travelling well in excess of their 40km/h speed limit (30km/h in built-up areas). Bikes or mopeds are not allowed on freeways at all. Only competition cyclists or posers wear bicycle helmets.

If you want to bring your own bike, consider the high risk of theft in Amsterdam – rental might be the wiser option. You can bring it along on the train for a nominal charge and (most) ferries charge nothing. Airlines usually treat it as normal accompanied luggage – inquire in advance, and also ask what to do if bike and luggage exceed your weight allowance or you could be charged a fortune for the excess.

For organisations offering local advice and rentals, see Bicycle & Moped in the Getting Around chapter. See also the Cycling Tours special section for suggested cycle excursions outside the city.

HITCHING

Hitching is never entirely safe in any country and we don't recommend it. Travellers who decide to hitch should understand that they are taking a small but potentially serious risk.

Many Dutch students have a government-issued pass allowing free public transport. Consequently the number of hitchhikers has dropped dramatically and car drivers are no longer used to the phenomenon. Hitchers have reported long waits.

On Channel crossings from the UK, the car fares on the Harwich-Hook of Holland ferry as well as the shuttle through the Channel Tunnel include passengers, so you can hitch to the Continent for nothing at no cost to the driver (though the driver will still be responsible if you do something illegal).

Looking for a ride out of the country? Try the notice boards at the main public library at Prinsengracht 587, the Tropenmuseum or youth hostels. People also advertise to share fuel costs in the classifieds paper *Via Via* published on Tuesday and Thursday.

BOAT

Several companies operate car/passenger ferries between the Netherlands and the UK, and one of them also sails to/from Norway via the UK. Most travel agents have information on the following services but might not always know the finer points – it's easier to catch eels with your bare hands than to pin down ferry routes and times. Prices and deals fluctuate madly depending on cross-Channel competition. Reservations are essential for motorists, especially in the high season, though motorcycles can often be squeezed in at the last moment. For those without private transport, the ferry companies offer packages that include connecting trains and/or buses starting at UK£20 to UK£30 return on top of the ferry fare.

Stenaline (☎ 08705-707 070, W www.stenaline.com) sails between Harwich and Hook of Holland and has both a day and night service (about 3½ hours). Foot passengers pay upwards of UK£50 return. Fares for a car with up to five people are about UK£200 return, or UK£30 to UK£80 less with special deals. Options such as reclining chairs and cabins cost extra, and cabins are compulsory on night crossings. Stenaline also has one-way 'Landbridge' deals to/from Ireland plus Harwich starting at IR£180/300 for a car plus two people in the low/high season – contact Stenaline in Dun Laoghaire on ☎ 01-204 7777.

P&O North Sea Ferries (☎ 08701-296 002, W www.ponsf.com) operates an overnight ferry every evening (13 hours) between Hull and Europoort (near Rotterdam). Return fares start at UK£80/104 for a (foot) passenger in the low/high season in a shared cabin (no seat option) plus UK£98/135 for a car. There are discounts for students, and also on mid-week sailings for pensioners and car fares.

DFDS Scandinavian Seaways (☎ 08705-333 000, W dfdsseaways.co.uk) sails between

Newcastle and IJmuiden, the closest port to Amsterdam, departing Newcastle daily (15 hours). Return fares start at UK£64/114 for a (foot) passenger in the low/high season plus UK£70/110 for a car and include reclining seats (cabins extra).

The same company also sails between IJmuiden and Kristiansand (Norway) via Newcastle (39 hours, including a six-hour stopover in Newcastle). From IJmuiden, fares cost €77.13/131.58 for a car in the low/high season, while passengers pay €70.33/136.12. From the Netherlands, book on ☎ 0800-022 78 80 (free call); from Kristiansand, ☎ 038-17 17 60.

TRAVEL AGENTS

Many travel agents specialise in discounted fares; more of them don't but still manage to be competitive with interesting packages. The best advice is to shop around (eg, along the Rokin) or try the following agents:

Ashraf (Map 1; ☎ 623 24 50, fax 622 90 28) Meidoornweg 2, 1031 GG Amsterdam. Runs overland adventure tours to Africa, Asia and Latin America for people aged 25 to 55.

D-Reizen (Map 1; ☎ 200 10 12) Linnaeusstraat 112. Really friendly service and some good last-minute deals from Lufthansa, KLM and others.

Kilroy Travels (Map 2; ☎ 524 51 00) Singel 413. Specialist in adventure tours, RTW and one-way tickets; special deals for under-26s and students under 34. Check the great Web site at W www.kilroytravels.com.

It's also worth checking the following Web sites for special offers (if you don't know Dutch get someone who does to help you with the Dutch sites): W www.vliegtarieven.nl (in Dutch only; the country's largest site for special deals); W www.vliegwinkel.nl (Dutch); W www.basiqair.com, run by the Transavia charter airline; W www.bizztravel.nl (Dutch); W www.vliegtickets.org (Dutch); and W www.airfair.nl (Dutch).

Getting Around

THE AIRPORT

Amsterdam's airport, Schiphol, is 18km south-west of the city centre. It lies 5m below sea level on the bottom of a drained lake, the Haarlemmermeer, and employs 50,000 people. The spacious yet compact, one-terminal design ensures that everything is within easy reach, and the signposting couldn't be much clearer.

The arrivals hall, built around a V-shaped concourse with shops called Schiphol Plaza, is on the ground floor, with the Holland Tourist Information office (open 7am to 10pm daily) in arrivals hall No 2 more or less in the central area – if you haven't already booked accommodation, you can do so here. The departures hall is upstairs. Passengers travelling to/from Schengen countries (see Visas in the Facts for the Visitor chapter) are kept separate from other passengers and don't go through passport control, though they should carry their passport as a means of identification and to transfer from Schengen to non-Schengen lounges.

On arrival, yellow signs and transfer information monitors direct you to the transfer gates or desks (if you don't already have a boarding pass for your onward flight), green signs to the various amenities.

Schiphol is world-renowned for its tax-free shopping: the scale and variety of goods are second to none and many prices are beaten only by airports such as Dubai and Abu Dhabi. In addition there's every facility you'd expect (and even some you wouldn't) of one of the world's leading international airports – it consistently rates near or at the top of business travel surveys. There's an interesting aviation museum nearby (see Amsterdam for Children in the Facts for the Visitor chapter) and even a casino in the passenger-only section of the non-Schengen departure lounge, open 6.30am to 7.30pm, accessible to passengers aged over 18 with a valid boarding pass.

For airport and flight information, ring ☎ 0900-01 41 (€0.10 per minute) – from abroad ☎ +800-724 474 65 (€0.10 per minute) – or check 🆆 www.schiphol.nl.

Left Luggage

Luggage up to 30kg can be left at the staffed counter (☎ 601 24 43) in the basement, under the plaza, for a minimum of a day and a maximum of a month. The counter is open 6.15am to 10.45pm but staff may be called through the intercom at other times. Self-service lockers are spread throughout the terminal and are available for a maximum of seven days.

TO/FROM THE AIRPORT

A taxi into the city takes 20 to 45 minutes (maybe longer in peak-hour traffic) and costs about €25 if you're lucky. Trains to Centraal Station (beware of thieves!) leave every 10 minutes, take 15 to 20 minutes and cost €2.84. Train-ticket counters are in the central court of Schiphol Plaza – buy your ticket before taking the escalator down to the subterranean platforms (while you're at it, consider buying a *strippenkaart* for public transport in the city – see the following Public Transport section). If your hotel is some way out of the city centre, it could be worth taking a train to one of the other stations around the city (see Train in the following section) and transferring to a taxi from there. Trains also connect Schiphol to 75% of train stations in the country either direct or with one change, and to major cities in Belgium, France and Germany.

Tip: if you're flying with KLM and you bought your ticket in the Netherlands, your ticket gives free train transport within the country to/from the airport on your day of departure/arrival – just show it to the conductors when they turn up to check tickets.

Free shuttle buses travel to the Dorint, Golden Tulip, Hilton, Ibis, Mercure, Radisson SAS, Bastion and Crowne Plaza hotels. The Connexxion Airport Hotel Shuttle bus runs between the airport and 22 major hotels in the city every 40 minutes from early morning to mid-evening for €7.95/13.60 one way/return. For information, contact the Transport Desk (open 7.30am to 11.30pm), the Holland Tourist Promotion desk or ring Connexxion on ☎ 405 65 65 (6am to 9pm daily). There are many other bus services that could better suit your needs – check W www.schiphol.nl or ring the national transport information line on ☎ 0900-92 92 (€0.48 a minute). There are also buses to other parts of the country – including the new *South Tangent*, a high-speed bus that links Schiphol with Haarlem and the huge Floriade horticultural exhibition, and eventually with Amstelveen south of Amsterdam, and the Bijlmer, Diemen and IJburg to the east/south-east.

Another way to get to the airport is by Schiphol Travel Taxi, a minivan that transports a maximum of eight people from anywhere in the country to the departure terminal. You share the ride with others and prices vary with the pick-up point, but from central Amsterdam it's fixed at €24.96 one way. For bookings, ☎ 0900-724 474 65 (€0.10 per minute) or W www.schiphol.nl.

Car-rental offices at the airport are near the central exits of Schiphol Plaza, though beware their hefty airport tax (see Car Rental later in this chapter). One of the country's main road arteries, the A4 freeway linking Amsterdam, The Hague and Rotterdam, tunnels under one of the airport runways. Just north of the airport is the A9 to/from Haarlem in the west, which runs south of the city and connects with the A2 to Utrecht and the south-east of the country. A bit farther north of the A9 is the intersection with the A10 ring road around Amsterdam.

Parking

The P1 and P2 short-term parking garages (under cover) charge €1.70 per half-hour for the first three hours, then €2.04 per hour. The maximum charge is €22.69 a day for the first three days, €11.35 a day thereafter. Pay at the machines before going to your car. Credit card holders can also use the P7 garage directly under the terminal but this costs a fair bit more. The P3 long-term

parking area (open-air) is a fair distance from the terminal (follow the signs 'P – Lang Parkeren') but is connected by an automatic 'Parking Hopper' to a central staging area and from there by free, 24-hour shuttle bus to the terminal every 10 minutes. The parking charge is €39.70 for up to three days (minimum charge) and €5.54 for each day thereafter – a worthwhile alternative to parking in the city.

PUBLIC TRANSPORT

Amsterdam is compact and you can get to a lot of places on foot, but public transport (tram, *sneltram*, bus, metro and ferries), run by the GVB (Gemeentevervoerbedrijf – Municipal Transport Company), is comprehensive and efficient; see the Public Transport map at the back of the book. The only problem is within the canal belt: trams and buses stick to the 'spoke' roads, so if you want to cover distance along a canal you'll have to take a tram or bus into the centre and another back out again.

The hub of the transport system is Centraal Station (CS), where most tram and bus lines, the metro and ferries converge. The GVB information office (Map 2) in front of the station is open 7am to 9pm weekdays (to 7pm late October to March), from 8am on weekends, and sells all types of tickets and passes. Pick up the free *Tourist Guide to Public Transport Amsterdam* booklet and several free transport maps; the complete transport map covering all of Amsterdam costs a token €0.68.

For transport information, call the national transport information line on ☎ 0900-92 92, 6am to midnight weekdays, from 7am weekends. This costs €0.48 a minute, which can add up quickly if your query is complicated. Expect to be put on hold for a couple of minutes as other calls are answered ahead of you. Unfortunately the great Web version of this service, W www.openbaarvervoer.nl, is in Dutch only, as is the GVB Web site, W www.gvb.nl. A useful site that also operates in English is the unofficial Amsterdam Public Transport Information site, W www.apti.is.nl, though it's not quite up to date.

Tickets & Passes

Ticketing is based on zones. Most of central Amsterdam (the canal belt and surrounding districts) is one zone; travel to the older suburbs is two, and to the newer, outer suburbs is three.

The strip ticket *(strippenkaart)* is valid on all buses, trams and metros in the country, as well as trains within municipal areas (though in Amsterdam's case Schiphol is *not* included). Fold the ticket to the relevant strip and stick it into the yellow machine to cancel two strips for the first zone and an additional strip for each additional zone – always one strip more than the number of zones. Any number of people can travel on the one ticket, so long as you cancel the appropriate number of strips for each person. When you get to the bottom of the ticket, cancel the last strip and proceed with the next ticket. The validity for one, two or three zones is one hour, during which time you can transfer as often as you like.

Strip tickets (€5.67 for 15 strips, €16.68 for 45) are available at tobacco shops, post offices, train-station counters and ticketing machines, many bookshops and newsagencies and special outlets such as the GVB offices in front of Centraal Station and the GVB head office in the Scheepvaarthuis (Map 2), Prins Hendrikkade 108–114 (the latter is open 9am to 4.30pm weekdays). Drivers and conductors only sell two/three/eight-strip tickets for €1.36/2.04/5.45, or a day pass for €5.45 (actually an eight-strip ticket stamped vertically). Children and pensioners pay €3.52 for a 15-strip ticket that has to be bought in advance (children under four years travel free).

Travelling without a valid ticket (there are frequent spot checks) incurs a fine of €29.30 plus the ticket price payable immediately, and playing the ignorant foreigner won't work.

The GVB offices also sell day passes valid for all zones at €5 for one day, €7.95 for two and then in €2.27 increments up to €23.85 for nine days. Those eligible for a discount pay €3.41 for one day, €5.45 for two days, then in €1.36 increments up to €15 for nine days. Passes valid for one zone cost €8.51/28.16 a week/month (€5.38/17.83 with concession). The GVB offices can advise of several other options.

Night buses take over when regular transport stops running shortly after midnight. Drivers sell single tickets for €1.93, or you can stamp three strips off your strip card and pay a €1.02 supplement (which is more expensive). Day passes are valid during the night(s) following the day(s) indicated on the pass but attract the same €1.02 supplement. Five-journey cards for night buses bought in advance cost €7.95. The privately run Connexxion night buses cost more.

Tram

Most trams can be entered or exited through any of the doors, where there are yellow machines to stamp strip tickets. If you need to buy a ticket, enter at the front by the driver. An increasing number of trams, however, have a separate conductor in the back and can only be entered through the rear doors (there are one-way bars at the others); in that case, show your ticket to the conductor. When getting in or out, the bottom step locks the door in the open position and prevents the tram from leaving.

There are also a few *sneltram* ('fast tram', or light rail) lines in the southern and southeastern suburbs. Tickets are cancelled the same way as in ordinary trams except where the sneltram shares the metro line, in which case you use the yellow machines at the stairways to the platforms.

Always assume that pickpockets are active on busy trams.

Circle Tram The very useful Circle Tram No 20 does a loop through the city (20A clockwise and 20B counter-clockwise) along all the major tourist sites every 10 minutes 9am to 6pm. It accepts normal strip tickets (one zone, ie, two strips) and passes. Unfortunately, due to lack of passengers it might stop operating after 2002.

Bus

Trams don't venture to Amsterdam North and only a few go to the outer suburbs, so you're likely to need a bus there. Board through the front door and present your ticket to the driver.

Train

You're most likely to use the train in Amsterdam when travelling to/from Schiphol airport. The options are Centraal Station, at the hub of the public transport system; Lelylaan, De Vlugtlaan and Sloterdijk in the western suburbs; Zuid WTC and RAI (near the exhibition centre) in the southern suburbs; or Duivendrecht and Diemen-Zuid in the south-eastern suburbs. A sneltram connects RAI station to Amstelstation for trains to/from Utrecht and the east of the country, though such trains also call at Centraal Station.

You can use strip tickets to travel on trains in the Amsterdam region – cancel your ticket at the machines near the stairways to the platforms. Muiderpoort and Amstelstation are two strips to/from Centraal Station; Diemen, Diemen-Zuid, Duivendrecht, RAI, Zuid WTC, Lelylaan, De Vlugtlaan and Sloterdijk are three strips; and Bijlmer is four strips. Strip tickets are *not* valid to/from Schiphol, which requires a normal train ticket.

For more about train travel, see Train in the Getting There & Away chapter, and Getting Around the Country in the Excursions chapter.

Metro

The metro is useful mostly for getting to the international bus station at Amstelstation (one zone) or to the Bijlmer (three zones). In the city there's only one metro line (at least, until the north-south line comes into operation in 2009) but after Amstelstation it branches into three lines – one to the southern suburbs of Buitenveldert and Amstelveen and two to the south-eastern suburb of Bijlmer. Cancel your strip ticket at the machines near the stairways to the platforms.

CAR & MOTORCYCLE

See Car & Motorcycle in the Getting There & Away chapter for general information about road rules, documents etc.

Parking

Central Amsterdam's narrow canalside streets were not built for heavy vehicular traffic, and driving into the city is actively discouraged by the council's *autoluw* (car-sheltered) policy. Of course, the most effective way to reduce the number of cars is by limiting parking space and charging heavily for the privilege.

There's no free parking in Amsterdam within the A10 ring road, and even if it looks like parking is free because no warning signs are posted, there's a hungry automatic ticketing machine in the vicinity. This disgorges a receipt that you should place on the dashboard. In the city centre and some of the 19th-century neighbourhoods, parking charges are payable between 9am and 11pm Monday to Saturday, between noon and 11pm Sunday. This costs €2.60/1.60 per hour inside/outside the centre 9am to 7pm Monday to Saturday, and €1.60 per hour at other times regardless of location (check the notice on the machine: fees and conditions change frequently). Tip: any ticket bought from a machine after 11pm is valid the next day, so you don't have to rush out at 8.55am to top up your ticket.

The ticketing machine may not be visible immediately but do find it, otherwise a bright yellow *wielklem* (wheel clamp) will be attached to your car and it will cost about €63.50 (depending on the area) to have it removed. Don't expect to talk your way out of this: they've heard it all before. The infringement notice on your windscreen will give the location of the nearest City Surveillance *(Stadstoezicht)* office, where you must go in person if you want to pay cash. Foreigners with a credit card can pay at their car by ringing the phone number indicated on the notice.

There are four City Surveillance offices that can remove wheel clamps: Weesperstraat 105A (head office), between Weesperplein and Waterlooplein on the corner of Nieuwe Prinsengracht; Jan Pieter Heijestraat 94 in Old West (north of the Vondelpark); Beukenplein 50 out east near the Oosterpark; and Daniel Goedkoopstraat 7–9 in the south-eastern suburbs (metro: Spaklerweg). The latter office is the least conveniently located but it's the only one that's open 24 hours, seven days a week; the others open 8am to 8pm Monday to Saturday (maybe Monday to Friday by the time you read this).

If you don't report to one of these offices within 24 hours (or if you have parked where you're not allowed to) your car will be towed away and an average towing charge of €167.90 (depending on the kilometres) will be collected, plus €44.70 per 12 hours garage fee (first 12 hours 'free') in addition to the parking fine, which can make things very expensive indeed. Towed cars are taken to the inconvenient Daniel Goedkoopstraat office, so before jumping to the conclusion that your vehicle has been stolen, call ☎ 553 01 65 (24 hours).

You can buy a special street parking permit at any of the above City Surveillance offices for €19.50/106 a day/week (reduced rates for areas outside the canal belt or Museum Quarter). Monthly permits are also available. The ticketing machines also issue day permits but not other permits. Some hotels issue one- and three-day tourist passes for their guests that are no cheaper than regular day permits (but may be more convenient if you don't have the necessary coins), and a few luxury hotels have their own expensive arrangements.

You can avoid all this headache by parking in the outer suburbs and entering the city by tram or metro, as many people do. Three large, multistorey Park & Ride (P+R) sites cater for this: the Transferium parking garage under the Arena stadium in the Bijlmer (from the A1, A2 or A9, follow the 'P+R Transferium Arena' signs); near the VVV office at Stadionplein in the southwestern outskirts of the city (A10 exit 's108'); and at Sloterdijk in the north-west (A10 exit 's102'). These cost €5.70 for the day, including two return tickets by public transport to Centraal Station – an excellent deal. After the first day, however, the charge skyrockets to €14.75 a day.

Parking garages in the city centre (eg, on Damrak, near Leidseplein and under the Stopera) are often full and cost more than a parking permit, though they do provide

shelter and some security against theft and vandalism.

Do your sums, and you'll probably find that for stays of more than a few days the wisest option is to head for the long-term parking area at Schiphol airport (see the earlier To/From the Airport section).

Drivers with a disability and the appropriate windscreen marker may park for three hours free of charge in designated parking spots, or can pick up a day pass from the City Surveillance offices (which also provide a map) – but beware of spots with a registration number reserved for local residents because your car will be towed away.

Motorcyclists don't face parking problems: they can park on the pavement (sidewalk) free of charge provided they don't obstruct anybody. Security is a big problem with any parked vehicle, however, irrespective of the time of day, so don't leave luggage on the bike or rely only on the steering lock. If you have a portable bike cover, use it.

In case you were wondering, the average wait for a residential parking permit within the canal belt (one per house, €45.60 for three months) is more than four years!

For more about parking, including current rates, visit Ⓦ www.toamsterdam.nl.

Car Rental

There's no point renting a car to tour the city but it's a good way to make excursions into the countryside. Car-rental prices and deals change by the week; the following list represents a snapshot of what was available at the time of research, but it pays to ring around to find the deal that suits you best. Make sure you bring a credit card.

Local companies are usually cheaper than the multinationals (Avis, Budget, Hertz, Europcar) but don't offer as much backup or flexibility (eg, one-way rentals). Rentals at Schiphol airport incur an extra €39.80 'airport company tax' which none of the companies are happy about.

Avis (☎ 683 60 61) Nassaukade 380, not far from Leidseplein; (☎ 644 36 84) President Kennedylaan 783; (☎ 665 88 78) Pieter Braaijweg 91 in Duivendrecht; international reservations ☎ +800-235 28

47, 8am to 8pm Monday to Friday, 9am to 5pm Saturday – €119/day for the cheapest car with unlimited kilometres, insurance included. Otherwise it's €59/day plus €0.16/km (the first 200km are free), tax and insurance included.

Budget (☎ 612 60 66) Overtoom 121; (☎ 604 13 49) Schiphol Plaza; central number and international reservations ☎ +800-05 37 (free call within the Netherlands) – €102.10/day for the cheapest car with unlimited kilometres, insurance and tax included. Otherwise it's €34.94/day plus €0.15/km (first 200km free), tax and insurance included. A Renault Cariole specially adapted for a wheelchair in the back costs €44.92/day (preferably book a week in advance). Budget offers a much cheaper deal through the post office, where you buy a voucher that gets you the smallest Budget car for €29.50/45.38 a day/weekend including insurance, tax and 200km (€0.10 per extra kilometre). The vouchers are valid for six months and you must book your car directly at a Budget office at least 24 hours in advance. For more information call ☎ 0900-15 76, 8am to 8pm weekdays, and to 5pm Saturday.

Europcar (☎ 683 21 23) Overtoom 197; (☎ 316 41 90) Schiphol Plaza; international reservations ☎ 070-381 18 91 (weekdays only) – a Renault Twingo for €31.31/day plus €0.13/km (the first 200km are free).

Hertz (☎ 612 24 41) Overtoom 333; international reservations ☎ 201 35 12 (8am to 8pm Monday to Saturday) – a Renault Twingo for €35.85/day with 150km free (€0.18 per extra kilometre). Holders of a *Voordeel-Urenkaart* (see Tickets under Getting Around the Country in the Excursions chapter) pay €24.96. The branch at Schiphol Plaza has cars from €91.20/day with unlimited kilometres.

Kuperus BV (☎ 693 87 90) Middenweg 175 on the south-eastern side of town (tram No 9) – cheapest car is €24/day including insurance, tax and 100km (€0.13 per extra kilometre). Cars with unlimited kilometres begin at €121.60 for three days, all-inclusive.

Safety Rent-a-Car (☎ 636 63 63) Papaverweg 3B near the Galaxy Hotel, Amsterdam North – cheapest car is €40.22/day plus €0.10/km (after the first 100km), tax and insurance included. Unlimited-kilometre rentals also available at monthly rates.

The cheapest deal in the country is offered via the Internet at W www.easyrentacar.nl. This is part of the easyGroup (easyJet, easyEverything). Its Amsterdam base is at Wibautstraat 224 next to the Amstelstation but you can only book (or indeed contact the office) online. The longer in advance you book the cheaper it gets, and prices tend to be higher on weekends, but it offers a great little A-class Mercedes from €15.90/day plus €0.08/km after the first 100km, plus a €9.10 'preparation fee' regardless of the rental period. There are small discounts for late pick-up and early return. Check the site to find out what it would cost you (prices in British pounds).

Camper Van Purchase

Braitman & Woudenberg (☎ 622 11 68), Droogbak 4A at Singel diagonally opposite Hotel Ibis, sells camper vans to travellers with a guaranteed repurchase agreement. A good VW Westfalia costs €4500, and if you return it in good condition within three months you'll get 75% back, within six months 65%, and within a year 60%; longer periods are negotiable. Occasionally there are cheaper vans at around €2250.

Buying and selling a vehicle privately is possible if you have sufficient time and expertise. You can transfer registrations at a large post office but don't forget about motor vehicle tax for Dutch-registered vehicles, which is due quarterly, or the annual roadworthiness certificate (APK) for vehicles over three years old. For information about registration documents, call the Department of Road Transport on ☎ 0598-62 42 40, 8am to 5pm weekdays, or W www.rdw.nl. The Central Office for Motor Vehicle Tax is on ☎ 0800-07 49 (free call), also 8am to 5pm weekdays.

Motorcycle Rental

Renting a car is far cheaper than renting a motorcycle but sometimes a car just won't do, will it? Check the following:

Kuperus BV (☎ 668 33 11) Van der Madeweg 1–5 – Honda VT750, CB750 or Suzuki Marauder €75.60/day including 100km; credit card and international driving permit required. Three-day, unlimited-kilometre hire €330.45.

Motoport Amsterdam (☎ 465 66 67) Spaklerweg 91 near Duivendrecht station – BMW

650GS, Honda Transalp or Suzuki Bandit €52.20/day plus €0.12/km (the first 125km are free), tax and insurance included; on a weekly basis €282 with 875km free; €450 deposit required. Cash is fine, as are credit cards but no AmEx accepted.

TAXI

Amsterdam taxis are among the most expensive in Europe and the drivers are rude, but you'd probably be rude too if you had to put up with such frequent traffic delays and road closures. To call a taxi, look under Taxi in the phone book. The largest (and most arrogant) taxi group is Taxicentrale Amsterdam, ☎ 677 77 77. Apart from the cost of the call, this is no more expensive than walking to a taxi stand. You're not supposed to hail taxis on the street but nobody seems to care much; the taxi is available if the roof sign is illuminated. Taxis cost the same day or night, and a tip of 5% to 10% is expected.

BICYCLE & MOPED

Amsterdam has 550,000 bicycles, an ideal way to get around because nothing within the canal belt (and sometimes a fair way beyond) is more than 15 minutes by bike. See Bicycle in the previous chapter for general information about road rules etc. Most bikes carry a couple of locks that are worth more than the thing itself, indicative of the fact that 200,000 bicycles are stolen each year.

An alternative to renting a bike (see the following section) is to buy one, which is worth considering if you're spending more than a month or so in town. Bicycle shops sell second-hand bikes from around €80; add €35 to €60 for one or two good locks to attach the frame and front wheel (not just the front wheel) to a bridge railing or something solid. Drug addicts might offer bikes for considerably less – as little as €15 if they're desperate – but Amsterdam residents boycott such activity and detest tourists who 'acquire' their vehicle this way. It's also highly illegal and can land you in big trouble if the owner recognises their bike (which happens more often than you'd think).

If you arrive with your own bicycle, the Dutch automobile association ANWB (Map 4; ☎ 673 08 44), Museumplein 5, provides

---

Two-Wheeled Obstruction

Scene: Vijzelstraat during afternoon peak hour. *Plot:* Loud swearing in the most guttural Dutch. A gentleman on a bicycle has stopped for a red light; other cyclists swerve to avoid colliding into the back of him. 'Idiot! Scrotum! Can't you just keep going? You're a road hazard!'

The gentleman in question? The then mayor of Amsterdam, Schelto Patijn.

---

information and services if you can show a letter of introduction from your automobile association (or your cycling association, but that seems to depend on the person behind the counter).

Some of the bicycle rental agencies mentioned here organise tours and can help with cycling maps. See also Organised Tours later in this chapter, or the Cycling Tours special section towards the end of this book. Map shops such as Pied à Terre, Jacob van Wijngaarden and à la Carte (see Books – Travel in the Shopping chapter) have an extensive range of cycling maps. Serious cyclists who are into cycling policy and legislation can contact the local cyclists' association, the ENFB (☎ 685 47 94), Wilhelmina Gasthuisplein 84, 1054 BC Amsterdam (advice on activities, rental, purchase, tours, train transport etc), after 10am weekdays.

Bicycle Rental

Many visitors rent a bike towards the end of their stay and wish they had done so sooner, but the chaotic traffic can be challenging. Amsterdam cyclists have been weaving through this mess all their lives, and believe with some justification that the embarrassingly obvious rental bikes spell trouble. Take care, and watch those tram tracks: if they catch a wheel you'll go down and it will hurt.

All the companies listed below require ID plus a credit card imprint or a cash deposit. The NS (railways) Rijwielshop and Amstel Stalling are the cheapest (even including the noncompulsory but sensible insurance) but their bicycles can be a bit run-down towards the end of the tourist season. They're cheaper still if you buy a

Party time – Koninginnedag (Queen's Day)

Canal Parade, a water-borne gay pride parade

Cleaning the canals of flotsam

The Dutch are the world leaders in the cultivation of the much-loved tulip.

Much cheaper to use trams...

...than cars in Amsterdam.

A Vondelpark cyclist

Pedestrians dodge the cyclists and trams on Leidsestraat.

A relaxed way to see the city from a different perspective

huurfiets-dagkaart (rental-bicycle day card) with your train ticket, or show your ticket at the counter of your destination station and buy it there. This costs a mere €4.66; a *huurfiets-weekkaart* for one week costs €18.64, and in both cases there's a €22.69 deposit. Some stations rent out tandems too. This excellent system applies to 100 train stations around the country – worth remembering for excursions.

Prices are for basic 'coaster-brake' bikes (no gears, brake in the rear hub operated by pedalling backwards) and generally don't include insurance; gears and handbrakes, and especially insurance, cost more:

Amstel Stalling (Map 1; ☎ 692 35 84) Amstelstation – €5.56/23.60 a day/week which includes insurance, plus €45 deposit.
Bike City (Map 3; ☎/fax 626 37 21) Bloemgracht 68–70 in the Jordaan opposite the Anne Frankhuis – €6.82/27.27 a day/week, €22.75 deposit and no advertising on the bikes, so you can pretend you're a local.
Damstraat Rent-a-Bike (Map 2; ☎ 625 50 29) Pieter Jacobszdwarsstraat 7–11 near Dam Square – €6.80/30.62 a day/week, €22.70 deposit.
Holland Rent-a-Bike (Map 2; ☎ 622 32 07) Damrak 247 in the Beurs van Berlage – €5.67/29.50 a day/week, €22.70 deposit with a passport or €90.75 without.
MacBike (Map 2; ☎ 620 09 85, **w** www.macbike.nl) Mr Visserplein 2 next to Waterlooplein market – €5.67/27.22 a day/week, €22.70 deposit with passport, no deposit with credit-card imprint. Another MacBike outlet is at Weteringschans 2 (Map 4; ☎ 528 76 88) near Leidseplein.
Rijwielshop (Map 2; ☎ 624 83 91) Stationsplein 12 – access from the outside of Centraal Station at the far east end of the building near the city bus stops; €5.56/23.60 a day/week which includes insurance, plus €45 deposit.

Moped Rental

Moped Rental Service (Map 3; ☎ 422 02 66), Marnixstraat 208, rents simple mopeds for €5.67 an hour or €15.88/27.22 a half/full day, including insurance and a full tank of petrol – a fun way to get out of Amsterdam for a spin. Nifty little scooters are €6.80 an hour or €22.69/40.83 a half/full day. You don't have to wear a helmet on the moped though you do on the scooter, and you need a licence (car licence will do). It's

open 9am to 7pm daily in summer, to 6pm in winter.

BOAT
Ferries

The free ferry to Amsterdam North for pedestrians, bicycles and mopeds, marked *Buiksloterwegveer* (*veer* means ferry), goes straight across the IJ from the landing between Piers 8 and 9 at the rear of Centraal Station. A round trip would be an interesting way to kill 45 minutes or so while waiting for a train. It operates every five minutes 6.30am to 9pm, then every 10 minutes 9pm to 6.30am daily, and only takes a few minutes to get across. The *Adelaarswegveer* from Pier 8 goes diagonally across the IJ and takes a bit longer. It operates every seven or 15 minutes 6.27am to 8.57pm weekdays, every 15 minutes Saturday, but not Sunday.

Canal Boat, Bus & Bike

For information about regular canal tours, see Canal Tours in the following Organised Tours section.

The Lovers Museum Boat (Map 2; ☎ 622 21 81) leaves every 30 or 45 minutes (the schedules vary) from the Lovers terminal in front of Centraal Station at Prins Hendrikkade, opposite No 26, and stops at all the major museums. A day ticket for unlimited travel costs €12.50 (€10 if you buy it after 1pm). If you only join for one/two/three stops it costs €4.50/7/8. The day ticket gives 10% to 50% admission discounts to most museums en route. If you can handle several museums in a day it's not a bad deal because expert commentary is part of the package and you save on a canal tour.

The Canal Bus (☎ 623 98 86) does a circuit of the tourist centres between Centraal Station and the Rijksmuseum between 10.15am and 6.45pm. A day pass costs €12.48 (€18.15 including entry to the Rijksmuseum).

Canal 'bikes' (☎ 626 55 74) can be hired from kiosks at Leidseplein, Keizersgracht on the corner of Leidsestraat, the Anne Frankhuis and the Rijksmuseum, with four-seaters costing €5.68 per person per hour (minimum of two people recommended).

GETTING AROUND

Water Taxi

Amsterdam's canals are sadly under-utilised for transport – there's no equivalent of the Venetian *vaporetto*, *traghetto* or *gondola*. The closest you'll get is the overpriced water taxi that operates 8am to midnight from its home base at the Lovers terminal in front of Centraal Station (Prins Hendrik-kade opposite No 26). It's more of a charter boat and prices vary depending on the number of people and the duration. Dinner can be supplied on board, or you can go for an aquatic running dinner (three courses at three restaurants). Advance bookings are essential on ☎ 535 63 63.

WALKING

The cliche 'Venice of the north' is apt: like Venice, Amsterdam is a joy to discover on foot, and most of the sights are within easy walking distance in the compact city centre. You can also get lost as in Venice, but never as comprehensively. There's a lot of irregular brick or cobblestone paving, so avoid high heels – and watch out for dog-shit.

Accident statistics show that the Netherlands is the safest country in Europe for pedestrians, who are more than twice as likely to be run over by a car in Britain. Beware of bicycles though: they have traffic rights separate to those of pedestrians. A lot of them zigzag through Amsterdam, ignoring road rules in the same way that pedestrians ignore pedestrian lights. Paving that is coloured reddish is reserved for cyclists, who can get quite angry (there are very few polite cyclists) when pedestrians get in the way, which foreigner visitors often do inadvertently.

ORGANISED TOURS

The following organisations offer tours that provide a quick overview of the sights. Prices may vary depending on special exhibitions at the Rijksmuseum.

Tours & Travel Services (☎ 620 32 44) GVB information office in front of Centraal Station – three-hour city sightseeing tours by bus at 11am and 2.30pm, including a diamond factory (€11.35); also day trips beyond Amsterdam; run by the GVB, great value.

Holland International (☎ 625 30 35) Damrak 90 – 3½-hour bus tour including the Rijksmuseum and a diamond factory, at 2.30pm daily (€23); also a Panoramic City Tour including a canal tour and a diamond factory, at 9.30am daily (€20).
Keytours (☎ 623 50 51) Dam 19 next to Thomas Cook and the Krasnapolsky Hotel – 3½-hour city sightseeing tours: the morning tour at 9am is by bus and boat (€20.42), the afternoon tour at 2pm is by bus to the Rijksmuseum and a diamond factory (€22.68).
Lindbergh Tours (☎ 622 27 66) Damrak 26 – 2½-hour city sightseeing tours by bus at 10am and 2.30pm daily in summer (€14.75, or €18.15 with one-hour canal boat tour); slightly different programs in winter, including trips to Volendam.

Canal Tours

It might come as a surprise that many if not most Amsterdammers have never taken a canal tour. Little do they realise they're missing a totally different and very worthwhile perspective of the city. A horde of operators leave from in front of Centraal Station, along Damrak and Rokin and near the Rijksmuseum, and charge around €8 for a one-hour cruise. They're all fairly similar so choose whichever is convenient. Advance bookings are unnecessary unless you're planning something special.

The operators run slightly different routes, so if there's a canal you desperately want to see from the water, ask. There are evening cruises by candlelight, with wine and cheese (or even five-course dinners) to enhance the experience.

You can save money on a regular day cruise by going to one of the two official youth hostels (the Stadsdoelen or Vondelpark – see Hostels in the Places to Stay chapter) and buying your ticket from the receptionist. This will get you a 30% discount on the normal price, though theoretically you need to be staying at the hostel. The Lovers boat opposite Centraal Station charges €4.50 for students.

Bicycle Tours

See the Cycling Tours special section in this book for self-guided cycling tours around Amsterdam. Several operators offer guided tours from April to October. Yellow Bike Tours (☎ 620 69 40), Nieuwezijds Kolk 29 off Nieuwezijds Voorburgwal, is the largest of its kind and has three-hour bicycle tours around town for €16, or longer, six-hour tours to Broek in Waterland north of Amsterdam for €21.

Let's Go (☎ 600 18 09, W www.letsgo-amsterdam.com) offers a 6½-hour bike tour to Edam and Volendam, a 4½-hour Castle & Windmills tour east of the city, and a 4½-hour Tulips Tour, for €22 (train tickets not included). Tours start at the VVV office in front of Centraal Station and you take the train to the bikes. Several readers have recommended these tours highly.

Cycletours Holland (☎ 627 40 98, fax 627 90 32, W www.cycletours.com), Buiksloterweg 7A, 1031 CC Amsterdam, offers a variety of overnight tours around the Netherlands by bicycle and barge-boat

sleeping 15 to 30 people. It caters mostly to people who book in advance from abroad, so it's best to write ahead for a brochure, or check the Web site. A one-week tour starts at €590 (cabin with shared shower and toilet); there are also four- or five-day tours in April, May and September from €300.

Walking Tours

Let's Go (see the preceding Bicycle Tours section) has a Rembrandt Mystery walking tour that sounds interesting. Gilde Amsterdam (see Senior Travellers in the Facts for the Visitor chapter) does some great walking tours but their success depends on the personality of the guide – some can be very entertaining, others a bit ho-hum. The VVV can advise of many other options including its own 3½-hour Discovery Tour.

Things to See & Do

Amsterdam is one of those places where you never get bored going for a walk. It's full of hidden gems and unexpected delights. The attractions described in this chapter are the more 'important' ones, but visitors as well as residents keep finding interesting things that don't make it into guidebooks. No doubt you'll find some of your own, and begin to understand what keeps drawing people back to the city.

HIGHLIGHTS

According to the VVV, the most popular attractions in Amsterdam are (in order):

1. Canal tour
2. Artis zoo
3. Rijksmuseum
4. Diamond factory visit
5. Van Gogh Museum
6. Holland Casino Amsterdam
7. Concertgebouw
8. Anne Frankhuis
9. Stedelijk Museum
10. Seksmuseum Amsterdam ('The Venus Temple')

This ranking includes Dutch as well as foreign visitors. A subjective listing on behalf of foreigners might read as follows:

1. Canal tour
2. Rijksmuseum
3. A few 'brown cafés'
4. Nederlands Scheepvaartmuseum (maritime history)
5. Stedelijk Museum
6. Aimless wandering within the canal belt
7. Albert Cuyp market
8. Begijnhof
9. People-watching at Leidseplein
10. Free summer concert in the Vondelpark

THINGS TO AVOID

Some of the popular sights are overrated, such as Madame Tussaud Scenerama on Dam Square (the one in London is better); Holland Experience next to the Rembrandthuis (an overpriced multimedia hype-fest); the casino off Leidseplein (why come to Amsterdam for a casino?); and even the Anne Frankhuis (the queues in summer are horrendous – visit the Joods Historisch Museum instead). Also avoid:

- A canal cruise with a bunch of school kids screaming through the commentary
- The Kalverstraat and Nieuwendijk shopping streets on Saturday and Sunday – far too busy, and a domain of pickpockets
- Taxis – rude drivers and very expensive
- Driving a car within the canal belt – you'll get stuck behind a truck unloading beer barrels and parking will blow the budget; if you do park, the car will get broken into

Amsterdam for Free

It's easy to spend a fortune in Amsterdam but some of the most enjoyable things cost nothing. The following free activities and sights are described in this chapter in the following order:

- Catch a ferry across the IJ
- Hear a carillon recital while walking along a canal (the VVV has up-to-date schedules)
- Wander through the red-light district and try to admire the architecture
- Stroll through the Civic Guard Gallery
- Enjoy peace and quiet in the Begijnhof
- Admire the view at the intersection of Keizersgracht and Reguliersgracht
- Take a tour of a diamond factory
- Visit the Zuiderkerk
- See the NAP display in the Stopera
- Wander through the Rijksmuseum garden
- Catch a free lunch-time concert in the Concertgebouw or the Stopera
- Go to an open-air concert in the Vondelpark in summer
- Join over 2000 in-line skaters on a skate through the city each Friday night (weather permitting); meet outside the Filmmuseum in the Vondelpark at 8pm
- Watch horses being trained indoors at the Hollandse Manege

- Brightly coloured hire bikes with embarrassing rent-a-bike signs – Amsterdammers consider them a traffic hazard (not that Amsterdammers stick to road rules themselves but at least they know what they're doing); ask for something less obvious if you have a choice
- Paying by credit card – many proprietors refuse cards, or charge a hefty 'administration fee'
- Taking photos of prostitutes or loiterers in the red-light district
- Buying drugs on the street

Central Amsterdam

The city within the canal belt is referred to as Amsterdam Centrum. One of the charms of this part of town is that its history is still so evident in its layout. The Damrak, Dam Square and Rokin, which run down the middle of the old medieval core, used to form the final stretch of the Amstel River. The city arose around the dam built across the Amstel at what is now Dam Square. The east bank was called Old Side (Oude Zijde), the west bank New Side (Nieuwe Zijde).

The marshy environment required drainage canals to create reasonably solid land. Eventually the Old Side was bordered by the Kloveniersburgwal and Geldersekade, and the New Side by the Singel (Moat), which marked the extents of the medieval city. In the late 1400s and early 1500s this modest area received a city wall, with fortified gates at strategic points.

A century later the feudal wall that cost so much to build was torn down again as the city spilled into the surrounding marshes; some of the old fortified gates remain today. Towards the end of the 16th century, habitable islands were built to the east. These form the current Nieuwmarkt neighbourhood, which lies east of the square of the same name.

Finally, in the 17th century, an enormous urban construction project resulted in the semicircular canal belt, enclosed by the

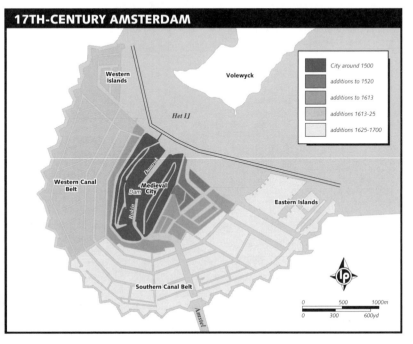

17TH-CENTURY AMSTERDAM

Volewyck

Het IJ

Western Islands

Western Canal Belt

Medieval City

Dam

Damrak

Rokin

Eastern Islands

Southern Canal Belt

Amstel

City around 1500
additions to 1520
additions to 1613
additions 1613-25
additions 1625-1700

0   500   1000m
0   300   600yd

Lijnbaansgracht and the zigzag Buitensingel (outer moat) now known as the Singelgracht.

DAMRAK, DAM SQUARE & ROKIN

Most visitors arrive at the 1889 **Centraal Station**. This Dutch-Renaissance edifice with Gothic additions was built to a design by Pierre Cuypers, also responsible for the Rijksmuseum, and AL van Gendt, who designed the Concertgebouw. Its structure – a central section flanked by square towers with wings on either side – is indeed similar to Cuypers' Rijksmuseum. It influenced the design of Tokyo's central station. Note the intricate gilded facade.

The site for the station was hotly debated at the time. Most council members favoured a station at Leidseplein or in the rapidly expanding southern suburbs, but the national government went for the current site, on three artificial islands in the IJ. This cut the city off from its historical harbour, though the focus of the harbour had already shifted eastwards and would later move well to the west.

You can leave Centraal Station at the rear, harbour side, hop on one of the free passenger ferries to Amsterdam North and experience the expanse of the IJ. It's quiet now, but in the 17th and 18th centuries this was the busiest harbour in the world.

Leaving the station at the front, city side, to your left are the cupola and twin towers of the neobaroque **St Nicolaaskerk** *(☎ 624 87 49, Prins Hendrikkade 73; admission free; open 11am-4pm Mon-Sat, 10.30am service Sun)*. Designed by AC Bleijs and built in 1887, it is the city's main Catholic church. The interior (wooden vaulting with square pillars of black marble) contains paintings of the Stations of the Cross and a high altar with a representation of the crown of Holy Roman Emperor Maximilian I. Given the recent origin of this church it's quite impressive.

Damrak (Map 2)

The Damrak (Dam Reach) stretches out in front of you towards Dam Square. This used

AMSTERDAMS HISTORISCH MUSEUM

Procession of the Lepers, Dam Square, painted by Adriaen van Nieulandt in 1633. Left to right: the old city hall, the Nieuwe Kerk, the Weigh House and the Damrak with small freighters drying their sails. The procession, to gather donations was last held in 1603.

to be the original harbour but soon became unsuitable for larger ships that tied up to palisades, along what is now Centraal Station, and unloaded onto lighters. Today the Damrak is an agonising stretch of gaudy souvenir shops, exchange bureaus and claustrophobic hotels.

Not so claustrophobic, however, is the grand **Victoria Hotel** *(Cnr Damrak & Prins Hendrikkade)*, which opened in 1890 to cash in on the Centraal Station project. Note the two **17th-century houses** *(Prins Hendrikkade 46 & 47)* in the facade of the hotel: the owners demanded too much money so the hotel developers simply built around them!

Continue down the Damrak to **Seksmuseum Amsterdam** *(The Venus Temple; ☎ 622 83 76, Damrak 18; admission €2.04; open 10am-11.30pm daily)*, well worth the admission fee for its bizarre collection of pornographic material. Welcome to Amsterdam!

In the late 19th century the southern half of the Damrak was filled in for the new exchange building, the 1903 **Beurs van Berlage** *(☎ 530 41 41, Damrak 243; adult/child €3.17/2.27; open 11am-5pm Tues-Sun)* named after the architect HP Berlage who was still designing it after work began. The functional lines and stark, square clock tower contrast with the more exuberant designs of the age, but it is considered one of the most important landmarks of Dutch city architecture. You'll understand why when you look more closely at the clever details inside and out. The large central hall, with its steel and glass roof, was the commodities exchange where coffee, tobacco, sugar, wine and colonial merchandise were traded. (The traders eventually deserted the building in favour of the neoclassical **Effectenbeurs**, or Stock Exchange, built in 1913 by Centraal Station's Pierre Cuypers on the east side of Beursplein.)

In the 1970s the foundations of Berlage's Bourse were sinking and it was slated for demolition, but it was saved by popular outcry. It is now a cultural centre (home to the Netherlands Philharmonic Orchestra) with concert performances and changing exhibitions such as Picasso's paintings, Frank Lloyd Wright's designs and Karel Appel's

A Medley of Museums

Everyone should find something to enjoy in Amsterdam's wide range of museums (visit the Web sites Ⓦ www.hollandmuseums.nl and Ⓦ www.amsterdammuseums.nl). Weekends tend to be the busiest times, along with Wednesday afternoons when many primary schools have the afternoon off and children are herded into museums. Many museums are closed on Monday.

Display captions may be in Dutch only – ask for an English-language brochure (often free) when you buy your ticket. Even so, captions are often short and you may wish to buy one of the guidebooks in the museum shop that explain things in more detail. Many museums have pleasant cafés (sometimes even restaurants) with gardens or courtyards – good places to relax and read up on the items on display.

A handful of museums are free but most charge admission and special exhibitions may cost extra. Discounts are frequently available for those aged over 65 or under 18, for students (rare), CJP Pass holders (see Student & Youth Cards in the Facts for the Visitor chapter) and holders of several other passes.

The Museumjaarkaart *(Museum Year Card; ☎ 0900-404 09 10, €0.45 per minute)* gives you free entry to 460 museums around the country for a year at €31.76 (€13.61 for those aged 24 and under). It's valid for most museums in Amsterdam (19 of them) including the major ones – Rijksmuseum, Van Gogh Museum, Stedelijk Museum, Scheepvaartmuseum etc – but not the Anne Frankhuis. At the others you'll usually get a discount, though special exhibitions might be an exception. After five or six museums the card will have paid for itself. Inquire at participating museums (one photo required).

The Museum Boat is also worth considering for the discounts offered with its day card (see Boat in the Getting Around chapter), but to maximise the discounts it's probably better to visit the Rijksmuseum separately because this can take a large chunk out of your day.

THINGS TO SEE & DO

works that are too large for regular museums. At the time of writing, Crown Prince Willem-Alexander was due to marry the Argentine Máxima Zorreguïeta here on '02-02-02' before proceeding to the Nieuwe Kerk (see later) for the church wedding.

The public entrance is on the Damrak side, next to the bicycle shop. Climb the clock tower for the view. In summer there's a pleasant *café* on the Beursplein side.

Dam Square (Map 2)

The Damrak ends in Dam Square (usually referred to simply as the Dam) where the original dam was built across the Amstel, giving the city its name. It was the central market square where everything happened. It used to be much smaller than today, reaching its current size only after buildings on all sides were gradually demolished. It

seems empty now, inhabited by thousands of cheeky pigeons and the occasional fun fair, though its recent refurbishment with tyre-shattering bricks and a slightly raised central section has resulted in a more pedestrian-friendly ambience.

The original dam was at the eastern end of the current square, with a sluice alongside so ships could pass through. From 1611 they had to lower their masts to pass under the new stock exchange built over the sluice, which was filled in for good in 1672.

The stock exchange itself was demolished in 1838 and the eastern end of the square is now dominated by a phallic obelisk, the **Nationaal Monument**. This was built in 1956 in memory of those who died during WWII and who are still honoured every year on 4 May. By the early 1990s it had become seriously weakened by rain and frost and

---

How to Murder Music: Street Organs & Carillons

Street organs and carillons are to the Dutch what bagpipes are to the Scots, and they elicit the same mixed feelings.

The elaborate street organs (*draaiorgels*, literally barrel organs) developed from hand-held barrel organs that were once popular throughout Europe but have now all but disappeared. Their atrocious tuning and repetitive repertoire contributed to their demise: people tended to pay organ grinders to stop rather than continue.

RICK GERHARTER

Richly decorated street organ

One of the factors that ensured their survival in the Netherlands was a leasing system established in Amsterdam in 1875: grinders leased their organs from owners who looked after maintenance and tuning, which ensured reasonable standards upheld by strict licensing laws. Even today, grinders are assigned limited hours in particular areas of the city so they are evenly distributed, and they can spend five minutes on the same spot before having to move on.

The repertoire includes anything from *Tulips from Amsterdam* and *The Blue Danube* to wacky renditions of the latest hits. Fluctuations in temperature and humidity still play havoc with tuning, sometimes resulting in a cat's-wail effect. Is it music? Who knows, but most will agree that a street organ at full tilt is a pretty impressive bit of machinery. They used to be operated by hand but now little generator motors do the hard work.

The Dutch infatuation with mechanical instruments extends to the out-of-tune carillons that adorn many public buildings, especially church towers. They're usually operated by machines, though a select group of carillonneurs pound the keys during occasional concerts. These live interpretations of the works of classical and modern composers are often played with a surprising amount of feeling if you consider the natural limitations of the instrument.

Carillons are wonderfully quaint and attractive in passing, but if your accommodation is in the shadow of a church that has one, the time chimes every 15 minutes can drive you up the wall. Thank God they fall silent at night.

was in danger of falling apart, but it was eventually restored (by a German firm – the irony!). The statues symbolise war (the four male figures), peace (woman with child) and resistance (men with dogs); the 12 urns at the rear contain earth from the 11 provinces and the Dutch East Indies.

The imposing hulk at the western end of the Dam is the **Royal Palace** *(Koninklijk Paleis; ☎ 620 40 60, Dam Square; adult/ child or senior €4.31/3.40, child under 6yrs free; open 11am-5pm daily mid-June–mid- Sept; 12.30pm-5pm Tues-Thur, Sat & Sun mid-Sept–mid-June)*. The palace – completed 1665, in use since 1655 –began life as the grand new city hall of republican Amster- dam. It replaced the old city hall on the same spot which conveniently burned down. No costs were spared by the architect, Jacob van Campen, for this display of Amster- dam's wealth that rivalled the grandest European buildings of the day. A century- and-a-half later it became the palace of King Louis, Napoleon Bonaparte's brother, who contributed one of the world's richest collections of Empire furniture but had the historic Weigh House in front of the build- ing demolished because it spoiled his view.

The building then passed to the House of Orange who stayed here occasionally. In 1935 the national government bought and restored it for state functions (officially Queen Beatrix lives here and pays a sym- bolic rent, though she really lives in The Hague). The stunning interior, particularly the richly decorated Civic Hall, is much more lavish than the stark exterior suggests and is well worth visiting. The official open- ing times are only a guideline and depend on government functions, so ring to check. There are free guided tours in English at 2pm Wednesday to Sunday in summer.

Next to the Royal Palace is the **Nieuwe Kerk** *(New Church; ☎ 638 69 09, Dam Square; admission €2.27; open 10am-6pm Fri-Wed, 10am-10pm Thur)*. Built in the early 15th century, it's the second-oldest church in the city and the coronation church of Dutch royalty. This late-Gothic basilica is only 'new' in relation to the Oude Kerk (Old Church; see later), with which it

competed to be the grandest church in the city. It was gutted by fire several times, and the planned, exceptionally high tower was never completed because funds were di- verted to the city hall next door.

Of interest are the magnificently carved oak chancel, the bronze choir screen, mas- sive organ, stained-glass windows, and mau- soleum of the city's greatest naval hero, Admiral Michiel de Ruijter, who died in 1676 fighting the French at Messina. Several other famous Amsterdammers are buried here, including poets Joost van den Vondel and Pieter Cornelisz Hooft. The building is used for exhibitions and for organ concerts, no longer as a church. Opening hours and admission fees may vary so ring to check.

Rokin (Map 2)

Beyond the Dam, the Damrak becomes the Rokin (a corruption of *rak-in*, 'inner reach'), most of which was filled in the 19th century. It is considerably more upmarket than the Damrak, with office buildings (the modern Options Exchange at No 61), pres- tigious shops (the wood-panelled tobac- conist Hajenius at No 92) and art dealers. A **column** on the pavement at Wijde Kapel- steeg commemorates the Miracle of Am- sterdam that made the city a place of pilgrimage in medieval times (see Early Trade in the History section of the Facts about Amsterdam chapter). The chapel built on the spot where the miracle of the incom- bustible Host took place has been demol- ished, but it occupied this small block between Wijde and Enge Kapelsteeg.

At Grimburgwal, where the water begins again, the bank opposite the Rokin is called Oude Turfmarkt. Near the Grimburgwal corner is the University of Amsterdam's **Allard Pierson Museum** *(☎ 525 25 56, W www.uba.uva.nl/apm, Oude Turfmarkt 127; adult/student/senior/child €4.31/3.17/ 1.36/0.45; open 10am-5pm Tues-Fri, 1pm- 5pm Sat & Sun)*, with the world's richest university collection of archaeological material. It's not in the same league as the country's largest collection of antiquities in Leiden, let alone the British Museum or the Louvre, but the exhibits (Egyptian,

Mesopotamian, Roman and Greek, among others) are far less overwhelming and provide a good insight into daily life in ancient times.

The Rokin terminates at Muntplein, a busy intersection dominated by the **Munttoren** (Mint Tower). This was part of the 15th-century Regulierspoort, a city gate that burned down in 1619. On what was left of the gate, the architect and tower-specialist Hendrick de Keyser built the tower which received its current name in 1672–73, when the French occupied much of the republic and the national mint was transferred here from Dordrecht for safekeeping.

OLD SIDE (OUDE ZIJDE)

East of the Damrak-Rokin axis is the Old Side of the medieval city. The name is misleading because the New Side to the west is actually older – see the following New Side section.

In the 1380s the Old Side began to expand eastwards towards the Oudezijds Voorburgwal (front fortified embankment) and soon farther towards to the Oudezijds Achterburgwal (rear fortified embankment).

Originally the city didn't extend farther south than Grimburgwal, where the filled-in part of the Rokin ends today. In the 1420s, however, the newly dug Geldersekade and Kloveniersburgwal added more space for the growing population.

Warmoesstraat (Map 2)

One of the original dikes along the Amstel – and thus one of the oldest streets in town – is Warmoesstraat, which runs parallel to Damrak behind the former warehouses that line the east bank of the river (the southern extension beyond the Dam is called Nes). The city's wealthiest merchants lived here, and anyone else who could afford to. Today it's a run-down strip of restaurants, cheap hotels and sex shops. **Geels & Co** (*☎ 624 06 83, Warmoesstraat 67; admission free; shop open 9am-6pm Mon-Sat, museum open 2pm-*

4.30pm Tues & Sat) is a tea and coffee shop with an interesting little museum upstairs.

Oude Kerk (Map 2)

A few paces east of here, through Enge Kerksteeg, is the mighty **Oude Kerk** (*Old Church; ☎ 625 82 84, Oudekerksplein 23; adult €3.62, student or senior €2.72, child free; open 11am-5pm Mon-Sat, 1pm-5pm Sun)*. This Gothic church was built early in the 14th century in honour of the city's patron saint, St Nicholas – the 'water saint', protector of sailors, merchants, pawnbrokers and children. It's the oldest surviving building in town, sadly demeaned by the red-light district that now surrounds it. The original basilica was replaced in 1340 by an intricately vaulted triple-hall church of massive proportions that was miraculously undamaged by the great fire of 1452.

Further extensions ground to a halt as funds were diverted to the Nieuwe Kerk, and a century later Calvinist iconoclasts smashed and looted many of the priceless paintings, statues and altars. The newly Calvinist authorities kicked out the hawkers and vagabonds who had made the church their home, and changed the official name from St Nicolaaskerk to Oude Kerk (as it was commonly known anyway). In the mid-17th century the Nieuwe Kerk took over as the city's main church.

Note the stunning Müller organ (1724), the gilded oak vaults (with remains of paintings above the southern aisle) and the stained-glass windows (1555). Check the lively 15th-century carvings on the choir stalls – some of them are downright rude. As in the Nieuwe Kerk, many famous and not so famous Amsterdammers lie buried here under worn tombstones, including Rembrandt's first wife, Saskia van Uylenburgh (died 1642). A Dutch Reformed service is held at 11am Sunday (doors close at 11am sharp).

The church's **tower**, built in 1565, is arguably the most beautiful in Amsterdam and is well worth climbing for the magnificent view. The 47-bell carillon, installed by the carillon master François Hemony in 1658, is considered one of the finest in the country. The bell in the top of the tower dates from 1450 and is the city's oldest.

At the time of writing, the tower was closed for much-needed renovations and it was unclear what the visiting arrangements would be when it reopened – in the past they were rather limited but it was certainly worth making the effort. Ring ☎ 612 68 56 to find out the latest. (For historic military reasons, most church towers in the country are still managed by city councils rather than by the churches themselves.)

Red-Light District (Map 2)

The city's (in)famous red-light district is bordered by Warmoesstraat in the west, Zeedijk/Nieuwmarkt/Kloveniersburgwal in the east and Damstraat/Oude Doelenstraat/ Oude Hoogstraat in the south. The area, known colloquially as the *wallen* or *walletjes* for the canals that run down the middle, has been sending sailors broke since the 14th century with houses of ill repute and countless distilleries. The distilleries have gone but prostitutes now display themselves in windows under red neon lights, touts at sex theatres lure passers-by with 'live show fucky-fucky podium', and sex-shop displays leave nothing to the imagination. Several years ago three men installed themselves behind windows as a sociological experiment; there was intense media interest and not a single woman dared enter. One of the prostitutes declared the experiment 'filthy'.

The ambience is laid-back and far less threatening than in red-light districts elsewhere. Crowds of sightseers both foreign and local mingle with pimps, drunks, weirdos, drug dealers and Salvation Army soldiers; police patrolling on foot chat with prostitutes. Streetwalking is illegal, so female sightseers are not automatically assumed to be soliciting and tend to be left alone if they exercise big-city street sense. Advice to all: don't take photos of prostitutes or loiterers, and don't enter into conversation with a drug dealer.

The mainly self-employed prostitutes are taxed on their earnings, undergo mandatory health checks and have a vocal union. Beneath the well-regulated veneer, however, is a world of exploitation, drug addiction and misery – for every happy hooker there's an unhappy one, perhaps a young Eastern European without the right papers, sucked into a vicious circle of high hopes and extortion.

For more about the local prostitution scene, visit the **Prostitution Information Centre** *(☎ 420 73 28, W www.pic-amsterdam .com, Enge Kerksteeg 3; open 11.30am-7.30pm Tues, Wed, Fri & Sat)*, run by a former prostitute. For €1.15 you can visit a copy of a prostitute's working quarters and look out from the window. The centre also caters for study groups from around the world (including police academies) and organises evening Red Light walks – ring for reservations.

The *wallen* area is actually a very pretty part of town and well worth a stroll for the architecture, if you need that sort of excuse. For a scenic view, face north on the bridge across Oudezijds Voorburgwal linking Lange Niezel and Korte Niezel.

Immediately to your left from here is the **Museum Amstelkring** *(☎ 624 66 04, Oudezijds Voorburgwal 40; adult €4.53, child, student or senior €3.40; open 10am-5pm Mon-Sat, 1pm-5pm Sun)*, home to **Ons' Lieve Heer op Solder** (Our Dear Lord in the Attic), one of several 'clandestine' Catholic churches established after the Calvinist coup in 1578. Church property was confiscated and Catholics were only allowed to worship in privately owned real estate so long as it wasn't recognisable as a church and the entrance was hidden. The wealthy hosier Jan Hartman had the house built in 1663, complete with a small church in the attic dedicated to St Nicholas. It remained in use until 1887, when the large St Nicolaaskerk on Prins Hendrikkade diagonally opposite Centraal Station opened its doors.

It then became a museum with the city's richest collection of Catholic church art, although occasional services, weddings and organ concerts are still held here. The museum is worth visiting for the 17th-century living quarters, including the Dutch Classical *Sael* or reception hall (note the matching rectangular patterns on the floor, walls and ceiling), and of course for the church in the attic – one of the few 'clandestine' churches that has remained intact.

Other places worth considering in the red-light district include the **Hash & Marihuana Museum** *(☎ 623 59 61, Oudezijds Achterburgwal 148; admission €5.67; open 11am-10pm daily)*. The **Erotic Museum** *(☎ 624 73 03, Oudezijds Achterburgwal 54; admission €2.27; open 11am-1am daily)* is less entertaining than Seksmuseum Amsterdam on Damrak (see the earlier Damrak, Dam Square & Rokin section).

Zeedijk (Map 2)

North of the red-light district is the Zeedijk, the original sea dike that curved from the mouth of the Amstel to Nieuwmarkt Square and continued from there along what are now St Antoniesbreestraat, Jodenbreestraat and Muiderstraat. The house at **Zeedijk 1** dates from the mid-1500s and is one of two timber-fronted houses still left in the city (the other, older one is in the Begijnhof).

The Zeedijk used to be (and to some extent still is) a street of wine, women and song, the first port of call for sailors after their long voyages. In the 1950s, wine and song predominated and many of the world's great jazz musicians played in pubs such as the **Casablanca** *(☎ 625 56 85, Zeedijk 26; open 4pm-1am daily)*. In the 1970s the street's dubious reputation hit rock-bottom when it became the centre of Amsterdam's heroin trade. A massive police campaign in the mid-1980s restored some of the old merriment and legitimate business is beginning to pick up again, but so too is the heroin trade at the Nieuwmarkt end of the street.

The Zeedijk is also the focus of Amsterdam's 10,000-strong Chinese community – at least, until the completion in 2008 of New Chinatown east of Centraal Station, a combination of offices, residences and entertainment facilities. Note the **Guan Yin Shrine** *(open noon-5pm Mon-Sat, 10am-5pm Sun)* at the Nieuwmarkt end of the Zeedijk, completed in 2000 and dedicated to the female buddha Guan Yin. It's the first Chinese temple in Europe to be built entirely along *feng shui* principles and is worth visiting for that reason alone.

The Winner by a Narrow Margin

Canal-boat commentators and other tourist guides like to point out the narrowest house in Amsterdam. They account for the phenomenon by explaining that property was taxed on frontage – the narrower the house the lower the tax, regardless of the height. There is some truth in this, but it seems as if each guide has a different 'narrowest' house. So which house holds the record?

The house at Oude Hoogstraat 22 east of Dam Square is 2.02m wide and 6m deep. Occupying a mere 12 sq metres it could well be the least space-consuming self-contained house in Europe (though it's a few storeys high). The house at Singel 7 is narrower still, consisting of just a door and a slim, 1st-floor window, but canal-boat commentators fail to point out that it's actually the rear entrance of a house of normal proportions. Farther along and on the other side of Singel at No 144 is a house that measures only 1.8m across the front; it widens to 5m at the rear and experts with nothing better to do will argue whether this counts.

The Kleine Trippenhuis (Small Trippenhouse) at Kloveniersburgwal 26 is 2.44m wide. It's opposite the 22m-wide house of the Trip brothers at No 29, one of the widest private residences in the city. The story goes that their coachman exclaimed, 'If only I could have a house as wide as my masters' door!' and that his wish was granted.

ROB VAN DRIESUM

Oude Hoogstraat 22

East of the Zeedijk is the Geldersekade, and at the mouth of this canal is a small brick tower, dating from around 1480, that used to form part of the city fortifications. It's the oldest such tower still standing and is called the **Schreierstoren** from an old Dutch word for 'sharp', a reference to this sharp corner that jutted out into the IJ. Tourist literature prefers to call it the 'wailing tower' (from *schreien*, to weep or wail) and claims that sailors' wives stood here and cried their lungs out when ships set off for distant lands, which makes a far more interesting story. The women even have a plaque dedicated to them.

The tower attracts plaques: another one explains that the English captain Henry Hudson set sail from here in 1609 in his ship the *Halve Maen* (Half Moon). The United East India Company had enlisted him to find a northern passage to the East Indies, but instead he bought Manhattan and explored the river that bears his name. On the return voyage his ship was seized in England and he was ordered never again to sail for a foreign nation.

His reports, however, made it back to base, and in 1614 the Dutch established a fort on Manhattan that developed into a settlement called New Amsterdam. In 1664 the West India Company's local governor, the fanatically Calvinist Pieter Stuyvesant, surrendered the town to the British who promptly renamed it New York. Stuyvesant retired to the market garden called Bouwerij (Agriculture), now known as the Bowery section of New York City. New Yorkers may be interested in the fact that the distance between the tip of Manhattan and Harlem is roughly similar to that between Amsterdam and Haarlem.

Nieuwmarkt Square (Map 2)

In the 17th century, ships used to sail from the IJ down Geldersekade to the Nieuwmarkt (New Market) to take on board new anchors or load and unload produce. (Nobody adds the world *plein* or 'square' to the name, which is confusing because the whole neighbourhood to the east and southeast is also known as Nieuwmarkt.)

The Nieuwmarkt's imposing **Waag** *(Weigh House; ☎ 422 77 72, Nieuwmarkt 4; admission free; open 10am-1am daily)* dates from 1488, when it was known as St Anthoniespoort (St Anthony's Gate) and formed part of the city fortifications. A century later the city had expanded farther east and the gate lost its original function. A section of Kloveniersburgwal was filled in to create the St Anthoniesmarkt (now the Nieuwmarkt). The central courtyard of the gate was covered and it became the city weigh house – the one on the Dam had become too small.

Guilds occupied the upper floor, including the surgeons guild who commissioned Rembrandt to paint *The Anatomy Lesson of Dr Tulp* (displayed in the Mauritshuis in The Hague) and added the octagonal central tower in 1691 to house their new Anatomical Theatre. The masons guild was based in the tower facing the Zeedijk – note the super-fine brickwork.

Public executions took place at the Waag from the early 19th century, after Louis Napoleon decreed that his palace on Dam Square was no longer a suitable spot for such gory displays. In later years it served other purposes – fire station, vault for the city archives, home to the Amsterdam Historical Museum and the Jewish Historical Museum. Today it houses a bar-restaurant illuminated by huge candle-wheels for medieval effect, and combines the medieval with the future as the Society for Old and New Media (see Internet Cafés in the Facts for the Visitor chapter). Unfortunately the Society's offices upstairs, including the Anatomical Theatre, are only open to the public during special events.

The area east and south-east of Nieuwmarkt Square was the centre of Jewish Amsterdam, which was virtually wiped out during the German occupation. Jews were assembled in front of the Waag for deportation.

South of Nieuwmarkt Square (Map 2)

Just south of the Nieuwmarkt, on the east side of Kloveniersburgwal, is the **Trippenhuis** *(Kloveniersburgwal 29)*. It was built in 1660–64 to house the wealthy Trip brothers,

TW
Facade detail of the Oostindisch Huis

Lodewijk and Hendrik, who made their fortune in metals, artillery and ammunition. The greystone mansion with Corinthian pilasters consists of two separate houses with false middle windows, and the chimneys are shaped like mortars to indicate their owners' trade. Note the narrow house across the canal at No 26 (see the boxed text 'The Winner by a Narrow Margin').

On the west side of Kloveniersburgwal beyond the intersection with Oude Hoogstraat (an extension of Damstraat) is the **Oostindisch Huis**, the former head office of the mighty VOC, the United East India Company. You could easily walk straight past it – there's no sign or plaque to identify it. The complex of buildings, attributed to Hendrick de Keyser, was built between 1551 and 1643. It was rented to the VOC in 1603 and now belongs to the University of Amsterdam. Enter the courtyard through the small gate at Oude Hoogstraat 24. Even here nothing indicates the historical significance of the place except for the small VOC emblem above the door ahead of you across the courtyard. Along the Kloveniersburgwal frontage, note the gables that defy convention by tilting backwards, which makes them seem higher.

Old Side, Southern Section (Map 2)

The Old Side south of Damstraat/Oude Doelenstraat/Oude Hoogstraat is distinctly residential and the red-light district seems miles away. The southern end of Oudezijds Voorburgwal used to be known as the 'velvet canal' for the wealthy people who lived here. Both the Oudezijds canals end at Grimburgwal and the junction is one of the strongholds of the **University of Amsterdam**, as evidenced by the jumble of parked bicycles.

The former municipal university (not to be confused with the orthodox-Calvinist Free University in the southern suburbs) has no central campus as such; its buildings are spread throughout the city but there's a large concentration of them here.

At the southern end of Oudezijds Voorburgwal is the **Universiteitsmuseum De Agnietenkapel** (☎ 525 33 39, *Oudezijds Voorburgwal 231; admission free; open 9am-5pm Mon-Fri; ring door bell for entry*), with changing exhibitions on the history of the university. The complex began life as a convent of St Agnes in 1397 and the beautiful Gothic chapel was added in 1470. When the Calvinists took over it was used as an admiralty warehouse.

In 1632 it also became home to the city library (moved from the Nieuwe Kerk) and the Athenaeum Illustre, the Illustrious Athenaeum, an offshoot of the University of Leiden. Classes were conducted in Latin to prepare students for higher education elsewhere. In 1864 the Athenaeum moved to Singel 421 (part of the present university library) and in 1877 it finally became the fully fledged Municipal University of Amsterdam – a long gestation for the university of such an eminent city.

Just south of the Agnietenkapel, where the three 'fortified embankments' *(burgwallen)* meet, is the **Huis aan de Drie Grachten** *(House on the Three Canals; ☎ 624 57 81, Oudezijds Achterburgwal 249; admission free; open 1pm-5pm Mon, Wed & Fri)*. This beautiful 1609 building was owned by a succession of prominent Amsterdam families, and is now an antiquarian bookshop.

Across Oudezijds Achterburgwal, just before the corner with Grimburgwal, is a small, arched gateway called the **Oudemanhuispoort** (Old Man's House Gate) leading to a passage of the same name that extends to Kloveniersburgwal. Note the spectacles above the gateway: an almshouse for elderly men and women was built here in 1601 from the proceeds of a public lottery. It was rebuilt in the mid-18th century and in 1879 became the seat of the university. The administration has since moved to other premises but the buildings here, referred to simply as 'de Poort', can lay claim to being the heart of the university.

A **market** has operated in the passage since the mid-1700s, specialising in gold, silver, books and knick-knacks but now devoted entirely to second-hand books. It's well worth a browse (11am to 4pm weekdays). Halfway along, an entrance leads to a lovely 18th-century courtyard dominated by a bust of Minerva (originally there was a bust of Rembrandt but the Roman goddess of wisdom was considered more appropriate). The university lecture rooms surrounding the courtyard are closed to the public.

A few steps south of the Oudemanhuispoort, at the end of Grimburgwal, another gateway leads to the former inner-city hospital, the **Binnengasthuis**, dating from 1582. In 1981 the university took over and the area is now a mini-campus, with university buildings, living quarters, a large refectory *(mensa)* and an information centre (see Universities in the Facts for the Visitor chapter).

NEW SIDE (NIEUWE ZIJDE)

West of the Damrak-Rokin axis is the New Side of the medieval city. It was actually settled slightly earlier than the Old Side – the names date from the construction of the Nieuwe Kerk and the division of the city into two parishes.

In the early 14th century the western boundary was formed by a watercourse running along Nieuwezijds Voorburgwal (filled in 1884), but this was soon extended westwards to the Nieuwezijds Achterburgwal (now also filled and known as Spuistraat). Around 1450 the Singel (Moat) was cut. This linked up with the Geldersekade and Kloveniersburgwal in the east to complete the moat around the medieval city, which received proper walls with fortified gates some 50 years later.

Nieuwendijk (Map 2)

The very first houses in Amsterdam probably stood on a strip of raised land, no more than 25m wide, on the western bank of the Amstel between the Dam and Oudebrugsteeg. This, the oldest dike in the city, parallel to the current Damrak, later acquired the name of its northern extension, Nieuwendijk. It used to link up with the road to Haarlem, and its shops and other businesses became adept at fleecing travellers on their way to Amsterdam's market on Dam Square. Today this pedestrianised shopping street still suffers from a distinctly downmarket image, though some of the narrow streets leading to the west can be as picturesquely medieval as it gets.

Singel, Northern Section (Map 2)

The top section of Nieuwendijk, between Martelaarsgracht and Singel, is sometimes referred to as Korte Nieuwendijk (Short Nieuwendijk). Head south from here along the east (odd-numbered) side of Singel, where the former city wall used to run, and you'll pass a house at No 7 (next to the Liberty Hotel) that's no wider than its door – except that this is actually the rear entrance of a house of normal proportions.

The domed church next door is the **Ronde Lutherse Kerk** *(Round Lutheran Church; ☎ 623 15 72, Cnr Singel & Kattengat; admission free; open 9am-1pm Mon-Fri & Sun)*, built in 1668–71 to replace the old Lutheran church on Spui Square. It's the only round Protestant church in the country and is pure 17th-century baroque, though the white interior is suitably sober. The church was rebuilt after a disastrous fire in 1822 but falling attendances forced its closure in 1936 (ironically the old church on Spui Square is still in use by Lutherans). It now serves as a conference centre for the nearby Renaissance Hotel.

Across the canal is the **Poezenboot** *(Cat Boat; ☎ 625 87 94, Singel 40; open 1pm-4pm daily)* owned by an eccentric woman who looks after several hundred stray moggies. They seem endearingly content with life on the water and visitors are welcome to stroke them in return for a donation towards cat food.

Farther along Singel is **Torensluis**, one of the widest bridges in the city. Here used to stand a tower that formed part of the city's fortifications; the bridge was later built around it. The tower was demolished in 1829, leaving a 42m-wide esplanade. The view northwards is camera material.

The ghastly statue that dominates the bridge represents Multatuli (Latin for 'I have suffered greatly'), the pen name of the brilliant 19th-century author Eduard Douwes Dekker, who would indeed suffer greatly if he stood here now. A local captain's son who served in the East Indies colonial administration, Multatuli exposed colonial narrow-mindedness in a novel about a coffee merchant. After being sacked he wrote letters and essays. The nearby **Multatuli Museum** (☎ 638 19 38, Korsjespoortsteeg 20; admission free; open 10am-5pm Tues, noon-5pm Sat & Sun) is a must for fans of Dutch literature.

Magna Plaza (Map 2)

Back towards Dam Square, facing the Royal Palace, is the imposing orange and white facade of **Magna Plaza** (☎ 626 91 99, Nieuwezijds Voorburgwal 182; open 11am-7pm Mon, 10am-7pm Tues, Wed, Fri & Sat, 10am-9pm Thur, noon-7pm Sun). This was the former GPO, built in 1895–99 by the government architect CH Peters, a pupil of Pierre Cuypers. It used to be one of the grandest post offices in Europe but has now been converted into a luxurious shopping centre dominated by clothing boutiques. Pop inside to admire the grand hall and look at some of the interesting shops. Several decades ago the Nieuwezijds Voorburgwal itself was the country's 'Fleet Street' where many newspapers had their head offices (they're now out in the suburbs).

Kalverstraat (Map 2)

South of Dam Square is Kalverstraat, the extension of Nieuwendijk and the country's most expensive shopping street rent-wise, at €1500 per square metre per year – no wonder the shops go broke with such depressing regularity. This was one of the original dikes along the Amstel – together with Nieuwendijk, Warmoesstraat and Nes – which makes it one of the oldest streets in the city. The name (Calves Street) presumably refers to the cattle that were led to

market on Dam Square. (In the 15th century there was a cattle market in the southern section of Kalverstraat beyond Spui Square but the name is older.)

Like Nieuwendijk, pedestrianised Kalverstraat has traditionally been a shopping street, albeit a more upmarket one that's well worth visiting on weekdays (it's too busy on Saturday and not much better on Sunday). The southern tip between Kalverstraat and Singel near Muntplein has been transformed into a shopping complex called the **Kalvertoren** (Singel 457; open 11am-7pm Mon, 10am-7pm Tues, Wed & Fri, 10am-9pm Thur, 10am-6pm Sat, noon-6pm Sun). It's worth visiting the snack bar at the top of the tower for the 360-degree rooftop view enjoyed by pigeons, though not for the food (better to use the Vroom & Dreesmann food court downstairs).

South along Kalverstraat from Dam Square, about two-thirds of the way to Spui Square, is a gateway to the right that leads to the **Amsterdams Historisch Museum** (☎ 523 18 22, Ⓦ www.ahm.nl, Kalverstraat 92; adult/child €6.12/3.06, child under 6yrs free; open 10am-5pm Mon-Fri, 11am-5pm Sat & Sun). (On the opposite side of Kalverstraat used to be the chapel commemorating the Miracle of Amsterdam.) This surprisingly interesting museum, with attractive displays about the history of the city (including wall tablets), is housed in the former civic orphanage that existed here till 1960. Be sure to ask for the English-language booklet. The restaurant (free entry) serves delicious pancakes.

If you want to give this a miss, it's still worth walking into the courtyard (note the cupboards in which the orphans stored their possessions) and from there to the Begijnhof through the **Civic Guard Gallery** (admission free; open 10am-5pm Mon-Fri, 11am-5pm Sat & Sun). The static group portraits of civic guards displayed here will help you appreciate just how dynamically Rembrandt handled this sort of thing in The Nightwatch, which is displayed in the Rijksmuseum. The gallery used to be a ditch separating the boys' and girls' sections of the orphanage.

Begijnhof (Map 2)

Hidden behind the intersection of Spui and Nieuwezijds Voorburgwal is the enclosed **Begijnhof** *(☎ 623 35 65; admission free; open 1pm-6.30pm Mon, 9am-6.30pm Tues-Fri, 9am-6pm Sat & Sun)*, a former convent dating from the early 14th century. The Nieuwezijds Voorburgwal curved westwards to include it in the city boundary. It's a surreal oasis of peace, with tiny houses grouped around a well-kept courtyard. Amsterdam has many such enclosed *hofjes* (literally 'little courtyards'), or almshouses (old people's homes run by charities), but this is the only one where the public is still welcome, though no tour groups or camera crews.

Linger a while to recover from the hustle and bustle of the city. Note the house at **No 34**: it dates from around 1465, making it the oldest preserved wooden house in the country. There's a collection of biblical wall tablets on the blind wall to the left.

The Beguines were a Catholic order of unmarried or widowed women from wealthy families, who cared for the elderly and lived a religious life without taking monastic vows; the last true Beguines died in the 1970s. They owned their houses, so these could not be confiscated after the Calvinist coup. Their **Gothic church** *(Engelse Kerk; ☎ 624 96 65, Begijnhof 48; admission free; open 11am-6pm daily, Presbyterian service in English 10.30am Sun)* at the southern end of the courtyard, however, was taken away from them and they were forced to worship in the **'clandestine' church** opposite (note the dog-leg entrance), where paintings and stained-glass windows commemorate the Miracle of Amsterdam. The Gothic church was eventually rented out to the local community of English and Scottish Presbyterian refugees – the Pilgrim Fathers worshipped here – and still serves as the city's Presbyterian church. Some of the pulpit panels were designed by a young Piet Mondriaan.

Spui Square (Map 2)

Until 1882, the elongated Spui Square (usually referred to simply as the Spui, pronounced *spow*, approximately) used to be water. In the 14th century it marked the southern end of the city, together with Grimburgwal, its north-eastern extension across Rokin. The name means 'sluice' (or rather, the area inside a sluice) and it connected the Amstel with the watercourse running along Nieuwezijds Voorburgwal, the western side of the city, and later with the Singel.

A **book market** is held 10am to 6pm Friday on the section of the square in front of

---

Wall Tablets

Before street numbers were introduced in 1795, many of Amsterdam's residences were identified by their wall tablets. These painted or carved stone plaques (dating from the mid-17th century) were practical decorations to identify not only the inhabitants' house but also their origin, religion or profession. Beautiful examples of these stones are still found on many of the buildings along the main canals. Occupations are the most frequently occurring theme: tobacconists, milliners, merchants, skippers, undertakers and even grass-mowers.

As well as being colourful reminders of the city's former citizens, these tablets also provide hints about the city's past. A stone depicting a mail wagon at Singel 74 commemorates the commencement of the postal service between Amsterdam and The Hague in 1660. Farther down the street a tablet portraying the scene of Eve tempting Adam with an apple attests to the time when that part of the street operated as a fruit market (known as the 'apple market').

Many wall tablets dotted throughout the city celebrate the life of famous citizens like the maritime hero Michiel Adriaenszoon de Ruyter and biologist Jan Swammerdam, but the most appealing are memorials to domestic life and common vocations of the age.

the Begijnhof entrance, where the Beguines used to have an outer garden, but the heart of the square is its western part where Nieuwezijds Voorburgwal and Spuistraat meet. The statuette in the middle, the *Lieverdje* (Little Darling), is an endearing rendition of an Amsterdam street-brat. It was donated by a cigarette company and became the focal point for Provo 'happenings' in the mid-1960s. The area is now a meeting point for the city's intelligentsia, who congregate in the pubs at the western end of the square and in the surrounding bookshops, including the landmark Athenaeum bookshop and newsagency.

The classicist building between Voetboogstraat and Handboogstraat is the **Maagdenhuis**, the Virgins' House, built in 1787 as a Catholic orphanage for girls and now the administrative seat of the university. In 1969 it was occupied by students, a watershed in the development of students' rights in the country. Police cordoned off the building but the occupiers held out for five days, with supplies ferried across a bridge that supportive workers built over the alley. The handsome **Lutheran Church** next door, on the corner of Singel, was built in 1633. It is still used as a church but also by the university for ceremonies such as doctoral promotions, which benefit from its good acoustics.

Singel, Southern Section

Around the corner is the current **University Library (Map 2)** *(Singel 421-425)*, at least for the time being. Citizen's militias used to meet here: the 'hand-bow' militia in No 421 and the 'foot-bow' militia in No 425 (the latter also served as headquarters for the West India Company and is now obliterated by the modern facade). Their firing ranges at the rear reached to Kalverstraat – the current Handboogstraat and Voetboogstraat are named after the militias. The building at No 423 was constructed by Hendrick de Keyser in 1606 as the city arsenal and was later used as royal stables.

On the opposite side of the canal are the soaring turrets of the neo-Gothic **Krijtberg** church **(Map 3)** *('chalk mountain'; ☎ 623 19 23, Singel 448; open for Mass noon-1pm*

& 5pm-6pm Mon-Fri, noon-1pm & 4pm-5pm Sat, 9am-1pm & 4.30pm-5.30pm Sun). Officially known as the St Franciscus Xaveriuskerk, it was completed in 1883 to a design by Alfred Tepe and replaced a 'clandestine' Jesuit chapel on the same site. The lavish paintings and statuary, recently restored to their full glory, make this one of the most beautiful churches in the city. One of the houses that stood here belonged to a chalk merchant, hence the common name.

You could turn left here to go back to Kalverstraat along **Heiligeweg (Map 2)**, the Holy Way travelled by pilgrims on their annual procession to the chapel of the Miracle of Amsterdam. The route used to extend all the way from the village of Sloten, southwest of the city, along what is now the Overtoom (once a canal for towboats carrying produce) and through the current Leidsestraat, but only this final section has retained the original name. A procession still takes place every year on the Sunday closest to 15 March and attracts Catholics from Holland and abroad.

Halfway to Kalverstraat along Heiligeweg is a gateway on your right, dating from the early 17th century and attributed to Hendrick de Keyser. This once gave access to the Rasphuis, a model penitentiary where beggars and delinquents were put to work to ease their return to society. One of their backbreaking jobs was to rasp brazil wood for the dyeing industry – hence the name, Rasp House. Later it became a normal prison and in 1896 a public swimming pool; now it's a gateway to the Kalvertoren shopping centre.

Back along Singel, the opposite side of the canal towards Muntplein is occupied by the floating **Bloemenmarkt (Map 4)** *(Flower Market; open 9am-5pm daily; closed Sun in winter)*. Amsterdam has had many flower markets since the Tulipmania in the 17th century (see the boxed text 'Mad about Tulips' for more about this speculative madness). The market here dates from the 1860s and specialises in flowers, bulbs, pots, vases and some plants. It's a very pretty sight and the place is packed with tourists and pickpockets. Prices are steep by Amsterdam standards but the quality is good.

Mad about Tulips

MW

A search on the Internet for the term 'Tulipmania' will turn up lots of articles about the speculative nature of Internet and e-commerce stocks. Indeed, when it comes to investment frenzy, the Dutch tulip craze of 1636–37 stands alongside the South Sea Bubble of 1720 and the boom preceding the Great Crash of 1929 as the greatest folly of all time.

Tulips originated as wild flowers in Central Asia and were first cultivated by the Turks, who filled their courts with these beautiful spring blossoms ('tulip' is Turkish for turban). In the mid-1500s the Habsburg ambassador to Istanbul brought some bulbs back to Vienna where the imperial botanist, Carolus Clusius, learned how to propagate them. In 1590 Clusius became director of the Hortus Botanicus in Leiden – Europe's oldest botanical garden – and had great success growing and cross-breeding tulips in Holland's cool, damp climate and fertile delta soil.

The exotic flowers with their frilly petals and 'flamed' streaks of colour attracted the attention of wealthy merchants, who put them in their living rooms and hallways to impress visitors. As wealth and savings spread downwards through society so too did the taste for exotic products, and tulips were no exception. Growers rose to service the demand.

Ironically, the frilly petals and colour streaks were symptoms of an infection by the mosaic virus transmitted by a louse that thrived on peaches and potatoes – healthy tulips are solid, smooth and monotone. Turks already knew that the most beautiful tulips grew under fruit trees but the virus itself wasn't discovered until the 20th century.

The most beautiful tulips in 17th-century Holland were also the weakest due to heavy cross-breeding, which made them even more susceptible to the virus no-one knew about. They were notoriously difficult to cultivate and their blossoms unpredictable. A speculative frenzy ensued, and people paid top florin for the finest bulbs which would change hands many times before they sprouted. Vast profits were made and speculators fell over themselves to out-bid each other. The fact that such bidding often took place in taverns and was fuelled by alcohol no doubt added to the enthusiasm.

At the height of the Tulipmania in November 1636, a single bulb of the legendary *Semper augustus* fetched the equivalent of 10 years' wages for the average worker; a couple of *Viceroy* bulbs cost the equivalent of an Amsterdam canal house. One unfortunate foreign sailor made himself rather unpopular with his employer by slicing up what he thought was an onion in order to garnish his herring. An English amateur botanist, intrigued by an unknown bulb lying in his host's conservatory, proceeded to bisect it, and was put in jail until he could raise 4000 guilders.

This bonanza couldn't last, and when several bulb traders in Haarlem failed to fetch their expected prices in February 1637, the bottom fell out of the market. Within weeks many of the country's wealthiest merchants went bankrupt and many more people of humbler origin lost everything they thought they had acquired. Speculators who were stuck with unsold bulbs, or with bulbs that had been reserved but not yet paid for (the concept of options was invented during the Tulipmania), appealed for government action but the authorities refused to become involved in what they considered to be gambling.

The speculation disappeared, but love of the surprising tulip endured and it remained an expensive flower. Cool-headed growers perfected their craft. To this day, the Dutch continue to be the world leaders in tulip cultivation and supply most of the bulbs planted in Europe and North America. They also excel in other bulbs such as daffodils, hyacinths and crocuses.

So what happened to the flamed, frilly tulips of the past? They're still produced but have gone out of fashion, and are now known as Rembrandt tulips because of their depiction in so many 17th-century paintings.

WESTERN CANAL BELT

Towards the end of
the 16th century, the
city burst out of its
medieval walls with a
flood of Jewish refu-
gees from Portugal
and Spain and Protes-
tant refugees from
Antwerp. In the 1580s,

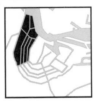

after the Calvinists took power and re-
assessed the city's needs, new land was
reclaimed from the IJ and Amstel in the east
(see the Nieuwmarkt Neighbourhood section later in this chapter), while in the west
the Singel became a residential canal with
the addition of a new moat that was to
become Herengracht.

In 1613 the authorities embarked on an
ambitious expansion project that more than
tripled the city's area. Based on a plan drawn
up by the city carpenter, Hendrick Jacobsz
Staets, Amsterdam received a belt of parallel canals from the IJ to the IJ, one after the
other like layers of an onion around the
medieval city core. These canals with their
many bridges and connecting roads (intended as shopping streets) were all built in
one huge effort. Parcels of land were sold
along the way to finance the project and
buildings arose gradually. The whole city
was enclosed by a new outer moat, the
zigzag Buitensingel (outer moat), now
known as the Singelgracht. The moat's outer
quays became the current Nassaukade, Stadhouderskade and Mauritskade.

Work began at the north-western end adjoining the new harbour works and headed
south from the radial Brouwersgracht. By
1625 the western canal belt was completed
down to the radial Leidsegracht when
money ran out. The project was picked up
again later but at a much slower pace, and
by the end of the 17th century it petered out
just short of its original goal (see the Southern Canal Belt section later in this chapter).

These new canals clearly segregated society into haves and have-nots. Until then,
merchants lived more or less in their warehouses, mingling with their labourers and
suppliers in the thick of the city's activities.

Now the wealthiest among them escaped
the sweat and the stench by building residential mansions along the delectable
Herengracht (named after the Heeren XVII,
the '17 Gentlemen' of the United East India
Company). The Keizersgracht (the 'emperor's canal' in honour of Maximilian) was
similarly upmarket, though the houses
along its later extension beyond Leidsegracht were a bit more pedestrian. Businesses that could be annoying or offensive
were banned, and bridges were fixed to
exclude large vessels – though this didn't
prevent barges from unloading and loading
goods at the warehouses that were built
even along these canals.

The Prinsengracht (so named to keep the
House of Orange happy) was a 'cheaper'
canal with smaller residences, warehouses
and workshops. It acted as a barrier against
the downmarket Jordaan that lay beyond –
a housing estate for the city's many labourers, including those employed in this massive extension project.

Western Islands (Map 3)

The wharves and warehouses of the Western Islands (Westelijke Eilanden), built into
the IJ north of the western canal belt, were
a focus of the harbour in the first half of the
17th century. The wealthy Bicker brothers,
mayors of Amsterdam, even built their very
own **Bickerseiland** to cater for their ships.

The area has a character all its own and
is well worth a wander. Many warehouses
have been converted to residences, and the
ones that haven't had much done to them
are in demand as studios for sculptors and
painters. The **Prinseneiland** and **Realeneiland** (named after the 17th-century merchant Reynier Reael) are the prettiest of the
islands – the narrow bridge linking the two,
the **Drieharingenbrug** (Three Herrings
Bridge), is a modern replacement for the
pontoon that used to be pulled aside to let
ships through.

By all means visit the photogenic **Zandhoek**, the 17th-century sand market on the
eastern waterfront of Realeneiland. The
Zandhoek escaped demolition this century
thanks to Jan Mens' 1940 novel *De Gouden*

Reael, named after the bar-restaurant at No 14. Galgenstraat (Gallows Street), which runs across Prinseneiland to Bickerseiland, used to provide a view over the IJ to the gallows at Volewyck, the uninhabited tip of what was to become Amsterdam North, where bodies of criminals executed on Dam Square were propped up and left to the mercy of crows and dogs.

Haarlem Quarter (Maps 2 & 3)

The Haarlem Quarter (Haarlemmerbuurt) between the Western Islands and Brouwersgracht gets few visitors, which is just as well because it offers a glimpse of life in central Amsterdam without tourists. **Haarlemmerstraat** and its western extension, **Haarlemmerdijk**, were part of the original sea dike along the IJ, from the Zeedijk in the east all the way to the western extremities of the IJ north of Haarlem. They have become a lot quieter now that the road artery to/from Haarlem runs north of here. Pedestrians have flocked back, mainly local residents lured by a good range of shops, pubs and restaurants.

Halfway along Haarlemmerstraat is the **Herenmarkt**, which leads to Brouwersgracht at the head of Herengracht. This was planned as a market in the 1613 canal-belt project but it never took off. Now it's a quiet oasis and a prestigious Amsterdam address. The building at the north end of the square used to be a meat hall before it became the **Westindisch Huis**, head office of the West India Company, from 1623 to 1654. In 1628 Admiral Piet Heyn captured the Spanish silver fleet off Cuba and the booty was stored here in the cellars. Every Dutch person knows the nursery rhyme celebrating Heyn's small name and big deeds, sung by soccer supporters at international matches as a warning not to underestimate this small country.

Walk through the east entrance into the courtyard with its statue of Pieter Stuyvesant, the unpopular governor of New Netherlands, which included the Hudson Valley, Delaware (captured from the Swedes) and several Caribbean islands. Today the building houses the John Adams Institute, a Dutch-US friendship society (see Cultural Centres in the Facts for the Visitor chapter).

The busy road to Haarlem led through the **Haarlemmerpoort** (Haarlem Gate) on Haarlemmerplein, where travellers heading into town had to leave their horses and carts. The current structure dates from 1840 and was built as a tax office and a gateway for King William II to pass through on his coronation. It's officially known as the Willemspoort but Amsterdammers never liked the building and still refuse to call it that, even now that it has been converted to housing. It replaced the most monumental of all the city gates, built by Hendrick de Keyser in 1615 but demolished some 200 years later.

In the 17th century a canal was dug from here to Haarlem to transport passengers on horse-drawn barges. In the 19th century the railways took over, but the original canalside road, Haarlemmerweg, is still a major road (which, for obvious reasons, no longer passes through the gate itself).

Beyond Haarlem Quarter (Map 3) It's worth going west across the traffic bridge next to the gateway and turning right, past the statue of Ferdinand Domela Nieuwenhuis (1846–1919) – a Frisian minister who converted to socialism and then to anarchism and played a leading role in the militant 19th-century workers' movement – and under the railway bridge. Turn immediately left and follow Zaanstraat for a few minutes until you come to the intersection with Oostzaanstraat, where you'll find a housing estate known as **het Schip** (the Ship), one of the highlights of Amsterdam School architecture.

This triangular block, loosely resembling a ship, was completed in 1920 to a design by Michel de Klerk for a housing corporation of railway employees. The pointed tower at the short side of the block has no purpose whatsoever, apart from aesthetically linking the two wings of the complex – and serving as a major symbol of the Amsterdam School. There are several other Amsterdam School-designed housing blocks in this area.

The former post office at the 'bow' of the 'ship' still has the original interior, all meticulously designed by De Klerk. It now houses the Documentation Centre for Social

Housing, with a permanent exhibition of Amsterdam School architecture called **Poste Restante** *(☎ 475 09 24, Spaarndammer-plantsoen 140; adult/concession €2.27/1.59; open 2pm-5pm Wed, Thur & Sun)*. The modest display consists of several videos, also in English, as well as books and postcards and a free email service in the former conference cubicle (originally used for financial discussions with the postmaster), but it's worth visiting just for the interior – note the clever double doors in the conference cubicle and phone booth, the geometrical designs of the leadlight windows and cast-iron counters, and the weird shapes of the tiled walls. Outside on the pavement is a small collection of typical Amsterdam School street furniture (letterboxes, fire alarms, urinals etc). Be sure to walk into the attractive courtyard next to the post office: the fairy-tale garden house with its sculpted roof was intended as a meeting room where residents could discuss housing issues and other matters of common interest.

After visiting the Schip, if it's a pleasant summer's day, walk back about 500m along Zaanstraat, go under the railway line and meander through beautiful Westerpark for a refreshment on the terrace of the former gas factory, the Westergasfabriek.

Brouwersgracht (Maps 2 & 3)

The Brewers' Canal, named after the breweries that used to operate here, was an industrious canal full of warehouses, workshops and factories banned from the residential canal belt. These included smelly breweries, distilleries, tanneries, potash works, whale-oil and sugar refineries, and warehouses for spices, coffee and grain.

The buildings were solidly constructed and many were converted to apartments in the 1970s and '80s. Note the almost uninterrupted row of former warehouses from No 172 to 212. Houseboats add to the lazy, residential character of this picturesque canal.

Herengracht (Maps 2 & 4)

The first section of Herengracht, south from Brouwersgracht, shows a mixture of expensive 17th- and 18th-century residences interspersed with warehouses – note the 18th-century warehouses at Nos 37 and 39, and the early-17th-century warehouses at Nos 43 and 45. On the opposite side of the canal, beyond pretty Leliegracht and at the first bend, is the White House and the adjacent Bartolotti House.

The **White House** *(Herengracht 168)*, named for its sandstone facade, was built in 1620 and modified in 1638 to a design by Philips Vingboons. It now houses the **Theatermuseum** *(☎ 551 33 00, Herengracht 170; adult €3.85, student, senior or child €2.95; open 11am-5pm Tues-Fri, 1pm-5pm Sat & Sun)*. Even if you're not interested in the history of Dutch theatre, it's worth visiting for the stunning interior which was completely restyled in the 1730s, with intricate plasterwork and extensive wall and ceiling paintings by Jacob de Wit and Isaac de Moucheron; a magnificent spiral staircase was added then too. In summer, the lovely garden out the back is the perfect spot to reflect on life.

The museum spills over into the **Bartolotti House** *(Herengracht 170-172)*, which has one of the most stunning facades in the city – a red-brick, Dutch-Renaissance job that follows the bend of the canal. It was built in 1615 by Hendrick de Keyser and his son Pieter by order of the wealthy brewer Willem van den Heuvel, who later assumed the name of his Bolognese father-in-law so he could inherit his bank and develop it into a trading empire. The house was later split down the middle and both residences were inhabited by prominent Amsterdam families.

Just beyond these houses, Herengracht is crossed by **Raadhuisstraat**, a 'spoke road' built in 1894–96 to link the Jordaan with the Dam. Note the shopping arcade on the far side, which follows the S-curve of Raadhuisstraat towards Keizersgracht. It was designed by AL van Gendt (the Concertgebouw architect) for an insurance company, with sculptures of vicious animals to stress the dangers of life without insurance. Smoke bombs greeted Princess Beatrix's wedding coach as it passed this arcade in 1966.

Continuing along Herengracht, the even-numbered side between Huidenstraat and

Leidsegracht shows an interesting mix of architectural styles. The quartet of sandstone neck gables at Nos 364–370 is known as the Cromhouthuizen, designed in 1662 by Philips Vingboons for Jacob Cromhout. They now house the **Bijbels Museum** (☎ 624 24 36, Herengracht 364-370; adult €4.31, child or student €2.72, child under 6yrs free; open 10am-5pm Mon-Sat, 1pm-5pm Sun), which even atheists might consider visiting for the beautiful 18th-century ceiling paintings by Jacob de Wit. The museum focuses on biblical archaeology from the Middle East and Egypt, models of temples, and a collection of Dutch bibles including the *Delft Bible* printed in 1477.

The house at **No 380–382** is unique in that it's designed like a French chateau in early French Renaissance style (a fairly faithful copy of the castle at Blois) instead of following Dutch Renaissance lines. It was built in the 1880s for Jacob Nienhuys, who made his fortune as a tobacco planter and wanted to live in the most luxurious canal house that money could buy. It was the first house in Amsterdam with electric lighting and had its own generator room. His neighbours took a dim view of such bright displays and spread the rumour that the authorities had prohibited him placing a solid gold gate in front of the house.

Keizersgracht (Maps 2 & 3)

The three **Greenland warehouses** (Keizersgracht 40-44), with their step gables, belonged to the Greenland (or Nordic) Company, which dominated Arctic whaling from the early 17th century when Amsterdam's whalers edged out the Basques. In 1680, Amsterdam's whaling fleet counted 260 ships and employed 14,000 sailors. Whalers from Zaandam proved more competitive after the company's monopoly was lifted in 1642, though Amsterdam continued whaling till the early 1800s.

Whale oil was much sought after for a variety of uses (soap, lamp oil, paint), as was whalebone or baleen (corsets, cutlery). Oil-storage wells in these Keizersgracht warehouses (there were five in a row – the ones at Nos 36 and 38 have been demol-

ished) held 100,000L of the precious stuff, and more barrels sat alongside the whalebone on the top floors. The authorities moved the storage facilities to the Western Islands in 1685 to maintain the upmarket character of the canal belt. Many houses at this end of Keizersgracht used to belong to whaling executives and still bear decorations related to their trade.

Farther south on the opposite side of the canal, halfway between Herenstraat and Leliegracht, is the **House with the Heads** (Keizersgracht 123), one of the finest examples of Dutch-Renaissance architecture. The beautiful step gable, with its six heads at door level representing the classical muses, is reminiscent of Hendrick de Keyser's Bartolotti House on Herengracht. This is not surprising: the original owner, Nicolaas Sohier, was related to the Bartolottis and commissioned De Keyser to design the house, though the architect died in 1621 and the job was presumably completed by his son Pieter a year later. Folklore has it that the heads represent six burglars, decapitated in quick succession by an axe-wielding maid of Sohier's as they tried to break into the cellar. Appropriately, the building now houses the city's conservation office (Bureau Monumentenzorg), which aims to preserve the city's listed buildings.

The tall **Greenpeace Building** (Keizersgracht 174-176), which houses the organisation's international headquarters as well as the Dutch branch, is a rare example of Art Nouveau architecture in Amsterdam (The Hague has a much richer collection). It was built in 1905 for a life insurance company – the facade's huge tile tableau shows a guardian angel who seems to be peddling an insurance policy.

On the same side of the canal, note the pink granite triangles of the **Homomonument** at Westermarkt just before you get to Raadhuisstraat. It commemorates those persecuted for their homosexuality by the Nazis – homosexuals had to wear a pink triangle, while Jews wore the Star of David. (See Gay & Lesbian Travellers in the Facts for the Visitor chapter for more about this monument.)

Beyond Raadhuisstraat and still on the same side of the canal, the **Groote Keyser** *(Keizersgracht 242-252)* is a row of houses that became famous as a squatters' fortress. Squatters occupied the empty buildings in November 1978 and couldn't be served with eviction notices until the authorities found out their full names. Notices were served a year later, but the squatters stayed put and had a well-organised support network. They fortified the buildings and set up a pirate radio station, the Vrije Keyser (Free Keyser), which scanned the police frequencies and broadcast instructions to their supporters – the station played a key role in the massive riots that accompanied Queen Beatrix's coronation on 30 April 1980. Eventually the owners and authorities gave up: in October 1980 the council bought the buildings, legalised the squatters and renovated the houses on their behalf.

A bit farther along Keizersgracht, just beyond Berenstraat, is the **Felix Meritis building** *(☎ 623 13 11, Keizersgracht 324; box office open 9am-7pm daily)*, a centre for performing arts. It was built in 1787 by Jacob Otten Husly for an organisation called Felix Meritis (Latin for 'Happy through Merit'), a society of wealthy residents who promoted the ideals of the Enlightenment through the study of science, arts and commerce. It became the city's main cultural centre in the 19th century. The colonnaded facade served as a model for that of the Concertgebouw, and its oval concert hall (where Brahms, Grieg and Saint Saëns performed) was copied as the Concertgebouw's Kleine Zaal (Small Hall) for chamber music.

The building later passed to a printing company and was gutted by fire in 1932. After WWII it became the headquarters of the Dutch Communist Party (and the offices of the party newspaper), and from 1968 to 1989 the Shaffy Theatre Company staged its avant-garde productions here. Today, the reconstituted Felix Meritis Foundation promotes European performing arts.

Opposite Felix Meritis, at No 317, is the residence where Tsar **Peter the Great** of Russia surprised his host, Christoffel Brants, by sailing right up to the house in the pas-senger barge from Utrecht to pay his respects. The Brants family used to live in Rusia and shared Peter's interest in ships. In 1697 the young tsar had already paid an incognito visit to the world centre of ship-building to serve as an apprentice shipwright; this time, in 1716–17, his visit was official.

The city dignitaries greeted him with compliments in cultured French; he answered in earthy Dutch expletives, drank beer straight from the jug at the evening banquet and passed out on the floor beside his bed. The next day he moved to the Russian ambassador's house at Herengracht 527 and trashed the place with bouts of drunken revelry over the following months. A similar lot befell Brants' country mansion (called 'Petersburg') along the Vecht River, though Brants received handsome financial recompense and a title.

Prinsengracht (Map 3)

Prinsengracht, named for William the Silent, Prince of Orange and forefather of the royal family, is the least upmarket of the main canals and also the liveliest. Instead of stately offices and banks, there are shops and cafés where you can sit outside in summer. The houses are smaller and narrower than along the other canals, and apartments are still relatively affordable by canal standards; houseboats line the quays. Together with the adjoining Jordaan neighbourhood (see the following section), this is an area where anyone can feel comfortable.

The **Noorderkerk** *(☎ 626 64 36, Noordermarkt 48; admission free; open 11am-1pm Sat, 10am-noon & 7pm-8.30pm Sun)*, near the northern end of the canal, was completed in 1623 to a design by Hendrick de Keyser as a Calvinist church for the 'common' people in the Jordaan (the upper classes attended his Westerkerk farther south). It was built in the shape of a broad Greek cross (four arms of equal length) around a central pulpit, giving the whole congregation unimpeded access to the word of God in suitably sober surroundings. This design, unusual at the time, would become common for Protestant churches throughout the country. A sculpture near the entrance commemorates the bloody Jordaan riots of July 1934, when five people died protesting the government's austerity measures, including a 12% reduction of already pitiful unemployment benefits.

The **Noordermarkt** *(Noorderstraat; open 8am-1pm Mon, 10am-3pm Sat)* has been a market square since the early 1600s. It now hosts a lively flea market on Monday morning where you can find some wonderful bargains. Early on Saturday morning there's a bird market (caged birds, rabbits etc – a holdover from the former livestock market), followed till early/mid afternoon by a 'farmer's market' *(boerenmarkt)* with organic produce, herbs etc.

On the opposite side of Prinsengracht, between Prinsenstraat and Leliegracht, is a row of former **warehouses** stretching from No 187 to No 217.

The **Anne Frankhuis** *(☎ 556 71 00,* **W** *www.annefrank.nl, Prinsengracht 263; adult/child €5.67/2.27, child under 10 years free; open 9am-9pm daily Apr-Aug, 9am-7pm daily Sept-Mar)* is probably the most famous canal house in Amsterdam with half a million visitors a year. The house itself is now contained in a modern, square shell. Interest focuses on the *achterhuis,* the 'rear house' or annexe where the Jewish Anne Frank and her family went into hiding from 1942 to 1944 to escape deportation by the Germans. The queues in summer can be exasperating but they should be OK if you arrive before opening time or late in the day.

Anne would listen to the carillon in the tower of the **Westerkerk**, at 85m the highest church tower in the city *(☎ 624 77 66, Westermarkt; church admission free, tower €1.35; church open 11am-3pm Mon-Fri Apr-June & Sept, 11am-3pm Mon-Sat Jul & Aug; tower open 10am-5pm Mon-Sat Apr-Sept).* It's topped by the imperial crown that Habsburg emperor Maximilian I bestowed to the city's coat of arms in 1489. The tower, the tourist logo of Amsterdam today, affords a tremendous view over the city, including the differing layouts of the canal

---

Anne Frank

Anne Frank's father, Otto Frank, was a manufacturer of pectin (a gelling agent used in jam) who had the foresight to emigrate with his family from Frankfurt to Amsterdam in 1933. In December 1940 he bought what is now known as the Anne Frankhuis and moved his business from the Singel to here. By then the German occupiers had already tightened the noose around the city's Jewish inhabitants, and even though he signed the business over to his non-Jewish partner, Otto was forced in July 1942 to go into hiding with his family – his wife and daughters Anne (aged 13) and Margot (16).

They moved into the specially prepared rear of the building, along with another couple, the Van Daans, and their son Peter, and were joined later by a Mr van Dussel. The entrance hid behind a revolving bookcase, and the windows of the annexe were blacked out to prevent suspicion among people who might see it from surrounding houses (blackouts were common practice to disorient Allied bombers at night).

Here they survived until they were betrayed to the Gestapo in August 1944. The Franks were among the last Jews to be deported and Anne died in the Bergen-Belsen concentration camp in March 1945, only weeks before it was liberated. Otto was the only member of the family to survive, and after the war he published Anne's diary which was found among the litter in the annexe (the furniture had been carted away by the Nazis). Addressed to the fictitious Kitty, the diary – written in Dutch but translated into 55 languages since – traces the young teenager's development through puberty and displays all the signs of a gifted writer in the making. It has been reissued in recent years, complete with passages deleted by her father about her awakening sexuality and relationship problems with her mother.

In 1957 the then owner donated the house to the Anne Frank Foundation, who turned it into a museum on the persecution of Jews in WWII and the dangers of present-day racism and anti-Semitism.

belt and the streets in the Jordaan. The climb during the 60-minute tour (last tour leaves at 4pm) is strenuous, though.

The church is the main gathering place for Amsterdam's Dutch Reformed community. It was built as a showcase Protestant church for the rich to a 1620 design by Hendrick de Keyser, who copied his design of the Zuiderkerk but increased the scale. De Keyser died in 1621 and the church was completed by Jacob van Campen in 1630. The square tower dates from 1638 – De Keyser would surely have made it hexagonal or octagonal. The nave, 29m wide and 28m high, is the largest of any Dutch Protestant church and is covered by a wooden barrel vault (the marshy ground precluded the use of heavy stone).

The huge main organ dates from 1686, with panels decorated with biblical scenes and instruments by Gerard de Lairesse. The secondary organ is used for Bach cantatas.

Rembrandt, who died bankrupt at nearby Rozengracht, was buried in the church on 8 October 1669 but no-one knows exactly where – possibly near his son Titus' grave.

On the quiet northern side of the square is the house where French philosopher **René Descartes** resided *(Westermarkt 6)* in 1634. He was one of many foreign intellectuals who found the freedom to develop and express their ideas in Amsterdam (others included Locke, Comenius, Voltaire and Marx), or who had their works published here. According to Voltaire, the residents were so preoccupied with profit that they'd never notice him even if he spent his entire life here.

Farther south along Prinsengracht is the **Pulitzer Hotel** *(Prinsengracht 315-331)*, which began business in 1971 and now occupies 17 adjoining canal houses, all connected with internal staircases and passages. The gables have been meticulously restored, along with some of the interior features. In August a free classical concert is held from barges in the canal in front of the hotel, as part of the Grachtenfestival (see Public Holidays & Special Events in the Facts for the Visitor chapter).

Diagonally across the canal, at Johnny Jordaanplein (which commemorates a popular singer of local ballads), is the **Houseboat Museum** *(☎ 427 07 50, Ⓦ www.houseb oatmuseum.nl, Prinsengracht opposite No 296; adult/child under 152cm €2.50/2.05; open 11am-5pm Wed-Sun Mar-Oct, 11am-5pm Fri-Sun Nov-Feb)*. This is a surprisingly interesting little museum, housed in a sailing barge built in 1914, that shows you can live quite comfortably on the water and enjoy all the modern conveniences. Its interior epitomises the Dutch term *gezelligheid* (cosiness, conviviality).

If you continue south along the opposite (eastern) side of the canal you might notice a number of very narrow **alleyways** between Berenstraat and Leidsegracht, closed off with gates. They were officially intended as side entrances for servants' quarters at the rear but such quarters were rented out as accommodation and workshops to the city's poor. These hidden slums, in damp cellars and clustered around dark courtyards, violated the municipal codes of the canal belt but nobody took much notice, probably because they were opposite the southern reaches of the Jordaan – had they been on Herengracht or Keizersgracht it might have been a different story.

Jordaan (Map 3)

The Jordaan neighbourhood was planned and built as a working-class district during the canal-belt project in the early 17th century. Here the canal-diggers and bridge-builders, carpenters and stonemasons settled with their families. Here too came the tanneries, breweries, sugar refineries, smithies, cooperages and other smelly or noisy industries banned from the upmarket canal belt, along with the residences of the artisans and labourers who worked in them.

The name Jordaan wasn't used until a century later and its origin is unclear. The most popular theory is that it's a corruption of the French *jardin* (garden). After all, many French Huguenots settled here in what used to be the market gardens beyond the city walls – the street pattern follows the original grid of ditches and footpaths, and many streets carry names of flowers. Some historians contend that the name had biblical connotations and referred to the Jordan River. For centuries, the Jordaan remained a thoroughly working-class area and the authorities saw it as the unruly heart of the city. It was the first precinct where tarred roads replaced brick paving because the latter could be turned into barricades and police-smashing projectiles during riots. Early this century one in seven Amsterdammers lived in the Jordaan, 1000 people packed to the hectare (100x100m) in squalid conditions.

New housing estates in Amsterdam's northern, western and southern suburbs brought some relief after WWI, and in the 1960s and '70s many Jordanese moved to the outlying 'garden suburbs' and the polders of Flevoland. Their places were taken by students, artists and tertiary-sector professionals who began to transform the Jordaan into a trendy area, though there are still enough working-class and elderly people for it to retain some of its original flavour.

Popular conceptions of the Jordaan linger: it is the 'heart and soul' of the 'real' Amsterdam epitomised in schmaltzy oompah ballads, where life happens on the streets or in corner pubs (rather than in the overcrowded homes) and where common folk still share their experiences; where houses are tiny but tidy, with lace curtains and flowers in window boxes, behind which auntie Greet eyes the street and her front door with the help of a *spionnetje* ('little spy' mirror) attached to the window-sill; and where living, working, shopping, schooling and entertainment are integrated in the one neighbourhood.

Such popular conceptions still hold true, as you will discover when you wander through the Jordaan and soak up the real-life atmosphere of people going about their daily business. Take your time and don't worry if you get lost (which you will): there are plenty of inviting pubs and restaurants, offbeat shops and weird little art galleries to grab your attention.

The Jordaan boasts a number of lively **markets**, such as:

De Looier (☎ 624 90 38, Elandsgracht 109) 11am to 5pm Saturday to Thursday. Bargain antiques and bric-a-brac at indoor stalls.

Lindengracht (Lindengracht) 11am to 4pm Saturday. General market, very much a local affair.
Noordermarkt (Noorderstraat) 9am to 1pm Monday, 10am to 3pm Saturday. See the earlier Prinsengracht section.
Westermarkt (Westerstraat) 9am to 1pm Monday. Cheapish clothes and textiles, some real bargains.

In the late 19th and early 20th centuries many of the Jordaan's ditches and narrow canals were filled in, mainly for sanitary reasons, though their names remain: Palmgracht, Lindengracht, Rozengracht (now a busy thoroughfare), Elandsgracht. **Bloemgracht** was the most upmarket of the canals (the 'Herengracht of the Jordaan') and, for that reason, was never filled in: here wealthy artisans built smaller versions of patrician canal houses. Note the row of three step gables at No 87–91, now owned by the Hendrick de Keyser Foundation and known as the Three Hendricks, though they were built in 1645, long after the famous sculptor/ architect had died.

The southern tip of the Jordaan beyond Rozengracht is quieter and perhaps less interesting than the area to the north. It was (and to some extent still is) an area of workshops and artists' studios.

The Jordaan also has a high concentration of **hofjes**, almshouses consisting of a courtyard surrounded by houses built by wealthy benefactors to house elderly people and widows – a noble act in the days before social security. Some hofjes are real gems, with beautifully restored houses and lovingly maintained gardens. The entrances are usually unobtrusive and hidden behind doors. Hofjes became such a popular tourist attraction in recent years that residents complained and in theory they are now closed to the public (the one exception being the famous Begijnhof, discussed in the earlier New Side section). If the entrance is unlocked, however, and if there are only one or two of you and you exercise discretion, most residents probably won't mind if you take a quick peek. Try the following:

Lindenhofje Lindengracht 94–112. Dating from 1614, this is the oldest surviving hofje.

THINGS TO SEE & DO

Suyckerhofje Lindengracht 149–163. A charming hofje founded in 1670.

Karthuizerhofje Karthuizersstraat 89–171. A hofje for widows, dating from 1650 and on the site of a former Carthusian monastery.

Claes Claeszhofje Eerste Egelantiersdwarsstraat 3. Also known as Anslo's Hofje, this has three courtyards dating from around 1630.

St Andrieshofje Egelantiersgracht 107–141. The second-oldest surviving hofje, finished in 1617, and founded by the cattle farmer Jeff Gerritzoon.

Venetiae Elandsstraat 106–136. Founded in the mid-1600s by a trader with Venice, this hofje features a very pretty garden.

SOUTHERN CANAL BELT

The canal project (see the earlier Western Canal Belt section) stopped at the radial Leidsegracht in 1625 through lack of funds but was picked up again later. Even then, work on the southern section progressed much more slowly: it had taken a mere 12 years to construct the

Bending the Golden Rules

Amsterdam has always had a shortage of land suitable for building purposes. When the authorities embarked on their expensive canal-belt project, they drew up detailed regulations to ensure that this scarce commodity would return maximum revenue. Parcels of land had to be large enough to attract top guilder, but small enough to maximise the number of sales flowing to the municipal coffers rather than to speculators.

On the outer bank of Herengracht, for instance, plots were limited to a width of 30 feet and a depth of 190 feet (these were pre-metric days). There were no limits to the height of buildings over the first 110 feet, but anything erected on the remaining 80 feet had to be less than 10 feet high to ensure the unprecedented luxury of large gardens (even today, the gardens behind many Herengracht houses are magnificent). Buyers also had to pay for the brick quayside in front of their plots but the city paid for the street. Subdivisions were prohibited in order to keep these properties desirable and maintain their value.

So much for the theory. In practice, the very wealthiest Amsterdammers got dispensation, as can be seen in the immense palaces along the 'Golden Bend' of Herengracht between Leidsestraat and Vijzelstraat. Elsewhere, regulations were interpreted creatively – for instance, by buying two adjacent plots and building one house with two fronts; or conversely by building one house with two entrances, subdividing the edifice into upstairs and downstairs and selling the two separately.

AMSTERDAMS HISTORISCH MUSEUM

Herengracht on the corner with Leidsegracht, painted in 1783 by Isaak Ouwater

canals down from Brouwersgracht, along with their interconnecting roads and the adjoining Jordaan area, but it took another 40 years to complete the southern canal belt towards the Amstel and beyond the opposite bank. Interest then fizzled out and the only canal that ever made it to the eastern IJ was the (Nieuwe) Herengracht.

The corner of Herengracht and Leidsegracht is a tranquil spot, surrounded by 17th- and 18th-century houses. You may notice that the buildings along Leidsegracht, as well as those along the southern canal belt, are almost entirely residential with very few of the warehouses or combined warehouses and residences found in the western section. The facades are also more restrained and stately, and less boisterously decorated.

Herengracht (Map 4)

Along the southern section of Herengracht more than anywhere else, the buildings are larger than in the western section. By the mid-17th century some of Amsterdam's merchants and shipping magnates had amassed stupendous fortunes and they saw to it that the authorities (often these same merchants and magnates) relaxed their restrictions on the size of canalside plots.

The Herengracht between Leidsestraat and Vijzelstraat, known as the **Golden Bend**, was the site of some of the largest private mansions in the city. Most of them now belong to financial and other institutions. Dutch architectural themes are still evident but the dominant styles are Louis XIV, XV and XVI – French culture was all the rage among the city's wealthy class.

You can look at the interior of one of these houses by visiting the **Goethe Institut** (☎ 623 04 21, Herengracht 470; see Cultural Centres in the Facts for the Visitor chapter). When this house was built in 1669 it was much larger and included No 468 next door.

Another Golden Bend house open to the public is the **Kattenkabinet** across the canal (Cats' Cabinet; ☎ 626 53 78, Herengracht 497; admission €4.53; open 9am-2pm Mon-Fri, 1pm-5pm Sat & Sun). This museum, devoted to the feline presence in art, was

---

The Great Art Fraud

Herengracht 470, which currently houses the Goethe Institut, used to include adjacent No 468. The house was later split, and during WWII a German art dealer 'acquired' No 468. The Amsterdam painter Han van Meegeren sold him a painting by the 17th century Delft master Jan Vermeer that the German passed on to Nazi ringleader Hermann Göring in return for two million guilders' worth of paintings plundered elsewhere.

Van Meegeren was accused of collaboration after the war, but he declared that he had painted the Vermeer himself and in fact had painted the other Vermeers that had appeared out of nowhere in recent years. To prove his case he painted another 'Vermeer' under supervision.

His work completely fooled the art historians of the day, including the prestigious Boijmans-van Beuningen Museum in Rotterdam which bought one of the paintings in 1937 (Christ at Emmaus) and gave it top billing. It was the greatest art fraud in Dutch history, all the more remarkable for the fact that Vermeer only produced 35 known paintings in his lifetime. Out of respect for Van Meegeren's talent, and the fact that he had swindled Göring, the judge sentenced him to a lenient one year in prison. Van Meegeren died before serving his sentence. See W www.mystudios.com/gallery/han for more on this gifted forger.

---

founded by a wealthy financier in memory of his red tomcat, John Piermont Morgan III. Cat fanciers will go gaga over the displays but it's also worth visiting for the magnificent interior and views of the garden.

Back on the even-numbered side of Herengracht, the corner with Vijzelstraat is dominated by the colossal (some would say monstrous) **ABN-AMRO bank building** that continues all the way to Keizersgracht. It's classed as a monument but is currently empty, and its future role remains unclear. It was completed in 1923 as head office for the Netherlands Trading Society, a Dutch overseas bank (successor to the United East

India Company and West India Company) that became the ABN Bank in the mid-1960s and merged with its competitor, the AMRO Bank, in 1991. The ABN-AMRO is the largest bank in the country and the largest foreign bank in the USA. It 'only' ranks 17th in the world on capital and 13th on total assets (8th and 7th in Europe respectively) but has one of the biggest international networks (the combination of finance and trade has always been a Dutch speciality).

Beyond Vijzelstraat, past the mayor's residence at No 502, is the **Geelvinck Hinlopen Huis** (☎ *639 07 47, Herengracht 518; open by appointment)*, a 17th-century house with stylish rooms, a formal garden and art in the coach house. Though not as impressive as Museum Willet-Holthuysen a bit farther along the canal (see later) or the Museum Van Loon (see the following section on Keizersgracht), it's far more serene, and worth a look if you can be bothered organising a private tour (€68.05, up to 15 people).

A few steps past this house is the start of the radial **Reguliersgracht**, the beautiful 'canal of the seven bridges' cut in 1664. You can just about count them all when you stand on the Herengracht bridge. Canal tour boats halt here for photos because it's easier to count them from below, especially at night when the bridges are lit up and their graceful curves are reflected in the water. This canal was almost filled at the turn of the 20th century to accommodate a tram line.

Walk down Reguliersgracht to take in its serenity and lively mix of architectural styles. Sights include:

- the house at No 34 with its massive eagle gable commemorating the original owner, Arent van den Bergh (*arend* is one of the Dutch words for eagle), and its unusual twin entrance against the side walls with V-shaped stairway for the upstairs and downstairs dwellings
- the superb scene back towards Herengracht from the east-west bridge at Keizersgracht, and the photogenic lean of the two houses on the corner (not to mention the 15 bridges visible from here)
- the Dutch/German woodwork fantasy at No 57–59 reminiscent of the city's medieval wooden houses, built in 1879 for a carpentry firm (the

same architect, Isaac Gosschalk, also designed the building at No 63)
- the Amstelveld with the white, wooden Amstelkerk at Prinsengracht (see the following Prinsengracht section)
- the statuette of a stork set into the corner house at No 92 (storks were a protected species but canal-boat operators fantasise that a midwife lived here)

The extension of Reguliersgracht across Herengracht towards the centre of town used to be water but is now **Thorbeckeplein**, with a statue of Jan Rudolf Thorbecke, the Liberal politician who created the Dutch parliamentary system in 1848. He faces outwards and wouldn't like the look of his square, though the second-rate nightclubs have all but disappeared and the banning of cars has made it more pleasant than it used to be. The **art market** here *(open 10.30am-6pm Sun Mar-Oct)* offers mostly modern pictorial work.

Beyond Thorbeckeplein is **Rembrandtplein**, originally called Reguliersplein and then Botermarkt because the butter market was held here. The proud statue of the painter, gazing pensively towards the Jewish quarter where he lived until circumstances forced him to the Jordaan, was unveiled in 1852 and the square was renamed in 1876. It's lined with pubs, grand cafés and restaurants, and attracts outer suburbanites looking for a noisy good time.

The street running west from Rembrandtplein to the Munt is Reguliersbreestraat. (Before the construction of the canal belt, the nuns of the Regulier, or 'Regular', order had a monastery outside the city walls roughly where Utrechtsestraat now crosses Keizersgracht, which explains the frequent use of the name in this area.) About a third of the way along on the left is the **Tuschinskitheater** (☎ *623 15 10, 0900-14 58, €0.23 per minute, Reguliersbreestraat 26-28; film tickets €5.67-17.01; open noon-10pm daily)*, established in 1921 and still the most glorious cinema in the country. The building's blend of Art Deco and Amsterdam School architecture, with its recently refurbished camp interior decorations, is a visual feast, even before you've seen a film on one of its screens. There used to be very worthwhile guided tours on Sunday and Monday in July and August, but the theatre was closed for renovations as this book was being updated and the owners weren't sure whether they would be reintroduced so check beforehand. Either way, you might as well go for the whole experience by watching a film in the main auditorium, Tuschinski 1.

Back at the Herengracht bridge over Reguliersgracht, continue eastwards across **Utrechtsestraat**, a lively street with interesting shops, restaurants and cafés that's worth a wander (turn right for this).

The **Museum Willet-Holthuysen** *(☎ 523 18 22, Herengracht 605; adult/child €4.08/ 2.04, child under 6yrs free; open 10am-5pm Mon-Fri, 11am-5pm Sat & Sun)* is named after Abraham Willet's widow who bequeathed this beautiful house with its sumptuous interior to the city 100 years ago. Dating from 1687, it has been remodelled several times and underwent extensive renovations a few years ago. Some furnishings and artefacts come from other bequests which explains the uncoordinated mix of 18th and 19th-century styles. It's all very impressive but a bit unnatural – the Museum Van Loon (see the following Keizersgracht section) gives a better idea of the real thing. You can see the formal French garden with its sundial for free through the iron fence at the Amstelstraat end.

Keizersgracht (Map 4)

The intersection of Keizersgracht and Leidsestraat has a couple of remarkable buildings. The **Metz department store** *(☎ 520 70 36, Keizersgracht 455; open 11am-6pm Mon, 9.30am-6pm Tues, Wed, Fri & Sat, 9.30am-9pm Thur, noon-5pm Sun)* was built in 1891 to house the New York Life Insurance Company (hence the exterior and interior eagles) but soon passed to the purveyor of luxury furnishings. The functionalist designer and architect Gerrit Rietveld added the gallery on the top floor where you can have lunch with a view.

Across the canal is the former **PC Hooft store** *(Keizersgracht 508)*, built for a cigar manufacturer in 1881 by AC Bleijs (the architect of the St Nicolaaskerk near Centraal

Station). The name refers to poet, playwright, historian and national icon Pieter Cornelisz Hooft, whose 300th birthday was commemorated in this Dutch-Renaissance throwback with Germanic tower. The playful facade reliefs depict the various stages of tobacco preparation. It now houses a 'smart drug' shop selling magic mushrooms and the like.

Farther along on this side of the canal, beyond Leidsestraat, is the solid yet elegant **Keizersgrachtkerk** *(Keizersgracht 566)*. It dates from 1888 and was built to house the orthodox-Calvinist Gereformeerd community who left the Dutch Reformed Church two years before (see Religion in the Facts about Amsterdam chapter).

The next side street is **Nieuwe Spiegelstraat**, lined with shops selling luxury antiques and other collectables. Even if you don't have the inclination (or the money!) to buy anything, at least have a look at the goods on offer. The extension of this street, the pretty Spiegelgracht with more antique shops and especially art galleries, leads to the Rijksmuseum.

Farther along Keizersgracht, across windswept Vijzelstraat, is the **Museum Van Loon** *(☎ 624 52 55, Keizersgracht 672; adult €4.53, child or student €2.99, child under 12yrs free; open 11am-5pm Fri-Mon)* built in 1672 – along with the house next door, No 674 – for a wealthy arms dealer. The portraitist Ferdinand Bol, a faithful student of Rembrandt, rented the place for a while. In the late 1800s it was acquired by the Van Loons, one of the most prominent patrician families, who lived in a style befitting their status; their stables across the canal at No 607 now house an art gallery. The house, with its period rooms and family portraits, provides a good impression of canalside living when money was no object, and the rococo rose garden is typical of the greenery 18th-century Amsterdammers aspired to.

Note the austere, two-storey **Amstelhof** on the opposite side of the river where Keizersgracht meets the Amstel. It was built in 1683 as an almshouse and is still in use today for Dutch Reformed elderly women (and men, in the basement). It illustrates how the canal project ran out of steam by the time it reached the Amstel. Much of the land beyond was given over to charities or turned into recreational area: the wealthy had already bought their plots and built their mansions, and the Dutch Republic went into consolidation mode against the British and French, which meant there was little new wealth (only increased wealth for those who already had money).

Prinsengracht (Map 4)

The odd and even house numbers along Prinsengracht are more out of step than along the other canals (where they follow one another fairly closely) due to the many Jordaan streets that lead off it. This is exacerbated by additional streets beyond Leidsegracht, and the result is that house No 1133 sits opposite No 868 when Prinsengracht reaches the Amstel.

Near the corner with Leidsegracht is the **Paleis van Justitie** (Court of Appeal) at No 436, a huge, neoclassical edifice rebuilt in 1829 by the city architect Jan de Greef. It began life in 1666 as the city orphanage and was designed for 800 orphans, but by the early 19th century more than half the city's 4300 orphans were crammed in here. A royal decree in 1822 relocated orphans over the age of six to other towns.

A hundred metres or so down Leidsestraat is **Leidseplein**, one of the liveliest squares in the city and the undisputed centre of nightlife. It has always been busy: in the 17th century it was the gateway to Leiden and other points south-west, and travellers had to leave their carts and horses here when heading into town.

The pavement cafés at the northern end of the square are perfect for watching interesting street artists and eccentric passers-by. There are countless pubs and clubs in the area that continue till daylight, and a smorgasbord of restaurants in the surrounding streets. There are cinemas and other entertainment venues, and even a casino built in the shape of a roulette table. Everybody finds something to enjoy at Leidseplein.

The **Stadsschouwburg** (City Theatre; ☎ 624 23 11, Leidseplein 26; box office open

10am-6pm Mon-Sat) with its balcony arcade dates from 1894. People criticised the building – as they criticised every city theatre before or since – and the funds for the exterior decorations never materialised. The architect, Jan Springer, couldn't handle this and retired. The theatre is used for large-scale plays and operettas. South across Marnixstraat, the **American Hotel** (☎ 556 30 00, Leidsekade 97) is an Art Nouveau landmark from 1902 foreshadowing the Amsterdam School's use of brick. No visit to Amsterdam is complete without a coffee in its stylish **Café Americain** (☎ 556 32 32).

Back at Prinsengracht, eastwards on the far side of the canal, the ebullient neo-Renaissance facade is all that remains of the former **milk factory** (Prinsengracht 739-741), built in 1876 to a design by Eduard Cuypers. Until then, milk was brought into town from the surrounding countryside in wooden barrels and sold on the streets from open buckets – not very hygienic.

Farther east, beyond the intersection of Prinsengracht and Reguliersgracht, is the Amstelveld with the wooden **Amstelkerk** (☎ 520 00 70, Amstelveld 10; admission free; open 9am-12.45pm & 1.30pm-5pm daily). The city planners had envisaged four new Protestant churches in the southern canal belt, linked to one another by Kerkstraat, but the only one they actually built was the Oosterkerk, way out on Wittenburgergracht near the IJ (Map 5; see the later Eastern Islands section). The Amstelkerk was a temporary structure, erected in 1670 so the congregation had somewhere to meet while the permanent church arose next to it, but the funds remained elusive and the 'temporary' church still conducts services today. Gothic alterations were made to the interior in the 1840s.

The authorities never completely dropped their plans for a permanent church and kept the **Amstelveld** free of buildings. In 1876 the Monday market moved here from Rembrandtplein. This lively 'free market' had vendors from out of town peddling a wide range of goods (it still operates in the summer months, focusing on plants and flowers). A small statue by the Amstelkerk commemorates Professor Kokadorus, a.k.a.

Bird's-eye view from Westerkerk tower

Take home your own canal house.

Tower of Westerkerk

Café-Restaurant Amsterdam, housed in a former water-processing plant

The Rijksmuseum, the country's leading art museum

Rembrandt's *Nightwatch* can be seen in the Rijksmuseum.

Meijer Linnewiel (1867–1934), the most colourful market vendor Amsterdam has known. People would buy anything from spoons to suspenders ('to hang up your mother-in-law') just to watch his performances interlaced with satirical comments about the politics of the day. Sadly, the annihilation of the Jewish community in WWII put an end to the city's rich tradition of creative vending (though if you understand Dutch you can still pick up some great lines in the markets of the Jordaan).

In summer the Amstelveld is a pleasant space where children play soccer, dogs run around, and patrons laze in the sun at Moko restaurant against the south side of the Amstelkerk. The Catholic church across the canal, **de Duif** *(the Dove; Prinsengracht 756)*, was first built in 1796, shortly after the French-installed government proclaimed freedom of religion. It was the first Catholic church with a public entrance for over two centuries, and was rebuilt to its current design in the mid-1800s. In the 1970s the Church authorities wanted to sell the building but the priest and other staff continued to hold services in defiance and saved the church.

Continue to the Amstel, and you'll see to your right the **Amstelsluizen**, which cross the river to Theater Carré (built as a circus in 1868, rebuilt in brick in 1887 and now used mainly as a theatre). These impressive sluices date from 1674 and allowed the canals to be flushed with fresh water from the Amstel rather than salt water from the IJ, which made the city far more livable (see Ecology & Environment in the Facts about Amsterdam chapter). They were still operated by hand until recently.

To your left is the **Magere Brug** (Skinny Bridge), the most photographed drawbridge in the city. It links Kerkstraat with Nieuwe Kerkstraat and dates from the 1670s, when it was a very narrow pedestrian drawbridge. Rebuilt and widened several times, it was finally torn down in 1929 to make way for a modern bridge, only to be rebuilt again in timber. It's still operated by hand and makes a very pretty sight during the day as well as at night when it's lit up. Stand in the middle and feel it seesaw under the passing traffic.

NIEUWMARKT NEIGHBOURHOOD

For information on Nieuwmarkt Square, see the earlier Old Side section. East of this square is the Nieuwmarkt neighbourhood, enclosed by the Geldersekade and Kloveniersburgwal in  the west, the Amstel in the south, the Valkenburgerstraat (the feeder road of the current IJ-Tunnel) in the east and the IJ in the north. It was the birthplace in 1975 of the organised squatter movement in response to the metro line. The planned line snaked through much of the neighbourhood and required the demolition of many squatter-occupied houses (see Cultural Revolution in the History section of the Facts about Amsterdam chapter).

New, subsidised housing estates arose after completion of the line and today the west and south of the neighbourhood are dominated by modern inner-city architecture, some of it interesting and some less than successful.

Until WWII the area was the focal point of Amsterdam's Jews, a thriving community who enjoyed more freedom here than elsewhere in Europe and made the city a centre for diamonds, tobacco, printing and clothing. They also gave Amsterdam an exceptional variety of lively markets, some of which still exist as sad reminders (eg, the flea market on Waterlooplein).

Lastage (Map 2)

The Nieuwmarkt neighbourhood grew haphazardly. Immediately east of Nieuwmarkt Square was an area known as the Lastage, a jumble of wharves, docks, rope yards and warehouses that lay beyond the medieval city wall and the protective sea dike that ran along the current Zeedijk, St Antoniesbreestraat, Jodenbreestraat and Muiderstraat. In the 1510s, after an attack by troops from Gelderland, the Lastage was fortified by means of the wide **Oude Schans** canal and guarded by a gun turret, the **Montelbaanstoren** – its octagonal tower was added

Jewish Amsterdam

The Nazis brought about the almost complete annihilation of Amsterdam's Jewish community. Before WWII there were about 140,000 Jews in the Netherlands of whom about 90,000 lived in Amsterdam, where they formed 13% of the population. (Before the 1930s this proportion was about 10% but it increased with Jews fleeing the Nazi regime in Germany.) Only some 5500 of these Amsterdammers survived the war, barely one in 16.

They played an important role in the city over the centuries. In medieval times few Jews lived here but their expulsion from Spain and Portugal in the 1580s brought a flood of Sephardic refugees. More arrived when the Spaniards retook Antwerp in 1585. They settled on the newly reclaimed islands in the current Nieuwmarkt neighbourhood where land was cheap.

The monopolistic guilds kept most trades firmly closed to these newcomers but some of the Sephardim were diamond-cutters, for which there was no guild. Other Sephardic Jews introduced printing and tobacco processing, or worked in similarly unrestricted trades such as retail on the streets, banking and medicine. The majority, however, eked out a meagre living as labourers and small-time traders on the margins of society, and lived in houses they could afford in the Nieuwmarkt area, which developed into the Jewish quarter. Still, they weren't confined to a ghetto and, with some restrictions, could buy property and exercise their religion – freedoms unheard of elsewhere in Europe.

The 17th century saw another influx of Jewish refugees, this time Ashkenazim fleeing pogroms in Central and Eastern Europe. Thus the two wings of the diaspora were reunited in Amsterdam but they didn't always get on well. Sephardim resented the increased competition posed by Ashkenazic newcomers, who soon outnumbered them and were generally much poorer, and the two groups established separate synagogues. Perhaps because of this antagonism, Amsterdam became a major Jewish centre in Europe.

The guilds and all remaining restrictions on Jews were abolished during the French occupation, and the Jewish community thrived in the 19th century. There was still considerable poverty and the Jewish quarter included some of the worst slums in the city; but the economic, social and political emancipation of the Jews helped their burgeoning middle class, who moved out into the Plantage area and later into the suburbs south of the centre.

The Holocaust left the Jewish quarter empty, a sinister reminder of its once bustling life. Many of the houses, looted by Germans and local collaborators and deprived of their wooden fixtures for fuel in the final, desperate months of the war, stood derelict until they were demolished in the 1970s.

Some estimates put the current Jewish population of Amsterdam at 30,000, but many are so integrated into Dutch society that they don't consider themselves distinctly Jewish. Amsterdam slang incorporates many terms of Hebrew or Yiddish origin, such as the alternative name for Amsterdam, Mokum (from *makom aleph*, the best city of all); the cheery goodbye, *de mazzel* (good luck); *gabber* (friend, 'mate') from the Yiddish *chawwer*, companion; and the ultimate put-down, *kapsones maken* (to make unnecessary fuss, from *kapsjones*, self-importance).

in 1606, presumably to a design by Hendrick de Keyser. Today the spot offers panoramic views over expanses of water.

North-west of here, across Waalseilandsgracht on the corner of Binnenkant and Prins Hendrikkade, is the **Scheepvaarthuis**, the Shipping House, completed in 1916 to a design by Johan van der Mey. Note the many facade sculptures. This remarkable building, which utilises the street layout to resemble a ship's bow, was the first building in the Amsterdam School style and is still one of the finest examples of this architectural movement. It used to house a consortium of shipping companies but is now home to the municipal transport company that runs the trams and buses.

Nieuwmarkt Islands (Maps 2 & 6)

In the 1580s, the sudden influx of Sephardic Jews from Spain and Portugal prompted the newly Calvinist authorities to reclaim land from the IJ in the form of several rectangular islands east of Oude Schans, one of which, **Uilenburg**, is still recognisable as an island today. Shipyards that operated here soon moved out to the new Eastern Islands (see the Eastern Islands section later in this chapter), making way for another wave of Jewish refugees, this time Ashkenazim from Central and Eastern Europe.

On Uilenburg, the vast **Gassan diamond factory** (*☎ 622 53 33, Nieuwe Uilenburgerstraat 173-175; admission free; open 9am-5pm daily*), abutting a synagogue, was the first to use steam power in the 1880s. The factory was recommissioned in 1989 after thorough renovations. See Diamonds in the Shopping chapter for more information about diamonds and free guided tours of the diamond factories.

Southern Nieuwmarkt Neighbourhood (Map 2)

South of here, inside the sea dike, the 16th-century authorities reclaimed land from the Amstel: the island of Vlooienburg (the current Waterlooplein), with canals and transverse streets that would become the heart of the Jewish quarter. This was not enough, however, to satisfy the needs of the rapidly growing city and two decades later the authorities gave the go-ahead for the ambitious canal-belt project (see the earlier Western Canal Belt and Southern Canal Belt sections).

The street that runs from Nieuwmarkt Square in the direction of Waterlooplein is St Antoniesbreestraat, once a busy street that lost its old buildings during the construction of the metro line – the new houses incorporate rubber blocks in the foundations to absorb vibrations caused by the metro. One

exception is the **Pintohuis** (*☎ 624 31 84, St Antoniesbreestraat 69; admission free; open 2pm-8pm Mon & Wed, 2pm-5pm Fri, 11am-2pm Sat*), which used to belong to a wealthy Sephardi, Isaac de Pinto, who had it remodelled with Italianate pilasters in the 1680s. In the 1970s a planned freeway to Centraal Station required the demolition of this building but the controversy stopped the freeway. It's now a library annexe – pop inside to admire the beautiful ceilings.

A passageway in the modern housing estate across St Antoniesbreestraat leads to the **Zuiderkerk**, the Southern Church built by Hendrick de Keyser in 1603–11. His tower, 1m out of plumb, dates from 1614. This was the first custom-built Protestant church in Amsterdam – still a Catholic design but without the choir – and served as a blueprint for De Keyser's Westerkerk. The final church service was held here in 1929 and at the end of WWII it served as a morgue.

It now houses the **Municipal Centre for Physical Planning and Public Housing** (*☎ 552 79 87, Zuiderkerkhof 72; admission free; open 11am-4pm Mon, 9am-4pm Tues, Wed & Fri, 9am-8pm Thur*) with a very interesting exhibit on all aspects of urban planning. A large, computerised laser map answers questions about the city in English. You can also climb the **tower** (*admission €1.35; open 2pm, 3pm, 4pm Wed-Sat June-Sept*) for a great view over the city.

The former cemetery east of the church adjoins Theo Bosch's community housing project, the **Pentagon** (1983), with an arty waterfall along the courtyard wall. You'll either love it or hate it but you can't ignore it. Visiting architects often have a look.

South of here, across the beautiful **Raamgracht** that city planners wanted to fill in the 1950s, is the narrow **Verversstraat** with a mix of old and new architecture typical of this area. The name, Painters' Street, refers to the polluting paint factories that were limited to this street (originally a canal) beyond the city walls.

The covered walkway over the street used to link sections of the **Leeuwenberg sewing-machine factory**, slated for demolition but saved by squatters who now live here legally (it's an impressive building viewed from the Zwanenburgwal end). At the end of Verversstraat, turn right to the steel drawbridge over the pretty **Groenburgwal**, which affords a good photo opportunity back towards the Zuiderkerk. You can clearly see the slight tilt in its tower.

Jodenbreestraat St Antoniesbreestraat opens on to the wide Jodenbreestraat, a remnant of the freeway-to-be. Note the picturesque, leaning lock-keeper's house on the left, where you can have a quiet beer out in the sun in summer.

Across the road is **Museum Het Rembrandthuis** (☎ 520 04 00, Ⓦ www.rembrand thuis.nl, Jodenbreestraat 4-6; adult/student/ child €6.80/5.67/1.13, child under 6 years free; open 10am-5pm Mon-Sat, 1pm-5pm Sun), a beautiful house dating from 1606 where Rembrandt lived (downstairs) and worked (upstairs). He bought the house in 1639 for a fortune thanks to his wealthy wife, Saskia van Uylenburgh, but chronic debt got the better of him and he had to bail out and move to the Jordaan in 1658. The years spent in this house were the high point of his career, when he was regarded as a star and ran the largest painting studio in Holland, before he ruined it all by making enemies and squandering his earnings.

The museum is well worth visiting for the almost complete collection of Rembrandt's etchings (250 of the 280 he is known to have made), though unfortunately not all of them are on display. There are also several drawings and paintings by his pupils and his teacher, Pieter Lastman, and an etching by Albrecht Dürer. The museum has been expanded with a modern section to the left including the entry hall and the etchings display. The house itself has been completely restored, and thanks to the list of Rembrandt's possessions drawn up by the debt collector, as well as several drawings and paintings by the master himself, the interior now looks as it did when he lived there.

Next to the Rembrandthuis is **Holland Experience** (☎ 422 22 33, Waterlooplein 17; adult €7.94, child or senior €6.80, with entry to Rembrandthuis €11.34; open 10am-

6pm daily). This multimedia hype-fest tries to cram all of this little land's big attractions into an overpriced mish-mash of sights, sounds and smells. A plotless half-hour film lurches from tulips to windmills to threatened dikes, without narration or explanation, but with artless extras parading as cutting-edge entertainment. Cheap perfume is puffed into the auditorium while the tulips are on screen. When an on-screen dike crumbles, room temperature plummets, the audience is sprinkled with water, and a Sony-augmented thunderstorm rages. A plaster ballerina wobbles on rails in front of a filmed rehearsal of Swan Lake. Holland Experience is a superlative example of what can happen with many machines and few ideas, and as entertainment it's very lame and expensive.

Waterlooplein South of Jodenbreestraat is Waterlooplein, once known as Vlooienburg and the heart of the Jewish quarter. It's now dominated by the gleaming gold front tooth in the canal belt, the **Stopera** (☎ 551 80 54, Waterlooplein 22; performances €11.34-49.90; box office open 10am-6pm Mon-Sat, 11.30am-6pm Sun), an oversized city hall and music theatre that opened in 1986 after endless controversy. It was designed by the Austrian architect Wilhelm Holzbauer and his Dutch colleague Cees Dam, who won a competition back in 1968 with a submission that, in the words of one critic, had 'all the charm of an Ikea chair'.

You might wish to attend a music performance in the theatre, or at least a free lunchtime concert on Tuesday, but in any case have a look at the little display in the arcade between city hall and the theatre that shows the country's water levels (for more about this subject, see the boxed text 'Sea Level & NAP' under Geography in the Facts about Amsterdam chapter).

The original Waterlooplein covered the eastern portion of Vlooienburg and was created in 1882 by filling a couple of canals. This was the site of the major Jewish flea market where anything was available. The **flea market** (open 9am-5pm Mon-Fri, 8.30am-5.30pm Sat) survived the war and is now held north and west of the Stopera

Baruch de Spinoza

title). LE Visser was a Jewish president of the supreme court who was dismissed by the Nazis. He refused to wear the Star of David and berated the Jewish Council for helping the occupiers carry out their anti-Jewish policies. He died before the Germans could wreak revenge on him.

On the eastern side of the square is the majestic **Portuguese-Israelite Synagogue** (☎ 624 53 51, Mr Visserplein 3; adult/child €3.40/2.27; open 10am-4pm daily, 9am service Sat), built between 1671 and 1675 by the Sephardic community. It was the largest synagogue in Europe at the time and is still impressive. The architect, Elias Bouman, was inspired by the Temple of Solomon but the building's classicist lines are typical of Amsterdam. It was restored after the war and is still in use today. The large library of the Ets Haim seminary is one of the most important Jewish libraries in Europe and contains many priceless works.

South of the synagogue is the triangular Jonas Daniël Meijerplein, named after the country's first Jewish lawyer (actual name Joune Rintel), who did much to ensure the full emancipation of the Jews in the Napoleonic period.

On the square, Mari Andriessen's **Dockworker statue** (1952) commemorates the general strike that began among dockworkers on 25 February 1941 to protest the treatment of Jews. The first deportation round-up had occurred here a few days earlier. The anniversary of the strike is still an occasion for wreath-laying but has become a low-key affair with the demise of the Communist Party.

On the southern side of the square, across busy Weesperstraat, is the interesting and impressive **Joods Historisch Museum** (Jewish Historical Museum; ☎ 626 99 45, W www.jhm.nl, JD Meijerplein 2-4; adult €4.53, student or senior €2.49, child €1.13-2.04, child under 6yrs free; open 11am-5pm daily; closed Yom Kippur), a beautifully restored complex of four Ashkenazic synagogues linked by glass-covered walkways. These are the Grote Sjoel (Great Synagogue, 1671), the first public synagogue in Western Europe; the Obbene Sjoel (Upstairs Synagogue,

selling a wide range of goods. It's popular, not least among tourists. Prices are a bit higher than at other markets but it's definitely worth a wander. Beware of pickpockets.

The neoclassical **Mozes en Aäronkerk** (☎ 624 75 97, Waterlooplein 205), a Catholic church built in 1841 on the north-eastern corner of Waterlooplein, shows that this wasn't an exclusively Jewish area. It is still used as a church (with an impressive organ) and also as a centre for social and cultural organisations who often hold exhibitions. It replaced the 'clandestine' Catholic church that occupied two houses named Mozes and Aäron at what is now the rear of the church along Jodenbreestraat.

One of the buildings demolished to make way for the new church was home to the Jewish philosopher **Baruch de Spinoza** (1632–77), who was born in Amsterdam but spent much of his life making lenses in The Hague after the rabbis proclaimed him a heretic. He is best known for his work *Ethics*, which proposes that the concept of God possesses an infinite number of attributes.

Jewish Centres The busy roundabout east of the church is Mr Visserplein ('Mr' stands for *meester*, or 'master', the Dutch lawyer's

1686); the Dritt Sjoel (Third Synagogue, 1700 with a 19th-century facade); and the Neie Sjoel (New Synagogue, 1752), the largest in the complex, but still dwarfed by the Portuguese Synagogue across the square.

The Great Synagogue contains religious objects as well as displays showing the rise of Jewish enterprise and its role in the Dutch economy. The New Synagogue focuses on different aspects of Jewish identity and the history of Jews in the Netherlands. There's also a kosher coffee shop serving Jewish specialities.

The area south-east of here, the 'new' canals (Nieuwe Herengracht, Nieuwe Keizersgracht and Nieuwe Prinsengracht) intersected by the busy Weesperstraat traffic artery, was where the canal-belt project petered out around 1700. The canals on this far side of the Amstel were less in demand among the city's wealthy residents and went to charities or were settled by well-off Jews from the nearby Jewish quarter.

THE PLANTAGE (MAPS 5 & 6)

The 19th century discovery of diamonds in South Africa led to a revival of Amsterdam's diamond industry and the Jewish elite began to move into the Plantage (Plantation), where they built imposing town villas.

Until then the Plantage had been a district of parks and gardens. In the 18th century, wealthy residents rented parcels of land here to use as gardens, and the area developed into a weekend getaway with tea houses, variety theatres and other establishments where the upper class relaxed in green surroundings.

The University of Amsterdam's **Hortus Botanicus** *(Botanical Garden; ☎ 625 84 11, ⓦ www.hortus-botanicus.nl, Plantage Middenlaan 2A; adult/child €4.53/2.27; open 9am-5pm Mon-Fri, 11am-5pm Sat & Sun May-Oct; 9am-4pm Mon-Fri, 11am-4pm Sat & Sun Nov-Apr)* was established in 1638 as a herb garden for the city's doctors and moved to this south-west corner of the

Plantage in 1682. It became a repository for tropical seeds and plants (ornamental or otherwise) brought to Amsterdam by the West and East India Companies' ships. Commercially exploitable plants such as coffee, pineapple, cinnamon and oil palm were distributed from here throughout the world. The herb garden itself, the Hortus Medicus, won world renown for its research into cures for tropical diseases.

The garden is a must-see for anyone with an interest in botany. There are guided tours (€1.13 on top of entry fee) at 2pm Sunday, though it's more a place for study than for pleasant relaxation – if you're after the latter, go to the Vondelpark (see later in this chapter) or the botanical garden in Leiden (see the Excursions chapter). Still, there's a lot to see: the wonderful mixture of colonial and modern structures includes the restored, octagonal seed house; a hyper-modern, three-climate glasshouse (1993) with subtropical, tropical and desert plants; a monumental palm house with a 400-year-old cycad, the world's oldest plant in a pot (it blossomed in 1999, a rare event); a butterfly house that's a hit with kids and stoned adults; an orangery with a very pleasant terrace; and of course the Hortus Medicus, the medicinal herb garden that attracts students from around the globe.

The complex of buildings in front of the garden includes the **Association for Nature & Environmental Education** *(☎ 622 81 15, Plantage Middenlaan 2C)*, which organises guided walks and other educational activities, and the **Nature & Environmental Education Centre** *(☎ 622 54 04, Plantage Middenlaan 2E)*, an information centre for environmental and nature education.

Several buildings in the area serve as reminders of its Jewish past. The **Nationaal Vakbondsmuseum** *(National Trade Union Museum; ☎ 624 11 66, Henri Polaklaan 9; adult/concession or union member €2.27/ 1.36; open 11am-5pm Tues-Fri, 1pm-5pm Sun; closed public holidays)* used to house the powerful General Netherlands Diamond Workers' Union, one of the pioneers of the Dutch labour movement under the chairmanship of Henri Polak. The displays won't be of great interest to foreigners but the building itself is definitely worth a look. The architect HP Berlage designed it as the union's headquarters in 1900 and it soon became known as the 'Burcht van Berlage', Berlage's Fortress – a play on Beurs van Berlage, the bourse along Damrak by the same architect.

Berlage considered it his most successful work and it's easy to see why, from the diamond-shaped pinnacle and the magnificent hall with its brick arches and decorated staircase, to the murals, ceramics and leadlight windows by famous artists of the day.

Around the corner is the **Verzetsmuseum** *(Resistance Museum;* ☎ *620 25 35, Plantage Kerklaan 61A; adult/child €4.08/2.27, child under 7yrs free; open 10am-5pm Tues-Fri, noon-5pm Sat-Mon)*, which provides an excellent insight into the difficulties faced by those who fought the German occupation from within. Labels in Dutch and English help with the exhibits, many of them interactive, that explain such issues as active and passive resistance, how the illegal press operated, how 300,000 people were kept in hiding, and how such activities were funded (a less glamorous but vital detail). The museum shows in no uncertain terms how much courage it takes to actively resist an adversary so ruthless that you can't trust neighbours, friends or even family. There's also a library.

Across the road is the entrance to **Artis Zoo** *(*☎ *523 34 00, Plantage Kerklaan 38-40; adult/child €12.90/9.07, child under 4yrs free; open 9am-5pm daily)*. The zoo was founded by an association called Natura Artis Magistra (Latin for 'Nature is the Master of Art') back in 1838, which makes it the oldest zoo on the European continent. Famous biologists studied and worked here among the rich collection of animals and plants. Unfortunately some of the cramped enclosures hardly seem to have progressed since the 19th century, but the zoo's layout – with ponds, statues and winding pathways through lush surroundings (remnants of some of the former Plantage gardens) – is very pleasant. Concerts and art exhibitions are also held here, in line with the original aim of the association: to link nature and art.

A highlight of the zoo is the fascinating **aquarium**, the oldest in the country (1882), with some 2000 fish; its many exhibits include a cross-section of an Amsterdam canal. There's also a **planetarium** (Dutch commentary with a summary in English), and zoological and geological **museums**. The entrance fee includes the hourly shows at the planetarium.

The **Hollandsche Schouwburg** *(Holland Theatre;* ☎ *626 99 45, Plantage Middenlaan 24; admission free; open 11am-4pm daily)* played a tragic role during WWII. Originally the house of the director of Artis zoo across the road, it became the Artis Schouwburg in 1892 and was soon one of the centres of Dutch theatrical life. In WWII, however, the Germans turned it into a theatre by and for Jews, and from 1942 they made it a detention centre for Jews awaiting deportation. Some 60,000 of them passed through here on their way to Westerbork transit camp in the east of the country and from there to the death camps.

After the war no-one felt like reviving the theatre. In 1961 it was demolished except for the facade and the area immediately behind it. A 10m-high pylon in the former auditorium commemorates the country's Jews who were killed by the Germans. There's a memorial room and an exhibition room with videos and documents that display the building's tragic history.

Diagonally across the road is the brightly coloured **Moederhuis** *(Mothers' House; Plantage Middenlaan 33)*, a refuge for young, single women awaiting childbirth. It was completed in 1981 to a design by Aldo van Eyck and incorporates the original 19th-century building to the right.

East of the Plantage

At the eastern end of Plantage Middenlaan, past the Artis aquarium and across the canal, is Alexanderplein with the **Muiderpoort** (Map 5), a grim, Doric city gate dating from 1771. Just north-east of here, along Sarphatistraat, is the 250m facade of the **Oranje-Nassau Kazerne**, barracks built to house the French garrison but only finished in 1814, a year after the French left. They've now been converted to homes, offices and studios. The former drill yard along Singel-gracht accommodates a remarkable row of six modern apartment blocks, each designed by an architect from a different country (from the Muiderpoort end: Japan, Greece, France, USA, Denmark, UK). This was the city's first large-scale experiment in residential architecture in recent times, foreshadowing what's now happening in the Eastern Harbour region (see later).

Just north of here, on Funenkade, stands an 18th-century grain mill known as **De Gooyer**, the sole survivor of five windmills that once stood in this part of the city. Originally south-west of here, it was moved to its current spot in 1814 when the Oranje-Nassau barracks stopped the wind. In 1985 the former public baths alongside were converted into **Bierbrouwerij 't IJ** *(☎ 622 83 25, Funenkade 7; admission free; open 3pm-8pm Wed-Sun)*, a small brewery producing 10 different beers, some seasonal and strong (up to 9% alcohol by volume), that can be tasted in the windmill. There are tours 4pm Friday.

North-East of the Plantage

When the Plantage was constructed in the 1680s, the original sea dike was moved north to what are now the Hoogte Kadijk and Laagte Kadijk (the 'high section' and 'low section' of the 'quay dike'). The stretch of water between the Plantage and this new sea dike is the **Entrepotdok**, established in the 1820s as a storage zone for goods in transit. The 500m-long row of warehouses, once the largest storage depot in Europe, has been converted into desirable apartments and studios.

On the outer side of the dike is **Museum-werf 't Kromhout** *(☎ 627 67 77, Hoogte Kadijk 147; adult/child €4.53/2.72; open 10am-3pm Tues)*, an 18th-century wharf that still repairs boats in its western hall. The eastern hall is a museum devoted to ship-building and even more to the indestructible marine engines that were designed and built here. It reopened in 2001 after a three-year refurbishment. Anyone with an interest in marine engineering will love the place; others will probably want to move on.

EASTERN ISLANDS (MAP 6)

The rapid expansion of seaborne trade led to the construction of new islands in the east of the harbour in the 1650s: the islands of Kattenburg, Wittenburg and Oostenburg.

The United East India Company set up shop on the eastern island of **Oostenburg**, where it established warehouses, rope yards, workshops and docks for the maintenance of its fleet. Private shipyards and dockworkers' homes dominated the central island of **Wittenburg** – city architect Daniël Stalpaert's **Ooster-kerk** (1671) on Wittenburgergracht was the last, and the least monumental, of the four 'compass churches' (the others were the Noorderkerk, Westerkerk and Zuiderkerk).

Admiralty offices and buildings arose on the western island of **Kattenburg**, and warships were fitted out in the adjoining naval dockyards that are still in use today.

The Republic's naval arsenal was housed in an imposing building completed in 1656 to a design by Daniël Stalpaert. The admiralty vacated the building in 1973 and since 1981 it has housed the **Nederlands Scheep-vaartmuseum** *(Netherlands Shipping Museum; ☎ 523 22 22, Kattenburgerplein 1; adult/senior/student/child €6.57/5.67/4.87/ 3.62 including entry to the* Amsterdam*; open 10am-5pm daily June-Aug, 10am-5pm Tues-Sun Sept-May)*. This has one of the most extensive collections of maritime memorabilia in the world. If you only have time to visit two or three museums in Amsterdam, make this one of them.

It traces the history of Dutch seafaring from the ancient past to the present. Maritime trade, naval combat, fishing and whaling are all explained in interesting displays, including an engaging audiovisual re-enactment of a trip to the East Indies. There are some 500 models of boats and ships, and a stunning collection of charts and navigational material.

The full-scale replica of the East Indiaman moored alongside the museum, completed in 1991, represents the United East

India Company's 700-tonne *Amsterdam*, one of the largest ships of the fleet. It set sail on its maiden voyage in the winter of 1748–49 with 336 people on board but got stuck off the English coast near Hastings; there it became a famous shipwreck that has been much researched in recent years. Actors in 18th-century costume do their best to re-create shipboard life.

West of this museum, the structure resembling a ship's bow on top of the IJ-Tunnel entrance is the science and technology centre **NEMO** *(☎ 531 32 33, Oosterdok; adult/student/child €8.48/6.78/4.54-5.67, child under 4yrs free; open 10am-5pm Tues-Sun)*. Designed by the Italian architect Renzo Piano who also worked on the Centre Pompidou in Paris, it offers many interactive displays that are a delight for children and grown-ups. The (free) rooftop 'plaza' affords a great view over the city, and on summer nights DJs play as patrons lounge on beanbags.

EASTERN HARBOUR DISTRICT (MAP 6)

The Eastern Harbour District north and east of the Eastern Islands has seen a lot of building activity in recent years – and lots of discussions between urban planners, financiers and council politicians over how to reconcile grandiose projects with affordable housing. By and large, affordable housing lost out with a relatively low proportion of 30% social housing spread throughout the area, and many of the delectable apartments here are now worth €400,000 and more. The whole district, with more than 8000 dwellings and 17,000 inhabitants, is a showcase of modern residential architecture and makes a very worthwhile excursion. Opinions are divided but everyone seems to form one.

North of Kattenburg is the **Oostelijke Handelskade** (Eastern Trade Quay), where the new passenger terminal caters for enormous cruise ships that dwarf the terminal itself. West of the terminal, the Muziek-gebouw Amsterdam (Music Building Amsterdam), due for completion in 2003, will house the Bimhuis (jazz) and IJsbreker (avant-garde) music centres.

The **Jan Schaefer Bridge**, named after a gung-ho municipal housing councillor in the 1980s who was responsible for an unprecedented number of social-housing projects (favoured motto: 'You can't live in claptrap'), links this area to the Java Eiland farther north. The southern end of the bridge passes through an old warehouse, which had to be reinforced at great expense to withstand the vibrations. The bridge itself has two removable sections that can be floated out of the way for special events, such as the Sail Amsterdam gathering of tall ships held every five years (next due in 2005). West of this warehouse is another warehouse that's home to a centre for interior design where you can ogle (but not buy) the creative products of the country's top manufacturers.

The **Java Eiland** consists of new housing estates separated by canals and enclosing sheltered parks. Its western tip is awaiting an as-yet-unknown project befitting its prominent location – municipal planners are looking for a landmark such as the Sydney Opera House – and is used meanwhile for temporary events such as the annual Drum Rhythm Festival.

The eastern third of this island is known as the **KNSM Eiland**, named after the Royal Netherlands Steamship Company which based its ships here in the late colonial period. This, too, has been transformed by apartment blocks that charm visiting architects, with expensive, private housing on the northern side and social housing on the southern side. Some interesting cafés have opened up here too.

The **Open Haven Museum** *(Open Harbour Museum; ☎ 418 55 22, KNSM-laan 311; adult/concession €1.81/1.13; open 10am-5pm Tues-Fri)* portrays the social and economic history of the harbour and its current transformation with creative use of material from the KNSM collection. It's rather boring unless you're interested in harbours, though you do get a great view from the Compass Room.

South of here, the low-rise housing estates on the former **Sporenburg** peninsula and **Borneo Eiland** have the highest density in the world for dwellings that aren't stacked on top of one another, with 100 houses per hectare (100x100m). None of the expensive apartments here is freestanding but they're designed in such a way to ensure privacy. The planning motto could be described as 'green is blue', meaning that instead of gardens there are roof terraces and lots of water and sky – in fact, trees and shrubs planted by residents are often removed because they 'spoil the harbour look' or 'obstruct pedestrians'. Sporenburg and Borneo have also been described as 'a sea of houses with

meteorites', the 'meteorites' being a number of huge apartment blocks, each of them architectural experiments with varying degrees of success. One of the most remarkable is Frits van Dongen's **The Whale** on Sporenburg, a zinc-coated, 12-storey construction that rears its head and tail. It encloses a landscaped garden that's off-limits to visitors and residents alike. A central cable-TV system with four satellite dishes ensures that residents can plug into 180 channels.

A tall pedestrian bridge at the far end of Sporenburg links this peninsula to Borneo. The bridge doesn't have a popular name yet, but **the Dinosaur** would be apt as it looks

Eastern Harbour Cycling Tour

The sights described in the text are most pleasantly explored by bike along the following route. You could try and walk but it would take at least three hours, as opposed to one to two hours by bike including stops.

Cross the Jan Schaefer Bridge (Map item No **1**) east of the ship-passenger terminal and turn right onto Sumatrakade on the northern side of Java Eiland. Note the four canals along here and the bridges built with arts funding, and have a look at some of the gardens within the apartment blocks. From west to east they're themed as winter, autumn, summer and spring gardens. If you prefer, you could use the cycle path connecting them all.

Via Azartplein, continue on to KNSM Eiland and the Open Haven Museum (**2**). The dark-brown social-housing block opposite the museum is called Piraeus (**3**) and was designed by Hans Kollhoff

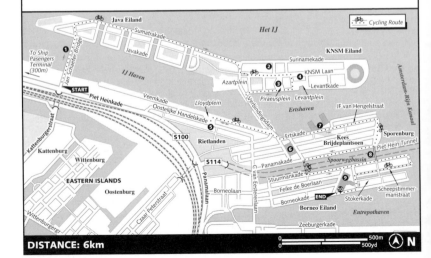

DISTANCE: 6km

like a huge sauropod kissing the other side. It's a work of art (built partly with arts funding) and walking across is quite an experience. Not only is it rather high and exposed (vertigo sufferers take note), and will sway precariously if rocked from side to side, but the steps are of unequal length and you can't see them properly on the way down. Great fun. The bridge is closed in bad weather.

At the far end of Borneo, **Scheepstimmermanstraat** ('Ships Carpenter Street') consists of so-called 'free lots', where purchasers were allowed to design and build whatever they liked (within reason). This has resulted in some amazing solutions to problems such as car parking, maximising

sun and ensuring an uninterrupted view of water and sky. It's all rather bizarre, and if you're with a friend the two of you will probably disagree strongly on the houses you do and don't like.

The 1.5km Piet Heintunnel under the water between Sporenburg and Borneo (the longest tunnel in the country) links the Eastern Harbour District to **IJburg**, a huge new housing project on a string of artificial islands in the IJmeer. Two of these islands are linked by the stunning Brug 2001 (Bridge 2001), a futuristic steel construction designed by Nicholas Grimshaw & Partners.

On completion, IJburg will be home to 45,000 people in 18,000 dwellings served by

Eastern Harbour Cycling Tour

and Christian Rapp. The building on stilts east of it **(4)** used to be the KNSM cafeteria and now houses artists' studios. Turn right towards the water; in front of the former cafeteria the stepped square that slopes down to the water hosts open-air events.

Continue west towards the Verbindingsdam (Connecting Dam) and go across to Sporenburg. Turn right onto Veemkade, and behind the shopping centre you'll see the tower of the Lloyd Hotel **(5)** on Oostelijke Handelskade. Before WWII this was a hotel for penniless Polish and Hungarian emigrants awaiting their KNSM ship for South America; during the war it was an SS prison, after the war a prison for collaborators and finally a youth prison. Now it's being resurrected as a trendy hotel-restaurant for artists, writers and publishers.

Return to Sporenburg and cycle around the zinc-coated Whale **(6)**. Look through the gate at the inaccessible garden, a landscaping work of art. A bit farther along Ertskade is the Chair **(7)**, a U-shaped apartment block designed by Steven Holl that encloses a small harbour.

Continue to the tip of Sporenburg, a pleasant picnic spot with a view over the mouth of the Amsterdam-Rhine Canal. Lock your bike and walk across the Dinosaur Bridge **(8)** to Borneo Eiland and back (you could carry your bike across but that detracts from the fun). The Kees Brijdeplantsoen (Kees Brijde Park) that runs diagonally to the northern side of Sporenburg is named after a 13-year-old boy shot here during the 1944–45 Hunger Winter for rustling coal (Sporenburg was a major railway yard).

Return to the Whale and cross the Dinosaur's sister bridge to Borneo Eiland. The water in this basin is actually quite shallow because the Piet Heintunnel runs through the length of it. Turn left on Stuurmankade, past Koen van Velzen's Pacman Block **(9)** – named after the ancient computer game because of its enclosed interior with a single opening on the southern side – and continue to the end. Come back through Scheepstimmermanstraat and admire (or detest) the crazy architecture along this street of free plots. About halfway along, you can cross the bridge to Stokerkade and observe these houses from the water side.

Back at the Pacman Block, proceed to the southern side and grab a seat at De Oceaan pub **(10)** for a well-deserved refreshment, in one of the original buildings still left on Borneo.

11 primary schools, its own cemetery and even a beach. A majority of Amsterdammers voted against the project in a referendum, but not enough people voted so the plan went ahead – though city planners had to work twice as hard to improve their blueprints. Inhabitants of Durgerdam, a picturesque old village across the water, were furious about losing their view.

19th-Century Districts

The canal belt was a far-sighted project that sufficed for two and a half centuries. There was no real pressure to expand beyond the canals until the 1860s, when the industrial revolution began to attract workers back to the city. In 1830 there were 200,000 inhabitants – 20,000 less than in the 18th century, due to Napoleon's disastrous Continental System. In 1860 this had picked up to 245,000, in 1880 to 320,000, and in 1900 to over 500,000.

This time the city's expansion was un-coordinated. There were several grand plans but none got past the proposal stage; instead, private initiative and speculation reigned supreme. The Pijp, between the Amstel and Hobbemakade, was the first area to be added, in the 1860s, full of dreary and shoddily built tenement blocks for the city's labourers. Farther west came the Vondelpark in the 1860s and 1870s, surrounded by upmarket housing. The last two decades of the 19th century were a free-for-all as investors grabbed other land beyond the canal belt and built new cheap housing, often with very few restrictions.

Many of these areas have now been renovated or replaced with modern social-housing estates and have become decidedly more pleasant. Old West (Oud West) around Kinkerstraat is a good example, as are the Frederik Hendrik and Staatslieden (Statespeople) neighbourhoods farther north. They have the potential to become trendy areas over the next decade, as has already happened with the Pijp.

OLD SOUTH (OUD ZUID)

This wedge-shaped district is roughly bordered by the Vondelpark in the west and Hobbemakade in the east. Some call it the Museum Quarter, Concertgebouw area or Vondelpark area, depending on which of these landmarks is closest. Fortunately it escaped the late-19th-century free-for-all. Wealthy investors wanted an upmarket area for themselves and saw to it that tenement blocks or businesses were prohibited here – a suitable spot for a grand national museum (the Rijksmuseum) and an equally grand new concert hall (the Concertgebouw).

In a rerun of the canal-belt scenario, the park and cultural centres were financed by the sale of plots of land to the highest bidders, who proceeded to build private mansions close to these attractive landmarks. It wasn't until the early decades of the 20th century, however, that the wealthy class deserted its mansions along Herengracht and Keizersgracht altogether.

In the 1920s, plots farther south that remained empty were filled with Amsterdam School-designed apartments commissioned by subsidised-housing corporations. Good examples can be seen along **JM Coenenstraat** (Map 4; architect JF Staal) and in the adjoining **Harmoniehof** (Map 4), featuring the robust designs of JC van Epen.

Museum Quarter (Map 4)

Rijksmuseum The Museum Quarter's gateway – literally, with its pedestrian and bicycle underpass – is the 1885 Pierre Cuypers-designed Rijksmuseum (*☎ 674 70 47*, **W** *www.rijksmuseum.nl, Stadhouderskade 42; adult €7.94, child under 18yrs free; open 10am-5pm daily*). It bears a striking resemblance to Centraal Station, which was indeed designed by the same architect and completed four years later, with a mixture of neo-Gothic and Dutch Renaissance. The neo-Gothic aspects (towers, stained-glass windows) elicited criticism from Protestants including the king, who dubbed the building 'the archbishop's palace' (Cuypers was Catholic, and proudly so in his approach to architecture).

The Rijksmuseum was conceived as a repository for several national collections, including the royal art collection that was first housed in the palace on Dam Square and then in the Trippenhuis on Kloveniersburgwal. It's the country's premier art museum and one that no self-respecting visitor to Amsterdam can afford to miss – in fact, 1.2 million visitors flock here each year.

Some 5000 paintings are on display in 200 rooms, and many other works of art, so it pays to be selective if you don't want to spend days here. Grab the free floor plan when you buy your ticket and home in on the areas that interest you most – there are five major collections but you'll need the floor plan to find your way around them. The museum shop on the 1st floor sells guidebooks that describe the collections in more detail.

The most important collection, Paintings, consists of Dutch and/or Flemish masters from the 15th to 19th centuries, with emphasis on the 17th-century Golden Age. Pride of place is taken by Rembrandt's huge *Nightwatch* (1650) in room 224 on the 1st floor, showing the militia led by Frans Banningh Cocq, a future mayor of the city – the painting only acquired this name in later years because it had become dark with grime (it's nice and clean now). Room 211 shows earlier (and more colourful) works by Rembrandt. Other 17th-century Dutch masters on this floor include Jan Vermeer *(The Kitchen Maid,* also known as *The Milkmaid,* and *Woman in Blue Reading a Letter),* Frans Hals *(The Merry Drinker)* and Jan Steen *(The Merry Family).*

The museum's other collections are Sculpture & Applied Art (delftware, beautiful dolls' houses, porcelain, furniture), Dutch History (though the Amsterdams Historisch Museum and Nederlands Scheepvaartmuseum do this better), Asiatic Art (including the famous 12th-century *Dancing Shiva),* and finally the Print Room *(open 10am-5pm Tues-Sun),* with changing exhibitions that can be surprisingly interesting

depending on which of the 800,000 prints and drawings are on display when you visit.

From late 2003 to 2006 most sections of the museum will be closed for a sweeping renovation that will cost an estimated €200m and bring more 'air' and 'light' into the sometimes rather gloomy rooms. Only the top 200 art pieces will be on display in the southern wing.

The **garden** at the back of the museum has flowerbeds, fountains and an eclectic collection of statues, pillars and fragments of demolished buildings and monuments from all over the country.

Street musicians perform in the pedestrian and bicycle underpass beneath the museum, their sounds echoing off the cavernous walls. This passage leads to the large **Museumplein**, which hosted the World Exhibition in 1883 and hasn't had a clear purpose since. It has recently been transformed into a huge park, with an underground Albert Heijn supermarket opposite the Concertgebouw. The name of the square is somewhat misleading because none of the museums actually face it.

Van Gogh Museum The next museum down is the Van Gogh Museum *(☎ 570 52 00,* W *www.vangoghmuseum.nl, Paulus Potterstraat 7; adult/child €7.03/2.27, child under 12yrs free; open 10am-6pm daily)* designed by Gerrit Rietveld (the recent expansion onto Museumplein, a separate exhibition wing designed by Kishio Kurosawa, is commonly known as 'the Mussel'). It opened in 1973 to house the collection of Vincent's younger brother Theo, which consists of about 200 paintings and 500 drawings by Vincent and his friends or contemporaries, such as Gauguin, Toulouse-Lautrec, Monet and Bernard.

Vincent van Gogh (pronounced 'khokh', rhyming with Scottish 'loch') was born in 1853 and had a short but very productive life. He didn't begin painting until 1881 and produced most of his works in the four years he spent in France, where he shot himself to escape mental illness in 1890 (he had already cut off his own ear after an argument with Gauguin). Famous works on display include *The Potato Eaters* (1885), a prime example of his sombre Dutch period, and *The Yellow House in Arles* (1888), *The Bedroom at Arles* (1888) and several self-portraits, sunflowers and other blossoms that show his vivid use of colour in the intense Mediterranean light. One of his last paintings, *Wheatfield with Crows* (1890), is an ominous work foreshadowing his suicide.

His paintings are on the 1st floor; the other floors display his drawings and Japanese prints as well as works by friends and contemporaries, some of which are shown in rotation. The **library** *(open 10am-12.45pm & 1.30pm-5pm Mon-Fri)* has a wealth of reference material for serious study.

Stedelijk Museum Next to the Van Gogh Museum is the Stedelijk Museum *(☎ 573 29 11, ⓦ www.stedelijk.nl, Paulus Potterstraat 13; adult €4.57, child or senior €2.27, extra for special exhibits; open 11am-5pm daily)*, the Municipal Museum that focuses on modern art – paintings, sculptures, installations, videos, photography etc – from 1850 to the present. It's one of the world's leading museums of modern art, with an eclectic collection amassed by its postwar curator, Willem Sandberg.

This includes works by Monet, Van Gogh, Cézanne, Matisse, Picasso, Kirchner and Chagall as well as other modern 'classics', including a unique collection of some 50 works by the Russian artist Malevich. There are abstract works by Mondriaan, Van Doesburg and Kandinsky, and a large, post-WWII selection of creations by Appel (including the former cafeteria decorated by him, next to the information desk to your left as you enter), De Kooning, Newman, Ryman, Judd, Warhol, Dibbets, Baselitz, Dubuffet, Lichtenstein, Polke and Rietveld's furniture. Be sure to visit Kienholz's famous *The Beanery* in Room 12, a surreal reconstruction of a bar that you walk into. Sculptures include works by Rodin, Renoir, Moore, Laurens and Visser. The pleasant café-restaurant, with a great mural by Appel, draws the glitterati of the (inter)national arts scene.

The museum displays most of its permanent collection in the summer months. At other times of the year many of the works make way for changing exhibitions that some people will consider pretentious nonsense while others will be ecstatic, though the planned expansion onto Museumplein in 2004 should provide space for everything (the gallery will be closed from Nov 2002 to March 2005). Grab a floor plan from the information desk to your left as you enter. There's a very well-stocked shop on the 1st floor.

Concertgebouw (Map 4)

The Concert Building *(☎ 671 83 45 – recording in Dutch, hold for English-speaking operator, ⓦ www.concertgebouw.nl, Concertgebouwplein 2-6; tickets €6.80-117.96; box office open 10am-7pm daily)*, at the end of Museumplein, attracts some 800,000 visitors a year, making it the busiest concert hall in the world. It was completed in 1888 to a neo-Renaissance design by AL van Gendt. In spite of his limited musical knowledge, he managed to give the Grote Zaal (Great Hall) near-perfect acoustics that are the envy of concert hall designers worldwide.

The best conductors and soloists consider it an honour to perform here. Under the 50-year guidance of composer and conductor Willem Mengelberg (1871–1951), the Concertgebouw Orchestra (with the epithet 'Royal' since 1988) developed into one of the world's finest orchestras.

In the 1980s the Concertgebouw threatened to collapse because its 2000 wooden piles were rotting. Thanks to new technology the piles made way for a concrete foundation, and the building was thoroughly restored to mark its 100th anniversary. The architect Pi de Bruin added a glass foyer along the southern side that most people hate though everyone agrees it's effective.

The Grote Zaal seats 2000 people and is used for concerts. Recitals take place in the 19x15m Kleine Zaal (Small Hall), a replica of the hall in the Felix Meritis building.

You can purchase tickets on the telephone between 10am and 5pm daily, or at the box office till 7pm (after 7pm you can only get tickets for that evening's performance). The VVV and Amsterdam Uitburo (see Tourist Offices in the Facts for the Visitor chapter) also sell tickets. There are free lunch-time concerts at 12.30pm Wednesday between September and June.

Vondelpark & Surroundings (Map 4)

This pleasant, English-style park, with ponds, lawns, thickets and winding footpaths, is about 1.5km long and 300m wide. Laid out on marshland beyond the canal belt in the 1860s and '70s as a park for the bourgeoisie when the existing city park, the Plantage, became residential, it was soon surrounded by upmarket housing. It's named after the poet and playwright Joost van den Vondel (1587–1679), the Shakespeare of the Netherlands.

In the late 1960s and early 1970s the authorities turned the park into an open-air dormitory to alleviate the lack of accommodation for hordes of hippies who descended on Amsterdam. The sleeping bags have long since gone and it's now illegal to sleep in the park, but there's still some evidence of Italian, French and Eastern European tourists stuck in the '70s.

The park is now used by one and all – joggers, in-line skaters, children chasing ducks or flying kites, couples in love, families with prams, acrobats practising or performing, teenagers playing soccer – and can be crowded on weekends but never annoyingly so. From June to August the park hosts free concerts in its **open-air theatre** (☎ 673 14 99, Ⓦ www.openluchttheater.nl), an experience not to be missed, and there are always people performing music throughout the park.

The functionalist *Round Blue Teahouse* (1936) is a wonderful little multilevel building that serves coffee, cake and alcohol; its terrace and balcony are great places for a beer on a sunny day, even in winter when the heaters are on. A stand at the pleasant *De Vondeltuin Cafetaria* (☎ mobile 06-546 622 62, Vondelpark 7), near the Amstelveenseweg entrance at the south-western end of the park, rents in-line skates and gloves for €4.52 an hour.

Close to Constantijn Huygensstraat is the former Vondelpark Pavilion (1881), now home to the **Filmmuseum** (☎ 589 14 00, Vondelpark 3; film tickets adult €5.67-7.94, concession or student €3.40-4.53; screenings 7pm-10pm Mon-Sat, 1pm-10pm Sun). It's not a real museum as such with displays but it has a large collection of memorabilia and a priceless archive of films that are screened in two theatres, often with live music and other accompaniments. One theatre contains the Art Deco interior of Cinema Parisien, an early Amsterdam cinema. The museum's charming *Café Vertigo* (☎ 612 30 21), with its theatrical balcony, is a popular meeting place and an ideal spot to spend a couple of hours watching the goings-on in the park; on summer evenings there are films on the outdoor terrace and jazz on Sunday during winter. Adjoining the museum is an impressive **library** and study centre (☎ 589 14 35, Vondelstraat 69-71; admission free; open 10am-5pm Tues-Fri, 11am-5pm Sat).

In 1980 the house at Vondelstraat 72, along with the intersection with Constantijn Huygensstraat, were the scene of one of the most dramatic episodes in the history of the squatter movement – see History in the Facts about Amsterdam chapter.

Also in Vondelstraat, near the Filmmuseum, is the **Vondelkerk** (1880), built to a design by Pierre Cuypers, which now accommodates offices. A few steps down the road is the neoclassical **Hollandse Manege** (☎ 618 09 42, Vondelstraat 140; open 9am-11pm daily) built in 1882 and designed by AL van Gendt, an indoor riding school inspired by the famous Spanish Riding School in Vienna. The building was fully restored in the 1980s, and it's worth walking through the passage to the door at the rear and up the stairs to the café, where you can sip a cheap beer or coffee while enjoying the beautiful interior and watching the instructor put the horses through their paces. Actual opening times can vary a bit from the official times – ring to avoid disappointment.

Beyond the opposite side of the park is narrow, 19th-century **PC Hooftstraat**, a shopping street for the cream of society and the nouveau riche (note the parked Daimlers and Ferraris).

Beyond the south-western extremities of the park, just north of the Olympic Stadium, is the former Haarlemmermeer Station which houses the **Tram Museum Amsterdam (Map 1)** *(☎ 673 75 38, Amstelveenseweg 264; return ticket adult/child €2.99/1.49; services operate 11am-5pm Sun mid-Apr–Oct, 1.45pm & 3.15pm Wed July & Aug).* Historic trams sourced from all over Europe run between here and Amstelveen – a great outing for kids and adults. A return trip takes more than an hour and skirts the large Amsterdamse Bos recreational area (contact the museum for a schedule).

DE PIJP (MAPS 4 & 5)

This district is enclosed by the Amstel in the east, Stadhouderskade in the north, Hobbemakade in the west and the Amstelkanaal in the south – it's actually a large island connected to the rest of the city by 16 bridges. The district's name, 'the Pipe' (originally the 'YY neighbourhood'), presumably reflects its straight, narrow streets that are said to resemble the stems of old clay pipes, but nobody really knows. There are a surprising number of attractions for an area that began as the city's first 19th-century slum.

Its shoddy tenement blocks, some of which collapsed even as they were being built in the 1860s, provided cheap housing not just for newly arrived workers drawn by the city's industrial revolution, but also for students, artists, writers and other poverty-stricken individuals. In the 1960s and '70s, as many of the working-class inhabitants left for greener pastures, the government began refurbishing the tenement blocks for immigrants from Morocco, Turkey, the Netherlands Antilles and Suriname. Now these immigrants are also moving out and the Pijp is attracting a wealthier breed of locals who are doing up apartments and lending the neighbourhood a more gentrified air.

In the past as now, the Pijp has often been called the 'Quartier Latin' of Amsterdam thanks to its lively mix of people – labourers, intellectuals, new immigrants, prostitutes (in the city's other and very depressing red-light district along Ruysdaelkade opposite Hobbemakade), and now an increasing number of higher-income professionals.

This interesting array is best viewed at the **Albert Cuyp market** *(Albert Cuypstraat; open 9am-5pm Mon-Sat)*, Amsterdam's largest and busiest market. The emphasis is on food of every description and nationality but clothes and other general goods are on sale too, often cheaper than anywhere else. If you want to experience the 'real' Amsterdam at its multicultural best, this market is not to be missed. As always at busy markets, beware of pickpockets.

The surrounding streets hide cosy neighbourhood cafés, small (and usually very cheap) restaurants that offer a wide range of cuisines, and an increasing number of stylish shops and bars.

Many tourists head for the **Heineken Experience** *(☎ 523 94 36, [W] www.heinekencorp.com, Stadhouderskade 78; admission €5; open 10am-6pm Tues-Sun)*, still commonly known as the Heineken Brewery. The self-guided tour ends with a beer 'tasting' session at which three glasses per person may be consumed. Visitors under 18 are only admitted under parental guidance.

The actual brewery closed in 1988 due to inner-city congestion and since then the building has been used only for the tours and administration; the company's directorate is in the low-key premises across the canal. Heineken beer is now brewed at a larger plant in 's-Hertogenbosch (Den Bosch) in the south of the country that opened in 1950, and since 1975 also at the largest brewery in Europe at Zoeterwoude near Leiden.

South of Albert Cuypstraat is the **Sarphatipark**, an English-style park named after the energetic 19th-century Jewish doctor and chemist Samuel Sarphati (1813–66). His diverse projects (a waste-disposal service, a slaughterhouse, a factory for cheap bread, trades and business schools, the Amstel Hotel, a mortgage bank) exasperated the dour city council, though many of these

Foeliedwarsstraat, a typical street in the Jewish quarter, painted by Alexander Hilverdink in 1889

Winter cityscape – Amsterdam shows a different face.

Shipping Museum's *Amsterdam*

De Waag, Nieuwmarkt Square

Hortus Botanicus, Plantage

NEMO science and technology centre

'Dinosaur' bridge linking Sporenburg and Borneo

ventures survive to this day. The street along the south side of the park is Ceintuurbaan, a traffic artery that holds little of interest except the **Kabouterhuis** *(Gnome House; Ceintuurbaan 251-255)* near the Amstel. Its whimsical woodwork facade incorporates a couple of gnomes playing ball, a reference to the surname of the original owner, Van Ballegooijen ('of ball-throwing').

South of here, the neo-Renaissance **Gemeentearchief** *(Municipal Archives; ☎ 572 02 02, Amsteldijk 67; admission free; open 10am-5pm Mon-Sat Sept-June, 10am-5pm Mon-Fri July & Aug)* housed in the former town hall of Nieuwer Amstel, a town annexed by Amsterdam during the late-19th-century expansion. Anyone interested in their family history or the history of the city can peruse the archives free of charge, and occasionally there are very interesting exhibitions.

South of Ceintuurbaan, the Pijp contains some of the most interesting examples of early 20th-century housing estates built in the Amsterdam School style. The imposing **Cooperatiehof**, surrounded by Burgemeester Tellegenstraat, was designed for the socialist housing corporation De Dageraad (The Dawn) by one of the main Amsterdam School architects, Piet Kramer. Another leading architect, Michel de Klerk, designed the idiosyncratic housing estates at **Henriëtte Ronnerplein** and **Thérèse Schwartzeplein**. As with other architecture of this school, the eccentric details are worth noting: vertically laid bricks, letterboxes as works of art, asymmetric windows, oddly shaped doorways, funny chimneys, creative solutions for corners and so forth.

OOSTERPARK DISTRICT (MAP 5)

This south-eastern district, named after the lush English-style park lying at its centre, was built in the 1880s. At the time, the city's diamond workers suddenly found they had money to spare thanks to the discovery of diamonds in South Africa. About a third of Jewish families

worked in the diamond industry in one way or another, and many of these could finally afford to leave the Jewish quarter for this new district beyond the Plantage (the delectable parklands where only the wealthiest could afford to live). Signs of this district's lower-middle-class heritage have long since disappeared and now it's depressingly similar to the other 19th-century slums that arose around the canal belt.

The only exception, apart from the park, is the **Tropenmuseum** *(☎ 568 82 15, W www.kit .nl, Linnaeusstraat 2; adult €6.80, senior or student €4.53, child €3.40, child under 6yrs free; open 10am-5pm daily)*, an impressive complex completed in 1926 to house the Royal Institute of the Tropics, still one of the world's leading research institutes for tropical hygiene and agriculture. Part of the building became a museum for the institute's collection of colonial artefacts, but this was overhauled in the 1970s to create the culturally aware and imaginatively presented displays you see today.

A huge central hall with galleries over three floors offers reconstructions of daily life in several tropical countries (a north African street, Javanese house, Indian village, African market etc). Separate exhibitions focus on music, theatre, religion, crafts, world trade and ecology, and there are special exhibitions throughout the year. Expert guides introduce children to tropical cultures in the separate **children's museum** *(☎ 568 82 33)* reserved for six to 12-year-olds. These programs are in Dutch only, though the 'summer school' also caters for foreign kids – ring to check. There's an extensive **library** *(☎ 568 82 54; open 10am-4.30pm Tues-Fri, noon-4.30pm Sun)*, a shop selling books and gifts and unique CDs, the pleasant *Soeterijn Café*, and the *Ekeko restaurant (☎ 568 86 44)* serving Third World cuisine.

The **Tropeninstituut Theater** *(☎ 568 82 15; box office open noon-4pm Mon-Sat)* has a separate entrance and screens films but also hosts music, dance, plays and other performances by visiting artists.

The museum itself is a good place to spend a lazy Monday when most of the other museums are closed. There's a useful notice board for travellers, with lift shares, people looking for travel partners etc.

Greater Amsterdam

The city's population stabilised at around 700,000 by 1920, which is still more or less the figure today. The authorities at the time didn't foresee this of course and cautiously expected 950,000 by the year 2000. Despite a slight pause during the Depression and WWII, the city kept gobbling up one outlying town after another as increased mobility fuelled urban sprawl.

NEW SOUTH (NIEUW ZUID) (MAP 1)

The Housing Act of 1901 set minimum standards for new houses and allowed for the compulsory purchase and demolition of old houses that didn't meet these standards. The act also forced municipal authorities to come up with proper blueprints for city expansion. One such plan was the Plan Zuid of 1917 for the south of the city, drawn up by the progressive architect Berlage and instigated by the labour party alderman FM Wibaut. The result was New South, between the Amstel and what was to become the Olympic Stadium.

Urban planners, architects and municipal authorities had not worked together so closely since the canal-belt project, successfully integrating solid housing and wide boulevards that enclosed quiet neighbourhoods with cosy squares. There was even a canal linking the Amstel in the east with the Schinkel in the west: the Amstelkanaal that split in two about halfway along and rejoined again behind the Olympic Stadium. Subsidised-housing corporations provided funding for innovative designs by architects

of the Amsterdam School. Many of these architects worked for the city housing department, and the council preferred their designs to the functionalist designs of Berlage himself.

Funding cutbacks in the 1930s meant that these architects couldn't be as creative as they had been in their earlier designs, but even today the area is as elegant as it was then. Streets such as Churchillaan, Apollolaan and Stadionweg are 'good' addresses. The area's main shopping street, Beethovenstraat, is lined with expensive shops and other establishments for elderly women in fur coats.

Among the first residents were Jewish refugees from Germany and Austria, many of them writers and artists, who settled around Beethovenstraat. The Frank family first lived at Merwedeplein farther to the east, where Churchillaan and Rooseveltlaan merge around the **'Skyscraper'** (1930), a 12-storey building with spacious luxury apartments designed by JF Staal.

South-west of here is the **RAI** exhibition and conference centre (*☎ 549 12 12, fax 646 44 69, Europaplein 8*), the largest such complex in the country. It opened in the early 1960s and new halls are still being added. There's always some sort of exhibition or trade fair going on.

AMSTELVEEN (MAP 1)

This suburb south of Amsterdam has a long history. In the 12th century it was a moor drained by the Amstel (*veen* means peat). Local farmers built canals to drain the land for agriculture, thus turning the Amstel into a clearly defined river. As the soil along the Amstel compacted, the farming community moved farther west, which is why the west bank of the Amstel at this latitude is relatively uninhabited today. There's not much to draw you to Amstelveen, but a couple of attractions are right up there.

First there's the **Amsterdamse Bos** (*Amsterdam Woods; visitors centre ☎ 643 14 14,*

Nieuwe Kalfjeslaan 4; admission free; visitors centre open 8.30am-5pm daily, park open 24 hours daily), a large recreational area built as a work-creation project in the 1930s. Amsterdammers flock here on weekends but it's so huge (940 hectares) that it never gets too crowded. Its only drawback is that it's close to Schiphol and a lot of low-flying aircraft.

There are lakes, wooded areas and meadows, an animal enclosure with bison, a goat farm, paths for walking, cycling and horse riding, a rowing course (the Bosbaan, with several water craft for hire), an **open-air theatre** *(☎ 626 36 47, 640 92 53)* with plays in summer, a sports park, a pancake house, a **forestry museum** *(☎ 676 21 52; admission free; open 10am-5pm daily)* with displays about the construction, flora and fauna of the area, and much more. To get here, take bus No 170, 171 or 172 from Centraal Station, or the historic tram from the Haarlemmermeer Station (see the earlier Vondelpark & Surroundings section). Bikes can be rented at the main entrance at Van Nijenrodeweg.

The other main attraction is the **CoBrA Museum** *(☎ 547 50 50,* **W** *www.cobra-muse um.nl, Sandbergplein 1-3; adult/child €5.67/ 1.59; open 11am-5pm Tues-Sun)*, in a creatively designed building just north of the A9 freeway's Amstelveen exit and opposite the Amstelveen bus terminal. The CoBrA artistic movement was formed in the postwar years by artists from Denmark, Belgium and the Netherlands – the name consists of the first letters of their capital cities. Members included Asger Jorn, Corneille, Constant and the great Karel Appel (see Painting in the Facts about Amsterdam chapter). The Stedelijk Museum has a good collection of their work but the CoBrA Museum is the treasure-trove, with paintings, ceramics, statuary, creative typography, the lot. Take bus No 170, 171 or 172 from Centraal Station.

AMSTERDAM NORTH (NOORD) (MAP 1)

In the dim, dark past, the area across the IJ now known as Amsterdam North was marshland with shifting contours. Roman sentries may have stared at it and glimpsed the bar-

barians beyond their empire. Several centuries ago its tip was known as Volewyck, a place where executed criminals were left to be devoured by crows and dogs. Few people actually lived here.

As ships became larger and the sandbanks in the IJ posed more of a problem, engineers built an 80km canal, the Noordhollands Kanaal (North Holland Canal), from Volewyck right up to Den Helder in the northern tip of Holland. It opened in 1824 but by 1876 it was replaced by the more efficient Noordzeekanaal (North Sea Canal) west to IJmuiden. Even so, Amsterdam North wasn't properly colonised until the turn of the 20th century, and the opening of the IJ-Tunnel in 1968 finally established a fixed connection.

The area is predominantly working-class, offering glimpses of authentic Dutch life away from the tourists in the old town, though its character is set to change with large-scale renovation and restructuring over the next decade. If you have time, it's worth spending half a day exploring the older parts of the area on foot or by bicycle.

Take the free pedestrian ferry marked 'Buiksloterwegveer' (between Pier 8 and Pier 9) from behind Centraal Station across the IJ to the Shell Oil installations at Buiksloterweg where you'll disembark next to the **Noordhollands Kanaal**. Climb up onto the first lock, the Willemsluis near the ferry wharf, for the view. Return to the main street and walk north 10 minutes on Van der Pekstraat. Ahead you'll eventually see the massive Golden Tulip Waterfront Hotel, formerly Amsterdam North's general hospital. Today it's used mostly by European tourists on bus tours.

A passageway to the right of the hotel leads into **Mosveld** where a large public market *(open 9am-5pm Tues-Sat)* is held. Market days are the best time to do this walk: you can mingle with local residents and will seldom see any tourists.

To return to central Amsterdam, catch bus No 34 or 35 from the stop next to the large **Egyptian Coptic Church** (the only one in Holland) on Mosplein. These buses go through the IJ-Tunnel straight back to Centraal Station.

If you have a bit more time, take any street east to the Noordhollands Kanaal, which you follow north through **Florapark**. You'll pass a public swimming pool and reach a small bridge which crosses another lock on the canal. The old road on both sides of this bridge is lined with picturesque little Dutch cottages. Don't cross the canal but continue north along its west bank and you'll come to a large windmill, the **Krijtmolen**, originally used to grind chalk, with a children's animal park alongside (free). Just north of here is Amsterdam North's massive public hospital where you can catch bus No 34 back to town. This interesting walk could easily fill a morning or afternoon; by bicycle it would take a couple of leisurely hours.

'GARDEN CITIES' (MAP 1)

The outer suburbs west of Amsterdam – **Geuzenveld**, **Bos en Lommer**, **Slotermeer**, **Osdorp** and **Slotervaart** – were planned in the 1930s as part of the city's grand General Extension Plan.
They were fully established after WWII to meet the continued demand for housing, made ever more acute by the demographic shift away from extended families. These spacious new estates, known as 'garden cities' *(tuinsteden)*, with carefully planned traffic systems, lakes, sporting fields, greenery and abundant natural light, represented the latest thinking in suburban living but seem rather dreary and windswept today.

Similar concepts dominated the massive Bijlmermeer housing project south-east of the city, now simply called the **Bijlmer**. The huge apartment blocks, laid out in a honeycomb pattern around artificial parks, were considered most progressive when the foundations were laid in the mid-1960s. By the time they were finished in the 1970s,

however, most people with a choice in the matter avoided such an environment and the area was doomed to become an instant slum, inhabited by Creole immigrants from the Netherlands Antilles, black immigrants from newly independent Suriname, and anyone else who couldn't afford to live elsewhere.

In 1992 the Bijlmer made world headlines when an El Al freighter jumbo crashed into one of the apartment complexes after take-off from Schiphol, just as residents were settling in to their evening meals. Officially 45 people died in the inferno but the figure was probably higher, despite the subsequent amnesty on illegal immigrants.

The western 'garden cities' as well as the Bijlmer will undergo massive renovation and restructuring over the next 15 years, with the pervasive apartment blocks making way for a blend of medium-density housing estates on a more human scale. In the case of the Bijlmer, building works have already begun and a huge entertainment centre is taking shape, including the Heineken Music Hall and a Pathé super-cinema.

Activities

Soccer, ice skating, cycling, tennis, swimming and sailing are just a few activities that keep the locals fit – and of course jogging, which is popular in the Vondelpark and other parks. The Amsterdamse Bos has several walking and jogging trails for serious exercise. **Het Twiske** (☎ 075-684 43 38), near Landsmeer north of Amsterdam, is another recreational area with nature trails, cycle routes, rentals of water craft, beaches, a children's swimming pool and playground. Take bus No 91 or 92 from Centraal Station.

The whole coast of Holland, from the Hook of Holland right up to Den Helder, is one long beach, backed by often extensive dunes that are ideal for walks. The closest seaside resort is Zandvoort (see the Excursions chapter) which can get packed in summer (forget about parking then – take the train), but more pleasant resorts can be found farther north, such as Castricum

Walking Tours

Amsterdam is tailor-made for walking. You can simply follow your nose or, if a particular area takes your fancy, you could explore it with this book. Or you can follow one or more of the official VVV walks designed by the ANWB (the Dutch automobile association) that are indicated on the maps in the back of this book and on occasional public maps at points en route. They take you through the most interesting parts of the city, though by necessity they do bypass some of the sights (make your own detours). Obviously they can be walked in either direction and you can combine them or jump from one to the other:

Red route – probably gives the best overview of some of the most popular areas. Starts at Centraal Station and goes along Nieuwendijk, the Dam, Kalverstraat, Spui Square (Begijnhof), Leidsestraat, Leidseplein and Museumplein, ending at the Concertgebouw. You could return via the Grey route.

Blue route – a bit of a west-east marathon. Starts at the Westerkerk (Anne Frankhuis) and heads into the city along Raadhuisstraat; passes Dam Square and continues east through the red-light district; on to Jodenbreestraat and the Jewish quarter; up towards the old harbour area north-east of the Plantage and on to the Tropenmuseum.

Green route – shorter alternative to the Blue route. Starts at Centraal Station and follows the Zeedijk to Nieuwmarkt Square (detour for the red-light district), through the Jewish quarter and then the Plantage before ending at the Tropenmuseum. It could be tacked on to the Blue route to make a full day trip.

Grey route – combines the old medieval centre with glimpses of authentic daily life just south of the canal belt; starts at Centraal Station and goes down Damrak and Rokin to Rembrandtplein; along beautiful Reguliersgracht; then past the Heineken Experience to the Albert Cuyp market (multicultural Amsterdam at its best); and on to the Concertgebouw (detour southwards to Harmoniehof for Amsterdam School architecture); you could return via the Red route.

Purple route – starts at either the ship-passenger terminal or Centraal Station and goes past the IJ-Tunnel entrance (NEMO science and technology centre) to Waterlooplein; then on to Rembrandtplein and Muntplein, and through Nieuwe Spiegelstraat (antiques) to Leidseplein; return via the Brown route or latch on to the Red route.

Brown route – goes past and through the Jordaan area (make your own detours), starting at Centraal Station and ending at Leidseplein.

See also the Eastern Harbour Cycling Tour in the Eastern Harbour District section earlier in this chapter, which you could do as a walking tour if you prefer. It gives a good idea of modern residential architecture in Amsterdam.

north of IJmuiden, or Egmond and Bergen a bit farther north near Alkmaar.

For information about sport and leisure activities and venues, visit the **city hall information centre** (☎ 624 11 11, Amstel 1) in the arcade between the Stopera and the city hall, or ring **Sportservice Amsterdam** (☎ 552 24 90). Local community centres (in the phone book under *Buurtcentrum*) organise fitness courses.

See Spectator Sports in the Entertainment chapter for details about soccer, field hockey or the Dutch sport of korfball.

FITNESS CENTRES

These centres are listed in the pink pages of the phone book under *Fitnesscentra*.

To pump iron, head for **Barry's Fitness Centre** (☎ 626 10 36, Lijnbaansgracht 350; day pass €9.07, month pass €56.71), though the loud disco music might not be to everyone's taste.

For aerobics and feel-good activities, including sauna, massage, physiotherapy and dietary advice, try **The Garden Gym** (☎ 626 87 72, Jodenbreestraat 158; day pass €8.16-11.34, month pass €47.64-56.71).

Saunas

Saunas are mixed and there's no prudish swimsuit nonsense, though they do cater for people who have a problem with this – ask.

Sauna Deco (Map 2) (☎ *623 82 15, Herengracht 115; admission 11am-2pm Mon-Fri/all other times €10.40/13.61; open 11am-11pm Mon-Sat, 1pm-6pm Sun)* is a respectable, elegant sauna with good facilities including a snack bar. The building itself is an early creation of the architect HP Berlage and its Art Deco furnishings used to grace a Parisian department store. You can also have massages and beauty therapies.

Eastern Bath House/Hammam (☎ *681 48 18, Zaanstraat 88; admission €10.20; open noon-10pm Tues-Fri, noon-8pm Sat & Sun)*, in the north-west beyond the Haarlemmerpoort, is an Eastern-style place for women only, offering a range of spa treatments.

Gay Saunas In a beautiful 18th-century canal house, **Mandate (Map 4)** (☎ *625 41 00, Prinsengracht 715; open 11am-10pm Mon-Fri, noon-6pm Sat, 2pm-6pm Sun)* is a very modern, gay-only gym and sauna. It is set up for real workouts, rather than cruising. **Thermos Day Sauna (Map 4)** (☎ *623 91 58, Raamstraat 33; admission €14.33; open noon-11pm Mon-Fri, noon-10pm Sat, 11am-10pm Sun)* is a large, popular place for sexual contacts, with porn movies and private (or not so private) darkrooms and a restaurant. The **Thermos Night Sauna (Map 4)** (☎ *623 49 36, Kerkstraat 58-60; admission €14.33; open 11pm-8am Sun-Fri, 11pm-10am Sat)* is similar to the day sauna except there's no restaurant.

SWIMMING POOLS

There are indoor pools and summer outdoor pools. It's always best to ring ahead to ensure the pool is open to the general public (English is almost always spoken) because there are often restricted sessions – nude, Muslim, children, women, seniors, clubs, lap swimming etc. Of course that might just be what you're after, but schedules for these sorts of sessions change constantly.

The **Bijlmersportcentrum** (☎ *697 25 01, Bijlmerpark 76, Bijlmer; adult/child €3.17-4.53/2.27; open 10am-5.30 daily; closed public holidays)* is a sports centre with indoor and outdoor pools, a small kids' pool and snack bars.

Brediusbad (Map 1) (☎ *684 71 72, Spaarndammerdijk 306; admission €1.13; open 10am-5.30pm daily May-Sept)* is an outdoor pool, north-west of the city centre.

East of the city centre, **Flevoparkbad (Map 6)** (☎ *692 50 30, Zeeburgerdijk 630; admission €2.27; open 10am-5.30pm daily May-Sept)* is an outdoor pool only.

Floraparkbad (Map 1) (☎ *632 90 30, Sneeuwbalweg 5, Amsterdam North; adult/child €2.94/2.49; open 10am-5.30pm daily May-Sept)* has indoor and outdoor pools, a kids' play area and a good sunbathing section.

West of the city centre, **Jan van Galenbad (Map 1)** (☎ *612 80 01, Jan van Galenstraat 315; adult/child €2.27/2.04, child under 3yrs free; open 10am-5.30pm daily mid-May–mid-Sept)* has an outdoor pool.

Marnixbad (Map 3) (☎ *625 48 43, Marnixplein 5-9; adult/child €2.15/1.81; open 7am-10.30pm daily Sept-June)*, at the western end of Westerstraat, has an indoor pool.

De Mirandabad (Map 1) (☎ *646 25 22, De Mirandalaan 9; adult or child €2.95, child under 3yrs free; open 9am-9pm daily May-Sept)* is a tropical 'aquatic centre', complete with beach and wave machine and indoor and outdoor pools, south of the city centre. It also has squash courts.

Sloterparkbad (Map 1) (☎ *506 35 06, Slotermeerlaan 2; adult or child €3.17, child under 2yrs free; open noon-7pm Mon, 10am-10pm Tues & Wed, 10am-7pm Thur & Fri, 10am-5.30pm Sat & Sun)* has indoor and outdoor pools, in an attractive recreational area with a yacht harbour in the western suburbs next to the terminus of tram No 14. In summer, on cold, rainy days the indoor pool will be open; the outdoor pools can get overcrowded but there's a less frequented nudist island reached by walking straight back past the pools and across a causeway.

An old indoor pool (1912) that has just been extensively restored to its original status, **Zuiderbad (Map 4)** (☎ *678 13 90, Hobbemastraat 26; adult/child/pensioner €2.50/2.27/1.59; open 7am-6pm Mon,*

7am-10pm Tue, Wed & Fri, 7am-6pm Thur, 8am-3.30pm Sat, 10am-3.30pm Sun, only for schools 9am-noon & 1pm-2.30pm Tue & Thur, special groups 9am-noon Wed), behind the Rijksmuseum, is unique and full of character.

SAILING

The Dutch are avid sailors – windsurfing is a national sport, but so is yachting which is curbed only by its expense (the word 'yacht', after all, comes from the Dutch *jachtschip*, 'chase ship'). This includes modern open boats and yachts but also the more traditional kind, which are revered here like nowhere else. On weekends a fleet of restored flat-bottomed boats, called the 'brown fleet' because of their (reddish) brown sails, crisscross the watery expanse of the IJsselmeer. Some are privately owned but many are rented, and sailing one is an unforgettable experience.

The cheapest options are *botters*, former fishing boats with long, narrow leeboards and sleeping space (usually for around eight people) below deck. Larger groups could rent a converted freight barge known as a *tjalk*, originally a Frisian design with jib and spritsail rig though modern designs are made of steel and have diesel motors. Other vessels include anything from ancient pilot boats to massive clippers.

Costs are quite reasonable if you can muster a group of fellow enthusiasts. Some places only rent boats for day trips but it's much more fun to go for the full weekend experience. The usual arrangement is that you arrive at the boat Friday at 8pm, sleep on board, sail out early the next morning, and visit several places around the IJsselmeer before returning on Sunday between 4pm and 6pm. Food is not included in the packages, nor is cancellation insurance (trips are cancelled if wind is stronger than 7 Beaufort), but you do get a skipper.

Contact the following companies (all outside Amsterdam; see the map in the Excursions chapter to locate the towns) to find the deal that suits you best, and bear in mind that everything is negotiable:

Hollands Glorie *(☎ 0294-27 15 61, fax 26 29 43, Ossenmarkt 6, Muiden)* has tjalks

and clippers at €567/907/1588-3857 per day/weekend/week, minimum of 15 people, with a 10% discount in March, April, October and November.

Holland Zeilcharters *(☎ 0299-65 23 51, fax 65 36 18, Monnickendam)* offers botters for €340/726 per day/weekend. Other options like modern yachts are €1815 per week.

Muiden Jacht Charter *(☎ 0294-26 14 13, fax 26 10 04, Naarderstraat 10, Muiden)* has tjalks for €613 to €760 per day, maximum of 23 people. Clippers per day cost €613 to €1361, maximum of 30 people.

Zeilcharter Volendam *(☎ 0299-36 97 40, fax 36 34 42, Enkhuizerzand 21, Volendam)* hires botters at €340 to €431 per day, maximum of 16 people. Yachts per day/weekend/week are €465/1134/2246, maximum of 12 people.

ICE SKATING

When the canals freeze over in winter (which doesn't happen often enough) everyone goes for a skate. Lakes and waterways in the countryside also fill up with colourfully clad skaters making trips tens of kilometres long. It's a wonderful experience, though painful on the ankles and butt if you're learning. Be aware that people drown under ice every year. Don't take to a patch of ice unless you see large groups of people, and be very careful at the edges and under bridges (such areas often don't freeze properly).

You can only rent skates at a skating rink. A pair of simple hockey skates costs upwards of about €50 at a department store (sports shops might have a wider selection but tend to be more expensive). Hockey skates are probably the best choice for learners: figure skates (with short, curved blades) are difficult to master, and speed skates (with long, flat blades) put a lot of strain on the ankles – but are definitely the go if you want to make serious trips. Check for second-hand skates on notice boards at supermarkets or at the Centrale Bibliotheek *(Central Library; ☎ 523 09 00, Prinsengracht 587)*. Old wood-framed skates that you tie under your shoes can be picked up cheaply at antique and bric-a-brac shops. Don't dismiss them: they're among the fastest skates around if they're freshly sharpened, and make great souvenirs.

The **Jaap Edenbaan (Map 1)** (☎ 694 9652, Radioweg 64; tram: No 9; adult/child €4.53/2.27; call for opening hours) in the eastern suburb of Watergraafsmeer has an indoor and outdoor rink.

In winter you can also skate on the pond on **Museumplein** for €2.20.

TENNIS & SQUASH

The huge **Borchland Sportcentrum** (☎ 563 33 33, Borchlandweg 8-12; metro: Duivendrecht or Strandvliet; open 8am-midnight daily), next to the Arena stadium in the Bijlmer (Ouderkerk aan de Amstel exit off A2/ E35 freeway towards Utrecht), has tennis, squash and badminton courts, bowling alleys and other facilities including a restaurant.

Tenniscentrum Amstelpark (☎ 301 07 00, Karel Lotsylaan 8; court hire per hour €18.14) has 42 open and covered courts and runs the country's biggest tennis school. It's conveniently close to the World Trade Center and RAI exhibition buildings.

Squash City (Map 1) (☎ 626 78 83, Ketelmakerstraat 6; court hire day/evening €10.66/12.93, with gym & sauna €12.07/ 16.78; open 8.45am-11pm Mon-Fri, 8.45am-8pm Sat & Sun) is at the railway line at Bickerseiland, west of Centraal Station.

More courts are listed under Tennisbanen and Squashbanen in the pink pages of the phone book.

CHESS

The **Max Euwe Centrum (Map 8)** (☎ 625 70 17, Max Euweplein 30A1; admission free; open 10.30am-4pm Tues-Fri & 1st Sat of month), off Leidseplein, has a permanent exhibition devoted to the history of chess and to the country's one and only world chess champion, for whom the centre is named. You can play against live or digital opponents. At other times, chess enthusiasts can be found in **Schaakcafé 't Hok** (☎ 624 31 33, Lange Leidsedwarsstraat 134).

GOLF

The main problem with golf in this country is lack of space and the consequent lack of affordable golf courses. The sport was long derided as something for the elite but has become increasingly popular in recent years.

Golfcenter Amstelborgh (☎ 563 33 33, Borchlandweg 6; round €9.07-20.40, club rental per half-set €6.80; open 8am-midnight daily) adjoining the Borchland Sportcentrum (see the earlier Tennis & Squash section) has nine holes.

Openbare Golfbaan Sloten (☎ 614 24 02, Sloterweg 1045; bus: No 142; round €10.20-12.93, club rental per half-set €5.67; open 8.30am-8pm Mon-Fri, 8.30am-6pm Sat & Sun May-Aug; 8.30am-8pm Mon-Fri Sept-Apr), on the south-west side of town, also has nine holes and you can play as many rounds as you like.

Look under Golfbanen in the pink pages of the phone book for several other options.

BUNGY JUMPING

Bungy Jump Holland (Map 1) (☎ 419 60 05, Westerdoksdijk 44; 1st jump/2nd jump/ 10 jumps €45.37/34.02/226.86; open noon-8pm Tues-Sun May & Oct, noon-8pm Fri-Tues June, noon-9pm daily July-Sept), at the waterfront half a kilometre west of Centraal Station, offers jumps from a crane suspended 75m above the water. If you can keep your nerves under control you'll never forget the view.

Courses

The Foreign Student Service is a support agency for foreign students that supplies information about study programs and intensive language courses. For more details about this organisation, or about study at academic level, see Universities in the Facts for the Visitor chapter.

LANGUAGE COURSES

Dutch is a close relative of English but that doesn't make it easy to learn. Regular courses take months and intensive courses last several weeks. Plan ahead and make inquiries well in advance.

The **Volksuniversiteit Amsterdam** (☎ 626 16 26, Rapenburgerstraat 73, 1011 VK

Amsterdam; *www.volksuniversiteitamst erdam.nl (Dutch); courses €102-318)* offers a range of day and evening courses that are well regarded and don't cost a fortune. The **Tropeninstituut** *(Royal Institute for the Tropics; Language Training department ☎ 568 85 59,* *www.kit.nl, Postbus 95001, 1090 HA Amsterdam; courses €206-1815)* has intensive training courses with a large component of 'cultural training', aimed specifically at foreigners moving to the Netherlands. They're fairly expensive but very effective. The **British Language Training Centre** *(☎ 622 36 34, Nieuwezijds Voorburgwal 328E, 1012 RW Amsterdam; courses €420-549)* is also expensive and has a good reputation.

OTHER COURSES

The above-mentioned **Volksuniversiteit** offers a range of courses, some in English.

The **Amsterdam Summer University** *(☎ 620 02 25,* *www.amsu.edu, Keizersgracht 324, 1016 EZ Amsterdam)* conducts all its courses and workshops in English. Subjects focus on arts and sciences, as befits the traditions of the Felix Meritis building that houses it.

Also inquire at museums: the **Stedelijk Museum** *(☎ 573 29 11,* *www.stedelijk.nl)*, for instance, conducts courses in art history.

The **city hall information centre** *(☎ 624 11 11, Amstel 1)*, in the arcade between the Stopera and the city hall, at the eastern end, has lots of information about informal courses and workshops (cooking, pottery, needlework, car repairs, stamp-collecting – you name it). Most or all are in Dutch but that isn't always an insurmountable problem. To find out about similar activities in your neighbourhood, contact the nearest community centre listed under *Buurtcentrum* in the phone book.

Places to Stay

Amsterdam is one of Europe's favourite short-break holiday destinations. But what price popularity? Small hotel rooms at over-inflated prices, that's what. At any given time (but especially over summer) the city is 2000 to 5000 hotel beds short and as a consequence even the most threadbare, squishy rooms command big prices. We've been honest about the choices available: if you want a nice, big, clean hotel room head to Rotterdam – or have buckets of euros on hand.

Be sure to book ahead: even camping grounds can be filled to capacity in summer. It's worth paying a bit extra for something reasonably central so you can enjoy the nightlife without having to rely on night buses or the most expensive taxis in Europe. This doesn't mean having to stay within the canal belt: accommodation in the Museum Quarter or around the Vondelpark, for instance, is still relatively close to the lively Leidseplein area.

Travellers arriving at Centraal Station may be accosted by touts offering accommodation. Some readers have reported good results this way, others have been ripped off. Maintain a healthy suspicion; if you have any doubts, walk away and use a reputable booking agent – see 'Hotels – Bookings' later in this chapter.

Theft isn't uncommon at camping grounds or in dormitories (bring your own padlock for the locker) but is rare in 'normal' hotel rooms. It's always wise to deposit valuables for safe keeping at the reception desk. Some hotels have coin-operated safety deposit boxes in the rooms (€0.45 per usage).

Ask about parking if travelling by car. In almost all cases parking is a major problem and the most you'll get is a (payable) parking permit out on the street – with all the attendant headaches and security risks – or a referral to the nearest parking garage (up to €35 a day) which may be a fair distance away. The top-end hotels have their own expensive parking arrangements but prefer to be warned in advance.

CAMPING GROUNDS

There are several camping grounds in and around Amsterdam, but the four listed here are the most popular and accessible. The Vliegenbos and Zeeburg sites attract crowds of young people, while the other two are more suited to older campers and families. Most sites also have cabins with different bed configurations, making them ideal for families.

Gaaspercamping (☎ 696 73 26, fax 696 93 69, Loosdrechtdreef 7, Gaasperdam) **Map 1** Tent sites €3.95-4.85, plus per person/vehicle €3.60/3.40. Open mid-Mar–Dec. Backpackers love this camp site in the south-eastern suburbs. It's in a large park-cum-recreational area with a café, restaurant, bar, barbecue facilities, supermarket, laundry and, wait for it, a lake with a beach for swimming and scuba diving. From Centraal Station, take Metro No 53 to Gaasperplas or night bus No 75.

Camping Het Amsterdamse Bos (☎ 641 68 68, fax 640 23 78, ⓔ msprado@wxs.nl, Kleine Noorddijk 1, Aalsmeer) **Map 1** Tent sites €2.70, plus per person/vehicle €4.10/2.25; cabins per double/quad €18.15/34. Open Apr-Oct. The downside: this camp site is a long way south-west of town and the noise from nearby Schiphol airport can be aggravating. The upside: wonderful recreational facilities in the Amsterdamse Bos. Go for a bike or horse ride, swim or just hang out at the site's pleasant bar and restaurant. The cabins have electricity but no bed linen. Take bus No 171 from Centraal Station.

Camping Vliegenbos (☎ 636 88 55, fax 632 27 23, Meeuwenlaan 138) **Map 1** Tent sites per person/vehicle €6.90/7.05, 4-person cabin €43.10. Open Apr-Sept. Convenient for people without a car, Vliegenbos, in Amsterdam North, is just a few minutes' bus ride from the city centre. There's a shop, restaurant, laundry, hot showers, cabins (with electricity, no bed linen) and 25 hectares of woodland to explore by bike.

Take bus No 32 or night bus No 72 from Centraal Station.

Camping Zeeburg (☎ 694 44 30, fax 694 62 38, W www.campingzeeburg.nl, Zuider IJdijk 20) **Map 1** Tent sites €2.95, plus per person/vehicle €3.60/3.40; cabins €29.50-88.45. Open Mar-Dec. Sleep 2m below sea level at Zeeburg. The grounds are on an artificial island east of the city and close to the Flevopark which has walking trails, a swimming pool and sporting facilities. Zeeburg has an animal farm (great for kids), a relaxed bar-restaurant, laundry, supermarket and bike-rental shop. Showers cost €0.70 and the log cabins, with electricity and bed linen, sleep up to six people. From Centraal Station, take bus No 22; from Amstelstation, bus No 37; from Dam Square, tram No 14.

HOSTELS
Official Youth Hostels
The Netherlands Youth Hostel Association (NJHC; W www.njhc.org) uses the Hostelling International (HI) logo for the benefit of foreigners but has kept the 'youth hostel' name. The head office (☎ 010-264 60 64, fax 264 60 61) is in Rotterdam but Amsterdam's Vondelpark hostel is the local port of call for hostel guides or reservations.

A youth hostel card (or rather, an International Guest Card) costs €13.60 at the hostels; alternatively, nonmembers pay an extra €3 a night for a bed and after six nights they're a member. HI or NJHC members can get discounts on international travel (eg, 10% discount on Eurolines tickets) and pay less commission on money exchange at the GWK offices. Members and nonmembers have the same rights at the hostels and there are no age limits.

Apart from the usual dormitories there are rooms for two, four, six and eight people. Be sure to book well ahead, especially in busy periods (spring, summer and autumn holidays).

Prices for the three hostels here include breakfast (usually buffet) and clean bed linen upon arrival.

City Hostel Vondelpark (☎/fax 589 89 55, Zandpad 5) **Map 4** Beds in 4-bed/6-bed/larger dorm €23.60/19.50/17.70, twin rooms €70.30. A blink away from the Vondelpark, this bustling, 475-bed hostel attracts over 300,000 guests a year – no wonder the lobby feels like a mini United Nations. All bedrooms are nonsmoking, have lockers, a shower, toilet and well-spaced bunks. There are lifts, a café, two restaurants, Internet and bike-hire facilities. There's no curfew but the no-visitors-at-night, no-drugs policy is strictly enforced. From March to October and during public holidays the maximum stay is three nights.

Stadsdoelen Youth Hostel (☎ 624 68 32, fax 639 10 35, Kloveniersburgwal 97) **Map 2** Dorm beds €16.10. Efficient Stadsdoelen is always bustling with backpackers and we can understand why. The staff are friendly and the eight, nonsmoking, ultra-clean rooms (each with 20 beds and free lockers) offer a modicum of privacy. There's a mix of single-sex and co-ed dorms and bathrooms, a big TV room, a bar, pool table, laundry, Internet facilities and a pretty lenient 2am curfew.

Haarlem Youth Hostel (☎ 023-537 37 93, fax 537 11 76, Jan Gijzenpad 3) Dorm beds €18.50. This pleasant, 31-room hostel in Haarlem, west of Amsterdam, appeals to family groups (they just love that 'silence after 10pm' rule). All rooms have a shower and toilet. There's a bar, TV room, video games and no curfew. It's a 10-minute walk from Santpoort Zuid train station (trains to/from Amsterdam take 15 minutes) or you can take bus No 2 to/from Haarlem Centraal.

Other Hostels
The following 'unofficial' hostels may be reluctant to take bookings over the phone and seem to prefer walk-in trade. Try getting there by 10am and you should stand a reasonable chance. Apart from these hostels, also check the Budget and Lower Middle hotels on the following pages: many have dorm beds at similar prices, in a less 'institutional' environment. Unless stated, prices at these hostels include breakfast and clean bed linen on check-in.

Anna Youth Hostel (☎ 620 11 55, Spuistraat 6) **Map 2** Dorm beds €15.90. Funky Anna's, with two co-ed rooms (20 beds each), has an inviting feel and caring proprietor. Unlike most hostels there's a quiet, respectful vibe and a wonderful, cheery, modern-Middle Eastern interior; it's a real winner. Rates include clean bed linen, towels and safety deposit box but no breakfast.

Bob's Youth Hostel (☎ *623 00 63, fax 675 64 46, Nieuwezijds Voorburgwal 92)* **Map 2** Dorm beds €15.90. Basic and tattered Bob's – just four blocks from Centraal Station – is a convenient place to crash if you roll into Amsterdam exhausted. Gaggles of backpackers appreciate the very relaxed policy on dope smoking but not the 3am curfew. Rates are the same for a bed in a six, eight or 18-bed dorm.

Christian Youth Hostel 'The Shelter City' (☎ *625 32 30, fax 623 22 82,* W *www .shelter.nl, Barndesteeg 21)* **Map 2** Dorm beds €12.70. The price is right at this rambling hostel, but *only* if you can handle Christian rock music piped through the PA system and enormous 'Jesus loves you' signs everywhere. The pros of staying here include large, airy, single-sex dorms (and bathrooms), filling breakfasts, free Internet facilities, a quiet garden courtyard, eternal salvation and a tough no-drugs or alcohol policy. The cons include a midnight curfew (1am Friday and Saturday), daily (non-obligatory) bible discussions – and the tough no-drugs or alcohol policy.

Christian Youth Hostel 'The Shelter Jordan' (☎ *624 47 17, fax 627 61 37,* W *www .shelter.nl, Bloemstraat 179)* **Map 3** Dorm beds €13.60. OK, we'll put up with the 'no-everything' (smokin', drinkin', splifrin') policy and 2am curfew at this small hostel because it's such a gem. Single-sex dorms are quiet and clean, breakfasts – especially the fluffy pancakes – are beaut and the garden patio is a relaxing retreat.

Flying Pig Downtown Hostel (☎ *420 68 22, fax 421 08 02,* W *www.flyingpig.nl, Nieuwendijk 100)* **Map 2** Dorm beds €16.10-20.85. Hang out with hundreds of dope-smoking, young backpackers at this very relaxed, very central, 30-room hostel. It could be cleaner, but no-one seems to mind, especially when there's so much fun to be had in the throbbing lobby bar (live DJs

Thursday and Friday), chilled-out, cushion-lined basement lounge and around that extra-large pool table.

Flying Pig Palace Hostel (☎ *400 41 87, fax 421 08 02,* W *www.flyingpig.nl, Vossiusstraat 46)* **Map 4** Dorm beds €16.10-19.75. The Palace has definitely seen better days. Most rooms are dark and small, but you may score an airy one with a balcony overlooking the Vondelpark. There are Internet and kitchen facilities, a heavy diet of Pearl Jam and Bob Marley on the sound system, and packs of relaxed smokers getting all cosy in the basement café.

HOTELS
Ratings & Facilities
The rating system for hotels goes up to five stars; accommodation that rates less than one star can call itself a pension or guesthouse but not a hotel. The ratings are not very helpful because they have more to do with the number of rooms and the amenities (lifts, phones in rooms, minibar etc) than with the actual quality of the rooms.

Many hotels (like many of the houses) have steep and narrow stairs but no lifts (elevators), which make them inaccessible for people with mobility problems. Check when you make inquiries. Of course, the top-end hotels have lifts, and some mid-range ones too.

Rooms usually come with TV, though in the cheaper places you might have to feed coins into a timer to help pay for the cable subscription. Then again, there might be no in-room TV even in some expensive hotels, so if this means a lot to you, check when making inquiries.

Hotels tend to be small – any hotel with more than 20 rooms is 'large'. Rooms with private showers usually include a toilet but not always, so ask when booking. If a room has a shower and toilet we've used the term 'private facilities'; if they're in the corridor we've used 'shared facilities'.

Hotel rooms in the top price bracket have their own bathrooms with real baths; cheaper hotels tend to have showers but might have a few rooms with baths for the same price – ask.

Bookings

The VVV offices in front of and inside CS, or the GWK (money-exchange office) inside, have hotel-booking services that can save you a lot of hunting around during busy periods. The VVV offices charge €11.35 commission per booking; the GWK office charges €4.54 commission per person with a maximum of €9.08. The Netherlands Reservation Centre (☎ 070-419 55 19, fax 419 55 44, W www.hotelres.nl, Postbus 404, 2260 AK Leidschendam) accepts bookings from abroad for the more upmarket hotels. Some readers have also recommended W www.amsterdam-hotels-guide.com, which lists over 250 hotels ranging from one to five stars and has links to the hotels.

Hotels tend to charge a bit more if you come to them through these services; often you can save money by booking directly with the hotel. Many of them won't accept credit card details over the phone (if they accept cards at all – check) and may insist on a deposit by cheque or money order before they'll confirm the booking.

When booking for two people, make it clear whether you want a twin (two single beds) or double (a bed for two). It should make no difference to the price, but the wrong bed configuration could be impossible to fix on the spot if the hotel is fully booked.

Prices

Generally you get what you pay for and you *really* don't get much. Hotels in the lowest price bracket (below €60 for a double) can be run-down, poorly maintained and invariably seem to suffer from mouldy smells due to the damp climate and the Dutch aversion to decent ventilation. Some hotels throw in breakfast – usually a buffet with cold-cuts, cheese, bread, spreads and hot drinks. Take advantage of it because few food establishments open earlier than 9am.

Single rooms cost about two-thirds of the rates quoted here for doubles; add a third to a half for triples. Hotels that accept children (many don't) often have special rates for families. Prices at many hotels drop a bit in the low season (roughly October to April excluding Christmas/New Year and Easter)

but it's always worth asking for 'special' rates, especially if you're staying a few nights. Top-end hotels, on the other hand, often rely on business travellers and tend to be markedly cheaper in the summer months and on weekends.

Most of the quoted rates include a 5% city hotel tax; at the most expensive hotels, however, this is added separately to the bill.

Hotels – Budget (Doubles under €60)

These places are popular with backpackers, and some have lounges filled with happy smokers who would be in jail if this weren't Amsterdam. Some hotels, however, are very strict about this sort of thing and lighting a joint could lead to instant expulsion, so check first.

Budget hotels often won't take bookings over the phone. Start door-knocking at 10am, or book into whichever place will have you and find something better at your leisure.

Inside the Canal Belt *Hotel BA* *(☎ 638 71 19, fax 638 88 03, e india@cistron.nl, Martelaarsgracht 18)* **Map 2** Dorm beds €20.40. BA is more hostel than hotel, with gangs of loud, brash backpackers, way-too-casual staff and bare-as-bones rooms. The price includes buffet breakfast, lockers and bed linen, but to be honest, you can do much better if you look around.

Hotel Beursstraat *(☎ 626 37 01, fax 690 90 12, Beursstraat 7)* **Map 2** Doubles with shared/private facilities €54.45/68.05. The rooms here have no phone or TV and there's no breakfast included, so why stay? Two good reasons: everything is extremely clean and well kept (a rarity in the red-light district) and there are no bad smells or drunken lager louts in the corridor (much, much rarer).

Hotel Brian *(☎ 624 46 61, fax 625 39 58, Singel 69)* **Map 2** Doubles with shared facilities €45.35. This ardently shabby and relaxed joint was recently renovated, but to be honest it's hard to tell. Anyway, it's churlish to quibble when the rates include a good breakfast buffet, advice from fun, knowledgeable staff, and the odd chance of scoring a room with skylights and canal views.

Frisco Inn *(☎ 620 16 10,* W *www.friscoho tel-amsterdam.com, Beursstraat 5)* **Map 2** Doubles with shared or private facilities €54.45. It's the luck of the draw at this lively, Irish-staffed hotel. You may snap up a largish room with street views and its own shower and toilet or have to settle for a small, smoky one with shared facilities. A four-leaf clover might help. The loud bar downstairs has satellite TV, Guinness and big breakfasts.

Hotel Groenendael *(☎/fax 624 48 22, Nieuwendijk 15)* **Map 2** Doubles with private facilities €52.15. Groenendael's small rooms are pretty clean, the clientele not too wild and the big breakfast sufficient for a day of sightseeing. It's close to Centraal Station and is one of the better-kept places in this bargain-basement category.

Hotel Hans Brinker *(☎ 622 06 87, fax 638 20 60,* W *www.hans-brinker.com, Kerkstraat 136)* **Map 4** Dorm beds €20.40, twins/triples/quads per person €34.50/29.50/23.80. A lobby that's always in a state of mayhem, spartan rooms that have all the ambience of a public hospital – and 538 beds almost always filled to capacity. Hans Brinker's crazy, frat-house feel is best evidenced in its bustling corridors and barn-like bar filled with boisterous backpackers. Rates include breakfast and bed linen.

Hotel Hortus *(☎ 625 99 96, fax 625 39 58,* W *www.hotelhortus.com, Plantage Parklaan 8)* **Map 5** Doubles with shared or private facilities €45.35. Facing the Botanical Garden, this recently renovated, comfy, 20-room hotel has small doubles with or without showers (luck of the draw). It's run by the same crew as hotels Brian and Liberty, so it's no surprise that the lounge is chock-full of young, happy stoners transfixed by the large-screen TV. Rates include a cooked breakfast.

Liberty Hotel *(☎ 620 73 07, Singel 5)* **Map 2** Doubles with shared facilities €45.35. Feel like a wake-up bong with your cornflakes? Grungy Liberty's the place for you, then. The hotel attracts sweet, dazed young things suffering attacks of the munchies and discussing their favourite coffeeshops. Spotless, big rooms are the last thing on their minds. A good thing too, really, because they won't find them here.

Hotel Pax *(☎ 624 97 35, Raadhuisstraat 37)* **Map 4** Doubles with shared facilities €54.45-63.50. Our favourite budget choice in hotel-lined Raadhuisstraat – run by two friendly, funky brothers – has a real artsy-student vibe. All eight rooms have a TV and each is individually decorated. The larger, airier rooms face the busy street with noisy trams, so bring some earplugs. Rates include breakfast.

Ramenas Hotel *(☎ 624 60 30, fax 420 22 61,* W *www.amsterdamhotels.com, Haarlemmerdijk 61)* **Map 3** Doubles with shared/private facilities €54.45/68.05. Ramenas, on increasingly hip Haarlemmerdijk, has been operating for over a hundred years, so it knows what it's doing. And it does it well. The 11 rooms – so sparsely decorated they make monasteries look ostentatious – are extra-big and scrupulously clean. Staff serve up friendly advice and satisfying Dutch breakfasts (included).

Outside the Canal Belt *Hotel Bema* *(☎ 679 13 96, fax 662 36 88,* W *www.bemaho tel.com, Concertgebouwplein 19B)* **Map 4** Doubles with shared/private facilities €56.70/65.80. This seven-room hotel in a higgledy-piggledy mansion house has a studiously bohemian feel. Expect extra-big doubles and breakfast in bed but no phone or TV in the room.

Hotels – Lower Middle (Doubles €60 to €90)

Hotels in this price range are pleasant enough for most people, though not all rooms will be worth the money compared with some of the better rooms in the previous category. Some come with breakfast, and have phones and TV, others don't – inquire when booking.

Inside the Canal Belt *Hotel de Admiraal* *(☎ 626 21 50, fax 623 46 25, Herengracht 563)* **Map 4** Doubles with shared/private facilities €61.25/77.15. Near bustling Rembrandtplein, nine-room Admiraal has a sweet, homely feel. The clean and bright canalside rooms (all with safes and TV, no phone) are furnished in an unpretentious, mix'n'match fashion. Ask to see the large 'family room' and be sure to take in the mammoth, Moroccan-style lamp in the breakfast room. Breakfast is €4.53 per person.

Hotel Adolesce (☎ 626 39 59, fax 627 42 49, Nieuwe Keizersgracht 26) **Map 4** Doubles with shared/private facilities €63.50/ 81.65. Enjoy breakfast on the sunny patio at this large, neat hotel, in a quiet location just off the Amstel. You could ask for a room at the front overlooking the canal but one of the rooms behind the patio would be just as pleasant. Rates include breakfast.

Hotel Fantasia (☎ 623 82 59, fax 622 39 13, Nieuwe Keizersgracht 16) **Map 4** Doubles with private facilities & breakfast €79.40. If Hotel Adolesce, five houses down the road, is full, try here.

Hotel Agora (☎ 627 22 00, fax 627 22 02, W www.hotelagora.nl, Singel 462) **Map 2** Doubles with shared/private facilities €74.85/107. Well-worn Agora really needs to update that 1980s, salmon-pink interior. If you can handle the colour scheme you may dig the large, five-person room (€35.40 per person) with canal views. Rates include breakfast and all rooms have phone and TV.

Amstel Botel (☎ 626 42 47, fax 639 19 52, W www.amstelbotel.com, Oosterdokskade 2-4) **Map 6** Doubles with private facilities & land/water view €70/80. This floating hotel is packed with dazed, Europe-in-four-days bus groups and packs of Brit boys celebrating bucks nights. Ambience-free rooms – the size of an airline toilet – have TV and phone; breakfast is €7 per person.

City Hotel (☎ 627 23 23, fax 330 93 23, W www.city-hotel.nl, Utrechtsestraat 2) **Map 4** Doubles with shared/private facilities €74.85/88.45. City Hotel, above the Old Bell pub, is a fab choice. It's clean, neat, well run and good value. All rooms, decorated with crisp blue and white bed linen, come with TV (no phone). We really like the airy, six-bed room (€40.85 per person) with skylights and curved metal girders overlooking Rembrandtplein. Rates include a buffet breakfast.

Hotel Clemens (☎ 624 60 89, fax 626 96 58, W www.clemenshotel.nl, Raadhuisstraat 39) **Map 3** Doubles with shared facilities €50-66, with private facilities €82-113. Stylish, steep-staired Clemens gears itself to all budgets. Take your pick of the chic, themed rooms (one with a sexy, decadent red-gold interior, another with delicate French antiques) all with TV, phone, safe, fridge and breakfast. The cute, closet-sized budget room has a private balcony and a beautiful glass ceiling.

Hotel Continental (☎ 622 33 63, fax 626 51 57, Damrak 40-41) **Map 2** Doubles with private facilities €68.05. Smack-bang in the centre of all things fun and bustling, this 20-room hotel offers very small, clean, bright rooms with TV and phone. A continental breakfast (included) in the pleasant breakfast room overlooking Damrak is a nice way to start the day.

Euphemia Hotel (☎/fax 622 90 45, W www.euphemiahotel.com, Fokke Simonszstraat 1) **Map 4** Doubles with private facilities €63.50-90.75. Euphemia's institutional layout certainly falls short of glamorous, but the rooms are neat and many are quite large. Other pluses? It's gay-friendly, has Internet facilities and a very sharp, very funny manager, though not everyone will appreciate his frankness. Buffet breakfast is €4.08 per person. Book over the Web and you'll get a 10% discount on the first night's stay.

Hemp Hotel (☎ 625 44 25, fax 471 52 42, W www.hemp-hotel.com, Frederiksplein 15) **Map 4** Doubles with shared/private facilities €63.50/65.80. Proof positive that Amsterdam is the capital of the northern 'hempisphere'. At this chilled-out hotel, hemp flour rolls (THC-free) are served with your (included) breakfast, the bar sells 11 hemp beers, and all five colourful and individually decorated rooms exude a 'just-back-from-Goa' vibe. Dope smokers apply now.

Hotel Hoksbergen (☎ 626 60 43, fax 638 34 79, W www.hotelhoksbergen.nl, Singel 301) **Map 2** Doubles with private facilities €86.20, apartments €136. You sure can't beat Hoksbergen's fantastic canalside location, but be warned: even sardines would have trouble squishing into the microscopically small rooms (with TV, phone and breakfast). If you get claustrophobic, the six-bed, self-contained apartments may be a better option.

International Budget Hotel (☎ 624 27 84, *fax 626 18 39,* **e** *ibh@budgethotl.a2000.nl, Leidsegracht 76)* **Map 4** Beds in 4-bed dorm €22.70, doubles with shared or private facilities €72.60. Reasons to stay: nice canal-side location; really close to nightlife; cool mix of backpackers from around the world smoking in the lounge; clean rooms in an attractive old canal house. Reasons not: your money will stretch further elsewhere. It's kind of cramped and dark, and breakfast is an additional €2.27 to €4.53.

Hotel Kap (☎ 624 59 08, *fax 627 12 89,* **w** *www.kaphotel.nl, Den Texstraat 5B)* **Map 4** Doubles with shower & shared toilet/private facilities €68.05/81.65. Ignore those garish, multicoloured bedspreads and take in the sweet ambience. We like the recently re-vamped, bright rooms with French windows and wicker furniture, the big buffet breakfast (included), the gorgeous courtyard garden and the courteous, gay-friendly owners.

Hotel Pension Kitty (☎ 622 68 19, *Plantage Middenlaan 40)* **Map 5** Doubles with shared facilities €70.30. Kind of spooky, and a whole lot kooky, this 10-room mansion house run by 81-year-old Kitty is kind of like a home away from home – assuming your home is full of kitsch clutter, fake fur rugs, prewar furniture and miles of ruby-red carpet. Rooms are big, comfortable and very lived-in.

Hotel Kooyk (☎ 623 02 95, *fax 638 83 37,* **e** *kooyk@hotmail.com, Leidsekade 82)* **Map 4** Doubles with shared facilities €70.30. In a street lined with worse-for-wear budget hotels, Kooyk is the definite champ. Winning features include big beds with clean linen, spotless carpet (trust us, it matters), good-sized rooms with TV, and a buffet breakfast (included) served in a pretty room lined with Delft tiles and antique prints. Ask to see the large, comfortable five-bed room (€29.50 per person). Other hotels along this street, though definitely a step down from Kooyk, include ***Hotel Impala*** (☎ 623 47 06, *fax 638 92 74, Leidsekade 77)* **(Map 4)**, with doubles with shared/private facilities for €72.60/81.65, all with breakfast, and ***Hotel King*** (☎ 624 96 03, *fax 620 72 77, Leidsekade 86)* **(Map 4)**, with doubles with shared facilities and breakfast for €74.85.

Hotel de Munck (☎ 623 62 83, *fax 620 66 47, Achtergracht 3)* **Map 4** Doubles with shared/private facilities €79.40/88.45. You'll think you've died and gone to rock'n'roll heaven once you spot Munck's brilliant breakfast room. It looks like a replica of a 1950s diner with a working jukebox, record covers lining the walls and Molly, the owner's dog, dancing to Elvis' *Little Sister*. There's even more to make you smile: a flower-filled courtyard and whip-smart, witty staff. All 14 rooms are bright and well kept and come with TV, phone and breakfast.

Hotel Nicolaas Witsen (☎ 626 65 46, *fax 620 51 13,* **w** *www.hotelnicolaaswitsen.nl, Nicolaas Witsenstraat 4-8)* **Map 4** Doubles with private facilities €83.95-93. All you style-aficionados may squirm at Nicolaas Witsen's outdated, pastel-hued decor and piped pop muzak (lobby only) but you'll squeal with delight over its amenities. Unlike most others in this category, the hotel has a lift and some rooms have baths. All 29 rooms are neat, kind of bland and come with TV, phone, safe and breakfast.

Hotel van Onna (☎ 626 58 01, **w** *www .netcentrum.com/onna, Bloemgracht 102-108)* **Map 3** Doubles with private facilities €80. It's a cruel joke, really it is. You've scored a sunny room overlooking one of Amsterdam's prettiest canals at this tidy, friendly hotel. Then as night falls, insomnia and 'church rage' set in. That's because nearby Westerkerk's bells peal every half-hour until 1.30am and start again at 6.30am! Come prepared with earplugs and you'll adore this place. Try and book the attic room with its old wooden roof beams and panoramic views over the Jordaan. Rates include breakfast but no phone or TV. The hotel is nonsmoking and doesn't accept credit cards.

Hotel Prinsenhof (☎ 623 17 72, *fax 638 33 68,* **w** *www.hotelprinsenhof.com, Prinsengracht 810)* **Map 4** Doubles with shared/private facilities €60/80. Drum roll. Envelope please. Prinsenhof wins our award for best in show. This beautiful 18th-century canal house with its dramatic electric luggage hoist suspended in the central staircase has affable staff, spacious rooms and breakfast (included) served in pleasant surrounds. The two attic rooms with their diagonal beams are the most popular (mind your head) but Room 1 gets our vote: it's huge, neat, overlooks the canal and is nattily decorated with antique furniture.

Hotel Rembrandt (☎ 627 27 14, fax 638 02 93, Plantage Middenlaan 17) **Map 5** Doubles with private facilities €63.50-90.75. Enjoying your morning meal in Hotel Rembrandt's stunning, wood-panelled breakfast room (with chandeliers and 17th-century paintings on the linen-covered walls) is a truly lavish experience. Other impressive features: rooms are spick and span, have a TV, phone, some even have a bath, and breakfast is included. Rooms 2 (a large double with a balcony overlooking a small garden) and 21 (four-person, split-level, sunny and surprisingly modern) offer plenty of bang for your buck.

Hotel de Westertoren (☎/fax 624 46 39, e hotelwestertoren@hotmail.com, Raadhuisstraat 35) **Map 3** Doubles with shared/private facilities €63.50/68.05. Facing a noisy tram line can be bothersome but you can't argue with breakfast in bed, a private balcony, your own TV and big, clean rooms. Rooms at the back are smaller but much quieter.

Hotel Winston (☎ 623 13 80, fax 639 23 08, w www.winston.nl, Warmoesstraat 123) **Map 2** Doubles with private facilities €88.45. Quirky Winston is party central for touring bands and up-for-anything tourists. Be sure to book one of the 'art' rooms: local artists, given free reign to outfit 10 rooms, have created a variety of super-raunchy, dubiously tasteful, colour-drenched sleeping spaces.

Outside the Canal Belt *Hotel Van Bonga* (☎ 662 52 18, fax 679 08 43, Holbeinstraat 1) **Map 1** Doubles with private facilities €70.30. Off Stadionweg, south-west of the city centre, this hotel is worth considering if you are an exhibitor needing a place near the RAI exhibition centre.

Hotel Museumzicht (☎ 671 29 54, fax 671 35 97, Jan Luijkenstraat 22) **Map 4** Doubles with shared/private facilities €68.05/88.47. The tiny, must-see, Art Nouveau corridor shower here almost rivals most rooms for size. Well-kept but well-worn rooms with no

phone or TV aren't much of a draw card but you're near the Rijksmuseum, and breakfast (included) in the homely dining room is rather nice.

Hotel Parkzicht (☎ 618 19 54, fax 618 08 97, e hotel@parkzicht.nl, Roemer Visscherstraat 33) **Map 4** Doubles with private facilities €83.90. Pleasant Parkzicht looks a bit run-down but offers great value. A split second from the Vondelpark, it has 13 big rooms with larger-than-average bathrooms and a charmingly raffish dining room overlooking a lush garden. Rates include breakfast.

Hotel Peters (☎ 673 34 54, fax 673 94 30, e hotelpeters@zonnet.nl, Nicolaas Maesstraat 72) **Map 4** Doubles with shared/private facilities €68.05/90.75. Looking more like a shared student house than a hotel, Peters seems way too shabby and laidback to be charging these rates. But spy the super-size rooms with TV and fridge (particularly the one with the small balcony overlooking the garden) and you may change your mind. Breakfast is included and spliff smokers are welcome.

Hotels – Upper Middle (Doubles €90 to €140)

These hotels – most of them small enough to offer personal attention – are big on comfort and low on formality. All rooms have a toilet and shower (and/or bath) and unless stated come with TV, phone and breakfast.

Inside the Canal Belt *Amsterdam Wiechmann* (☎ 626 33 21, fax 626 89 62, w www.hotelwiechmann.nl, Prinsengracht 328) **Map 3** Doubles €125-136. Wiechmann's canalside location is so marvellous that we'll forgive it the smallish rooms with florid, floral soft furnishings. It's worth staying just for the wacky lobby decorations: Russian samovar, pot-belly stove and full suit of armour. It's all very *Ghost & Mrs Muir*.

Hotel The Crown (☎ 626 96 64, fax 420 64 73, w www.hotelthecrown.com, Oudezijds Voorburgwal 21) **Map 2** Doubles with shared/private shower €90.75/99.80. Rooms at this Brit-run, red-light district hotel have shared toilets, and no TV or phone – and don't even bother asking for breakfast.

PLACES TO STAY

Prices just make it into our upper-middle price bracket but quality is firmly in the lower-middle. So what's the draw, you ask? It's plenty of fun. The downstairs bar – with Sky TV, pool table, dart board and hordes of celebrating stag-nighters – is only closed from 4am to 11am and spliff smoking is allowed in the tidy, newly painted and carpeted rooms.

't Hotel (☎ 422 27 41, fax 626 78 73, e th.broekema@hetnet.nl, Leliegracht 18) **Map 3** Doubles €130. Quiet and understated, 't Hotel is a genuine find. It's a 17th-century canal house with only eight rooms, all with comfortable, Art Deco-inspired furnishings. Be sure to book Room 7: it's a sun-filled space with a gabled roof and large windows overlooking the canal.

Hotel Orlando (☎ 638 69 15, fax 625 21 23, Prinsengracht 1099) **Map 4** Doubles €72.60-125. Oh Orlando, how do we love thee? Let us count the ways. One: biggish, canalside rooms, smallish rates. Two: hospitable, gay-friendly host. Three: breakfast in bed, room service and business facilities. Four: impeccably chic, boutique style.

Seven Bridges (☎ 623 13 29, Reguliersgracht 31) **Map 4** Doubles €113-168. Private, sophisticated Seven Bridges – one of the city's loveliest little hotels on one of its loveliest canals – has nine tastefully decorated rooms (all lush oriental rugs and elegant antiques). Morning sightseeing will seem superfluous once breakfast, served on fine china, is delivered to your room.

Hotel Toren (☎ 622 60 33, fax 626 97 05, w www.toren.nl, Keizersgracht 164) **Map 3** Doubles €120-143. Exquisitely renovated Toren – public areas all 17th-century antique-y with gilded mirrors, fireplaces and chandeliers, guest rooms all elegantly furnished with modern facilities – is this category's title-holder for price, room size and personal service. Go all out and book the room with the two-person jacuzzi and garden patio (€220).

Waterfront Hotel (☎/fax 421 66 21, w www.hotelwaterfront.nl, Singel 458) **Map 2** Doubles €102-118. Newly renovated Waterfront is a smart, stylish choice. Crisply decorated rooms with a soothing mix of modern and traditional details are largish and light-filled. Book the canalside room with the tiny, plant-covered balcony.

Zosa Hotel (☎ 330 62 41, fax 330 62 42, w www.zosa-online.com, Kloveniersburgwal 20) **Map 2** Doubles €136. What Zosa's six rooms lack in size, they make up for in pure visuals. Each is ineffably fashionable and individually designed. Feeling romantic? Book the 'Baroque' room with soothing lamps and lollypop-pink walls. Stressed out? The minimal, modern 'Zen' room is a tranquil balm. Our favourite, the 'Room of Wonders', is a modern Middle Eastern space with delicate murals and Moroccan lanterns.

Outside the Canal Belt *Hotel Arena* (☎ 850 24 00, fax 850 42 15, w www.hotelarena.nl, 's-Gravesandestraat 51) **Map 2** Doubles €107-155. Hotel Arena, bordering lush Oosterpark, has had more facelifts than your average Hollywood starlet. Originally a chapel and orphanage, then a backpackers hostel, it's now a super-modern, 121-room hotel with a fashionable restaurant, café and fun nightclub. Minimally furnished rooms – 'designer-industrial-hospital' chic – are more Ikea than *Wallpaper** magazine, but the large, split-level double rooms with separate lounge area are a sun-drenched delight. Rooms are phoneless, breakfast is €9 per person and there is wheelchair access throughout. Ask for a room in section A, B, E or F away from the noisy central hall.

Hotel de Filosoof (☎ 683 30 13, fax 685 37 50, w www.hotelfilosoof.nl, Anna van den Vondelstraat 6) **Map 4** Doubles €110-120. Staying at Filosoof may not make you any smarter, but the snappy surrounds will stimulate your senses. Each room is decorated after a famous philosopher or writer including Aristotle, Wittgenstein and Spinoza. Some rooms are festooned with lush furniture and over-the-top wallpaper, and others, such as the Zen room, are a minimal paean to serenity. Ask to see the large, less expensive (and less ornamented) rooms in the house across the street.

Hestia Hotel (☎ 618 08 01, fax 612 37 10, w www.hestia.demon.nl, Roemer Visscherstraat 7) **Map 4** Doubles €88.45-125.

Friendly, family-run Hestia, with 18 rooms decorated in fresh blue and white, is an ever-reliable choice. Scrupulously neat, well-sized doubles with balconies overlooking the Vondelpark are a quiet retreat after a day of sightseeing.

Owl Hotel (☎ 618 94 84, fax 618 94 41, Ⓦ www.owl-hotel.demon.nl, Roemer Visscherstraat 1) **Map 4** Doubles €107. You'll hoot with happiness at this wonderful hotel. The staff are warm and welcoming, and the dapper, eye-pleasing rooms come with lots of facilities (hairdryers, laptop plug-ins). Best of all, buffet breakfast is served in a serene, light-filled room overlooking a gorgeous garden.

Hotels – Top End (Doubles €140 to €270)

If you're looking for a bit of luxury, loads of privacy and lashings of personal service, these boutique hotels will put a smile on your dial. Expect extras like nonsmoking rooms, lifts, in-room dataports, minibars and room service. Unless stated, rates include breakfast.

Inside the Canal Belt *Ambassade Hotel (☎ 555 02 22, fax 555 02 77, Ⓦ www.ambassade-hotel.nl, Herengracht 341)* **Map 3** Doubles €180. Flick through the books in Ambassade's spiffy little library and you'll spy signed copies by Salman Rushdie and Umberto Eco. Literary luminaries and well-heeled tourists alike love this tastefully appointed hotel, spread over 10 canal houses. The beautiful antique furniture and fixtures are traditional without being cloying, and the sparkling lounge (with fresh flowers and chandeliers) is ideal for business meetings or afternoon tea. Breakfast is €14 per person.

Canal House Hotel (☎ 622 51 82, fax 624 13 17, Ⓦ www.canalhouse.nl, Keizersgracht 148) **Map 3** Doubles €134-179. Where to spend your time in this splendid boutique hotel? In the ornately furnished, 17th-century dining room resplendent with chandeliers, grand piano and garden views? The cosy, plush, burgundy-hued bar? Or the small but inviting, antique-filled guest rooms? All areas are equally charming and refined. Rooms have phones and computer connections but no TV.

Golden Tulip Schiller (☎ 554 07 00, fax 624 00 98, Ⓦ www.goldentuliphotels.nl/gtschiller, Rembrandtplein 26-36) **Map 4** Doubles €220-259. Although it's been restored to its original (1912) Art Deco splendour, with paintings by the artist-hotelier Frits Schiller adorning the walls, this hotel has blandly corporate rooms. Best lap up the atmosphere in the attached Brasserie Schiller (the stained-glass windows are magnificent) or out on bustling Rembrandtplein. Breakfast is €14.74 per person.

Outside the Canal Belt *Jan Luyken Hotel (☎ 573 07 30, fax 676 38 41, Ⓦ www.janluyken.nl, Jan Luijkenstraat 58)* **Map 4** Doubles €181-272. This Art Nouveau delight is currently undergoing much-needed modernisation. Stuffy, chintzy rooms are being smartened up with a crisp white and caramel colour scheme and sleek designer furniture. Amenities include a swish little gym (solarium, sauna and whirlpool), business lounge and an alluring bar with garden views. Buffet breakfast is €13.15 per person.

Okura Hotel (☎ 678 71 11, fax 678 83 07, Ⓦ www.okura.nl, Ferdinand Bolstraat 333) **Map 1** Doubles €250. The business traveller's choice. Okura's proximity to the RAI exhibition centre and its delicious, panoramic views of Amsterdam make it easy on the feet and on the eye.

Hotels – Deluxe (Doubles over €270)

Facilities like nonsmoking rooms, air-conditioning, fitness centres (some with pocket-sized swimming pools), conference and banquet rooms, and business centres (or at least 'desks') are par for the course at these hotels, as are brutally priced breakfasts (€11 to €23). Check their competitively priced weekend and summer packages, which may be comparable to rates in the Top-End category.

Inside the Canal Belt *American Hotel (☎ 556 30 00, fax 556 30 01, Ⓦ www.amsterdam-american.crowneplaza.com, Leidsekade*

PLACES TO STAY

97) **Map 4** Doubles €352-397. Sad to say, but recent renovations seem to have sapped all the charm and grandeur from this Art Deco monument. Small, ultra-expensive rooms have been facelifted with new (but cheapish-looking) furnishings and the lobby has been given a generic corporate makeover. Let's hope they leave its stunning *Café Americain* (see the Entertainment chapter) well alone.

Amstel Inter-Continental Hotel (☎ 622 60 60, fax 622 58 08, **W** *www.interconti.com, Professor Tulpplein 1)* **Map 4** Doubles €452-863. Everything about this five-star edifice is spectacular, from its imposing location overlooking the Amstel, to its magnificent colonnaded lobby and of course its wallet-walloping room prices. Lavishly decorated rooms, reverential service and luxe amenities such as a Michelin-awarded restaurant, chauffeured limousines and a heated indoor pool delight even the fussiest transatlantic celebrities and euro-royalty.

Blakes (☎ 530 20 10, fax 530 20 30, **W** *www.slh.com/blakesam, Keizersgracht 384)* **Map 3** Doubles €341-432. London hotelier Anouska Hempel's newest creation is a true temple of style with drop-dead gorgeous staff, rooms and restaurant. Slink through the 17th-century canal house's beautiful courtyard entrance and ensconce yourself in the stunning, 'East meets Dutch'-themed rooms. A sophisticated, two-tone colour palette, fluffy towels and silk pillows piled high, and spacious bathrooms create a serene, sumptuous environment.

Hotel de l'Europe (☎ 531 17 77, fax 531 17 78, **W** *www.leurope.nl, Nieuwe Doelenstraat 2-8)* **Map 2** Doubles €304-429. Oozing Victorian elegance, l'Europe welcomes you with a glam chandelier and marble lobby and gloriously large rooms. The attached *Excelsior Restaurant* and chichi gym with swimming pool are equally impressive.

Golden Tulip Barbizon Palace (☎ 556 45 64, fax 624 33 53, **W** *www.goldentuliphotels.nl/gtbpalace, Prins Hendrikkade 59-72)* **Map 2** Doubles €380. Stretching over 19 houses (some 17th-century) and incorporating the 15th-century St Olof Chapel, the Barbizon Palace seamlessly blends Old World charm with modern amenities. Traditionally decorated rooms (olive green and claret the overriding colours) could be bigger, but after luxuriating in the gym's Turkish bath you may not notice or care.

Grand Hotel Krasnapolsky (☎ 554 91 11, fax 622 86 07, **W** *www.krasnapolsky.nl, Dam 9)* **Map 2** Doubles €290-310. This gargantuan, historic hotel on Amsterdam's prime patch of real estate offers elegant if slightly noisy and compact rooms. Spectacular public spaces make up for any size issues you may have. The 19th-century 'winter garden' breakfast room, with its soaring steel-and-glass roof, and the tented *Shibli Bedouin Restaurant*, with hookah pipes, Persian carpets and comfy cushions, are gobsmackingly marvellous.

Grand Westin Demeure (☎ 555 31 11, fax 626 62 86, **W** *www.thegrand.nl, Oudezijds Voorburgwal 197)* **Map 2** Doubles €374. The Demeure – Amsterdam's former city hall (1808–1987) – was the scene of Queen Beatrix's civil wedding in 1966. You may feel a bit royal yourself as you wander through the cavernous lobby, grandiose stairwells and a spacious inner courtyard.

Pulitzer Hotel (☎ 523 52 35, fax 627 67 53, **W** *www.sheraton.com/pulitzer, Prinsengracht 315-331)* **Map 3** Doubles €272-385. Occupying a row of 17th-century canal houses, Pulitzer packs a mighty punch. It manages to combine big-hotel efficiency with boutique-hotel charm. Beautifully restored rooms with mod-cons galore, a cigar bar, art gallery, garden courtyards and wonderful restaurant are high on elegance and low on pomposity.

Seven One Seven (☎ 427 07 17, fax 423 07 17, **W** *www.717hotel.nl, Prinsengracht 717)* **Map 4** Doubles €352-567. Without doubt, the most wonderful hotel in Amsterdam. Hyper-plush, deliciously appointed rooms come with that rare luxury: space. Step into the splashy Picasso suite – with its soaring ceiling, commodious furniture, gorgeous contemporary and antique decorations, and bathroom as big as some European principalities – and you'll never, *ever* want to leave. Rates include breakfast, afternoon tea, house wine and oodles of one-on-one service.

Outside the Canal Belt *Hilton Amsterdam (☎ 710 60 00, fax 710 90 00, W www .hilton.com, Apollolaan 138-140)* **Map 4** Doubles €254-406. Controversy just keeps dogging this dependable hotel. It was 'flower-power' central in 1969 when John Lennon and Yoko Ono staged their 'bed-in' for world peace (you can rent the room). On a much sadder note, Herman Brood, Holland's most famous junkie-artist-musician, committed suicide here in 2001 by jumping off the roof – he used to frequent the hotel's popular bar (carrying a parrot on his head). As well as standard chain-hotel facilities, the Hilton also boasts its own marina with boats for hire.

Marriott Hotel (☎ 607 55 55, fax 607 55 11, W www.marriotthotels.com, Stadhouderskade 12) **Map 4** Doubles €250-375. Dutch congeniality and American big-hotel know-how combine to make the Marriott a fine choice, especially for business travellers. 'Executive' suites (€325 to €375) are large, modern and allow access to the super-quiet private lounges.

Gay & Lesbian Hotels

Hotels are pretty relaxed about same-sex couples (and would be breaking the law if they refused them) but some cater specifically for them.

Hotel Aero (☎ 622 77 28, fax 638 85 31, W www.aerohotel.nl, Kerkstraat 49) **Map 4** Doubles with shared/private facilities €65.80/ 74.85-97.55. The small, musty rooms here are being refurbished and enlarged. Newer quarters are much cleaner, roomier and have modern bathrooms. All rooms come with TV, phone and breakfast.

Amistad Hotel (☎ 624 80 74, fax 622 99 97, W www.amistad.nl, Kerkstraat 42) **Map 4** Doubles with shared/private facilities €70/115. Rooms at this new, bijou hotel in the middle of the gay action are dotted with hip designer flourishes like Philippe Starck chairs, CD players, chic soft furnishings (and TV, phone, safe and fridge). Highlights include breakfasting in the kitchen/dining room – with ruby red walls and make-a-friend communal table – while chatting with the two super-spunky owners.

Black Tulip Hotel (☎ 427 09 33, fax 624 42 81, W www.blacktulip.nl, Geldersekade 16) **Map 2** Doubles with private facilities €100-175. Bondage boys welcome: the nine well-appointed rooms feature a mind-boggling array of equipment (cages, slings, bondage chairs, hooks and masses of black leather and latex). Rates include buffet breakfast and nonsmoking rooms are available.

Liliane's Home (☎ 627 40 06, Sarphatistraat 119) **Map 5** Doubles with private facilities €100. This nine-bedroom private home, the sole women-only establishment in town, has loads of personality. Rooms with huge windows (some with balconies) include TV (no phone), fridge, books to read and a basket of breakfast goodies delivered to your door each morning.

Hotel Orfeo (☎ 623 13 47, fax 620 23 48, W www.hotelorfeo.com, Leidsekruisstraat 14) **Map 4** Doubles with shared/private facilities €68.05/93. Opened in 1969, central Orfeo has simple, small, wood-panelled rooms (with TV, phone, minibar) and the flirtiest breakfast room in town. Cruising over a bowl of cornflakes is a perky start to the day.

Hotel Quentin (☎ 626 21 87, fax 622 01 21, Leidsekade 89) **Map 4** Doubles with shared/private facilities €65.80/88.50-134. Arty Quentin, decorated with colourful murals and handmade furniture, offers a variety of well-sized rooms, some with balconies, canal views, phone and TV. It's popular with lesbians and international actors and musicians performing at nearby Theatre Bellevue and Melkweg.

Stablemaster Hotel (☎ 625 01 48, fax 624 87 47, e tony-starr@hotmail.com, Warmoesstraat 23) **Map 2** Doubles with shared facilities €88.45. Rooms here may be noisy and a bit worse for wear but they come with tons of extras (porno TV channel, phone, VCR, fridge, stereo, couch, tea and coffee-making facilities). Need more convincing? The attached bar holds 'jack-off' parties five nights a week.

LONG-TERM RENTALS

Rental accommodation costing less than €453 a month unfurnished is subject to a housing permit. This is only issued to legal residents who are bound to the region through work or study, and the price and size of the dwelling must match their income and needs (housing permits are not required in Amsterdam Zuidoost (south-east) but that's because it's a rather unattractive area). This means that as a foreigner you'll usually pay more – say, €850 a month for a smallish, two-bedroom flat in the Vondelpark area – and you might not like what you get. Apartments tend to be small, so sharing is rare.

Residents usually procure accommodation through housing corporations. Others have more luck through property ads in the daily newspapers *De Telegraaf* (especially Wednesday) and *De Volkskrant* or *Het Parool* (especially Saturday – look under *Te Huur*, For Rent), or through the classifieds paper *Via Via* (published Tuesday and Thursday). The national organisation of real-estate agents (W www.nvm.nl) lists properties but only in Dutch.

Speaking English can work against you in a variety of ways when apartment-hunting, so get a Dutch friend to help, and act swiftly because it's very much a seller's market. The owner will probably want a deposit of a month's rent, and the previous tenant may demand key money disguised as take-over costs for furnishings or recent handiwork.

Official information on renting is supplied by the Information Centre for Physical Planning and Housing (☎ 680 68 06, W www.swd.amsterdam.nl) in the Zuiderkerk, Zuiderkerkhof 72, open 11am to 4pm Monday; 9am to 4pm Tuesday, Wednesday and Friday; and 9am to 8pm Thursday. It might not be too helpful if you're not a resident but it will supply an updated list of recommended agents.

If speed is of the essence, try the following agents:

All-Inn Apartment Service (☎ 428 23 00, fax 428 23 04, W *www.apartment.nl*, *Singel 315*) Furnished apartments per month €1134-2722. All-Inn handles rentals throughout the city including studios and 'luxurious canalside apartments'; minimum rental is six months.

Amsterdam Apartments (☎ 626 59 30, fax 622 95 44, *Kromme Waal 32*) Furnished apartments per week €544. This agency has lots of self-contained, central apartments on its books. Minimum rental is one week.

Goudsmit Estate Agents (☎ 644 19 71, fax 644 23 76, W *www.goudsmit.com*, *A.J. Ernststraat 735*) Furnished apartments per month €1361-4537. Goudsmit caters mainly to corporate clients – check the Web site for photos of the accommodation. Minimum rental is one year.

IDA Housing Services (☎ 624 83 01, fax 623 38 44, e *ida@ida-housing.demon.nl*, *Den Texstraat 30*) Furnished apartments per month €907-1588. IDA rents everything from studio apartments outside the canal belt to lavishly furnished canal houses. Minimum rental is six months (sometimes shorter in summer).

Intercity Room Service (☎/fax 675 00 64, *Van Ostadestraat 348*) Flat-shares per month €295, furnished apartments per month €1134. This option is only if you need a room quick smart. Accommodation is available per month and also for shorter periods. Commission is two weeks' rent (one month's for apartments longer than six months). Agencies operating in this price bracket need a municipal permit, which this one has.

Riverside Apartments (☎ 627 97 97, fax 627 98 58, e *geuje@worldonline.nl*, *Amstel 138*) Furnished apartments per week €907-1361. This company specialises in 'luxury executive' accommodation in central Amsterdam; monthly rates attract a commission.

Places to Eat

FOOD

Let's face it, in the culinary world Dutch cuisine is pretty close to the bottom of the food chain. Concentrating on filling the stomach rather than titillating the taste buds, the national cuisine is based on a rudimentary meat, potato and vegetable theme. Don't fret though, almost every other world cuisine is represented in Amsterdam – and to be fair, the city has recently undergone a bit of a culinary revolution with enthusiastic chefs creating interesting, palatable menus. Prices are reasonable by European standards and servings are generous.

Smoking is still an entrenched habit in restaurants. Some places have nonsmoking sections but even the most self-righteous vegetarian establishments have trouble banning smokers altogether.

Where & When

Don't overlook the many *eetcafés*, pubs that also serve meals – see Cafés (Pubs) in the Entertainment chapter: most of them could just as well be listed here as places to eat. They're affordable, often lively and full of character. The grand cafés in particular are good places for a long lunch or Sunday brunch.

Amsterdammers like to eat out and they eat early: dinner, the main meal of the day, is served between 6pm and 10pm and popular places fill up by 7pm, so book ahead, arrive early or be prepared to wait at the bar. Alternatively you could try arriving late: films and concerts usually start at 8.30pm or 9.30pm and tables may become available then for a 'second sitting', but keep in mind that many kitchens close by 10pm (though the restaurants stay open longer). Vegetarian restaurants tend to close even earlier. In the top tourist months of July and (especially) August, however, many locals go on holidays and restaurants tend to be quieter.

Lunch is a modest affair, with sandwich and salad menus, though you may find places that serve full meals.

Many restaurants are open daily, but some are closed Sunday or Monday; ring to check.

Cuisines

Cuisines such as Italian, Spanish, Mexican, Thai, Chinese, Indian and Turkish will be similar to what you're used to, though they might be adapted to suit the Dutch palate and the availability of local ingredients. Most restaurants have one or more vegetarian dishes on the menu, though we also list several dedicated vegetarian places.

Dutch The standard Dutch meal consists of potatoes, meat and vegetables in large portions (though meat is expensive, so don't expect plate-filling steaks). Few restaurants serve exclusively Dutch cuisine but many menus include some Dutch staples, especially in winter, that are filling and good value:

stamppot ('mashed pot') – potatoes mashed with vegetables (usually kale or endive) and served with smoked sausage or strips of pork

hutspot ('hotchpotch') – similar to stamppot, but with carrots, onions and braised meat

erwtensoep – thick pea soup (a spoon stuck upright in the pot should fall over slowly) with smoked sausage and bacon

asperges – asparagus (usually white, very popular in spring), served with ham and butter

kroketten – croquettes: dough-ragout with meat (sometimes fish or shrimp) that's crumbed and deep-fried; also in the form of small balls called *bitterballen* served with mustard – a popular pub snack

mosselen – mussels, popular (and best eaten) from September to April; cooked with white wine, chopped leeks and onions, and served with a side dish of French fries *(frites* or *patat)*. Use an empty shell as a pincer to pluck out the bodies and don't eat mussels that haven't opened properly as they can be poisonous

Seafood doesn't feature as prominently as you'd expect in a seafaring nation, though there's plenty of it, except on Mondays when fish tends to be old and the locals avoid it – fish shops and herring stalls are closed then too. Popular fish include *schol*

Traditional Dutch Dishes

Winter may be the best season to cook up one of these hearty, homely Dutch dishes.

Dutch Pea Soup

This thick soup tastes even better the next day. Serve with hot, crusty bread.

3 cups split green peas
1 pig's trotter
1 pig's ear
1 cup diced bacon
1kg potatoes
2 leeks
2 onions
1 celeriac
4 frankfurters
salt and pepper to taste

* Wash peas, cover with water and soak overnight.
* Boil softened peas in 3L of water for one hour.
* Add pig's trotter, ear and bacon and continue to cook for two hours.
* Add sliced potatoes, diced leeks, diced onions and diced celeriac and simmer for a further one hour.
* Add sliced frankfurters to soup for the last five minutes. Season with salt and pepper.

Mashed Potatoes with Crispy Bacon

1 cup diced bacon
1kg floury potatoes
2 tbsp butter
milk to mix
cracked pepper and salt to taste

* Fry the bacon until crispy, set aside, reserve the fat.

* Peel and quarter potatoes; place in a large saucepan with water, bring to the boil and cook for 20 minutes.
* Drain and mash potatoes with butter and milk.
* Return to heat and fold through bacon and remaining fat. Season as required.

Dutch *Appeltaart*

1 packet shortcrust pastry
1½ tsp gelatine
1kg apples
1 tbsp lemon juice
2 tbsp sugar
2 tsp cinnamon
150g dried fruit soaked in 3 tbsp rum
¼ cup butter
1 tsp caster sugar
½ cup whipped cream

* Preheat oven to 175°C/350°F.
* Use three-quarters of the shortcrust pastry dough to line base and sides of a 24cm greased round cake tin; sprinkle with the gelatine.
* Peel and core apples, slice thinly, sprinkle with lemon juice and mix in sugar and 1 tsp of cinnamon.
* Place alternate layers of apple slices and dried fruit in tin, sprinkling each layer with some cinnamon and sugar. Use apples for the top layer and dot with butter.
* Roll the remaining dough into a rectangle, cut into 1cm-wide strips and lay in a lattice over fruit, sealing at ends; brush with some milk, and sprinkle caster sugar mixed with remaining cinnamon on top.
* Bake for 45 minutes or till golden.
* Cool and serve with a generous amount of whipped cream.

(plaice), *tong* (sole), *kabeljauw* (cod) and freshwater *forel* (trout). *Garnalen* (shrimps, prawns) are also found on many menus, often large species known by their Italian name of *scampi*. *Haring* (herring) is a national institution, eaten lightly salted or occasionally pickled but never fried or cooked; *paling* (eel) is usually smoked.

Don't dismiss herring or eel until you've tried them – see the Fast Food section later in this chapter.

Typical Dutch desserts are fruit pie (apple, cherry or other fruit), *vla* (custard) or pancakes. Many snack bars and pubs serve *appeltaart* (apple pie) and coffee throughout the day.

Fusion Fusion cuisine combines Asian/Pacific-Rim ingredients and cooking techniques with local produce on the one plate. Sometimes the dishes are wonderful, while other times it's a miserable melange of flavours and textures and could just as easily be labelled 'Confusion Cuisine'. Listed on the following pages are restaurants where the experiment is working successfully.

Indonesian This is a tasty legacy of Dutch colonial history. Some dishes, such as the famous *rijsttafel* ('rice table' – white rice with lots of side dishes), are colonial concoctions rather than traditional Indonesian, but that doesn't make them less appealing.

One slight problem, however, is that most places serving Indonesian food are Chinese-Indonesian, run by Chinese (some with Indonesian backgrounds) who have created bland dishes to suit Dutch palates. The food is OK and can be great value, but if you want the real thing, avoid places that call themselves *Chinees-Indonesisch* (or order Chinese dishes there instead).

Even at 'genuine' Indonesian restaurants, rijsttafel can be a bit of a rip-off and the ingredients don't always taste authentic – once you've had a really good one you'll know the difference. A few good rijsttafel places are mentioned in this chapter, but it's an expensive dish and if you eat elsewhere you're better off ordering *nasi rames* (literally, boiled rice), a plate of rice covered in several accompaniments that would be served in separate bowls in a rijsttafel. The same dish with thick noodles (more a Chinese-Indonesian variant and quite filling) is called *bami rames*.

Gado-gado (lightly steamed vegetables and hard-boiled egg, served with peanut sauce and rice) feels good in all respects. *Saté* or *sateh* (satay) is marinated, barbecued beef, chicken or pork on small skewers; unfortunately it's often cooked electrically and smothered in peanut sauce. Other stand-bys are *nasi goreng* (fried rice with onions, pork, shrimp and spices, often topped with a fried egg or shredded omelette) and *bami goreng* (the same thing but with noodles).

Indonesian food is usually served mild for sensitive Western palates. If you want it hot (*pedis*, pronounced 'p-DIS'), say so but be prepared for the ride of a lifetime. It's better to play it safe by asking for *sambal* (chilli paste), if it isn't already on the table, and helping yourself. Usually it's *sambal oelek*, which is red and hot; the dark-brown *sambal badjak* is based on onions and is mild and sweet. If you overdo it, a spoonful of plain rice will quench the flames; drinking distributes the oily sambal and only makes things worse.

Indonesian food should be eaten with a spoon and fork (chopsticks are Chinese) and the drink of choice is beer or water.

International Many restaurants fall into this category, with menus looking like a roll call for the United Nations. Dishes may include Indian curries, Italian pasta, Spanish tapas and Mexican enchiladas. Main courses usually come with salads that can be quite imaginative.

Surinamese Food from this former South American colony is similar to Caribbean food – a unique African/Indian hybrid – with Indonesian influences contributed by indentured labourers from Java. Chicken features strongly, along with curries (chicken, lamb or beef), potatoes and rice, and delicious *roti* (unleavened bread pancakes). It can be hot and spicy, but it's always wholesome and good value. Surinamese restaurants are small and specialise in takeaway food, though there might be a few tables and chairs. Most close early and some are only open for lunch.

Costs
Most of the prices quoted in this chapter are for main courses; add the cost of drinks and one or two other dishes and you could spend twice as much. Drinks other than draught beer *(pils)* will pad out the bill, and wine can be a blatant rip off, with bottles that cost €4.50 in the shops selling for up to €20. 'House wines' are no different: a half-litre carafe of acidic house red starts at €7, though some restaurants serve drinkable stuff.

Many places list a *dagschotel* (dish of the day) or *dagmenu* that will be good value, but don't expect a culinary adventure.

PLACES TO EAT

Service is included in the bill and tipping is at your discretion, though most people leave small change (5% or so) if the service hasn't been bad enough to warrant customer revenge; service can often be incredibly slow and unprofessional but that's normal here. The protocol is to say how much you're paying in total as you settle the bill.

Beware that many restaurants do *not* accept credit cards; check in advance.

DRINKS
Nonalcoholic
Amsterdam tap water is fine but it does have a slight chemical taste, so mineral and soda waters are popular. Dairy drinks include chocolate milk, Fristi (a yogurt drink), *karnemelk* (buttermilk) and of course milk itself, which is good and relatively cheap. A wide selection of fruit juices and soft drinks are available too.

Tea & Coffee For a city with such a rich tradition in the tea and coffee trade, tea is a bit of a disappointment. It's usually served as a cup of hot water with a tea bag, though many places do offer a wide choice of bags. If you want milk, ask *'met melk, graag'* (with milk, please); many locals add a slice of lemon instead.

The hot drink of choice is coffee – after all, it was the merchants of Amsterdam who introduced coffee to Europe in a big way, in the early 1600s. It should be strong and can be excellent if it's freshly made or horrendous if it has been simmering for a couple of hours. If you simply order *koffie* you'll get a sizable cup of the black stuff with a small airline container of *koffiemelk*, a slightly sour tasting cream similar to unsweetened condensed milk that enhances the flavour. *Koffie verkeerd* (coffee 'wrong') comes in a bigger cup or mug with plenty of real milk. If you order *espresso* or *cappuccino* you may be served a decent Italian version, but most cappuccinos are bland and covered in watery froth.

Alcoholic
Lager beer is the staple, served cool and topped by a two-finger-thick head of froth – supposedly to trap the flavour. Requests

of 'no head please' will meet with a steely response. *Een bier*, *een pils* or *een vaas* will get you a normal glass; *een kleintje pils* is a small glass and *een fluitje* is a small, thin, Cologne-style glass. Many places also serve half-litre mugs *(een grote pils)* to please tourists, but somehow draught lager doesn't taste the same in a mug and soon goes flat if you don't hurry up!

Popular brands include Heineken, Amstel, Grolsch, Oranjeboom, Dommelsch, Bavaria and the cheap Brouwersbier put out by the Albert Heijn supermarket chain. They contain about 5% alcohol by volume, so a few of those seemingly small glasses can pack quite a wallop. Tasty and stronger Belgian beers, such as Duvel and Westmalle Triple, are also very popular and are reasonably priced. *Witbier* is a somewhat murky, crisp beer that's drunk in summer with a slice of lemon; the dark, sweet *bokbier* is available in autumn.

Dutch gin (*genever*, pronounced yer-NAY-ver) is made from juniper berries and is drunk chilled from a tiny glass filled to the brim. Most people prefer *jonge* (young) genever, which is smooth and relatively easy to drink; *oude* (old) genever has a strong juniper flavour and can be an acquired taste. A common combination, known as a *kopstoot* (head banger), is a glass of genever with a beer chaser – few people can handle more than two or three of those. Brandy is known as *vieux* or *brandewijn*. There are plenty of indigenous liqueurs, including *advocaat* (a kind of eggnog) and the herb-based *Beerenburg*, a Frisian schnapps.

Wines in all varieties are very popular thanks to European unity, which has given French vintners and their overpriced products a run for their money. The average Amsterdam supermarket stocks wines from every corner of Europe (with excellent value from Spain and Bulgaria) and many countries farther afield, such as Chile, South Africa and Australia. The most expensive bottle in a supermarket rarely costs more than €8 and will be quite drinkable.

BREAKFAST & LUNCH
Amsterdam wakes up late and you'll have trouble finding places other than hotels that

serve anything before 9am or even 10am. Dutch hotel breakfasts typically consist of a selection of breads and toast with butter and jam, cheese and cold cuts, coffee or tea. A soft-boiled egg is sometimes part of the package, and Anglo-American eggs and bacon might be available on request. The Dutch version of fried eggs and meat, the *uitsmijter* served in snack bars and some pubs (see Fast Food), is not commonly eaten for breakfast but will keep you going for hours.

Despite the lack of early-morning eateries, you can still have breakfast if you know where to look (and don't get up too early). Amsterdam has a plethora of small, inexpensive restaurants serving hearty breakfasts and good quality sandwiches, soups and cakes for lunch. The more interesting ones are in the smaller side streets inside the canal belt and in the Jordaan neighbourhood. Some are only open for breakfast and lunch, while others open at 8am and serve food till 10pm. Most don't serve alcohol, but some have fully stocked bars.

Barney's (☎ *625 97 61, Haarlemmerstraat 102*) **Map 2** Mains €6.80-13.60. Need a joint with that morning juice? Barney's coffeeshop is your best bet. It does a roaring trade in massive, set breakfasts: Irish, Mexican, vegetarian and even one with rib-eye steak.

Dimitri's (☎ *627 93 93, Prinsenstraat 3*) **Map 3** Mains €3.40-10.45. Resembling a mini Parisian brasserie, sophisticated Dimitri's serves an international menu of gargantuan salads, pastas and burgers. Mornings see fashionable types nibbling on croissants or, if they're feeling particularly perky, ordering the champagne breakfast: coffee, juice, toast, bacon, smoked salmon and a glass of bubbly (€10.20).

Enorm (☎ *670 99 44, PC Hooftstraat 87*) **Map 4** Mains €3.15-6.35. Entering Enorm is like stepping into an oversize, shiny industrial refrigerator, except this one is full of scary society specimens liposuctioned to within an inch of their lives. Order a huge takeaway salad, sandwich and chocolate brownie and hotfoot it to the Vondelpark.

Foodism (☎ *427 51 03, Oude Leliestraat 8*) **Map 2** Mains €5.45-7.95. A hip little joint run by a fun, very relaxed crew of chefs and waiters. All-day breakfasts, filled sandwiches and salads make up the day menu; night-time sees patrons tucking into platefuls of pasta – try the eminently edible 'Kung Funghi' (with mushrooms, parsley, walnuts and cream).

Goodies (☎ *625 61 22, Huidenstraat 9*) **Map 3** Mains €4.10-5. Looking like a 1970s country kitchen, arty Goodies is always full of students munching on filled bagels named after cartoon characters (choose from Sleepy, Dopey or Bashful) and office workers enjoying pasta dishes at night.

Hein (☎ *623 10 48, Berenstraat 20*) **Map 3** Mains €3.40-6.80. This stylish café with its open, industrial-style kitchen is popular with media types doing business over brunch. The super-scrumptious crepes, stuffed with chicken and vegetables and served with salad, are prize-winning stuff.

Metz & Co Café (☎ *520 70 36, Keizersgracht 455*) **Map 4** Mains €5.65-15.90. Drink in that amazing, panoramic view! This café, on the top floor of swanky Metz & Co department store, has such glorious views over the city that you'd expect exorbitant prices. Yet the substantial set breakfasts, brunches and swish afternoon teas are well priced.

Café Morlang (☎ *625 26 81, Keizersgracht 451*) **Map 4** Mains €5.90-10. Around the corner from Metz & Co, smart Morlang offers a quiet retreat from the mayhem of Leidsestraat. Grab a fashion magazine, order the terrific omelette with wild spinach, mushrooms and Dutch cheese, and take in the gigantic portraits of staff members painted on the back wall.

New Deli (☎ *626 27 55, Haarlemmerstraat 73*) **Map 2** Mains €4.55-12.25. Slick, hip couples congregate at this modern and minimal café to air-kiss, read design magazines, gossip and share Italian and Asian-inspired dishes.

Nielsen (☎ *330 60 06, Berenstraat 19*) **Map 3** Mains €3.40-7.95. This sunny café, with its bright interior filled with fresh flowers, is definitely worth a visit. The tasty set breakfast – eggs, toast, fruit, juice and coffee (€7) – is hard to beat. During lunch a large variety of tasty salads and sandwiches are served: try the gigantic, fantastic chicken club sandwich.

Puccini (☎ *620 84 58, Staalstraat 21*) **Map 2** Mains €2.70-10.45. Refuel on Italian-inspired sandwiches and salads (with stacks of sun-dried ingredients) at this small, chic sandwich bar. It stays open for dinner until 8pm whenever there's an opera on at the nearby Stopera.

Café Reibach (☎ *626 77 08, Brouwersgracht 139*) **Map 3** Mains €2.25-10.45. This charming establishment serves a magnificent breakfast (€10.45): a platter laden with Dutch cheese, pâté, smoked salmon, eggs, coffee and fresh juice. It's also pleasant for afternoon cake and coffee (try the creamy cheesecake).

Villa Zeezicht (☎ *626 74 33, Torensteeg 7*) **Map 2** Mains €3.60-5. Villa Zeezicht is always packed and for good reason: it serves *the* best apple pie in the city. For €2.50 you get a mountain of cooked apples dusted in cinnamon, surrounded by warm flaky pastry and smothered in fresh cream – perfect for afternoon tea. Be warned, service is frustratingly shambolic.

Village Bagels (☎ *528 91 52, Stromarkt 2*) **Map 2** Mains €2.70-3.60. Bagel-chic hits Amsterdam with the arrival of this modern espresso bar/café. Grab a copy of the *Herald Tribune*, order the vegetarian 'Bleeker' bagel and make like a native New Yorker.

Café Walem (☎ *625 35 44, Keizersgracht 449*) **Map 4** Mains €4.30-14.95. Toasted sandwiches are the speciality at this popular, modern, industrial-style café. It does a neat line in soups and salads too – the sprightly, fresh tuna salad is particularly tasty. If the weather's nice, sit in the garden courtyard.

DINNER RESTAURANTS

For ease of use, the following restaurants are listed by location and then by cuisine, but Amsterdam is quite small and you don't need much initiative to visit a worthwhile restaurant wherever it is.

Medieval Centre

Argentinian You'll find at least one or two Argentinian steak houses dotted along all the tourist 'eat streets'. They're pretty formulaic: big grilled steaks, spareribs, salad bars and live South American bands on the weekend.

Gauchos (☎ *626 59 77, Geelvincksteeg 6*) **Map 4** Mains €11.10-24.05. Carnivores will be on cloud nine: Gauchos plates up three sizes of rib-eye steaks (€13.60-24.05) and as many spareribs as you like for €13.40. Vegetarians are catered for too: a big plate of polenta with char-grilled vegetables packs a mighty punch.

Asian *NOA* (☎ *626 08 02, Leidsegracht 84*) **Map 4** Mains €13.60-15.90. Noodle mania has swept Amsterdam and this casually chic, cavernous space (with its share-a-bowl menu of pan-Asian noodles) is the best place we know for an evening of super-slurping and flirting.

Wagamama (☎ *528 77 78, Max Euweplein 10*) **Map 4** Mains €8.15-11.35. Wagamama's Zen interior, as minimal as haiku, is sure to clear your brain, while a bowl of steaming ramen or udon noodles is sure to fill your stomach.

Chinese For 'real' Chinese, with the freshest ingredients at affordable prices, visit the strip of Chinese restaurants along the Zeedijk near Nieuwmarkt Square. Don't worry about reservations – if a place is full, the one next door will have space.

Hoi Tin (☎ *625 64 51, Zeedijk 122*) **Map 2** Mains €7-17. Cheap and cheerful Hoi Tin is perpetually packed with people tucking into unpretentious Cantonese fare. The huge menu – as big as China – features all your old faves like sweet and sour chicken and beef in black bean sauce.

New King (☎ *625 21 80, Zeedijk 115*) **Map 2** Mains €4.10-15.40. Every chef we know heads here for the whole steamed fish with mushrooms and a side serve of sizzling aubergine. Elbow in and see what all the fuss is about.

Oriental City (☎ *626 83 52, Oudezijds Voorburgwal 177-179*) **Map 2** Mains €4.55-20.45. This huge, unpretentious Hong-Kong style restaurant is always lively; join gaggles of local Chinese for daily dim sum (11.30am to 4.30pm) and classic Canto cuisine.

Si-Chuan Kitchen (☎ 420 78 33, Warmoesstraat 17-19) **Map 2** Mains €5-14.95. Spicy Sechuanese is served in quiet surrounds at this low-lit, family-run restaurant. Settle in, dig the so-tacky-it's-cool photo mural and order the spicy fried squid.

Dutch Dorrius (☎ 420 22 24, Nieuwezijds Voorburgwal 5) **Map 2** Mains €19.20-24.75. Dressed-up diners head to Dorrius for its fab old-world surroundings (marble floor, leather wallpaper and velvet upholstered chairs) and upscale Dutch dishes like duck confit with sauerkraut.

Haesje Claes (☎ 624 99 98, Nieuwezijds Voorburgwal 320) **Map 2** Mains €12.70-17.70. Haesje Claes' warm surrounds, lots of dark wooden panelling and antique knick-knacks, is just the place to sample comforting pea soup and endive stamppot.

Pannenkoekenhuis Upstairs (☎ 626 56 03, Grimburgwal 2) **Map 2** Mains €4.10-7.15. Climb some of the steepest stairs in town to reach this small-as-a-stamp restaurant. The lure? Flavoursome, filling pancakes (try the chicken ragout pancake) and kooky decorations (vintage teapots hanging from the ceiling).

De Roode Leeuw (☎ 555 06 66, Damrak 93) **Map 2** Mains €17-19. To escape the cacophony that is Damrak, duck into this dark, formal dining room. Note the striking wooden boats hanging from the ceiling (carved in 1911 by a Hungarian guest) as you linger over old-fashioned dishes like fish stew and marrowfat peas.

Keuken van 1870 (☎ 624 89 65, Spuistraat 4) **Map 2** Mains €5-9.50, set menu Mon-Fri €6.15. Open 12.30pm-8pm Mon-Fri, 4pm-9pm Sat & Sun. This former soup kitchen, an institution among the downand-out, serves dirt-cheap meals. The very simple (though hyper-fresh) Dutch dishes won't win awards but that's not the point.

d'Vijff Vlieghen Restaurant (☎ 530 40 60, Spuistraat 294-302) **Map 2** Mains €21.75-27.20. Spread out over five 17th-century canal houses, d'Vijff Vlieghen is a glorious dining experience. Ask to be seated in the Rembrandt Room (it has four original etchings) and join splurging business

groups being treated to silver service and chichi Dutch food.

Fusion Tom Yam (☎ 622 95 33 Staalstraat 22) **Map 2** Mains €25.85-29.50. Top-shelf, Asian-infused and inspired soups, curries and noodle dishes are the order of the day at this small, sophisticated restaurant.

Greek Grekas (☎ 620 35 90, Singel 311) **Map 2** Mains €8.60-10.90. Ignore Grekas' no-style, snack-bar ambience and sit down for generous portions of the best Greek home cooking in town. The chicken, spinach and rice stew is a hearty delight.

Indonesian Kantjil en de Tijger (☎ 620 09 94, Spuistraat 291) **Map 2** Mains €3.40-14.50. You'll be impressed by the Art Deco style and the enormous rijsttafel for two (22 dishes for €37.45). Pleasant service almost makes up for somewhat patchy cooking.

Sukasari (☎ 624 00 92, Damstraat 26) **Map 2** Mains €5.90-15.20. With its requisite Indonesian-style decorations (batik tablecloths and ornamental fans), this does a damn good mini-rijsttafel (€9.45) and a scrupulously authentic mixed meat satay (€9.30).

International Blauw Aan De Wal (☎ 330 22 57, Oudezijds Achterburgwal 99) **Map 2** Mains €18.60-22.70. Inventive dishes shine at this hidden-away, upmarket restaurant. The building, originally a 17th-century herb warehouse, is replete with old steel weights and measures, dramatic flower displays and a nonsmoking section. Be sure to order the chocolate brownie dessert: it's as rich as the clientele.

Pier 10 (☎ 624 82 76, De Ruijterkade Steiger 10) **Map 2** Mains €14.95-16.80. Perched like a pelican at the end of a pier behind Centraal Station, this romantic, shabby-chic restaurant offers superlative water views and a smart, eclectic menu. Book a table in the rotunda and watch the sun set over the North Sea Canal as freight barges pass by your window.

Supper Club (☎ 638 05 13, Jonge Roelensteeg 21) **Map 2** 5-course set menu €54.45. Brilliant concept, so-so food and service.

PLACES TO EAT

Imagine the decline of the Roman Empire as filmed by Fellini and you're getting close to the surreal, sensual atmosphere here. Enter the theatrical, all-white room, snuggle up on enormous mattresses and snack on platters of victuals as DJs spin platters of house music.

Italian *Caprese* (☎ *620 00 59, Spuistraat 261*) **Map 2** Mains €8.15-20.40. Perfectly edible pizzas, traditional pastas and just-like-mamma-makes meat dishes may not make Caprese the most inventive Italian restaurant in town, but it sure makes it one of the most popular.

Japanese *Stereo Sushi* (☎ *777 30 10, Jonge Roelensteeg 4*) **Map 2** Mains €6.80-11.35. It ain't the most authentic sushi bar in the city, but this blink-and-you'll-miss-it place is definitely the most fun. Get sozzled on sake as DJs spin deep house. That way you won't notice how small the serves of sushi and sashimi are.

North American *Caffe Esprit* (☎ *622 19 67, Spui 10*) **Map 2** Mains €4.35-10. Over-taxed waiters scurry around Esprit's terrace serving mega-size burgers, bagels and salads to too-thin glamour girls. Order the mammoth 'Mississippi' club sandwich: it'll keep you going for hours.

Seafood *De Visscher* (☎ *623 73 37, Kalverstraat 122*) **Map 2** Mains €6.80-10.45. Superior seafood snacks and delicious fried morsels are piled high at De Visscher. Don't be deceived by the fast-food counter at the front: there's a perfectly acceptable restaurant inside and lots of choices for famished kids.

Werkendam (☎ *428 77 44, Sint Nicolaasstraat 43*) **Map 2** Mains €13.60-27.20. There are all sorts of piscatorial pleasures to be had at this loud, industrial-style restaurant. If it swims, it's sure to be grilled, fried or poached and served up to you. The enormous seafood platter (€52.15) is a great way to taste-test the menu.

Nieuwmarkt Neighbourhood
International *Café Bern* (☎ *622 00 34, Nieuwmarkt 9*) **Map 2** Mains €5.45-12.25.

Indulge in a fondue frenzy at this delightfully well-worn brown café. People have been flocking here for over 25 years for the gruyere cheese fondue. After one gorgeous, gooey dip you'll know why.

Hemelse Modder (☎ *624 32 03, Oude Waal 9*) **Map 2** 3-course/4-course/5-course menu €23.60/27/30.35 per person. This beautifully decorated, modern restaurant (floor-to-ceiling mauve velvet curtains, well-spaced tables and displays of dramatic tropical flowers) serves palate-pleasing dishes at wallet-pleasing prices. The chocolate mousse ('heavenly mud', hence the restaurant's name) is a calorific delight.

Zosa Soupkitchen (☎ *330 62 41, Kloveniersburgwal 20*) **Map 2** Soups €2.05-5.35. Soup: it's the new sushi. Sunny, ultra-groovy Zosa has transformed itself into a modern soup kitchen and is doing a roaring trade ladling big bowls of broth (laksa, seafood, vegetarian) to appreciative locals and tourists.

Italian *Ristorante Gusto* (☎ *626 25 82, Kloveniersburgwal 7*) **Map 2** Mains €10.45-27.20. Funky, rustic Gusto – with its modern stained-glass windows and chichi chandeliers – does great, authentic Italian dishes. Try the spaghetti cooked in a huge wheel of parmesan cheese or the whole fish, oven-baked in a crust of sea salt.

Western Canal Belt
Dutch *Moeder's Pot Eethuisje* (☎ *623 76 43, Vinkenstraat 119*) **Map 3** Mains €3.60-10.90. This small, kitsch place has been serving up solid, inexpensive meals (beefsteaks, schnitzels and burgers) for over 30 years. The gruff proprietor has been slinging caustic comments for just as long.

The Pancake Bakery (☎ *625 13 33, Prinsengracht 191*) **Map 3** Mains €6.35-10. The Dutch know how to make delicious pancakes and this basement restaurant – in a restored warehouse – is one of the best places to try them. It has 79 varieties (try the 'Canadian', with bacon, mushrooms, onions and cheese) as well as omelettes, soups and desserts.

French *Bordewijk* (☎ *624 38 99, Noordermarkt 7*) **Map 3** Mains €18.15-26.30. The interior here is so minimal that you have little to do but appreciate the spectacular French/Italian cooking. The Bresse chicken with spring vegetables and truffles will impress.

Brasserie Mistinguett *(☎ 622 47 15, Westerstraat 136)* **Map 3** Mains €11.35-17.70. Paying perfect tribute to the brasserie tradition, this romantic, crisply decorated place plays Piaf while plating up robust Gallic goodies (pork terrine, steak tartare and creme brulee).

Christophe *(☎ 625 08 07, Leliegracht 46)* **Map 3** Mains €30.85-34. A Michelin star ensures that Jean-Christophe Royer's subtly swanky restaurant is constantly filled with dressed-up diners. They're wooed and wowed by dishes like roasted lobster with sweet garlic and potatoes.

Jean Jean *(☎ 627 71 53, Eerste Anjeliersdwarsstraat 12)* **Map 2** 3-course set menu €17.95. Honest and affordable Gallic comfort food is what this cosy neighbourhood bistro offers, such as traditional and competent crepes, soups, meat and fish dishes.

Fusion *Blakes (☎ 530 20 10, Keizersgracht 384)* **Map 3** Mains €30.85-35.40. It's swank central, baby. Take out a loan and head for the dazzlingly elegant interior with well-spaced power tables, ultra-smooth service, Asian-accented cuisine and an ever-present smattering of international celebs. You won't be disappointed.

Lof *(☎ 620 29 97, Haarlemmerstraat 62)* **Map 2** 3-course menu €30.85. Chef Sander Louwerens combines South-East Asian and Mediterranean flavours in complex and complementary ways. Evidence his brilliance in dishes like pike served with fennel and a delicate miso sauce.

Greek *De 2 Grieken (☎ 625 53 17, Prinsenstraat 20)* **Map 3** Mains €10.45-18.15. Craving a big plate of stewed mountain goat or some juicy lamb chops? This relaxed, family-run bistro caters to all your carnivorous desires with great grills – and fine homemade dips and desserts.

Indian *Koh-I-Noor (☎ 623 31 33, Westermarkt 29)* **Map 3** Mains €10.90-17.25. Yep, Koh-I-Noor's interior is about as gaudy as it gets, but the curries, tandoori and biryani dishes (especially the king prawn biryani) are about as good as you get in Amsterdam.

Indonesian *Cilubang (☎ 626 97 55, Runstraat 10)* **Map 3** Mains €7.25-18.15. Cute, cosy, celadon-hued Cilubang soothes the stomach and soul with a filling rijsttafel and attentive, personal service.

International *Balthazar's Kitchen (☎ 420 21 14, Elandsgracht 108)* **Map 3** 3-course set menu €20.40. Open Wed-Fri. Balthazar's modern-rustic look, attentive service and fresh takes on Mediterranean cuisine ensure a fantastic night out. Be sure to book.

De Belhamel *(☎ 622 10 95, Brouwersgracht 60, entrance on Binnen Wieringerstraat)* **Map 2** Mains €16.80-19.50. De Belhamel's gorgeous Art Nouveau interior is the perfect backdrop for excellent, French-inspired dishes like beef with poached shallots and a chanterelle-armagnac sauce. It's a wonderful first-date spot.

Burger's Patio *(☎ 623 68 54, Tweede Tuindwarsstraat 12)* **Map 3** 3-course menu €21.75. Despite the name, hamburgers are not the speciality here and there's no patio, but a small garden courtyard. What you will find is a sensibly priced set menu with French and Italian-inspired dishes.

Lulu *(☎ 624 50 90, Runstraat 8)* **Map 3** 3-course/4-course menu €27.25/31.80. Lulu's decorations – gaudy chandeliers and tacky cupids – are the perfect foil for the kitchen's serious and delicious, Italian-accented dishes. The beef carpaccio is so popular it almost has its own Web site.

Spanjer en van Twist *(☎ 639 01 09, Leliegracht 60)* **Map 3** Mains €10.45-13.15. Romantic canalside tables make Spanjer en van Twist one of the Jordaan's most popular destinations. It's just as lovely inside with Mondriaanesque stained-glass panelling and a spin-the-compass menu with everything from fish and chips to chicken enchiladas.

Stoop *(☎ 639 24 80, Eerste Anjeliersdwarsstraat 4)* **Map 3** Mains €7.70-21.55. Locals may actively discourage you from visiting Stoop. Why? It seems they want to keep this modestly priced bistro – with its robust, tasty mains (like the to-die-for organic roast chicken), creative vegetarian dishes and delish desserts – all to themselves.

Summmum (☎ 770 0407, Binnen Dommersstraat 13) **Map 3** Mains €17.25-20.40. Summum's melt-in-the-mouth ceviche of scallops is one of our favourite Amsterdam taste sensations. Punchy culinary creations, spunky waiters and the effortlessly sophisticated decor means bookings are essential.

Italian Toscanini Caffè (☎ 623 28 13, Lindengracht 75) **Map 3** Mains €10.90-37. Can't afford to rent a Tuscan villa this year? A meal at Toscanini is the next best thing. The modern-rustic interior, a former horse carriage storehouse, is a cinematic setting for classic Italian dishes like freshly made gnocchi and rabbit in white wine sauce.

Middle Eastern Nomads (☎ 344 64 01, Rozengracht 133) **Map 3** 5-course set menu €38.55. Wine, dine and recline at the Supper Club's decadently decorated, Moroccan-style restaurant. Lie on mattresses and graze on platters of mod Middle Eastern snacks while being entertained by belly dancers and DJs. It's a superbly sexy, fancy-trancey treat.

Seafood Albatros (☎ 627 99 32, Westerstraat 264) **Map 3** Mains €12.50-24. Albatros' garish decorations (plastic lobsters hanging in fishing nets) fall into the 'so-bad-it's-good' camp. But the lovingly cooked seafood dishes – like grilled tuna steak in a spicy red-wine sauce – fall into 'so-good-it's-good'. There's a smokefree section.

Spanish Casa Juan (☎ 623 78 38, Lindengracht 59) **Map 3** Mains €12.70-16.80. Casa Juan does fantastic Spanish food – some say the best in Amsterdam – at very reasonable prices. Juan's wife runs the floor while Juan whips up vast quantities of his speciality, seafood paella. Be sure to book.

Duende (☎ 420 66 92, Lindengracht 62) **Map 3** Tapas €2.05-10.45. Flamenco music (Saturday night), big shared tables and reasonably priced tapas guarantee Duende's

popularity. It's just the place to party with a big group of friends – or strangers.

Paso Doble (☎ 421 26 70, Westerstraat 86) **Map 3** Tapas €3.15-14.95. Paso Doble's staff should come with a health warning: they're so energetic that just watching them can be exhausting. If you follow their lead you too will be dancing with wild abandon on the old wooden tables before the night's out.

Thai Pathum Thai (☎ 624 49 36, Willemsstraat 16) **Map 3** Mains €11.35-15.90. This sweet, little neighbourhood restaurant serves much-loved and authentically cooked Thai standards like tom yum soup, pad thai and a good selection of green and red curries. It ain't flash but that's the way we like it.

Rakang Thai (☎ 627 50 12, Elandsgracht 29) **Map 3** Mains €13.60-20.40. Rakang's goofy decorations –chairs wrapped in white hospital bandages – and delicious cooking (go for the duck salad: a crunchy, spicy delight) keep it busy night after night.

Turkish Turquoise (☎ 624 20 26, Wolvenstraat 22) **Map 3** Mains €10.70-19.95. Once a cheap eetcafé, Turquoise has spruced itself up, painted its four rooms a stylish dark blue with gold trim and started charging very grown-up prices. Come on a Sunday night for live Turkish music and great dishes like chicken fillet stuffed with mushrooms and walnuts.

Vegetarian De Bolhoed (☎ 626 18 03, Prinsengracht 60-62) **Map 3** Mains €11.35-13.15, 3-course menu €15.95-18.15. De Bolhoed's verdant little canalside terrace, surrounded by wild rose bushes, is just the place to tuck into enormous, organic (even vegan) Mexican and Italian-inspired dishes. Leave room for the super ice-cream sundaes.

De Vliegende Schotel (☎ 625 20 41, Nieuwe Leliestraat 162) **Map 3** Mains €6.80-10.45. Service here can be so infuriatingly slow and slapdash that you may burst a blood vessel in frustration and undo any of the health benefits of eating here. But if you're prepared to wait (and wait), you'll enjoy some of the biggest and best serves of home-style vegetarian cooking this side of the Atlantic.

Westerpark

French-International *Café-Restaurant Amsterdam* (☎ 682 26 66, Watertorenplein 6) **Map 3** Mains €9.05-20.40. One of the city's hippest eateries is housed in a former water-processing plant. Expect classic French brasserie food (steak bearnaise, coq au vin and crepes) served in a vast, industrial-style space. Note the 100-foot wooden ceilings (with hanging metal hooks and chains) and the 22 huge floodlights rescued from the former Ajax and Olympic stadiums.

International *Blender* (☎ 486 98 60, Van der Palmkade 16) **Map 3** Mains €19.05-19.95. Blender's, cheeky, curvy, 1970s airport-lounge interior (think lots of orange swivel chairs) is just the place to sip cocktails, sample inventive food and socialise as DJs spin deep house and soul.

Café West Pacific (☎ 488 77 78, Haarlemmerweg 8-10) **Map 3** Mains €13.60-15.90. Funky West Pacific looks like an old school hall decorated by bohemian artists. Aqua walls, big, red laminex tables, well-worn leather banquettes and an enormous central fireplace are the backdrop for an international menu of soups, salads and meat dishes. DJs play nightly after 11pm.

Southern Canal Belt

Chinese *Sichuan Food* (☎ 626 93 27, Reguliersdwarsstraat 35) **Map 4** Mains €14.75-19.50. Michelin-star-awarded Sichuan Food has a suitably formal setting and, disappointingly, Sechuanese dishes adapted to Western palates. Still, there's a large selection of great fish dishes and a perfectly crispy Peking duck dish.

Dutch *De Blauwe Hollander* (☎ 623 30 14, Leidsekruisstraat 28) **Map 4** Mains €8.15-13.60. This no-nonsense, countrified little place serves dishes you'd eat in a Dutch home: pea soup, beef and onion casserole and roast veal in gravy. It's good value for this part of town and the food's always fresh – that's why it's always full.

French *Zuidlande* (☎ 620 73 93, Utrechtsedwarsstraat 141) **Map 4** Mains €20.65-

22.45. Creative and flavoursome French-Med dishes (we're gaga for the duck breast with caramelised apple syrup) are served in this romantic, upscale restaurant. It's a worthwhile and memorable splurge.

Indian *Memories of India* (☎ 623 57 10, Reguliersdwarsstraat 88) **Map 4** Mains €13.60-18.15, set menus 16.35-18.60. This chichi, glam, yet ineffably relaxed restaurant produces great, greaseless samosas and deftly spiced subcontinental standards like tandoori lamb chops and Bengal prawns (in lime, chilli and ginger). It does a fantastic vegetarian set menu too.

Indonesian *Bojo* (☎ 622 74 34, Lange Leidsedwarsstraat 51) **Map 4** Mains €6.60-10.45. Bojo is an institution among late eaters (it's open into the early hours of the morning). They head here post-nightclub for sizzling satays, filling plates of fried rice and steaming bowls of noodle soup. The quality may be uneven but the food is certainly well priced.

Coffee & Jazz (☎ 624 58 51, Utrechtsestraat 113) **Map 4** Mains €9.05-13.60. This hip little joint is just the place to hang out with friends. Get cosy on a couch, order the spicy chicken curry, an extra large mango juice and chill out to the great jazz music.

Tempo Doeloe (☎ 625 67 18, Utrechtsestraat 75) **Map 4** Mains €13.60-27.20. Regarded as one of the best Indonesian restaurants in the city, Tempo Doeloe charges accordingly. Dishes here come spicy yet you can still taste all those subtle flavours – mains like giant shrimps in coconut-curry sauce are perfect evidence. The extraordinary wine list is laden with well-chosen New World wines and a stunning collection of rare bottles. Reservations are essential.

Tujuh Maret (☎ 427 98 65, Utrechtsestraat 73) **Map 4** Mains €12.25-14.50. Dare we say it, Tujuh Maret, right next door to Tempo Doeloe, is less expensive but just as good and more consistently so. Take a seat on one of the wobbly wicker chairs and tuck into spicy Sulawesi-style dishes like dried, fried beef or chicken in red pepper sauce.

PLACES TO EAT

International *Moko (☎ 626 11 99, Amstelveld 12)* **Map 4** Mains €15.90-16.80. Without a doubt, Moko has the most stunning terrace (full of scenesters) in Amsterdam. Super-size cushions and long outdoor tables are *the* place to spend summer evenings. The Asian-inspired menu is very much an afterthought.

Pygma-lion (☎ 420 70 22, Nieuwe Spiegelstraat 5A) **Map 4** Mains €13.60-18.15. This modern, South African bistro plates up all those animals you normally have to go to a game park to see. Expect ostrich curry, springbok with sauerkraut and sandwiches filled with oven-roasted zebra. Squeamish stomachs will be sated by vegetarian options and the delicious, traditional 'tipsy' tart (chock full of dates, nuts and brandy).

Sluizer (☎ 622 63 76, Utrechtsestraat 43-45) **Map 4** Mains €13.60-31.75. This lively Amsterdam institution – with its super-romantic, enclosed garden terrace – comprises two restaurants: a Parisian-style 'meat' restaurant (No 43) and a fish restaurant (No 45) though both menus are offered in either. Spareribs are the speciality of the former and bouillabaisse the most favoured fish dish in the latter.

Szmulewicz (☎ 620 28 22, Bakkersstraat 12) **Map 4** Mains €10-15.40. Szmulewicz's menu ping-pongs around the globe: expect big serves of Indian curries, Mexican burritos and Indonesian satays. The ambience is fitting, especially in summer, when enthusiastic buskers play world music on the terrace.

Italian *Pasta e Basta (☎ 422 22 26, Nieuwe Spiegelstraat 8)* **Map 4** 3-course set menu €34. Entertaining, chaotic, neurotic and very operatic. At Pasta e Basta, opera singers serenade you while serving a variety of antipasto and pasta. Quite often the trilling is superior to the tortellini.

Pastini (☎ 622 17 01, Leidsegracht 29) **Map 4** Mains €10-11.35. Overlooking two canals, Pastini wins praise for its picturesque views and its perfectly cooked pastas. Share an antipasto starter (€10.45 for five dishes) and save room for the thrilling, filling desserts.

Piccolino (☎ 623 14 95, Lange Leidsedwarsstraat 63) **Map 4** Mains €5.45-14.95. Piccolino is affordable – and always packed. No surprises on the menu, just a whole lot of pastas and pizzas with all your favourite toppings. The pizza calzone is great.

Zet Isie (☎ 623 42 59, Reguliersdwarsstraat 23) **Map 4** Mains €12.70-17.70. This restaurant looks like a set designer's vision of a rustic trattoria – all whitewashed walls and wooden tables set with bowls of fresh vegetables (decoration only) and warm farmer's bread with olive tapenade. The menu has modern interpretations of Mediterranean dishes like carpaccio, pasta and tiramisu.

Japanese *Yoichi (☎ 622 68 29, Weteringschans 128)* **Map 4** Mains €12.70-18.15, set menu € 29.50-49.90. Classic and elegant Yoichi specialises in fastidiously prepared sushi and sashimi. Book the upstairs tatami room and order the 'Shogun Deluxe': this all-round winner features tasty morsels of yakatori, tempura, miso, sukiyaki and sashimi.

Mexican *Rose's Cantina (☎ 625 97 97, Reguliersdwarsstraat 38)* **Map 4** Mains €10.90-18.15. Big tables of margarita-fuelled office workers start their weekends here sharing mega-portions of fajitas, quesadillas and enchiladas. Try and score a table in the gorgeous garden courtyard: it's much quieter and rather romantic.

North American *Gary's Muffins (☎ 420 24 06, Reguliersdwarsstraat 53)* **Map 4** Mains €2.25-4.55. Gary's great fresh bagels, warm chocolate brownies and sweet and savoury muffins are pure manna for clubbers craving a healthy(ish) late-night mini-munch.

Seafood *Le Pêcheur (☎ 624 31 21, Reguliersdwarsstraat 32)* **Map 4** Mains €18.15-31.30. Le Pêcheur is renowned for its beautiful garden courtyard and wonderfully prepared fish. Menu highlights include the well-priced seafood platter (€18.80) and a treasonably tasty tarte tatin.

Spanish *Pata Negra (☎ 422 62 50, Utrechtsestraat 142)* **Map 4** Tapas €3.15-14.95.

Pata Negra is both an eyeful and a mouthful of fun. The alluringly tiled exterior is matched by an equally vibrant crowd inside. Weekends are quite a scene, with boisterous groups sharing jugs of sangria and tapas plates (the garlic-fried shrimps and grilled sardines are snack-a-licious).

Thai *Dynasty (☎ 626 84 00, Reguliersdwarsstraat 30)* **Map 4** Mains €9.05-22.70. Decorated on a lavish 'King and I' budget, Dynasty is resplendent with colourful murals and hundreds of rice-paper fans. The menu, a heady mix of South-East Asian cuisines, is as embellished as the interior. Dishes like 'thousand flower duck' and 'three meats in harmony' taste as good as they sound.

Take Thai (☎ 622 05 77, Utrechtsestraat 87) **Map 4** Mains €11.35-19.05. This modern, all-white restaurant plates up some of the best Thai food in the city. Choose from a variety of curries spiced according to your palate ('soft, spicy or killing', as the menu puts it). The Penang beef curry is a winner as is the fish fried in lemongrass and Thai basil.

Thai Corner (☎ 320 66 84, Kerkstraat 66) **Map 4** Mains €10.45-19.50. Don't dismiss this cute little place: it does seriously authentic Thai. Locals and restaurant critics swoon over squid with garlic pepper and tofu with Thai basil and stare agog at the over-the-top, carved wooden bar at the back of the room.

Vegetarian *Deshima Proeflokaal (☎ 625 75 13, Weteringschans 65)* **Map 4** Dishes €3.15-11.35, buffets €12.70 & 14.95. Postage-stamp-sized Deshima offers all manner of macrobiotic meals. The gentle food here may border on bland, but there's no denying it's healthy. The changing daily menu comprises sushi, miso soups, tofu and tempeh bakes and eight styles of salad.

Golden Temple (☎ 626 85 60, Utrechtsestraat 126) **Map 4** Mains €5.90-11.80. Friendly and family-run Golden Temple is a real find. Its international menu of Indian thali, Middle Eastern and Mexican platters is consistently good and inexpensive. Leave room for the wicked banana cream pie.

De Vrolijke Abrikoos (The Happy Apricot; ☎ 624 46 72, Weteringschans 76) **Map 4** Mains €12.70-19.50. A cheerful name for a lovely place. De Vrolijke Abrikoos isn't fully vegetarian (it serves meat and fish) but most of the ingredients are organic, including the wines. Snare a table on the little balcony and dig into a plate of crispy almond *latkes* (potato pancakes) served with vegetable terrine and a mango-mustard sauce.

Plantage, Eastern Islands & Eastern Harbour

International *Koffiehuis van den Volksbond (☎ 622 12 09, Kadijksplein 4)* **Map 6** Mains €7.70-13.60. This laid-back place, with an artsy vibe and a youngish clientele, began life as a charitable coffee house for dockers. It still offers good value – and a truly eclectic menu: Italian tomato soup, Moroccan lamb stew and vegetarian tortillas. The chocolate almond tart with warm chocolate sauce has fans all over town.

Gare de l'Est (☎ 463 06 20, Cruquiusweg 9) **Map 6** 5-course set menu €23.60. Four chefs who normally work elsewhere take turns preparing seasonal set meals here. Globe-trotting menus – one night it might be North African, the next Asian, then Mediterranean – keep diners coming back for more. An equally diverse blend of decorations (Portuguese tiles and glowing Middle Eastern lamps) adorn the interior.

Odessa (☎ 419 30 10, Veemkade 259) **Map 6** Mains €14.50-19.05. Odessa rocks. Literally. This groovy boat, with outdoor eating decks and a 1970s-themed, 'plush-porno' basement disco, is just the sort of place where Hugh Hefner would hold a debauched pyjama party. Make your own mischief here while enjoying the terrific meaty menu.

Panama (☎ 311 86 86, Oostelijke Handelskade 4) **Map 6** Mains €12.25-20.40. The Eastern Harbour gets its first grown-up restaurant with Panama. Enter the enormous, sleek, chic room and take in those amazing, circular, steel light fixtures. The atmosphere and food are just as impressive, with tables of Gucci-garbed couples splurging on oysters and lobster.

PLACES TO EAT

Plancius (☎ 330 94 69, Plantage Kerklaan 61A) **Map 6** Mains €13.60-17.25. In the Resistance Museum opposite the Artis Zoo, this new, dramatically stylish space is where TV execs head to cut deals over big serves of upmarket comfort food (such as lamb fillet served with green peas and new potatoes).

Old South
French *Le Garage (☎ 679 71 76, Ruysdaelstraat 54)* **Map 4** 2-course/3-course set menu €33/25-40. Spy Dutch soap stars, media biz-kids and a couple of international celebrities at this dramatically decorated and glamorous joint. The semicircular room – with bold red banquettes and mirrored walls – is the perfect place to indulge in French-inspired cuisine and the creamiest creme brulee in town.

International *Cobra Café-Restaurant (☎ 470 01 11, Hobbemastraat 18)* **Map 4** Mains €8.15-18.15. This arty, glass cube of a restaurant, full of original artwork by Corneille and Appel, sure is touristy. But when you're all museumed out and need a big salad or stew, you'll hardly notice.
Dwinger (☎ 618 0368, Overtoom 28) **Map 4** Mains €14.95-19.50. Eye-poppingly groovy media types have made this new restaurant a favourite pre-club pit stop. The food suffers somewhat from delusions of grandeur, but Dwinger's ultra-mod lounge is the best place we know to sip cocktails and slouch insouciantly.
Toomeloos (☎ 618 99 01, Overtoom 72-74) **Map 4** Mains €8.15-14.50. This relaxed, no-nonsense eatery serves inspired, tasty dishes to a mixed clientele. It's a favourite of ours for a good meal with professional service that won't break the bank. The lunch menu is worthwhile too.
Spring (☎ 675 44 21, Willemsparkweg 177) **Map 4** Mains €20.40-34. Strikingly spare yet unspeakably stylish, Spring is our favourite swish night out. Book a table by the open kitchen and watch Amsterdam's best and best-looking chefs whip up spruce, modern creations. Be sure to clock Amsterdam's most lavish loos downstairs.

De Pijp
This cosmopolitan part of town – once a bohemian stronghold – is quickly emerging as one of Amsterdam's most interesting and diverse foodie neighbourhoods.

Assyrian *Eufraat (☎ 672 05 79, Eerste van der Helststraat 72)* **Map 4** Mains €8.15-13.15. This no-frills, friendly eetcafé may not look like much but it's hailed far and wide for its excellent Middle Eastern-Assyrian food. A good-value portion of Assyrian pancakes stuffed to bursting with chicken and cheese is sure to hit the spot, as is a fuel-injected cup of Arabic coffee afterwards.

International *District V (☎ 770 08 840, Van der Helstplein 17)* **Map 4** 3-course menu €26. Apart from the cute waiters, everything you see at District V – plates, tables, lamps – is for sale. The rustic, split-level room decorated by local artists has a Mediterranean feel, roughly in keeping with the bold offerings from the kitchen. Be sure to book; it's worth it, just for that delectable nectarine tart.
Madam Jeanette (☎ 673 33 32, Eerste van der Helststraat 42) **Map 4** Mains €13.60-18.15. Clusters of ultra-foxy models have quickly made Madam Jeanette their spiritual home. While they're getting all schmoozey in the 1970s-style bar, grab a table and treat yourself to a cool cocktail and a plate of seriously good shrimp tempura.
De Ondeugd (☎ 672 06 51, Ferdinand Bolstraat 13-15) **Map 4** Mains €14.50-19.50. De Ondeugd is everyone's idea of a good idea. Scan the gargantuan pink-foil menu for lush offerings like foie gras and sirloin steak and take in the flamboyant interior: mirrored columns, erotic vintage photos and lots of chandeliers.
De Soepwinkel (☎ 673 22 93, Eerste Sweelinckstraat 19F) **Map 4** Soups €3.40-8.85. Slurping out loud is positively encouraged at sleek De Soepwinkel. A welcome alternative to fast-food joints, this airy, modern eatery does all manner of scrumptious, seasonal soups: try the chicken and coconut or the creamy Greek lemon.

Spanish *Más Tapas* (☎ *664 00 66, Saenredamstraat 37)* **Map 4** Mains €5.45-10.45. This cool, whitewashed sliver of a room is always full of funsters having a garlicky good time. The volume is loud, the tapas terrific.

Surinamese *Albert Cuyp 67* (☎ *671 13 96, Albert Cuypstraat 67)* **Map 4** Mains €4.10-6.80. If you're looking for stylish surrounds, turn away now. If, however, you're after fine Surinamese food, take a seat. A colossal portion of *roti kip* (chicken curry, flaky roti bread, potatoes, egg and cabbage) is the best replenishment you know after a couple of hours at Albert Cuyp market. *Albina* (☎ *675 51 35, Albert Cuypstraat 69)* **Map 4** next door does similar food and is equally good.

Other Areas

Ethiopian *Lalibela* (☎ *683 83 32, Eerste Helmersstraat 249)* **Map 4** Mains around €7.50. Never tried Ethiopian food before? This dirt-cheap place in Old West is as authentic as it gets, from the Aksumite hide paintings with Christian motifs to the large, pancake-base platters without cutlery (fingers only), the heavenly coffee with incense, and unique, trippy music.

French *La Rive* (☎ *622 60 60, Amstel Inter-Continental Hotel, Professor Tulpplein 1)* **Map 5** Mains €31.75-45.35. A Michelin star, fancy French cuisine and a formal dining room with views over the Amstel River make La Rive the perfect venue for an out-to-impress business lunch or big-night-out dinner.

International *Soeterijn Café-Restaurant* (☎ *568 83 92, Linnaeusstraat 2)* **Map 5** Mains €11.35-15.90. It's fun to dine here before attending a performance in the adjacent Tropeninstituut Theater. The weekly specials coincide with the performers' country of origin, so expect Turkish, Vietnamese, Indian or even Tibetan-themed meals.

De Kas (☎ *462 45 62, Kamerlingh Onneslaan 3, Frankendael Park)* **Map 1** Set menu €36.30. If you only eat out once in Am-

sterdam, De Kas is *the* place to do it. This totally organic restaurant in a chic glass greenhouse plates up the Netherlands' most delectable dishes. Make a night of it and book the chef's table (€102 with wine). You sit in the kitchen and sup away as the brilliant crew create culinary delights.

Vandemarkt (☎ *468 69 58, Schollenbrugstraat 8)* **Map 1** 3-course set menu €31.75. To market, to market. The chefs at this wonderfully modern, colourful restaurant near the Amstelstation create menus from whatever they've found fresh that morning at the market. Pray that the pannacotta with summer fruits is making an appearance.

Surinamese *Riaz* (☎ *683 64 53, Bilderdijkstraat 193)* **Map 4** Mains €5.65-10.45. For some of the best Surinamese-Indian and Surinamese-Indonesian cuisine in town, seek out this totally unpretentious local eatery in Old West. The menu is jam-packed with all types of curry, roti, nasi and bami combinations as well as wonderful Surinamese and Indian options.

GAY & LESBIAN RESTAURANTS

The following places are popular among the gay and lesbian community:

Getto (☎ *421 51 51, Warmoesstraat 51)* **Map 2** Mains €9.05-13.60. Join Elvis, Getto's famous white cat, as he slinks around the legs of some of the cutest gay boys in town. Getto's fab-trashy, 1970s disco-pad interior is just the place to indulge in a few fluffy cocktails and a big beef burger.

De Huyschkaemer ☎ *627 05 75, Utrechtsestraat 137)* **Map 4** Mains €10.90-13.60. De Huyschkaemer looks like it was decorated by bohemian roadies: industrial metal beams, ladders and theatrical lights jostle up against arty patterned walls and floors. It's macho-tacky but the food is indisputably elegant.

Saturnino (☎ *639 01 02, Reguliersdwarsstraat 5)* **Map 4** Mains €11.35-22.45. It's all the usual suspects menu-wise at this Italian bistro. Stunning gay couples pack the Art Nouveau-styled space for pizzas, pasta and playful flirting.

La Strada (☎ 625 02 76, *Nieuwezijds Voorburgwal 93-95)* **Map 2** Mains €12.25-15.90. A mixed lesbian, gay and hetero crowd enjoy the Euro-styled food, pleasant ambience and friendly service at this split-level restaurant. Fish dishes, such as pan-baked tuna on tagliatelle pasta, are reliably good.

Raap & Peper (☎ 330 17 16, *Peperstraat 23-35)* **Map 6** 3-course menus €31.75. The Mediterranean cuisine of Chef Jacqueline and her lady Danielle gets rave reviews in the local press, and for good reason. This is also one of the favourite places for lesbian wedding banquets.

SELF-SERVICE CAFETERIAS

Hema department store (☎ 623 41 76, *Nieuwendijk 174)* **Map 2** Open 9.30am-6pm Mon-Wed, Fri & Sat, 9.30am-9pm Thur, noon-6pm Sun. Hema, a couple of blocks south of Centraal Station, has a modern, inexpensive cafeteria with a decent selection of sandwiches and hot dishes. It also sells good-value wines and deli items.

Other department stores, like *Vroom & Dreesmann* and *Bijenkorf* (see the Shopping chapter), also have worthwhile cafeterias. See the following Self-Catering section for supermarkets that do good takeaway food.

Atrium (☎ 525 39 99, *Binnengasthuis university complex)* **Map 2** Mains €2.25-4.55. This is a student refectory (mensa) in the university, off the southern end of Oudezijds Achterburgwal. It serves up low-priced portions of meat or fish with vegetables, pasta or rice. Bland and forgettable but you can't complain about the price.

FAST FOOD

There are any number of sandwich shops *(broodjeszaken)* or snack bars to sate your immediate hunger. The latter serve greasy junk food (French fries etc) but the former – such as *Broodje van Kootje (Leidseplein 20 or Spui 28)* – do a reasonable job with buns rather than sandwiches. If you're in a particularly healthy mood, ask for a *bruin broodje gezond* (brown bun healthy), with salad filling.

Vlaamse frites (Flemish fries) are French fries made from whole potatoes rather than

the potato pulp you'll get if the sign only says 'frites'. They're supposed to be smothered in mayonnaise (though you can ask for ketchup or *pindasaus*, peanut sauce) and will fill your stomach for around €1.80. At *Vlaams Friteshuis (Voetboogstraat 31)* **(Map 2)**, a hole-in-the-wall takeaway off Spui Square, you can join queues of locals lining up for the best Flemish fries in town.

An *uitsmijter* (literally 'bouncer') is fried eggs – sunny, often gluggy, side up – with cheese or meat (usually ham, sometimes beef) and garnish. Many cafés and snack bars serve this and it makes a filling breakfast or inexpensive lunch for under €4.55.

Also try seafood at one of the seafood stalls around town. Raw, slightly salted herring (about €2, cut into bite-sized bits and served with optional onion and gherkin) might not sound appealing, but you may think differently once you've tried it. The same applies to smoked eel, which, like herring, is quite filling, especially in a bun. If you still can't bear the thought, go for shrimps or *gerookte makreel* (smoked mackerel).

Israeli or Lebanese snack bars specialise in *shoarma*, a pitta bread filled with sliced lamb from a vertical spit, salad and a choice of sauces. In some parts of the world it's known as a *gyros* or *döner kebab*. Such places also do a mean *felafel* (spiced chickpea patties, deep-fried).

Poffertjes are miniature pancakes, heaped on a plate and topped with butter and caster sugar – absolutely delicious. They're not a dessert but a snack served at special stalls or parlours using supposedly secret recipes. Try them at the *Carrousel (Weteringcircuit)* **(Map 6)**.

SELF-CATERING

Many visitors compensate for their expensive hotel rooms by buying at supermarkets and eating in their rooms. When you're paying at a supermarket the clerk may ask if you want savings stamps or loyalty points, but they're hardly worth it for residents let alone visitors. Beer bottles, crates and plastic soft drink containers are returnable for a (hefty) deposit that's added to the purchase price when you buy them – you'll usually find a bottle-return machine near the supermarket turnstiles. Oh, and bring your own shopping bag: for environmental reasons, supermarkets charge up to €0.22 for a plastic bag.

Albert Heijn *(AH; ☎ 421 83 44, Nieuwezijds Voorburgwal 226, Haarlemmerdijk 1, Jodenbreestraat 21, Nieuwmarkt 18,* **Map 2***; Westerstraat 79-87, Westermarkt 21,* **Map 3***; Vijzelstraat 117, Museumplein, Van Woustraat 148-150, Overtoom 454,* **Map 4***; Koningsplein 6,* **Map 2***)* The country's dominant supermarket chain seems pretty much to have sewn up the centre of Amsterdam. They've driven many neighbourhood shops and other supermarkets out of business, and the lack of competition shows in their occasional shabbiness and casual service. Still,

they're well stocked and open long hours, including weekends. The branch on Nieuwezijds Voorburgwal behind the Royal Palace has great stand-up or takeaway meals. The Museumplein branch is located underground in front of the Concertgebouw.

Hema department store (see Self-Service Cafeterias) has a good food section located at the back.

Dirk van den Broek *(☎ 673 93 93, Eerste van der Helststraat 25)* **Map 4** Located behind the Heineken Museum with another entrance at Marie Heinekenplein 25, this is one of the country's least expensive supermarket chains, and usually beats AH on price.

Aldi Supermarket *(Nieuwe Weteringstraat 28)* **Map 4** Near Vijzelgracht, this supermarket is cheaper than any of the others but quite depressing.

PLACES TO EAT

Entertainment

Whatever the weather, Amsterdam sizzles. It's the party capital of Europe, with an amazing roster of live music, arts festivals, cutting-edge theatre and film programs to excite even the most jaded culture vulture. Add to the mix a whole lot of ambient canalside pubs, chilled-out coffeeshops and hedonistic gay clubs and not even a rainy day can dampen Amsterdam's heat.

CAFÉS (PUBS)
Brown Cafés
Medieval Centre There are more brown cafés here than elsewhere but many are newcomers that pander to tourists.

Lokaal 't Loosje (☎ *627 26 35, Nieuwmarkt 32-34)* **Map 2** With its beautiful etched-glass windows and tile tableaus on the walls, this is one of the oldest and prettiest cafés in the Nieuwmarkt area. It attracts a vibrant mix of students, locals and tourists.

Near Spui Square are quite a few brown cafés worth seeking out:

Hoppe (☎ *420 44 20, Spui 18)* **Map 2** Go on. Do your bit to ensure Hoppe maintains one of the highest beer turnovers in the city. Since 1670, drinkers have been enticed behind that velvet curtain into the dark interior to down a few glasses – the entrance is to the right of the pub-with-terrace of the same name. In summer, Hoppe's crowd of boisterous business boys spills over onto the pavement of Spui Square but they coexist peacefully with left-wing journalists and writers at *Café De Zwart* (☎ *624 65 11)* just across the alley.

Pilsener Club (☎ *623 17 77, Begijnensteeg 4)* **Map 2** Also known as Engelse Reet, this small, narrow and ramshackle place doesn't allow you to do anything but drink and talk, which is what a 'real' brown café is all about. It only started in 1893 but has hardly changed since. Beer comes straight from the vat behind the draughting alcove and connoisseurs say they can taste the difference (most places have vats in a cellar or side room with long hoses to the bar).

De Schutter (☎ *622 46 08, Voetboogstraat 13-15)* **Map 2** This large student eetcafé has a relaxed vibe and inexpensive, tasty *dagschotels* (dishes of the day) like roast beef with horseradish mayonnaise. We're particularly fond of the stuffed toy animals dangling from the ceiling fans too.

Within the Canal Belt The Jordaan area, the adjoining Prinsengracht and nearby side streets are packed with wonderful cafés:

De Doffer (☎ *622 66 86, Runstraat 12-14)* **Map 3** Writers, students and artists congregate at this popular café (with adjoining bar) for affordable food and good conversation. The dining room with its old Heineken posters, large wooden tables and fresh flowers is particularly ambient at night.

Café Het Molenpad (☎ *625 96 80, Prinsengracht 653)* **Map 4** This place attracts a nice mix of artists, students and tourists. Lunch is the standard sandwich and salad affair but dinner dishes are more interesting, especially the fillet of red bass with a pistachio, white wine sauce.

Café 't Monumentje (☎ *624 35 41, Westerstraat 120)* **Map 3** Diagonally opposite Café Nol, this slightly scruffy café is always full of barflies, backgammon players and locals. It's a good spot for a beer and a snack after shopping at the Westermarkt.

Café Nol (☎ *624 53 80, Westerstraat 109)* **Map 3** Nol epitomises the typical Jordaan café with a must-see, kitsch interior. It's the sort of place where the original Jordanese (ie, before students, artists and professionals moved in) still sing oompah ballads with drunken abandon.

Het Papeneiland (☎ *624 19 89, Prinsengracht 2)* **Map 3** You won't be the only tourist visiting this café: it's a 17th-century gem with Delft-blue tiles and a central stove. The name, 'Papists' Island', goes back to the Reformation when there was a clandestine Catholic church across the canal, allegedly linked to the other side by a secret tunnel.

Café Society

When locals say *café* they mean a pub, also known as a *kroeg*, and there are over 1000 of them in the city. Proprietors prefer the term *café* (yes, they serve coffee as well, but very much as a sideline). Of course, when they say *coffeeshop* they mean another thing all together.

Many cafés have outside seating on a *terras* (terrace) that may be covered and heated in winter. These are great places to relax and watch passers-by, soak up the sun, read a paper or write postcards. Once you've ordered a drink you'll be left alone but you might be expected to order the occasional top-up. If all tables are occupied, don't be shy about asking if a seat is taken and sharing a table.

A good tradition in many cafés, especially the so-called grand cafés, is the indoor reading table with the day's papers and news magazines, including one or two in English.

The price for a standard beer varies from around €1.25 in the outer suburbs to €2.50 in the popular Leidseplein and Rembrandtplein areas. If you occupy a table or sit at the bar, it's common to put drinks on a tab and to pay when you leave. If things are busy or you sit outside you'll probably have to pay per service.

Opening hours depend on whether the café has opted to be a 'day business' (7am to 1am Sunday to Thursday, to 3am Friday and Saturday), an 'evening business' (8pm to 3am, Friday and Saturday to 4am) or a 'night business' (10pm to 4am, Friday and Saturday to 5am). Cafés are free to adjust their hours within these limits but very few open before 9am.

TYPES OF CAFÉS

Once upon a time cafés only served a few perfunctory snacks but many these days have proper menus. Those that take their food seriously (or would like their customers to think they do) call themselves **eetcafé** and their food can be very good indeed. Many cafés in the following categories serve food.

Brown Cafés

The most famous type is the brown café *(bruin café)*. The true specimen has been in business for a while, is stained by smoke (recent aspirants simply slap on the brown paint), has sand on the wooden floor, and provides an atmosphere conducive to deep and meaningful conversation. There might be Persian rugs on the tables to soak up spilled beer.

Grand Cafés

These are spacious with comfortable furniture. They're all the rage, and any pub that installs a few solid tables and comfortable chairs will call itself a grand café. Some are grand indeed, and when they open at 10am they're perfect for a lazy brunch with relaxing chamber music tinkling away in the background.

Other Cafés

At **theatre cafés** you'll see performing artists and other types who do a lot of drinking. **Women's cafés** cater to a mainly gay clientele, but straight women will feel perfectly comfortable there too (see the later Gay & Lesbian Venues section for listings). There are also a few **tasting houses** *(proeflokalen)* that used to be attached to distilleries (a holdover from the 17th century when many small distilleries operated around town), where you can try dozens of *genevers* and liqueurs. **Beer cafés** specialise in the brew, with many seasonal and potent brands on tap and in the bottle.

Irish and **English pubs** are currently so popular in Amsterdam that many pubs are undergoing extensive renovations and reopening with Guinness on tap and some Gaelic decorations. Don't worry though, we've only listed authentic ones. There's also been an explosion of ultra design-conscious, 'loungey' **night bars** in the past three years. Some are ultra-modern, some retro-loungey, others shabby-chic. Some cafés straddle a few of these categories and others are so unique – New-Age tearooms for instance – that they defy easy classification.

De Pieper (☎ *626 47 75, Prinsengracht 424)* **Map 4** Considered by some to be the king of the brown cafés, De Pieper is small, unassuming and unmistakably old (1664). The interior features stained-glass windows, fresh sand on the floors, antique Delft beer mugs hanging from the bar and a working Belgian beer pump (1875).

De Prins (☎ *624 93 82, Prinsengracht 124)* **Map 3** Close to Anne Frankhuis, this pleasant and popular brown café prepares good lunch-time sandwiches, a terrific blue cheese fondue and serves international dishes like vegetarian enchiladas at night.

De II Prinsen (☎ *624 97 22, Prinsenstraat 27)* **Map 3** With its large windows, mosaic floor and big terrace, this café looks suitably restrained. You may be surprised then by the pumping disco music inside; all those students munching on tasty sandwiches don't seem to mind though.

Van Puffelen (☎ *624 62 70, Prinsengracht 377)* **Map 3** This large café-restaurant, popular among cashed-up professionals and intellectual types, has lots of nooks and crannies for cosy drinks and big, communal tables for sharing meals like antipasto and extra-large salads.

De Reiger (☎ *624 74 26, Nieuwe Leliestraat 34)* **Map 3** Assiduously local, this café has a quiet, front bar and a noisy, more spacious dining section at the back serving meals like duck breast with red pesto sauce.

Café 't Smalle (☎ *623 96 17, Egelantiersgracht 12)* **Map 3** This charming café has such a pretty and convivial terrace that it's packed from early morning to late at night in summer. It opened in 1786 as a genever distillery and tasting house. The interior was restored during the 1970s with antique porcelain beer pumps and leadlight windows.

De Tuin (☎ *624 45 59, Tweede Tuindwarsstraat 13)* **Map 3** Always a good place to start the evening – join the youngish clientele enjoying the wide selection of Belgian beers, good food and funky soul music.

De 2 Zwaantjes (☎ *625 27 29, Prinsengracht 114)* **Map 3** Squish into this smoky, small, authentic Jordaan café on Friday, Saturday and Sunday nights and join over a hundred people belting out torch and pop standards. It's absolutely hilarious. Or go during the day and watch the locals play cards under the imposing leadlight awning over the bar.

These cafés in the southern canal belt are real stayers, some full of history, others ever-popular local haunts:

Eylders (☎ *624 27 04, Korte Leidsedwarsstraat 47)* **Map 4** During WWII, Eylders was a meeting place for artists who refused to toe the cultural line imposed by the Nazis, and the spirit lingers on. It's still an artists' café with exhibits and makes a suitably quiet retreat from the mayhem of Leidseplein.

Reynders (☎ *623 44 19, Leidseplein 6)* **Map 4** Opened in 1897, this venerable establishment has undergone a touristy Irish makeover. It still retains a smidgen of old-world charm though, and the pleasant terrace (heated in winter) makes for good people-watching.

Oosterling (☎ *623 41 40, Utrechtsestraat 140)* **Map 4** Opened in the 1700s as a tea and coffee outlet for the United East India Company, historic Oosterling is as authentic as it gets. These days it's packed with the after-work drinks crowd from the central bank across the road and is one of the very few cafés that has a bottle-shop (liquor-store) permit.

Grand Cafés

Café Americain (☎ *556 32 32, American Hotel, Leidsekade 97)* **Map 4** This Art Deco monument, opened in 1902, is the oldest and by far the most stylish grand café in Amsterdam. It's the sort of place that attracts rafts of celebrities, as the photos lining the walls of the recently renovated Nightwatch bar will attest. Café prices are stiff but it's worth visiting at least once for a drink or snack and the chance to rub shoulders with your favourite star at the marvellous, library-like reading table.

Café Dante (☎ *638 88 39, Spuistraat 320)* **Map 2** This big, Art-Deco-style space (with an art gallery on the 1st floor) is peaceful during the day, but between 5pm and 9pm weeknights it transforms into a lively bar full of stockbrokers and suits.

Café-Restaurant Dantzig (☎ 620 90 39, *Zwanenburgwal 15)* **Map 2** Glitzy Dantzig, on the Amstel, has a great riverside terrace that's always busy in summer and affords good views over the water and lots of sunlight. It's just the place to unwind after shopping at Waterlooplein market or catching a show at the Stopera.

Dulac (☎ 624 42 65, *Haarlemmerstraat 118)* **Map 2** This old bank building is outrageously decked out in a kooky, kind of spooky mixture of styles (think Turkish, Art Nouveau and Amsterdam School and you're getting close). Definitely worth a visit.

Café de Jaren (☎ 625 57 71, *Nieuwe Doelenstraat 20)* **Map 2** Watch the Amstel float by from the balcony and waterside terraces of this huge, bright, grand café. Find a foreign publication at the great reading table and settle down for a Sunday brunch (try the smoked salmon rolls) or an afternoon snack like banana cream pie.

Café ter Kuile (☎ 639 10 55, *Torensteeg 4)* **Map 2** Ter Kuile's large, canalside terrace is always busy with students, businesspeople and ladies-who-lunch enjoying a coffee and cake or more extravagant dishes like filet mignon with truffle sauce.

Luxembourg (☎ 620 62 64, *Spui 24)* **Map 2** Join gaggles of glam locals and tourists at this permanently busy café. Our advice is to check the reading table (or buy a paper at Athenaeum newsagency), procure a terrace seat in the sun, order the 'Royale' snack platter (bread, cured meats, Dutch cheese and deep-fried croquettes) and watch the goings-on in Spui Square.

Mediacafé De Kroon (☎ 625 20 11, *Rembrandtplein 17-1)* **Map 4** What a stunner! De Kroon, our favourite, secret-hideaway grand café, is a sumptuous delight: lots of upholstered velvet armchairs, chandeliers and ornaments with a biological bent (ancient microscopes and cabinets with pinned butterflies and animal skeletons). It has a covered balcony terrace with views over Rembrandtplein and pretty good food too (try the corn-fed chicken with mushrooms).

Café de Vergulde Gaper (☎ 624 89 75, *Prinsenstraat 30)* **Map 3** Decorated with old chemists' bottles and vintage posters, this former pharmacy has a pleasant terrace and amiable staff. It gets busy late afternoons with media types meeting for afterwork drinks and big plates of fried snacks.

Irish & English Pubs

The Blarney Stone (☎ 623 38 30, *Nieuwendijk 29)* **Map 2** This reputable Irish pub loved for its country-style interior bursts with Irish, Australians and locals enjoying a pint.

The Dubliner (☎ 679 97 43, *Dusartstraat 51)* **Map 4** Irish expats swear that the Guinness here is the best in town (the pipes are always clean) and that Fergal, the bar manager, is the wildest man around.

Durty Nelly's (☎ 638 01 25, *Warmoesstraat 117)* **Map 2** Huge, dark and always busy, this red-light district pub attracts foreign visitors from the cheap hotels in the area. It serves a first-rate Irish breakfast too.

Last Waterhole (☎ 624 48 14, *Oudezijds Armsteeg 12)* **Map 2** Hankering to hang out with Hell's Angels and homesick Brits? This has three pool tables, jam sessions (9pm to 1am Sunday to Thursday) and rock or blues cover bands (10pm to 2am Friday and Saturday). There's also a nightly happy hour (7pm to 9pm) and hostel beds (€13.60 to €18.15).

Molly Malone's (☎ 624 11 50, *Oudezijds Kolk 9)* **Map 2** Regularly packed with Irish folk, this dark, woody pub holds spontaneous folk music sessions – bring your own guitar.

Mulligans (☎ 622 13 30, *Amstel 100)* **Map 4** This is probably the most 'authentic' pub, at least music-wise. There's a congenial atmosphere, Guinness on tap, live Irish music, and dancing most nights from 9pm (no cover charge).

O'Donnell's (☎ 676 77 86, *Ferdinand Bolstraat 5 at Marie Heinekenplein)* **Map 4** This large Irish pub, just south of the Heineken Experience, has a few snugs (great if you can grab one), Sky TV and a terrace full of sociable types.

Old Bell (☎ 624 76 82, *Rembrandtplein 46)* **Map 4** This comfortable English pub is full of ephemera like dart boards, old signs and drinking mugs. It's popular among businesspeople and tourists but is less appealing on weekends when brazen Dutch youth take over.

Tasting Houses

De Drie Fleschjes (☎ 624 84 43, Gravenstraat 18) **Map 2** Behind the Nieuwe Kerk, De Drie Fleschjes dates from 1650, and is dominated by 52 old vats full of liqueurs and genevers that are rented out to businesses who take their clients here. Be sure to try the macaroon liqueur and take a peek at the collection of *kalkoentjes*, small bottles with hand-painted portraits of former mayors.

Proeflokaal Wijnand Fockinck (☎ 639 26 95, Pijlsteeg 31) **Map 2** This small tasting house (without seats or stools) has scores of different genevers and liqueurs – some quite expensive and all potent! Behind the tasting house is one of our favourite retreats: a pretty garden courtyard café serving well-prepared lunches and snacks (10am to 6pm daily). Wijnand Fockinck is through an arcade behind Grand Hotel Krasnapolsky.

Beer Cafés

't Arendsnest (☎ 421 20 57, Herengracht 90) **Map 2** This gorgeous, re-styled brown café, with its glowing, copper genever boilers behind the bar, specialises in Dutch beer. Be sure to try the herby, powerful 'Jopen Koyt', brewed from a 1407 recipe.

Gollem (☎ 626 66 45, Raamsteeg 4) **Map 2** Gollem, the pioneer of Amsterdam's beer cafés, is a minuscule space covered in beer paraphernalia (old coasters, bottles and posters). The 200 beers on tap or in the bottle attract lots of drinkers.

Maximiliaan (☎ 626 62 80, Kloveniersburgwal 6-8) **Map 2** This rambling brewery-pub with its dramatic copper kettles is one of only two breweries still operating in the city (the other is Bierbrouwerij 't IJ – see Things to See & Do chapter). Steeped in brewing history too – during the 16th century it was a brewery/cloisters run by nuns – it has a restaurant, tasting area, tours, beer seminars and home-brewed, seasonal beers on tap.

In de Wildeman (☎ 638 23 48, Kolksteeg 3) **Map 2** This former distillery tasting house has been transformed into a beautiful beer café with over 200 bottled beers and a smokefree area. Locals rave about the choice of Trappist ales and the potent French 'Belzebuth' (15% alcohol!).

Theatre Cafés

Blincker (☎ 627 19 38, Sint Barberenstraat 7-9) **Map 2** The Frascati Theatre's café, with its attractive, airy interior (lots of marble and plants), is a convivial spot for a post-theatre drink. It has a large collection of wines and decent food like sirloin steak with caper sauce.

De Brakke Grond (☎ 626 00 44, Nes 43) **Map 2** Part of the Flemish Cultural Centre, this café overlooking a quiet square does an honest trade in Flemish beer (try a magnum bottle from a Belgian abbey) and home-style food (largely fish and veal dishes).

Felix Meritis Café (☎ 626 23 21, Keizersgracht 324) **Map 3** Join performing artists from around Europe and the city's cultural cognoscenti imbibing in this beautiful, refined room, dominated by a dramatic cast-iron chandelier.

De Smoeshaan (☎ 625 03 68, Leidsekade 90) **Map 4** Theater Bellevue's café gets pretty lively with theatre visitors and artists before and after the shows. It has a good restaurant upstairs too.

Other Cafés

Himalaya (☎ 626 08 99, Warmoesstraat 56) **Map 2** Just the place to put some yin back into your yang. Sip a cup of 'vitality' tea, snack on a vegie burger and contemplate the Buddha statues at this calm, New-Age tearoom overlooking Damrak.

Café De IJsbreker (☎ 668 18 08, Weesperzijde 23) **Map 5** The IJsbreker centre for contemporary music has a great riverside terrace (at least until it moves to new premises in 2003) that's glorious in summer for a long lunch. Join the country's leading experimental musicians and other arty types quaffing wine and dipping into cheese fondue.

Café-Restaurant Kapitein Zeppo's (☎ 624 20 57, Gebed Zonder End 5) **Map 2** This site, off Grimburgwal, has assumed many guises over the centuries: it was a cloister during the 15th, a horse-carriage storehouse in the 17th and a cigar factory in the 19th. These days it's one of the liveliest pick-up joints in town, full of young students downing Belgian beers. There's live music Sunday from 4pm (cover groups and big bands).

De Koe (☎ 625 44 82, Marnixstraat 381) **Map 4** De Koe is loved by locals for its fun pop quizzes, darts tournaments, good restaurant and free performances by local rock bands (from 4pm Sunday, winter only).

Pompadour (☎ 623 95 54, Huidenstraat 12) **Map 3** Join society ladies sipping topnotch tea and nibbling away at Belgian chocolates and pastries at this gloriously chichi little tearoom.

Café Schiller (☎ 624 98 46, Rembrandtplein 26) **Map 4** The walls of this wonderful Art Deco café are lined with portraits of Dutch actors and cabaret artists from the 1920s and '30s, and the bar stools are occupied by journalists, artists and students enjoying a tipple.

Café Thijssen (☎ 623 89 94, Brouwersgracht 107) **Map 3** The glowing umber, Art Deco-inspired interior with stained-glass windows and big tables is a crowd-puller. It's busy on weekends with groups meeting up for a late brunch and staying on till dinner.

Waag (☎ 422 77 72, Nieuwmarkt 4) **Map 2** This former 15th-century weigh house is now an impressive café-restaurant combining old-world charm (over 300 candles hang from wrought-iron candelabras) with new-world technology (free Internet access with your drink, though the terminals are in a sorry state and could well be gone by the time you read this). It serves pretty good sandwiches (try the Club) and salads too.

Designer Bars

Absinthe (☎ 777 48 70, Nieuwezijds Voorburgwal 171) **Map 2** This calm, chilled-out basement bar is the coolest place to indulge in Europe's coolest drink: gooey-green absinthe. It's served without the highly prohibitive wormwood.

Finch (☎ 626 24 61, Noordermarkt 5) **Map 3** This funkalicious bar, with its retro decor, is just the spot to hang out and knock back a few beers after a visit to the market.

Lime (☎ 639 30 20, Zeedijk 104) **Map 2** Small but perfectly formed Lime, with its ever-changing, kitsch-cool interior and upbeat grooves, is the perfect pre-club pit stop.

Magic Minds (☎ 521 70 10, Prins Hendrikkade 20-21) **Map 2** Massive, monochrome (white-only) Magic Minds is where media mavens and club kids gather weeknights for fancy drinks, dinner and dancing.

NL Lounge (☎ 622 75 10, Nieuwezijds Voorburgwal 169) **Map 2** NL's 13m-long, solid-glass bar, underlit for dramatic effect, is rather special. So too are the gangs of glamourpusses grooving to two-step and deep house on the weekend.

De Ruimte (☎ 489 36 19, Eerste Constantijn Huygensstraat 20) **Map 4** Hard to spot from the street, this former university building has been transformed into an enormous, industrial-style bar. Rub shoulders with arty-bohemian types as DJs spin funk and hip-hop.

Wolvenstraat 23 (☎ 320 08 43, Wolvenstraat 23) **Map 3** Part 1970s love-pad, part slick lounge, this fun day-into-night bar plays host to students, biz-kids and hipsters.

Nieuwezijds Voorburgwal has three of the city's hippest 'see and be seen' bars. They get insanely busy on summer nights. When you see hundreds of punters spilling out onto the sidewalk (and often the street) you'll know you've found the right place:

Bar Bep (☎ 626 56 49, Nieuwezijds Voorburgwal 260) **Map 2** With its olive-green vinyl couches and ruby-red walls, Bep resembles a kitsch, 1950s Eastern European cabaret lounge. It serves food during the day but really starts heating up with groovy film makers, photographers and artists after 6pm.

Diep (☎ 420 20 20, Nieuwezijds Voorburgwal 256) **Map 2** Just next door to Bar Bep, Diep does first-rate quirky decorations. Expect chandeliers made of bubble wrap, a 6-foot fibreglass hammerhead shark, illuminated electronic signs above the bar and a similarly creative crowd.

Seymour Likely (☎ 627 14 27, Nieuwezijds Voorburgwal 250) **Map 2** A laid-back mix of down-tempo house, funky breakbeats and sleazy lounge music ensures that this late-opening, club-style lounge is always full of dressed-up kids enjoying a pre- or post-club drink.

Marnixstraat, near Leidseplein, also has a clutch of funky and busy bars. Join the perpetually clamorous din of 20-something arts students, designers and stylish city workers drinking and dancing at **Lux** (☎ 422 14 12, *Marnixstraat 403*), **Kamer 401** (☎ 320 45 80, *Marnixstraat 401*) and **Weber** (☎ 627 05 74, *Marnixstraat 397*), all **Map 4**.

COFFEESHOPS

Abraxas (☎ 625 57 63, *Jonge Roelensteeg 12*) **Map 2** Hands down the most beautiful coffeeshop in town, this has three floors of modern, Middle-Eastern-style decorations with live DJs, a games room and extra-friendly staff.

Barney's (☎ 625 97 61, *Haarlemmerstraat 102*) **Map 2** Ever-popular Barney's is more famous for its enormous all-day breakfasts

(the traditional Irish is the most popular) than its quality weed and hash. Go figure.

The Bulldog (☎ 627 19 08, *Leidseplein 13-17*) **Map 4** Amsterdam's most famous coffeeshop chain has five branches around town; this is the largest, with Internet facilities, two bars, pool tables and fabulous fluorescent decorations.

Global Chillage (☎ 777 97 77, *Kerkstraat 51*) **Map 4** Toke on some 'Super Skaff' hash as you inhale the ambience. It's like a little forest with trippy murals, chilled-out music (African and jazzy beats) and happy smokers relaxing on comfortable couches.

Greenhouse (☎ 627 17 39, *Oudezijds Voorburgwal 191*) **Map 2** One of the most

Amsterdam Coffeeshops

'Wow, this coffee's strong!'

Many establishments that call themselves *koffieshop* (as opposed to *koffiehuis*, espresso bar or sandwich shop) are in the cannabis business, though they do serve coffee. There are also a few *hashcafés* serving alcohol that are barely distinguishable from pubs.

You'll have no trouble finding a coffeeshop; they're all over town, seemingly on every corner. It's a safe bet that an establishment showing palm leaves and perhaps Rastafarian colours (red, gold and green) will have something to do with cannabis – take a look at the clientele and ask at the bar for the list of goods on offer, usually packaged in small bags for €4.53 or €11.34 (the better the quality, the less the bag will contain). You can also buy ready-made joints in nifty, reusable packaging (a good idea because the stuff can be potent).

'Space' cakes and cookies are sold in a rather low-key fashion, mainly because tourists have problems with them. If you're unused to their effects, or the time they can take to kick in and run their course, you could be in for a rather involved experience. Ask the staff how much you should take and heed their advice, even if nothing happens after an hour. Some coffeeshops sell magic mushrooms – quite legal because they're an untreated, natural product. If you're after mushies and other mind-altering products, see Smart Drug Shops in the Shopping chapter.

Most cannabis products used to be imported but these days the country has top-notch home produce, so-called *nederwiet* (NAY-der-weet) developed by horticulturists and grown in greenhouses with up to five harvests a year. Even the police admit it's a superior product, especially the potent 'superskunk' with up to 13% of THC, the active substance (Nigerian grass has 5% and Colombian 7%). According to a government-sponsored poll of coffeeshop owners, nederwiet has captured over half the market and hash is in decline even among tourists.

Price and quality are OK – you won't get ripped off in a coffeeshop like you would on the street. Most shops are open 10am to 1am Sunday to Thursday, to 3am Friday and Saturday.

popular coffeeshops in town – smokers love the funky music, multicoloured mosaics, psychedelic stained-glass windows and the high-quality weed and hash. The alcohol licence doesn't hurt either.

Grey Area (☎ 420 43 01, Oude Leliestraat 2) **Map 2** Owned by a couple of laid-back American guys, this tiny shop introduced the extra-sticky, flavoursome 'Double Bubble Gum' weed to the city's smokers.

Homegrown Fantasy (☎ 627 56 83, Nieuwezijds Voorburgwal 87A) **Map 2** Quality Dutch-grown product, pleasant staff and good tunes make this popular with backpackers from nearby hostels. Patrons make use of the 3-foot glass bongs to smoke hydroponic weed like 'Blue Haze' (which gives an 'inspiring' buzz).

Kadinsky (☎ 624 70 23, Rosmarijnsteeg 9) **Map 2** Hidden away near Spui Square, this attractive, little coffeeshop has a good selection of hash and grass and moreish, flying-saucer-sized, choc-chip cookies.

Rokerij (Singel 8) **Map 2** African and South American vibes predominate at this relaxed coffeeshop close to Centraal Station. The painted mural/collage on the wall is sure to trip you out after a smoke of the sweet, crispy 'Star Dust' grass.

La Tertulia (Prinsengracht 312) **Map 3** This mother-and-daughter-run coffeeshop is a backpackers' favourite. Sit outside by the Van Gogh-inspired murals or relax by the mini-fish pond inside, play some board games and take in those Jurassic-sized crystals by the counter.

CLUBS

Amsterdam's club scene is, disappointingly, an increasingly commercial affair, with happy house, classic funk and R&B-garage dominating. Thursday and Saturday are the most popular club nights and not much happens before midnight.

Most of the venues listed here close at 4am on Thursday and Sunday, 5am on Friday and Saturday. If you're looking for recovery parties, keep an eye out for flyers at record shops, smart-drug and club-wear stores or ask around the club at closing time. Dress standards are decidedly casual and

you may feel out of place in head-to-toe designer clothes. Some clubs charge exorbitant admission (up to €20), others are free. If there's no entrance fee, it's good etiquette to slip the doorman a couple of euro as you leave. Also, have a bit of change (€0.45) handy if you plan to visit the toilet.

Only in Amsterdam: staff from the Adviesburo Drugs (☎ 623 79 43), Entrepotdok 32A, open 2pm to 5pm Tuesday to Friday, can check the purity of ecstasy pills for a fee of €2.27.

Arena (☎ 694 74 44, Hotel Arena, 's-Gravesandestraat 51) **Map 5** Arena's formula of crowd-pleasing tunes – a jumble of rock, house and techno – lures loads of merry students and hotel guests to this club.

Club De Ville (Westergasfabriek, Haarlemmerweg 8-10, W www.clubdeville.nl) **Map 3** One-off club nights are held here: fetish parties, Drum Rhythm nights and extravagant, jam-packed 'Speedfreax' bashes.

Dansen bij Jansen (☎ 620 17 79, Handboogstraat 11) **Map 2** Amsterdam's most famous student nightclub is more than 25 years old and still thumping nightly. Its secret? Cheap drinks (happy hour 11pm to midnight), a fun selection of classic disco

Dance Valley Festival

It's big and it's getting bigger, baby! Dance Valley is Europe's largest outdoor daytime dance music festival: over 130 of the world's best DJs and bands perform in 15 tents and two outdoor stages to 80,000 dance-music lovers. Held on a Saturday each August at the green, valley-like Spaarnwoude Recreational Area, the festival (☎ 0900-300 12 50, W www .dancevalley.nl, tickets €45.40) presents 14 full-on hours of techno, drum'n'bass, jungle, house, trance, garage, roots and hip-hop.

The 2001 event got completely out of control, with organisers unprepared for the massive influx – in pouring rain, with minimal facilities and public transport. The press devoted front-page articles to the fiasco and the mayor proclaimed that future events would only be allowed if the organisers got their act together. Let's hope they do.

ENTERTAINMENT

and house and a relaxed dress code. Valid student cards are required for entry.

De Duivel *(☎ 626 61 84, Reguliersdwars-straat 87)* **Map 4** Droves of B-boys and fly girls cram this small bar, with its spooky, stained-glass portrait of the devil, for a menu of hip-hop, rap, ska and drum'n'bass.

Escape *(☎ 622 11 11, Rembrandtplein 11)* **Map 4** Resident DJs host weekly sessions of thumping house and techno at this massive and massively popular club. A dressed-up crowd, serious about dancing, takes Saturday's 'Chemistry' night by storm (especially when international DJs like Armand Van Helden play).

iT *(☎ 625 01 11, Amstelstraat 24)* **Map 4** Originally the city's most famous gay club (Saturday still gay only), this huge venue now attracts gangs of glam club kids relishing hours of hands-in-the-air, happy house.

Mazzo *(☎ 626 75 00, Rozengracht 114)* **Map 3** Still a firm favourite, this relatively small club programs a fierce roster of first-rate DJs playing everything from deep house to Latin beats and experimental electro. Catch 'DJazzedelic' (first Sunday of month) for brilliant, rare grooves or 'Cinematic Clubbing' (first Wednesday of month), a night of ambient beats and trippy films.

Melkweg *(☎ 531 81 81, Lijnbaansgracht 234A)* **Map 4** Thursday's 'Soundclash' is by far the best reggae night around with truckloads of dancehall, ragga, dub and jungle. Saturday sees two rooms open: one with indie faves and old-school floor-fillers, the other with two-step, hip-hop and funky beats.

Ministry *(☎ 623 39 81, Reguliersdwars-straat 12)* **Map 4** Speed garage, R&B, funk and disco classics make up the selection at this small, well-designed club.

Odeon *(☎ 624 97 11, Singel 460)* **Map 2** This relaxed, friendly venue offers three floors of dancing options; choose from dance classics, house or hip-hop.

Panama *(☎ 311 86 86, Oostelijke Handelskade 4)* **Map 6** A brilliant and luxe venue for stylish 30- and 40-somethings, Panama has a salsa-tango dance salon, a restaurant and glam nightclub that programs Cuban big bands, Brazilian circus acts and a soulful selection of DJ talent.

Paradiso *(☎ 626 45 21, Weteringschans 6)* **Map 4** Regular student-indie club nights here on Wednesday and Thursday play a diet of The Clash, Nirvana and Fatboy Slim. Semi-regular night 'Paradisco' is almost always sold out, especially when the line-up includes DJs like Theo Parrish and hip-hop supremo Biz Markie. The best night is arguably the monthly 'Kindred Spirits', when DJs Wix and KC the Funkaholic mix a deep selection of hip-hop and jazzy beats.

Vakzuid *(☎ 570 84 00, Olympic Stadium 35)* **Map 1** A spanking new, glamorous club-restaurant overlooking the 1928 Olympic Stadium, this has a large dance floor and loads of comfortable lounges to pose on.

Café West Pacific *(☎ 488 77 78, Haar-lemmerweg 8-10)* **Map 3** They push back the chairs and tables at this funky restaurant, transforming it into a club after dinner. The music varies from nu-skool house to breakbeat.

Winston *(☎ 623 13 80, Warmoesstraat 127)* **Map 2** Changing theme nights and a fine line-up of local DJs make Winston a popular destination. Our fave night, 'Ex Porn Star' (first Saturday of month), promises an eyeful of salaciously dressed party-people and an earful of groovalicious tunes.

Bloemen Marvellous Beach Gigs

Can't afford Ibiza this year? Don't worry, Amsterdam's club promoters have come up with the next best thing: clubbing at Bloemendaal Beach. Each Sunday from June to October, thousands of flamboyant, party-mad clubbers crowd into and spill out of massive and quite sophisticated beach-tents from midday to midnight. Each tent has a different musical style: Republiek attracts hordes of house fans with brilliant local DJs like Mary Sol; Solaris mixes it up with hip-hop beats, drum'n'bass and disco classics; Woodstock keeps the party sticky and sexy with soulful house; and De Zomer flavours its tent with funk, dub, salsa and Latin beats.

To get there from Centraal Station, take the train to Haarlem Station. From there catch bus No 81 and get off at Bloemendaal aan Zee.

Café Thijssen in the Jordaan

Nightlife near the Oude Kerk

Cockring, a popular gay nightclub

LIVE JAZZ

Café Alto

Sax is big at Jazz Café Alto.

café de jaren

Café de Jaren, a spacious grand café overlooking the Amstel

ELLIOT DANIEL

'Golden Fleece' condom shop

MARTIN MOOS

The shop of Analik, one of the city's leading fashion designers

MARTIN MOOS

Hema, the nation's equivalent of K-Mart or Woolworths

JON DAVISON

Heaven for cheese lovers

NIKKI HALL

Hand-made chocolates

GAY & LESBIAN VENUES

Amsterdam's gay scene is the biggest in Europe, with close to 100 gay and lesbian bars, cafés, clubs, shops and hotels. Queer club nights are held weekly at some of the larger nightclubs but they generally don't last long, changing their name or theme every few months. Ask around or contact the Gay & Lesbian Switchboard (☎ 623 65 65) to find out about the latest 'in' places. See Gay & Lesbian Travellers in the Facts for the Visitor chapter for details of more information sources.

The following centres of gay and lesbian culture are always busy and a good place to start exploring.

Reguliersdwarsstraat

This street, also known simply as the Straat, has some of Amsterdam's most famous gay establishments. It attracts rafts of tanned, buff, beautiful boys who schmooze and cruise their way along the street; follow their lead and meet for happy hour at one of the various bars, eat dinner at a gay-run restaurant and finish the night off in a sweaty, sexy club.

April (☎ 625 95 72, *Reguliersdwarsstraat 37*) **Map 4** April is equally famous for its 'shuffle bubble' happy hour (6pm to 7pm Monday to Thursday, 6pm to 8pm Sunday) and the beautiful guys who cram into the space to flirt and drink, although it has lost out a bit to Soho across the street. The revolving bar can make for a giddy experience after too many cocktails.

Downtown (☎ 622 99 58, *Reguliersdwarsstraat 31*) **Map 4** This daytime eatery used to plate up great food; these days it's better known for its large terrace, friendly staff, good coffee and cake.

Exit (☎ 625 87 88, *Reguliersdwarsstraat 42*) **Map 4** This multistorey nightclub plays underground house and has a selection of bars, dance floors and an always busy darkroom. 'Drag Planet' (Thursday) and 'NSDP' (Sunday) tend to be the busiest, most entertaining nights.

Havana (☎ 620 67 88, *Reguliersdwarsstraat 17*) **Map 4** Havana boasts a camp Art Deco bar with gorgeous bar staff, thumping club music and outrageously decadent dress-up parties. There's a trendy women's night Friday in the upstairs disco.

Other Side (☎ 421 10 14, *Reguliersdwarsstraat 6*) **Map 4** This gay coffeeshop sells hash, grass and energy drinks and plays a mix of disco, funk and soul.

Poonani Club (☎ 623 39 81, *Reguliersdwarsstraat 12*) **Map 4** Mixed dance nights are held every Thursday at Ministry; see the earlier Clubs section.

Soho (☎ 626 15 73, *Reguliersdwarsstraat 36*) **Map 4** Kitschly decorated – imagine an old-world English library on the Titanic – this enormous, two-storey bar pumps with a young, ridiculously pretty clientele and an increasing number of straights who drink and flirt on the upstairs Chesterfield sofas.

Amstel & Rembrandtplein

This is real queen territory with a selection of interesting bars. Some are camp (sing-alongs to Dutch pop songs), some are cloney (lots of moustaches) and some are refined and quiet (attracting gay businessmen who pop in after work for a quick drink).

Back Door (☎ 620 23 33, *Amstelstraat 32*) **Map 4** This club, next to iT, hosts Sunday's jam-packed 'Tea Dance'. Hot boys, thumping house music and sexy staff dressed in flamboyant costumes are the draw.

Club Showtime (☎ 620 01 71, *Halve Maansteeg 10*) **Map 4** During the week young professionals congregate at this popular bar for after-work drinks; on the weekend it's a busy spot for pre-club refreshments.

iT (☎ 625 01 11, *Amstelstraat 24*) **Map 4** One of the most extravagant and commercial clubs in town, this features weekly gay nights; Saturday's 'Gay Gang Bang' is always packed with sweaty, spunky guys.

Lellebel (☎ 427 51 39, *Utrechtsestraat 4*) This hip drag café just off Rembrandtplein has drag shows Friday, Saturday and Sunday.

Montmartre (☎ 620 76 22, *Halve Maansteeg 17*) **Map 4** This is quite an experience: bar staff and patrons sing Dutch ballads and pop songs (think Abba) at the top of their voices; it's like a camp, festive Eurovision song contest.

ENTERTAINMENT

Café Rouge (☎ *420 98 81, Amstel 60*) **Map 4** An older, mixed gay crowd enjoys beer and blasting Dutch pop ballads at this brown café decorated with hundreds of photographs.

Vivelavie (☎ *624 01 14, Amstelstraat 7*) **Map 4** This lively place is probably the most popular lesbian café in town. It has flirty girls, loud music and large windows. In summer the outdoor terrace buzzes.

You II (☎ *421 09 00, Amstel 178*) **Map 4** This women-only nightclub has a roster of not entirely exciting theme nights: tropical, top 40 or R&B. The crowd can be a little lacklustre too.

Warmoesstraat

Kinky Amsterdam congregates in the red-light district at a variety of clubs catering to lovers of leather, rubber, piercings, slings, darkrooms and hard-core porn.

Argos (☎ *622 65 95, Warmoesstraat 95*) **Map 2** Leather boys of all ages head here for the famous darkrooms, cabins and kinky toys. The monthly and aptly named 'SOS' (Sex On Sunday) is always wild – dress code: nude!

Cockring (☎ *623 96 04, Warmoesstraat 96*) **Map 2** This nightclub, playing techno, hard house and trance, has live strip shows and a cruisey, hot darkroom for young leather boys.

Getto (☎ *421 51 51, Warmoesstraat 51*) **Map 2** This groovy restaurant and bar is loved more for its fun nightly entertainment (tarot readers, DJs, bingo competitions, cocktail happy hours) than the quality of its food. It's patronised by a hip and up-for-it crowd.

Getto Dance (☎ *623 13 80, Warmoesstraat 127*) **Map 2** At Winston – see Clubs, earlier – the gang from Getto restaurant holds a funky lesbian night every second Thursday of the month. Expect cute gals and slamming female DJs.

Other Areas

The gay establishments tend to cluster around the above three areas but there are others dotted around the inner city.

COC (☎ *623 40 79, Rozenstraat 14*) **Map 3** The Amsterdam branch of the national

gay and lesbian organisation holds a variety of gay, lesbian and mixed club nights every weekend – such as the Saturday night 'Just Girlsz' for under-26 women in the coffee-shop, and the ever-popular disco which attracts women of all ages. It also has a wealth of information on gay health, local support groups and special events.

Cuckoo's Nest (☎ *627 17 52, Nieuwe-zijds Kolk 6*) **Map 2** A small, busy bar with the largest 'playroom' in Europe. You could spend a whole night exploring the labyrinth of cubicles and 'glory holes'.

Planet Pussy (☎ *531 81 81, Lijnbaans-gracht 234*) **Map 4** Courtesy of Amsterdam's busiest lesbian nightclub entrepreneur, Puck Verdoes, flirty chicks dig DJ Natarcia's housey-garage tunes at Melkweg. The night is held every third Sunday of the month, 9pm to 2am.

Queen's Head (☎ *420 24 75, Zeedijk 20*) **Map 2** A beautifully decorated, old-world-style café run by the infamous, outrageous, pierced and tattooed drag queen Dusty. Her bingo nights (Tuesday) are legendary, as is the free 'Bitterball Buffet' on Sunday.

Saarein II (☎ *623 49 01, Elandsstraat 119*) **Map 3** During the late 1970s Saarein II was the focal point of the feminist movement, and it's still a premier meeting place for lesbians. The café itself dates from the early 1600s and the interior has been kept almost intact. It offers a small menu with tapas, great soups and daily specials. Bar staff Puck and Dia can give you tips on lesbian nightlife.

De Spijker (☎ *620 59 19, Kerkstraat 4A*) **Map 4** Leather boys and clones feel right at home at this friendly bar. Entertainment is in the form of pool tables, hard-core videos and a very busy darkroom.

De Trut (*Bilderdijkstraat 165E*) **Map 3** Queue for this mixed, lesbian and gay Sunday-night club institution held in the basement of a former squat well before its 11pm opening time and be prepared for the strict 'door police'; heteros are definitely not welcome.

Vandenberg (☎ *622 27 16, Lindengracht 95*) **Map 3** Run by a gruff proprietor, this no-frills eetcafé is popular among older lesbians but men come here too. It does hearty meals for under €13.60.

The Web (☎ 623 67 58, St Jacobsstraat 6) **Map 2** A cruisey, well-established leather and clone bar with darkrooms, 'Bear nights' and a Sunday evening buffet (food, we think).

MUSIC

For a description of the local music scene, see Music in the Facts about Amsterdam chapter. At many of the venues listed below, just turn up at the door and pay to get in. You might want to book ahead, however, for famous acts or highbrow performances – check the *Uitkrant* (see Useful Publications in the Facts for the Visitor chapter) to see what's happening where, or consult the weekly agenda in the *Parool* newspaper's Saturday *PS* magazine. Apart from the *Uitkrant*, the Amsterdam Uitburo also publishes a bi-monthly pop and jazz listing available free from record shops, cafés and music venues.

For further information and bookings, contact the venues direct (box office hours are normally 10am to 6pm Monday to Saturday and an hour before the performance); or the Uitburo, also called AUB Ticketshop (Map 4), Leidseplein 26, open 10am to 6pm Friday to Wednesday, 10am to 9pm Thursday; or ring the Uitlijn (☎ 0900-01 91, €0.40 per minute, 9am to 9pm daily).

Classical & Contemporary

A pleasant feature of the Amsterdam music scene is the free lunch-time concert, usually chamber music, from 12.30pm to 1.30pm (not June, July or August, when everyone goes on holidays). The Muziektheater offers free concerts of 20th-century music on Tuesday in the Boekmanzaal; on Wednesday the Concertgebouw has chamber music or classical concerts (often public rehearsals), sometimes also jazz, but you won't be the only visitor taking advantage of this; and on Friday the Bethaniënklooster puts on anything from medieval to contemporary, while the IJsbreker specialises in contemporary music.

Bethaniënklooster (☎ 625 00 78, Barndesteeg 6B) **Map 2** A small former monastery near Nieuwmarkt Square with a glorious ballroom, it's the perfect place to take in some Stravinsky or Indian sitar.

Beurs van Berlage (☎ 627 04 66, Damrak 243) **Map 2** This former commodities exchange houses two small concert halls with comfortable seats and underwhelming acoustics. Resident companies the Netherlands Chamber Orchestra and the Netherlands Philharmonic (under the direction of Hartmut Haenchen) play a varied menu of Mozart, Beethoven, Bach, Mahler and Wagner.

Concertgebouw (☎ 671 83 45, Concertgebouwplein 2-6) **Map 4** This world-famous concert hall with near-perfect acoustics is home to the Royal Concertgebouw Orchestra led by Riccardo Chailly. See it perform works by Ravel, Stravinsky and Shostakovich. Alternatively, watch visiting international soloists and chamber groups perform in the Recital Hall.

Koninklijk Theater Carré (☎ 622 52 25, Amstel 115-125) **Map 5** This theatre presents a regular diet of crowd-pleasing opera, operetta, ballet, musicals and cabaret. Expect productions like *The Barber of Seville* and *Madam Butterfly*.

Muziekcentrum De IJsbreker (☎ 693 90 93, Weesperzijde 23) **Map 5** Itching to hear some avant-garde jazz or a bit of modern Turkish guitar? This centre for contemporary music is the answer. In 2003 it will move to a new complex in the Eastern Docklands (west of the ship-passenger terminal) together with the Bimhuis jazz centre.

Muziektheater (☎ 625 54 55, Waterlooplein 22) **Map 2** This swanky, large-scale theatre in the Stopera is the official residence of the Netherlands Opera, National Ballet and Netherlands Ballet Orchestra. Renowned international dance companies like Merce Cunningham and Martha Graham perform here too.

Stadsschouwburg (☎ 624 23 11, Leidseplein 26) **Map 4** The National Travelling Opera calls this lovely theatre home. They and other international companies perform a regular roster of opera and operetta here.

Check the Amsterdam Uitburo for performances in ***churches*** (not just organ recitals), including the Oude Kerk, Nieuwe Kerk, Engelse Kerk (English/Scottish Presbyterian church in the Begijnhof), Round Lutheran Church, Waalse Kerk (Walloon Church; ☎ 030 236 22 36, Oudezijds Achterburgwal 157), Amstelkerk etc.

Rock

Information and tickets are available at the Amsterdam Uitburo or at the venues, but for large pop concerts you can also telephone the Ticketlijn on ☎ 0900-300 12 50 (€0.45 a minute).

Arena Stadium (☎ 311 13 33, Arena Blvd 1, Bijlmermeer) This ultimate stadium venue seats 52,000 and produces shows that are big on lights, screens and production – crowd-pulling performers like the Rolling Stones, Back Street Boys and Bon Jovi. Operas like *Carmen* and *Aida* are also staged here as are mega-dance parties like 'Sensation'.

Heineken Music Hall (☎ 409 79 79, Arena Blvd, The Corridor 9, Bijlmermeer) A steady stream of international acts (St Germain, Linkin Park, Manic Street Preachers) perform at this new, mid-sized entertainment venue which is praised for its high-quality acoustics and amazing lights.

Korsakoff (☎ 625 78 54, Lijnbaansgracht 161) **Map 3** Still grungy after all these years, this hard-rock and alternative-music venue attracts a young clientele for lashings of punk, metal and goth.

Melkweg (Milky Way; ☎ 531 81 81, [W] www.melkweg.nl, Lijnbaansgracht 234A) **Map 4** Melkweg's a cinema, art gallery, café, multimedia centre and a superlative pop and rock venue. There's live music almost every night (everything from Afro-Celtic to thrash) and an always impressive, eclectic international line-up: expect performers like Afrika Bambaataa, Jeff Beck, Aimee Mann and Weezer, sometimes within the same week!

Paradiso (☎ 626 45 21, Weteringschans 6) **Map 4** This large former church has been the city's premier rock venue since the 1960s. Big-name acts like PJ Harvey, John Cale, Sonic Youth and David Bowie all come here to strut their stuff.

Westergasfabriek (☎ 586 07 10, Haarlemmerweg 8-10) **Map 3** This former gas factory hosts two or three rock concerts a year in the old, round gas-holder, as well as other arts events and raves. It also used to host the brilliant Drum Rhythm Festival (acts included DJ Herbert, Jazzanova and Black Eyed Peas) before this moved to the Java Eiland.

Jazz, Blues & Latin American

Jazz is popular in Amsterdam and there's a lot happening in cafés around town; blues thrives less. The world's largest jazz festival is the North Sea Jazz Festival in The Hague in July (see Public Holidays & Special Events in the Facts for the Visitor chapter), and throughout that month many international greats take the opportunity to take to the stage in Amsterdam too.

Bimhuis (☎ 623 33 73, Oude Schans 73-77) **Map 2** Amsterdam's main jazz venue attracts Dutch and international jazz greats like Bob Berg, Steve Solo and Kenny Wheeler. It has an excellent auditorium and a pretty spiffy bar. Bimhuis will move to a new location in the Eastern Docklands (west of the ship-passenger terminal) in 2003.

Bourbon Street Jazz & Blues Club (☎ 623 34 40, Leidsekruisstraat 6-8) **Map 4** Catch blues, funk and rock and roll performances here. There are weekly jam sessions and unplugged nights too.

Brasil Music Bar (☎ 626 15 00, Lange Leidsedwarsstraat 70) **Map 4** Get jiggy at this popular little club; there's live Brazilian and Caribbean music weeknights and R&B and two-step DJs on weekends.

Casablanca (☎ 625 56 85, Zeedijk 26) **Map 2** This jazz café has an illustrious history but its glory days are definitely over. There's still live jazz (Sunday to Thursday) and big-band performances (Monday and Wednesday) but it's mainly a karaoke bar, albeit a fun one.

Cotton Club (☎ 626 61 92, Nieuwmarkt 5) **Map 2** Squish into this dark, bustling brown café every Saturday (4pm) for live, vibrant jazz.

Heeren van Aemstel (☎ 620 21 73, Thorbeckeplein 5) **Map 4** Office workers and students cram this grand-café-style club to enjoy the rather bland roster of live big bands and pop and rock covers bands.

Jazz Café Alto (☎ 626 32 49, Korte Leidsedwarsstraat 115) **Map 4** A slightly older crowd of jazz lovers toe-taps to serious jazz and blues at this small brown café; try to catch tenor saxophonist Hans Dulfer.

Maloe Melo (☎ 420 45 92, Lijnbaansgracht 163) **Map 3** This small, smoky venue is home to the city's blues scene with local and international musos playing everything from Cajun zydeco and swing to Texas blues and rockabilly.

Meander (☎ 625 84 30, Voetboogstraat 5) **Map 2** Get all snake-hipped at the ever-popular Sunday salsa night, or visit this multilevel club on other nights for DJs spinning funk, garage, soul and jazzy beats.

World Music

Amsterdam is a major European centre for music from exotic parts of the world. See Music in the Facts about Amsterdam chapter for information sources, or contact the Amsterdam Uitburo about gigs in the venues listed below, as well as at Paradiso and Latin bars.

Akhnaton (☎ 624 33 96, Nieuwezijds Kolk 25-27) **Map 2** A young, multi-culti crowd jams this club every weekend to catch live hip-hop, Latin and Afrocentric acts.

Tropeninstituut Theater (☎ 568 85 00, Tropenmuseum, Linnaeusstraat 2) **Map 5** Come here for sterling live music, mainly South American, Indian and African. Make a night of it too: the adjoining restaurant serves food to suit the performances.

Melkweg (☎ 531 81 81, Lijnbaansgracht 234A) **Map 4** If Mongolian throat singers rock your world, then Melkweg, the city's premier venue for world music, is your spiritual home. Every week sees shows by a veritable United Nations of musicians and during June it co-presents the funky-flavoured Amsterdam Roots Festival.

THEATRE

There are about 50 theatres in Amsterdam – the ones listed here are merely a selection. Performances are mostly in Dutch, sometimes in English (especially in summer) and sometimes it doesn't matter. Check the *Uitkrant*, the Saturday *PS* magazine in the *Parool* newspaper, the Amsterdam Uitburo or the venues direct for current performances.

Amsterdamse Bos Theatre (☎ 626 36 47, 640 92 53) **Map 1** This large open-air amphitheatre in the park stages plays in Dutch (Chekhov, Shakespeare) in summer.

De Balie (☎ 553 51 51, Kleine Gartmanplantsoen 10) **Map 4** International productions spotlighting multicultural and political issues are the focus here. De Balie also holds short film festivals, political debates, has new-media facilities and a stylish bar (see Cultural Centres in the Facts for the Visitor chapter).

Theater Bellevue (☎ 530 53 01, Leidsekade 90) **Map 4** Come here for experimental theatre, international cabaret and modern dance, mainly in Dutch. Bellevue's light kids' plays like 'Miffy: The musical' are introducing a new generation to theatre.

Boom Chicago (☎ 423 01 01, Leidseplein 12) **Map 4** English-language stand-up and improv comedy is performed here year-round. The café, boomBar, serves fresh, reasonably priced food.

Brakke Grond (☎ 622 90 14, Flemish Cultural Centre, Nes 45) **Map 2** A fantastic array of experimental video, modern dance and exciting, young theatre is performed in Brakke Grond's striking, all-red, 150-seat theatre.

Felix Meritis (☎ 623 13 11, Keizersgracht 324) **Map 3** The former cultural centre of the city now presents innovative, modern theatre, music and dance with lots of co-productions between Eastern and Western European artists.

Frascati (☎ 626 68 66 day, 623 57 23 evening, Nes 63) **Map 2** This experimental theatre spotlights young Dutch directors, choreographers and producers. There are multicultural dance and music performances, as well as a monthly hip-hop, rap and breakdancing night.

De Kleine Komedie (☎ 624 05 34, Amstel 56) **Map 4** This internationally renowned theatre, founded in 1786, focuses on concerts, dance, comedy and cabaret, sometimes in English.

Koninklijk Theater Carré (☎ 622 52 25, Amstel 115-125) **Map 5** The largest theatre in town puts on big-budget, international shows, cabaret, circuses and musicals; think Andrew Lloyd Webber and you're on the right track. Backstage tours of the Koninklijk Theatre Carré are available 3pm Saturday and Wednesday.

Melkweg (☎ *531 81 81, Lijnbaansgracht 234A*) **Map 4** This world-renowned cultural centre programs fresh and modern dance performances and multimedia productions.

Tropeninstituut Theater (☎ *568 82 15, Tropenmuseum, Linnaeusstraat 2*) **Map 5** The Tropenmuseum's theatre explores non-Western culture in plays, dance and film.

Stadsschouwburg (☎ *624 23 11, Leidseplein 26*) **Map 4** The city's most beautiful theatre, built in 1894 and refurbished in the 1990s, features large-scale productions, operettas, summer English-language productions and performances by the stolid Toneelgroep Amsterdam.

Universiteitstheater (☎ *623 01 27, Nieuwe Doelenstraat 16*) **Map 2** Home to the Institute for Dramatic Art, this theatre presents some performances in English.

Vondelpark Theatre (☎ *673 14 99,* Ⓦ *www.openluchttheater.nl, Vondelpark*) This large open-air amphitheatre in the middle of the Vondelpark presents a wide range of free summer performances. Expect stand-up comedy, musical theatre, dance workshops and pop concerts.

Westergasfabriek (☎ *586 07 10, Haarlemmerweg 8-10*) **Map 3** A former gas factory, Westergasfabriek hosts a wide range of experimental theatre and music performances, events and festivals.

CINEMAS

There's always a good choice of films screening in Amsterdam, including plenty of 'art' movies for discriminating cinephiles. The 'film ladder' – the listing of what's on – is pinned up at cinemas and in many pubs, or you can check it in Thursday's paper, when weekly programs change. *AL* means *alle leeftijden*, all ages, and 12 or 16 indicates the minimum age for admission.

Films are almost always screened in their original language with Dutch subtitles; the exceptions are children's matinees where

the latest Disney creation may come with Dutch voices.

Ticket prices are quite expensive (€6.35 to €9.07) but the mainstream Hollywood cinemas around Leidseplein normally have half-price matinee tickets for their first screening on weekdays.

The following cinemas (merely a selection) are worth seeking out:

Bellevue/Calypso (☎ *623 48 76, Marnixstraat 400-402*) **Map 4** These two comfortable, mainstream cinemas screen a steady diet of Hollywood fare.

Cinecenter (☎ *623 66 15, Lijnbaansgracht 236*) **Map 4** Euro and American art-house fare is the flavour of the day at this recently modernised cinema complex. The last Monday of the month is devoted to queer films.

Filmmuseum (☎ *589 14 00, Vondelpark 3*) **Map 4** The esteemed Filmmuseum's program appeals to a broad audience. It schedules cult shlock-horror movies (Friday night), cutting-edge foreign films (Iran, Korea), and specials devoted to screen legends and genres such as Bollywood musicals.

Het Ketelhuis (☎ *684 00 90, Westergasfabriek, Haarlemmerweg 8-10*) **Map 3** Documentaries, cult-alt favourites, international and Dutch art-house flicks are shown here.

Kriterion (☎ *623 17 08, Roetersstraat 170*) **Map 5** This Amsterdam School/Art Deco building screens cult movies, kids' flicks and 'sneak previews' of up-coming films (10pm Tuesday). Its lively and popular café is worth a visit too.

The Movies (☎ *638 60 16, Haarlemmerdijk 161*) **Map 3** Interesting, arty films are mixed in with independent American and Brit pics at this beautiful Art Deco cinema. Its restaurant, Wild Kitchen, is highly regarded also.

Tuschinskitheater (☎ *623 15 10,* ☎ *0900-14 58 – €0.23 a minute, Reguliersbreestraat 26-28*) **Map 4** Extensively refurbished, Amsterdam's most famous cinema – screening mainstream blockbusters – is a monument worth visiting for its sumptuous Art Deco interior alone, especially its main auditorium, Tuschinski 1.

De Uitkijk (☎ *623 74 60, Prinsengracht 452*) **Map 4** This cosy art-house stalwart is the city's oldest surviving cinema (1913). In an old canal house, it attracts film buffs who know their Fuller from their Fellini.

SPECTATOR SPORTS

See Activities in the Things to See & Do chapter for sports you can engage in as well as watch. Spectator sporting events worth seeking out apart from soccer (of course) are field hockey and the unique Dutch sport of korfball. For general information on sports clubs and upcoming events, contact the Amsterdam Sport Council on ☎ 552 24 90.

Soccer (Football)

Local club Ajax is usually at or near the top of the European league. Other Dutch leaders are PSV (the Philips Sport Association) from Eindhoven and Feijenoord from Rotterdam, and if any of these clubs play against one another it's a big event. Dutch soccer is 'cool' and 'technical', characterised by keep-the-ball and surgical strikes. Local hooligans, however, are every bit as hot-headed as their British counterparts but you should be quite safe if you buy seat tickets (as opposed to standing-room tickets).

Arena Stadium *(☎ 311 13 33, Arena Blvd 1, Bijlmermeer; metro: Bijlmer)* Ajax plays in this stadium, which seats 52,000 spectators and has an Ajax museum with cups and other paraphernalia. It's a massive, expensive, high-tech complex with a retractable roof, built over a highway. Soccer games usually take place Saturday evening and Sunday afternoon during the playing season (early September to early June, with a win-

ter break from just before Christmas to the end of January).

Readers have recommended the one-hour guided tour of the stadium (☎ 311 13 36) for €7.95/6.80 per adult/child, between 9am and 6pm daily, except on game days or major events. The tour includes a walk on the hallowed turf and entry to the museum.

Hockey

Dutch (field) hockey teams compete at world-championship level. In contrast to soccer, which is played mainly by boys in school yards, streets and parks, hockey is still a somewhat elitist sport played by either sex on expensive club fields. The season is similar to that for soccer.

Hockey Club Hurley *(☎ 645 44 68, Nieuwe Kalfjeslaan 21, Amsterdamse Bos)* This is a good contact for information and matches, with mixed, informal games from 9pm to 10.30pm Monday and Tuesday and children's games Saturday morning.

Korfball

This sport elicits giggles from foreigners who don't understand how appealing the game can be. It's a cross between netball, volleyball and basketball, where mixed-sex teams toss a ball around and try to throw it into the opposing team's hoop which is 3.5m off the ground; players can only mark opponents of the same sex. There's a lively local club scene. For information, contact the **Amsterdam Sport Council** *(☎ 552 24 90)* or try **SVK Groen-Wit** *(☎ 646 15 15, Kinderdijkstraat 29)*.

Shopping

During the 17th century, Amsterdam was the warehouse of the world, stuffed with imperial riches from far-off colonies and nearby neighbours. The Dutch empire has since crumbled but its capital remains a shopper's paradise. In particular, Amsterdam's speciality shops and markets truly stand out. Sure, you can probably find glowing Mexican shrines or banana-flavoured condoms back home, but Amsterdam has whole shops devoted to such items and, of course, dope, pornography, flower bulbs, clogs, rounds of cheese and obscure types of *genever* (Dutch gin). Fantastic bargains are rare here but it may be worth chasing pictorial art, music, vintage clothes, diamonds and collectors' books.

Potheads can purchase smoking paraphernalia at most corner tobacco shops, but keep in mind that flights from Amsterdam attract more than their fair share of attention from customs officials elsewhere.

The most popular shopping streets are lowbrow Nieuwendijk and slightly less lowbrow Kalverstraat, with department stores and clothing boutiques that cater for large crowds on Saturday and Sunday (good days to avoid). Leidsestraat is more upmarket with less junk, though the goods are still rather mainstream. Well-heeled shoppers head for the expensive shops and boutiques along PC Hooftstraat, and antique and art buffs check Nieuwe Spiegelstraat and Spiegelgracht. The Jordaan neighbourhood is full of quirky shops and galleries, as are the radial streets in the canal belt, especially in the western section.

Souvenirs are sold everywhere, most of them tacky, but try a Delft-blue tulip vase or bulbs to plant back home (home legislation permitting).

As for markets, the Albert Cuyp is not to be missed, with its food and other goods from all corners of the globe. The floating flower market along Singel is unique, though photographers will be frustrated by the crowds and the fact that most of the market is in the shade. Waterlooplein flea market specialises in bric-a-brac, army clothes and music; other markets might be cheaper but don't stock as wide a selection.

Most stores are open seven days a week (at least in the city centre) but many start late on Monday. Hours are normally 1pm to 6pm on Monday, 10am to 6pm on Tuesday, Wednesday, Friday and Saturday, 10am to 9pm on Thursday and, in the city centre, noon to 6pm on Sunday, but there are many variations.

If you intend to do serious shopping (eg, diamonds) and live outside the EU, see Taxes & Refunds under Money in the Facts for the Visitor chapter about reclaiming the 19% value-added tax.

ART GALLERIES & ANTIQUE STORES

Amsterdam is full of art galleries, from tiny operations with one person's work, to huge, commercial, museum-like complexes. Opening hours are normally noon to 6pm Tuesday to Sunday, and many galleries close for one month over summer. Most of the city's best antique stores are found in Nieuwe Spiegelstraat and the nearby side streets.

Art Kitchen (☎ 622 34 22, Herengracht 160) **Map 3** This basement gallery has blown a breath of fresh air into the Amsterdam arts scene. A fine roster of local and international artists exhibits works on paper, sculpture and installation art.

Art Works (☎ 624 19 80, Herengracht 229-231) **Map 3** This small gallery displays figurative paintings and sculptures by Dutch, Spanish, Belgian and Swiss artists.

Arti et Amicitiae (☎ 623 35 08, Rokin 112) **Map 2** This well-established artists' club exhibits contemporary art, everything from computer graphics to cutting-edge work by graduate students.

Aschenbach & Hofland Galleries (☎ 412 17 72, Bilderdijkstraat 165C) **Map 3** These galleries focus on contemporary figurative tendencies and photography.

Astamangala (☎ 623 44 02, Kerkstraat 168) **Map 4** This has ancient art and ethnographical objects from the Himalayan region.

Decorativa (☎ 420 50 66, Nieuwe Spiegelstraat 7) **Map 4** An amazing and massive jumble of European antiques, collectables and weird vintage gifts fills this large space.

Eduard Kramer (☎ 623 08 32, Nieuwe Spiegelstraat 64) **Map 4** Specialising in antique Dutch wall and floor tiles, Eduard Kramer is bursting with vintage homewares.

EH Ariëns Kappers (☎ 623 53 56, Nieuwe Spiegelstraat 32) **Map 4** This pretty gallery stocks original prints, etchings, engravings, lithographs, maps from the 17th to 19th centuries and Japanese woodblock prints.

Galerie Zwiep (☎ 320 87 59, Kerkstraat 149) **Map 4** This beautiful space is filled with Primitive and Oceanic sculpture, masks and statues. The Amazonian feather masks are especially alluring.

Gallery Nine (☎ 627 10 97, Keizersgracht 570) **Map 4** Come here for abstract painting and sculpture by emerging and established Dutch and Belgian artists.

Jaski (☎ 620 39 39, Nieuwe Spiegelstraat 27-29) **Map 4** This large, commercial gallery sells paintings, prints, ceramics and sculptures by the most famous members of the CoBrA movement.

Josine Bokhoven (☎ 623 65 98, Prinsengracht 154) **Map 3** Across the canal from the Anne Frankhuis, this gallery features contemporary art and the work of emerging, young artists.

Kunsthaar (☎ 625 99 12, Berenstraat 21) **Map 3** Collective exhibitions of abstract and realistic contemporary Dutch and European art are held here.

Lieve Hemel (☎ 623 00 60, Nieuwe Spiegelstraat 3) **Map 4** You'll find exemplary contemporary Dutch realist painting and sculpture at this smart gallery.

The Living Room (☎ 623 15 47, Fokke Simonszstraat 10) **Map 4** There are six interesting galleries in this building; this one features figurative work (everything from symbolism to realism) by Dutch and German artists.

Montevideo (☎ 623 71 01, Keizersgracht 264) **Map 3** This institute for media art puts on funky shows with fashion designers and club promoters.

Nanky de Vreeze (☎ 627 38 08, Lange Leidsedwarsstraat 198-200) **Map 4** This large, impressive gallery displays modern, representative art by European and Asian artists.

Parade (☎ 427 46 46, Prinsengracht 799) **Map 4** Big-name American and German pop and postmodern artists and photographers are the draw here: Donald Judd, Andy Warhol and Jasper Johns.

Paul Andriesse (☎ 623 62 37, Prinsengracht 116) **Map 3** Contemporary art's the go here – think video installations and avant-garde sculpture by international and Dutch artists like Thomas Struth, Fiona Tan and Hellen van Meene.

Prestige Art Gallery (☎ 624 01 04) Reguliersbreestraat 46) **Map 4** This gallery near Rembrandtplein specialises in 17th- to 20th-century oil paintings and bronzes.

Reflex Modern Art Gallery (☎ 627 28 32, Weteringschans 79A) **Map 4** This prominent gallery opposite the Rijksmuseum is filled with contemporary art, aimed at tourists.

Steltman (☎ 622 86 83, Teniersstraat 6) **Map 4** The focus here is on unusual surrealist and romantic paintings, figurative modern art and design.

BOOKS

Amsterdam is still a major printing centre in Europe. Unfortunately books are expensive, and you may wish to steer clear of English-language titles if you're used to US or British prices. However, bibliophiles will delight in the large number of bookshops, both new and antiquarian, with knowledgeable and enthusiastic staff. Following are some well-known outlets, but keep an eye out for obscure, second-hand shops, where you can find some bargains. See also the later Markets section for dedicated book markets.

English-Language

The American Book Center (☎ 625 55 37, W www.abc.nl, Kalverstraat 185) **Map 2** Always jam-packed, this shop holds interesting sales, has a good travel-guide section and stocks many US newspapers and magazines. It's often cheaper than its competitors and offers 10% student discount.

The English Bookshop (☎ 626 42 30, Lauriergracht 71) **Map 3** This canalside shop has a well-chosen selection of art books, magazines and novels.

Waterstone's (☎ 638 38 21, Kalverstraat 152) **Map 2** Resembling a beautiful library, Waterstone's is the specialist in English-language books and is strong on travel guidebooks, maps and novels. British titles are often discounted.

Gay & Lesbian

The American Book Center (see under English-Language) The 'Pink Camp' in the basement stocks rare trash as well as sophisticated works (Henry James' *The Bostonians*).

Intermale (☎ 625 00 09, W www.interm ale.nl, Spuistraat 251) **Map 2** There are two floors of gay photo books, sexy magazines, videos and pornographic postcards.

Vrolijk (☎ 623 51 42, W www.xs4all.nl/ ~vrolijk, Paleisstraat 135) **Map 2** Most of the major gay and lesbian magazines worldwide are available here, as well as novels, guidebooks and postcards. Climb the stairs for art, travel, poetry and videos.

Second-hand & Antiquarian

Antiquariaat Kok (☎ 623 11 91, Oude Hoogstraat 14-18) **Map 2** A wide and engaging range of antiquarian stock (literature, coffee-table books, old prints etc) is sold here, including biology, art and architecture titles.

The Book Exchange (☎ 626 62 66, Kloveniersburgwal 58) **Map 2** A rabbit warren of second-hand books, this has temptingly priced occult, sci-fi and detective novels.

De Slegte (☎ 622 59 33, Kalverstraat 48) **Map 2** This specialist in second-hand or remaindered titles has lots of dirt-cheap books including some gems.

Vrouwen in Druk ('Women in Print'; ☎ 624 50 03, Westermarkt 5) **Map 3** A ramshackle second-hand bookshop, this place specialises in women's titles (with a reasonable English section): history, biographies and fiction.

Travel

à la Carte (☎ 625 06 79, Utrechtsestraat 110) **Map 4** Travellers head here for guidebooks, maps, globes and beautiful photo books.

Evenaar Literaire Reisboekhandel (☎ 624 62 89, Singel 348) **Map 3** There's a wide selection of coffee-table books, travel literature and guidebooks, as well as antique travel books here.

Jacob van Wijngaarden (☎ 612 19 01, Overtoom 97) **Map 4** This geographical bookshop has a large collection of guidebooks and maps and funky blow-up globes.

Pied à Terre (☎ 627 44 55, Singel 393) **Map 2** This shop specialises in hiking and cycling books, topographical maps and travel guides.

Other Bookshops

Architectura & Natura (☎ 623 61 86, Leliegracht 22) **Map 3** This charming canalside shop has architecture, landscape and coffee-table books on the ground floor, antiquarian art and architecture titles upstairs.

Athenaeum (☎ 622 62 48, Spui 14-16) **Map 2** This enormous, multilevel store has a vast assortment of unusual books. The separate newsagency has the city's largest selection of international newspapers and magazines.

Au Bout du Monde (☎ 625 13 97, Singel 313) **Map 2** Find a new religion or guru here; this tranquil shop stocks books on Eastern and Western philosophy, alternative medicine and has a selection of esoteric gifts.

Boekie Woekie (☎ 639 05 07, Berenstraat 16) **Map 3** This shop/gallery deals in handmade books, postcards, monographs and *objets d'art*.

Broekmans & Van Poppel (☎ 675 16 53, Van Baerlestraat 92-94) **Map 4** This is the best address in town for classical and popular sheet music and books about musicians.

Computercollectief (☎ 638 90 03, Amstel 312) **Map 4** Come here for computer books, magazines, software and friendly service. Prices are higher than in the USA, though.

Lambiek (☎ 626 75 43, Kerkstraat 78) **Map 4** Serious collectors of comic books rush here for titles by Crumb, Avril and Herriman; it doubles as an informal museum.

Martyrium (☎ *673 20 92, Van Baerlestraat 170-172*) **Map 4** There's a good English section, but even better, almost half of this large, quiet store is devoted to discounted stock: categories include art books, dictionaries, biographies and cooking titles.

Scheltema (☎ *523 14 11, Koningsplein 20*) **Map 4** The largest bookshop in town is a true department store with many foreign titles, New-Age and multimedia sections, and a restaurant.

Stadsboekwinkel (☎ *572 02 29, Amsteldijk 67*) **Map 5** Run by the city printer, this is the best source for books about Amsterdam's history, urban development, ecology, politics etc, some in English.

Xantippe Unlimited (☎ *623 58 54, Prinsengracht 290*) **Map 3** This lovely canalside bookshop has a large selection of (mainly Dutch) women's books, everything from classical fiction to modern research and gay books too.

CAMPING & OUTDOOR
The Dutch enjoy outdoor pursuits and don't mind paying for the right gear. Quality and prices tend to be high.

Bever Zwerfsport (☎ *689 46 39, Stadhouderskade 4*) **Map 4** Everything you need for a local hike or a Himalayan expedition is here: camping, outdoor gear, clothes, shoes.

Carl Denig (☎ *626 24 36, Weteringschans 115*) **Map 4** Opened in 1912, this is Amsterdam's oldest and best outdoor retailer, though you pay for the quality. There are five floors of packs, tents, hiking/camping accessories, snowboards and skis.

Demmenie (☎ *624 36 52, Marnixstraat 2*) **Map 4** For professional outdoor gear for the serious enthusiast, this specialises in mountaineering, with tents, shoes and clothes.

Perry Sport (☎ *618 91 11, Overtoom 2*) **Map 4** Camping goods are downstairs at this general sports store, perhaps cheaper than Bever Zwerfsport nearby but the quality may not be as good.

CHILDREN
There are lots of trendy kids' clothing, toy and book shops in the city. Particularly interesting are the stores selling wooden toys,

replica canal houses and puppets. Most children's clothing stores sell miniature versions of current street fashion at close to adult prices. For less expensive kids' or baby wear, visit some of the markets (see later).

BamBam (☎ *624 52 15, Magna Plaza, Nieuwezijds Voorburgwal 182*) **Map 2** Luxurious clothes and handmade furniture for pampered little princes and princesses are sold here.

Exota Kids (☎ *420 68 84, Nieuwe Leliestraat 32*) **Map 3** Hip parents shop here to ensure their children look as chic as they do. Its own label, Petit Louie, is worn by Amsterdam's grooviest kids.

Kitsch Kitchen Kids (☎ *622 82 61, Rozengracht 183*) **Map 3** Explore this crammed cacophony of colourful and crazy Mexican toys, dress-ups, furniture and birthday presents.

Knuffels (☎ *427 38 62, Nieuwe Hoogstraat 11*) **Map 2** This entrancing shop delights adults and kids alike with soft toys, puppets, beautiful mobiles, teddies and jigsaw puzzles.

Mechanisch Speelgoed (☎ *638 16 80, Westerstraat 67*) **Map 3** This fun shop is crammed full of nostalgic and wind-up toys like snowdomes, glowlamps, masks and finger puppets.

Miffy Shop (☎ *671 97 07, Beethovenstraat 71*) **Map 1** Dutch illustrator Dick Bruna's most famous character, Miffy, is celebrated in books, toys and kids' merchandise.

Oilily (☎ *422 87 13, Kalvertoren shopping centre, Singel 457*) **Map 2** Amsterdam's cutest kids are decked head-to-toe in Oilily's ultra-colourful and long-lasting outfits.

Pinokkio (☎ *622 89 14, Magna Plaza, Nieuwezijds Voorburgwal 182*) **Map 2** This pleasant shop stocks wooden and educational toys, rocking horses, replica canal houses, mobiles and of course, lots of Pinocchio dolls.

Prenatal (☎ *626 63 92, Kalverstraat 40*) **Map 2** This well-priced chain store sells trendy baby and kids' clothes, maternity wear, toys, prams etc.

De Speelmuis (☎ *638 53 42, Elandsgracht 58*) **Map 3** There's an outstanding array of doll's houses, miniature toys, puppets and jigsaw puzzles. Kids love the little wooden pushcarts and bikes.

Storm *(☎ 624 10 74, Magna Plaza, Nieuwezijds Voorburgwal 182)* **Map 2** European and American designer clothes for hip preteens and teenagers feature here. Less expensive are the sweet and colourful dress-up costumes.

TinkerBell *(☎ 625 88 30, Spiegelgracht 10)* **Map 4** The mechanical bear blowing bubbles outside this shop fascinates kids, as do the intriguing technical and scientific toys inside.

CLOTHING

Amsterdam is not the place to buy extravagant designer clothes. The Calvinist ethos frowns on conspicuous consumption and demands value for money, and as a consequence, clothing is stylish but low-key and very reasonably priced. A stroll down Kalverstraat indicates the city's abundance of inexpensive chain stores.

The city is in a league of its own, however, in funky and alternative apparel, often second-hand and sold at markets and in countless small boutiques. The choice seems endless – simply go for a walk in the Jordaan or along the radial streets in the canal belt.

High Street Fashion, Street & Club Wear

America Today *(☎ 638 84 47, Magna Plaza, Nieuwezijds Voorburgwal 182)* **Map 2** Try this one-stop shop for Levi's-engineered jeans, Calvin Klein underwear, Triple 5 Soul hoodies and Carhartt pants. Stock up on imported snacks like root beer, cookies and chocolate bars too.

D.E.P.T. *(☎ 528 79 07, Heiligeweg 49)* **Map 2** Good-quality, stylish pieces (cotton T-shirts, woollen sweaters, well-cut suits) in the latest colours make this the perfect pit stop for savvy, elegant shoppers.

Exota *(☎ 620 91 02, Hartenstraat 10)* **Map 3** This funky clothes emporium for men, women and kids mixes well-known labels like Lee, Kookai and French Connection with more alternative brands and cutsie Japanese giftware.

Fun Fashion *(☎ 420 50 96, Nieuwendijk 200)* **Map 2** This busy shop has street, surf and skate wear for guys and girls. Brands include Carhartt, Stussy, Oakley and Birkenstock.

Hennes & Mauritz *(☎ 624 06 24, Kalverstraat 125)* **Map 2** One of the better fashion chain stores, this has up-to-the-minute clothes for all ages. The quality can be questionable but prices are remarkably low.

Housewives on Fire *(☎ 422 10 67, Spuistraat 102)* **Map 2** *The* place to purchase tickets to one-off club nights, deck yourself out in techno-style clothes and top it all off with a wild 'do' at the in-house hairdressing salon.

Mango *(☎ 427 27 60, Kalvertoren shopping centre, Singel 457)* **Map 2** This sells all the latest trends in women's street wear, club gear and office separates at reasonable prices.

Seventyfive *(☎ 626 46 11, Nieuwe Hoogstraat 24)* **Map 2** At this true temple to trainers, stimulate your sports-shoe obsession with brands like Royal Elastics, Gola, W&LT, Rizzo and, of course, Nike and Adidas, all at prices lower than in the UK.

Zara *(☎ 530 40 50, Kalverstraat 69)* **Map 2** This large Spanish retailer has a great eye for fresh-off-the-catwalk styles. Expect weekly deliveries of sensibly priced, fashionable separates for guys and girls.

Designer Clothes & Shoes

Analik *(☎ 422 05 61, Hartenstraat 34-36)* **Map 3** Analik, Amsterdam's pre-eminent fashion designer, creates stylish pieces for smart young things. Check out the swish handbags and accessories by Dutch artists and innovative designers in her new store next door.

Cora Kemperman *(☎ 625 12 84, Leidsestraat 72)* **Map 4** This successful Dutch designer specialises in floaty, layered separates and dresses in raw silk, cotton and wool.

Laundry Industry *(☎ 420 25 54, Spui 1)* **Map 2** Hip, urban types head here for well-cut, well-designed clothes. Watch glam couples coveting soft leather coats and perfectly fitted suits.

Local Service *(☎ 620 86 38, Keizersgracht 400-402)* **Map 3** Media types hunt for the latest Paul Smith, Fake London, Ghost and Stone Island collections here.

Mare (☎ 528 78 02, Leidsestraat 79) **Map 4** This sleek, modern shop has friendly staff and sexy labels for men and women (Voyage, Gaultier, Friends of Bruce, Gigli).

Van Ravenstein (☎ 639 00 67, Keizersgracht 359) **Map 3** Chic men and women shop here for upmarket Belgian designers like Dries Van Noten, Ann Demeulemeester and Dirk Bikkembergs.

Razzmatazz (☎ 420 04 83, Wolvenstraat 19) **Map 3** These flamboyant and expensive designer outfits and avant-garde club clothes for women and men include the Westwood, Frankie Morello and Andrew Mackenzie labels.

Reflections (☎ 664 00 40, PC Hooftstraat 66-68) **Map 4** This surprisingly unintimidating store attracts the haute-couture crowd with its collections of Issey Miyake, Dolce e Gabbana and Comme des Garçons.

Shoebaloo (☎ 626 79 93, Leidsestraat 10) **Map 4** We like the chic shoes here: imports like Fendi, Helmut Lang, Miu Miu and Prada Sport, and the less expensive, just-as-wearable house label.

Vintage Clothes

Lady Day (☎ 623 58 20, Hartenstraat 9) **Map 3** This is the premier location for unearthing spotless vintage clothes from Holland and elsewhere. The leather jackets, floral '50s frocks and woollen sailors' coats are well-priced winners.

Laura Dols (☎ 624 90 66, Wolvenstraat 7) **Map 3** Compulsive style-watchers head here for fur coats, '20s beaded dresses, lace blouses and '40s movie-star accessories like hand-stitched leather gloves.

Zipper (☎ 627 03 53, Nieuwe Hoogstraat 8) **Map 2** It's vintage clothes for funksters here, with a good range of jeans, T-shirts and customised club gear.

DEPARTMENT STORES

With the possible exception of Metz & Co and sections of the Bijenkorf, the department stores stick to mainstream products.

Bijenkorf (☎ 621 80 80, Dam 1) **Map 2** The city's most fashionable department store, this has a small restaurant or snack bar on each floor and the design-conscious will enjoy the well-chosen clothing, toys, household accessories and books. Head to the 'Chill Out' section for club and street wear.

Hema (☎ 638 99 63, Nieuwendijk 174) **Map 2** The nation's equivalent of Woolworths or K-Mart has undergone a facelift and now attracts as many design aficionados as bargain hunters. Expect low prices, reliable quality and a wide range of products including good-value wines and delicatessen goods.

Kalvertoren (Singel 457) **Map 2** This popular, modern shopping centre contains a small Hema, Vroom & Dreesmann and big-brand fashion stores like Replay, Quicksilver, Levis, Timberland and DKNY.

Magna Plaza (☎ 626 91 99, Nieuwezijds Voorburgwal 182) **Map 2** This grand 19th-century building, once the main post office, has over 40 upmarket fashion, gift and jewellery stores. Our faves include Ordning & Reda (swanky, colourful stationery) and Shu Uemura (stylish makeup).

Maison de Bonneterie (☎ 531 34 00, Rokin 140) **Map 2** Exclusive and classic clothes for the whole family are featured here. Men are particularly well catered for with labels like Ralph Lauren, Tommy Hilfiger and Armani, best purchased during the brilliant 50%-off sales. Note the amazing chandeliers and beautiful glass cupola.

Metz & Co (☎ 520 70 36, Keizersgracht 455) **Map 4** This boutique-y store does a fine line in luxury furnishings and homewares, upmarket designer clothes and gifts. Don't miss the top-floor lunch room with its splendid view (see the Places to Eat chapter).

Vroom & Dreesmann (☎ 622 01 71, Kalverstraat 201) **Map 2** Slightly more upmarket than Hema, this national chain is popular for its clothing and cosmetics. Its fabulous cafeteria, La Place, serves well-priced, freshly prepared salads, hot dishes and pastries.

DIAMONDS

Amsterdam has been a major diamond centre since Sephardic Jews introduced the cutting industry in the 1580s (one of the few occupations open to them at the time). The 'Cullinan', the largest diamond ever found (3106 carats), was split into more than 100 stones here in 1908, after which the master cutter spent three months recovering from stress. The 'Kohinoor' or Mountain of Light was cut here too – a very large, oval diamond (108.8 carats), acquired by Queen Victoria, that now forms part of the British crown jewels.

There are about a dozen diamond factories in the city, five of which offer guided tours – the Gassan tour is probably the most interesting. The tours are free and are usually conducted 9am to 5pm seven days a week, but ring ahead for details.

Diamonds aren't necessarily cheaper in Amsterdam than elsewhere but prices are fairly competitive. At least you will have seen how they're worked, and when you buy from a factory you get an extensive description of the purchase so you know exactly what you're buying. The Diamond Stock Exchange (Diamantbeurs Amsterdam; ☎ 696 22 51) is in the Bijlmer at Hogehilweg 14, 1101 CD Amsterdam.

The factories are: *Amsterdam Diamond Center* (☎ 624 57 87, Rokin 1) **(Map 2)**; *Coster Diamonds* (☎ 305 55 55, Paulus Potterstraat 2-6) **(Map 4)**; *Gassan Diamonds* (☎ 622 53 33, Nieuwe Uilenburgerstraat 173-175) **(Map 2)**; *Stoeltie Diamonds* (☎ 623 76 01, Wagenstraat 13-17) **(Map 4)**; *Van Moppes & Zoon* (☎ 676 12 42, Albert Cuypstraat 2-6) **(Map 4)**.

FOOD & DRINK

While Dutch cuisine is nothing to write home about, some of the following shops are hard to resist.

Australian Homemade (☎ 428 75 33, Singel 437) **Map 2** There's nothing particularly Australian about these chocolates, but they're decidedly delicious, as is the freshly made ice cream.

Bakkerij Paul Anné Entrees (☎ 623 53 22, Runstraat 25) **Map 3** This healthy organic bakery has delicious breads, sandwiches and scrumptious apple turnovers.

De Belly (☎ 330 94 83, Nieuwe Leliestraat 174) **Map 3** This organic supermarket in the Jordaan has a great bakery and a superior selection of gourmet items.

De Bierkoning (☎ 625 23 36, Paleisstraat 125) **Map 2** Head here for hundreds of different Belgian, German, English and Dutch beers, glasses, mugs and books on home brewing.

Le Cellier (☎ 638 65 73, Spuistraat 116) **Map 2** This large store sells genevers, liqueurs, a large selection of New World wines and over 75 types of beer.

Eichholtz (☎ 622 03 05, Leidsestraat 48) **Map 4** This small deli is bursting with everything homesick Brits and Americans yearn for, like Oreo cookies, Betty Crocker cake mix, Lea & Perrins sauce and Baxters tinned soup.

Geels & Co (☎ 624 06 83, Warmoesstraat 67) **Map 2** Operating from this glorious, aromatic store for over 140 years, this distinguished tea and coffee merchant also sells chocolate, teapots and coffee plungers. Be sure to visit the interesting little museum that's upstairs.

De Kaaskamer (☎ 623 34 83, Runstraat 7) **Map 3** A small shop full of hundreds of cheeses from around Europe and Holland and deli items like pâté, cured meats and baguettes, this does a roaring trade at lunch time selling filled sandwiches.

Hart's Wijnhandel (☎ 623 83 50, Vijzelgracht 27) **Map 4** Listen to classical music as you peruse the large selection of genevers and French and Italian wines at this peaceful shop.

Meeuwig & Zn (☎ 626 52 86, Haarlemmerstraat 70) **Map 2** Over 50 types of olive oil from around the world are stocked in this lovely shop, along with bottles of gourmet vinegar, mustard and chutney, and fresh olives.

Puccini Bomboni (☎ 427 83 41, Singel 184) **Map 2** We go gaga over Puccini Bomboni's large, handmade chocolate bonbons with rich fillings. Try the unforgettable spicy bonbon with peppers or the ultrasweet calvados cup.

Simon Lévelt (☎ 624 08 23, Prinsengracht 18) **Map 3** This old-fashioned tea and coffee merchant has knowledgeable staff and first-rate products.

De Waterwinkel (☎ 675 59 32, *Roelof Hartstraat 10*) **Map 4** Thirsty? With over 100 types of bottled water (mineral, sparkling, still and flavoured), this calm, pretty store will quench your thirst.

Wijnkoperij Otterman (☎ 625 50 88, *Keizersgracht 300*) **Map 3** Come here for French wines with character and organic wines without preservatives.

MARKETS
No visit to Amsterdam is complete if you haven't experienced one or more of its lively markets. The following is merely a selection. For more information about some of these markets, see the relevant entries in the Things to See & Do chapter. Oh, and watch out for pickpockets.

Albert Cuypmarkt (*Albert Cuypstraat*) **Map 4** Open 9am-5pm Mon-Sat. This general market has food, clothing, hardware and household goods at cheap prices. It's a great place to watch Amsterdam's melting pot in action.

Antiques market (*Noordermarkt*) **Map 3** Open 8am-1pm Mon. Try this Jordaan market for antiques, fabrics and second-hand bric-a-brac.

Antiques market (*Nieuwmarkt Square*) **Map 2** Open 9am-5pm Sun May-Sept. There are many genuine articles here and lots of books and bric-a-brac.

De Looier antiques market (☎ 624 90 38, *Elandsgracht 109*) **Map 3** Open 11am-5pm Sat-Thur. The indoor stalls in the De Looier complex sell jewellery, furniture, art and collectibles.

Art markets (*Thorbeckeplein & Spui Square*) **Maps 4 & 7** Open 10.30am-6pm Sun Mar-Oct. These quiet markets, dealing in mostly modern pictorial art, are a bit too modest in scope to yield real finds.

Bloemenmarkt (*Along Singel near Muntplein*) **Map 4** Open 9am-5pm daily summer, 9am-5pm Mon-Sat winter. The city's floating flower market is colourful in the extreme.

Boerenmarkt (*Farmer's Market; Noordermarkt & Nieuwmarkt Square*) **Maps 2 & 3** Open 10am-3pm Sat. Pick up homegrown produce, organic foods and picnic provisions from these markets.

Book market (*Oudemanhuispoort*) **Map 2** Open 11am-4pm Mon-Fri. Held in the old arcade between Oudezijds Achterburgwal and Kloveniersburgwal (blink and you'll miss either entrance), this is the place to find that 19th-century copy of *Das Kapital* or a semantic analysis of Icelandic sagas.

Book market (*Spui Square*) **Map 2** Open 10am-6pm Fri. The selection here is good but not very cheap.

Mosveldmarkt (*Mosveld, Amsterdam North*) **Map 1** Open Tue-Sat. This (untouristy) typical Dutch market sells mostly food and clothing. Take bus No 34/35 from Centraal Station to the first stop after the IJ-Tunnel.

Plant market (*Amstelveld*) **Map 4** Open 3pm-6pm Mon Easter-Christmas. All sorts of plants, pots and vases are sold here.

Stamp and coin market (*Nieuwezijds Voorburgwal 276*) **Map 2** Open 10am-4pm Wed & Sat. This little street-side market, just south of Wijdesteeg, sells stamps, coins and medals.

Waterlooplein flea market (*Waterlooplein*) **Map 2** Open 9am-5pm Mon-Fri, 8.30am-5.30pm Sat. Amsterdam's most famous flea market is full of curios, second-hand clothing, inexpensive Doc Martens, music, electronic stuff slightly on the blink, hardware and cheap New-Age gifts.

MUSIC
CD prices can be steep for popular material, but collector's items are another story, thanks to the wide variety of shops with interesting (and obscure) stock. Also, many shops and markets sell second-hand CDs that can be absolute bargains.

Blue Note (☎ 428 10 29, *Gravenstraat 12*) **Map 2** This is *the* place for jazz (Dutch, European and American), Japanese pressings and a smattering of acid jazz and related dance CDs.

Broekmans & Van Poppel (☎ 675 16 53, *Van Baerlestraat 92-94*) **Map 4** Head to the 1st floor for a comprehensive selection of classical music from the Middle Ages to today.

Concerto (☎ 623 52 28, *Utrechtsestraat 52-60*) **Map 4** This rambling shop, spread over several buildings, has Amsterdam's best selection of new and second-hand CDs and records; you could spend hours browsing in here. It's often cheap, always interesting and has good listening facilities.

FAME Music (☎ 638 25 25, *Kalverstraat 2-4, at Dam Square*) **Map 2** This megastore has an enormous number of titles with broad (and mainstream) collections of pop, jazz, classical, CD-ROMs and videos. It also sells tickets to big concerts.

Get Records (☎ 622 34 41, *Utrechtsestraat 105*) **Map 4** This deceptively large store has an eclectic and wide range of rock, folk, country and blues CDs.

Kuijpers (☎ 679 46 34, *Ferdinand Bolstraat 6*) **Map 4** A specialist in hard-to-find Dutch classical recordings, this shop also focuses on baroque and chamber music.

Roots (☎ 620 44 70, *Jonge Roelensteeg 6*) **Map 2** Small as a stamp, Roots stocks an impressive array of reggae, dancehall, soukous and African CDs. It also sells concert videos and knows about reggae club nights.

Rush Hour Records (☎ 427 45 05, *Spuistraat 98*) **Map 2** Join Amsterdam's best DJs scouring the racks of just-released, imported dance music (deep house, hip-hop, soul-jazz and broken beat). Knowledgeable staff give great tips on the best nightclubs.

Soul Food (☎ 428 61 30, *Nieuwe Nieuwstraat 27C*) **Map 2** Fuel your funky appetite with imported rap, R&B, house, two-step and garage titles while listening to budding DJs honing their skills on the turntables.

Tropenmuseum (☎ 568 82 15, *Linnaeusstraat 2*) **Map 5** This museum has one of the most interesting selections of ethnic-music CDs for sale anywhere – everything from Ethiopian to Cambodian pressings.

SMART-DRUG SHOPS

Smart-drug shops began popping up all over the city in the mid-1990s and are now an established addition to the coffeeshop scene. They sell legal, organic hallucinogens like magic mushrooms, herbal joints, seeds (poppy, marijuana, psychoactive), mood enhancers and aphrodisiacs. Note that, while it's legal to buy magic mushrooms over the counter in Amsterdam, the

same products are probably illegal to bring back home.

The stores listed here sell all manner of mood- and mind-enhancing products as well as books (on shamanism, psychedelia, spiritualism), jewellery, trancey videos and bongs. Before you buy, ask the staff to explain exactly what dosage to consume and what to expect from your trip.

Botanic Herbalist (☎ 470 88 89, *625 44 25, Cornelis Troostraat 37*) **Map 4** Highly recommended for its potent psychoactive plants (especially the rare salvia) and huge range of hemp products, this shop has developed 'the Pollinator' (€15.40 to €36.30), a machine that extracts the active ingredient from the waste-leaf material of marijuana and transforms it into high-quality hash.

Chills & Thrills (☎ 638 00 15, *Nieuwendijk 17*) **Map 2** A busy shop, always packed with tourists trying in vain to hear each other over the thumping techno music, this sells herbal trips, mushrooms, psychoactive cacti, amino-acid/vitamin drinks, novelty bongs and lifesize alien sculptures. Check out the mini-vaporiser, a smoke-free way to consume grass.

Conscious Dreams (☎ 626 69 07, *Kerkstraat 93*) **Map 4** Enhance whatever might need enhancing at Amsterdam's original smart shop; enthusiastic staff explain everything about the stock which includes magic mushrooms, trippy herbs and cacti. There are books on psychedelia and esoteria, club flyers advertising upcoming trance/ambient nights, and Internet facilities.

Kokopelli (☎ 421 70 00, *Warmoesstraat 12*) **Map 2** Conscious Dreams' second store is a large, beautiful space in the middle of the red-light district. As well as selling mushrooms and smart drugs, Kokopelli has an art gallery, Internet facilities, books (on how to take, make and fake psycho-active drugs) and a chilled-out lounge area overlooking Damrak.

The Magic Mushroom Gallery (☎ 427 57 65, *Spuistraat 249*) **Map 2** There are fresh and dried magic mushrooms on sale (it's recommended that first-timers try the Mexican ones for a relaxed, happy trip) as well as mushroom-growing kits, herbal ecstasy and smart drinks.

TRADITIONAL SOUVENIRS

Need a traditional reminder of your visit to Amsterdam? Best pick up a pair of clogs, some tulip bulbs or a Delft vase then.

Bloemenmarkt (Singel, near Muntplein) **Map 4** The traders at the floating flower market should be able to tell you if you can take the flower bulbs back home: Ireland and the UK allow an unlimited amount of bulbs to be brought back in, as do Canada and the USA (but you need a certificate, which will be provided). Japan permits up to 100 certified bulbs while Australia and New Zealand ban the importation of bulbs altogether.

Galleria d'Arte Rinascimento (☎ 622 75 09, Prinsengracht 170) **Map 3** This pretty shop sells Royal delftware, all manner of vases, platters, brooches, Christmas ornaments and interesting 19th-century wall tiles and plaques.

Heinen (☎ 627 82 99, Prinsengracht 440) **Map 4** With four floors of delftware, all the major factories are represented and all budgets catered for (spend €4.10 on a spoon or €2676 on a replica 17th-century tulip vase).

De Klompenboer (☎ 623 06 32, St Antoniesbreestraat 51) **Map 2** Bruno, the eccentric owner of this cute clog shop, gets his mum to hand-paint all the shoes (the cow print ones are pretty funky). Brush up on the history of clogs at the tiny museum that has samples of miniature wooden shoes and a 700-year-old pair.

SPECIALITY SHOPS

At a loss for souvenirs or gifts for yourself? Try some of the following:

Art Multiples (☎ 624 84 19, Keizersgracht 510) **Map 4** You could spend hours here flipping through thousands of postcards with unusual subject matter; take a peek at the raunchy 3-D ones. It also sells beautiful art posters and museum-shop gifts.

Aurora Kontakt (☎ 623 59 89, Vijzelstraat 27) **Map 4** This shop has a huge assortment of electronic and computer gizmos at competitive prices.

Beaufort (☎ 625 91 31, Grimburgwal 11) **Map 2** Exquisite hand-crafted contemporary jewellery is created on site; the necklaces and rings are particularly beautiful.

Christodoulou & Lamé (Rozengracht 42) **Map 3** Handwoven Tibetan silk pillows, velvet throws and hand-beaded saris from this treasure-trove of sumptuous soft furnishings will transform your home into a plush sanctuary.

Condomerie Het Gulden Vlies (☎ 627 41 74, Warmoesstraat 141) **Map 2** Perfectly positioned in the red-light district, this shop stocks hundreds of different types of condoms, lubricants and saucy gifts. Check its amazing Web site, ⓦ www.condomerie.nl.

Foto Professional (☎ 624 60 24, Nieuwendijk 113) **Map 2** Happy snappers and professionals head here for the country's largest selection of second-hand cameras and lenses. There's also new photographic gear and a repairs department.

Frozen Fountain (☎ 622 93 75, Prinsengracht 629) **Map 3** An ever-changing collection of progressive furniture, interior design products and giftware by Dutch and international designers. Current favourites include super-sized corduroy bike bags and delicate, screen-printed crockery.

Hajenius (☎ 623 74 94, Rokin 92) **Map 2** Renowned for its tobacco products and paraphernalia, including traditional leaf cigars (house brand) and clay pipes, this beautiful Art Deco shop is a puffer's paradise.

3-D Hologrammen (☎ 624 72 25, Grimburgwal 2) **Map 2** This fascinating (and trippy) collection of holographic pictures, jewellery and stickers will delight even the most jaded peepers.

Kitsch Kitchen (☎ 428 49 69, 1e Bloemdwarsstraat 21) **Map 3** Transform your home into a colourful temple of kitsch with fun Mexican tablecloths and pink plastic chandeliers from India.

Maranón Hangmatten (☎ 420 71 21, Singel 488) **Map 4** Those who love hanging around should explore Europe's largest selection of hammocks.

De Ode (☎ 419 08 82, Levantkade 51, KNSM Island) **Map 6** Looking for a coffin or funeral with a difference? You can purchase a bookcase that converts to a coffin when you join the library in the sky, or a coffin on wheels with bicycle towbar – perfect for pedalling friends to their last bike rack.

Santa Jet (☎ *427 20 70, Prinsenstraat 7*) **Map 3** The interior's vivid colours are worth a visit alone as are the Mexican shrines, religious icons, Day of the Dead paraphernalia, candles and love potions.

De Witte Tanden Winkel (☎ *623 34 43, Runstraat 5*) **Map 3** Sparklier smiles are guaranteed with a large range of toothbrushes (designer brands and cute kids' ones), toothpastes and advice.

THIRD WORLD & NEW AGE

This is one of the best cities for getting in touch with the Third World, nature and the inner you, often all at once.

African Heritage (☎ *627 27 65, Zeedijk 59*) **Map 2** Breathtakingly cramped, this store is chock-full of African curios, clothing, masks, wooden toys and musical instruments.

Fair Trade Shop (☎ *625 22 45, Heiligeweg 45*) **Map 2** This charitable shop features quality, stylish Third-World products including clothes, comestibles, toys, CDs and interesting ceramics. The company works directly with producers and provides ongoing business training.

Himalaya (☎ *626 08 99, Warmoesstraat 56*) **Map 2** What a surprise: a peaceful, New-Age oasis amid the red-light district. Stock up on crystals, incense and oils, ambient CDs and books on the healing arts, then visit the lovely tearoom.

Jacob Hooy & Co (☎ *624 30 41, Kloveniersburgwal 12*) **Map 2** This charming chemist's shop – with its walls of massive, wooden drawers – has been selling medicinal herbs, homeopathic remedies and natural cosmetics since 1743. It now has a massage room too.

Cycling Tours

The area around Amsterdam seems built-up when you look at a map but takes on a different perspective from a bicycle. Amsterdam is surrounded by some very pretty countryside, and you can make numerous one-day or even half-day trips through serene, flat and unbelievably green landscape, with church steeples and the occasional windmill on the horizon. Cycling through these surroundings you'll understand how Dutch artists learned to paint such dramatic skies.

We describe a few routes here to get you started; they begin and end in Amsterdam. See also the Eastern Harbour District section of the Things to See & Do chapter for a route taking in the sights in that area.

Information

If the routes described here whet your appetite, many of the bike-rental shops can advise of several other options and will sell the accompanying route maps (see Bicycle Rental in the Getting Around chapter). Some outfits also organise bicycle tours (see Organised Tours in the same chapter).

The Dutch motoring organisation ANWB (see Other Information Sources in the Facts for the Visitor chapter) sells a welter of excellent route maps as well as camping, recreation and sightseeing guides aimed especially at cyclists, though these will be in Dutch – not that it matters with the maps. Its *ANWB Fietsmap Amsterdam en Omgeving* (ANWB Cycling Map Amsterdam and Surroundings) costs €11.32 and contains four detailed topographical maps on a scale of 1:50,000. These show 21 cycling routes varying in length from 25km to 95km, and the numbers of these routes correspond to the ANWB cycling signs along the way (six-sided, green paint on white background).

RICK GERHARTER

Previous page: A healthy, pollution-free and cheap way to explore both city and countryside (photo by Christian Aslund)

Left: You may need to replace one of these if you're unlucky

Preparations

See the Getting Around chapter for details on renting bikes. If you want to go farther afield than these routes (for instance, to tour the bulb fields) it might make more sense to rent from a local train station.

A standard, coaster-brake bike will be fine if trips aren't too long. Gears are useful for riding against the wind (very common in this flat country) but cost a bit more to rent. Ask for a tyre repair kit and pump. Few locals wear a bicycle helmet, though they're sensible protection especially for children.

Wind and rain are all-too-familiar features of Dutch weather. A lightweight nylon jacket will provide protection, but be sure to use a variety that breathes (Gore-Tex for example) or the sweat will gather, even in a strong wind. The same applies to cycling trousers or shorts. On other than warm days, a woollen cap or balaclava is a good idea as your ears will freeze.

Carry a backpack with a sweater, camera and packed lunch, and off you go.

AMSTEL ROUTE
30km, 3-4 hours

This is an attractive, convenient route, beginning in the southern suburb of Amstelveen and taking in a selection of the Amstel River and some unexpectedly bucolic surrounds.

Departure point is the **Amstelpark**, a pretty municipal park about 300m south of the A10 motorway. Cycling isn't allowed in the park, which has a rose garden, open-air theatre, cafés and other facilities.

A couple of kilometres south of the route's start, cycling along the quiet east bank of the Amstel, you'll come to **Ouderkerk aan de Amstel**, a pretty, affluent village (actually a few centuries older than Amsterdam) with plenty of riverside cafés and handsome houses.

At Ouderkerk, cross the bridge over the Bullewijk River and turn left (east) opposite the ancient Jewish cemetery, leaving the Amstel behind and following the right bank of the Bullewijk.

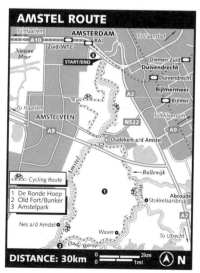

You pass under the A9 motorway and about 1km farther on, at a spot with a pleasant restaurant, the Waver River comes in from the right (south) and you follow that. By now you'll have great views of **De Ronde Hoep**, a wild, sparsely populated peat area drained by local settlers about 1000 years ago (the Waver and Bullewijk were the drainage rivers). It attracts many birds, impervious to Amsterdam's skyscrapers looming in the distance. The Waver narrows and becomes the Oude Waver, and when you come to the two hand-operated bridges, you'll clearly see that the land is below water level.

At the south-westernmost part of our route lies a squat riverside **bunker**, one of 38 defensive forts built around Amsterdam at the turn of the 20th century (they were already outmoded by the 1920s). Here you join the Amstel again and turn right (north), following the eastern bank back in the direction of Amstelveen. Just north of here, the village of **Nes aan de Amstel** across the river has some delightful wooden, café-filled terraces – admire them from a distance, as there's no bridge close by.

Crossing north under the A9, the final leg of the journey provides a view towards the western edges of Amsterdam-Zuidoost, home to the depressing suburb of Bijlmer. You could continue past Ouderkerk and return the way you came, along the east bank of the Amstel, but an interesting little diversion would be to cross the bridge at Ouderkerk to the west bank and curl around the fringes of the green Amstelland area, with oodles of all-too-cute garden allotments. The Amstelpark, your starting (and finishing) point, lies just to the north.

WATERLAND ROUTE
37km, 3½-5 hours
(incl Marken & Volendam, 55km, 7-10 hours)

This trip through the eastern half of Waterland is culture-shock material: 20 minutes from the centre of Amsterdam you step back in time a couple of centuries, with isolated farming communities and flocks of birds amid ditches, dikes and lakes.

Take the free Buiksloterwegveer ferry from behind Centraal Station across the IJ, and continue 1km along the west bank of the Noordhollands Kanaal. Do a loop onto and over the second bridge, continue along the east bank for a few hundred metres and turn right, under the freeway and along Nieuwendammerdijk past the Vliegenbos camping ground. At the end of Nieuwendammerdijk, do a dogleg and continue along Schellingwouderdijk. Follow this under the two major road bridges, when it becomes Durgerdammerdijk and you're on your way.

The pretty town of **Durgerdam**, spread along the dike, looks out across the water to IJburg, a major land-reclamation project that will be home to 45,000 people in a few years' time. Farther north, the dike road passes several **lakes** and **former sea inlets** – low-lying, drained peat lands that were flooded during storms and now form important bird-breeding areas. Colonies include plovers, godwits, bitterns, golden-eyes, snipes, herons and spoonbills (in north-western Europe,

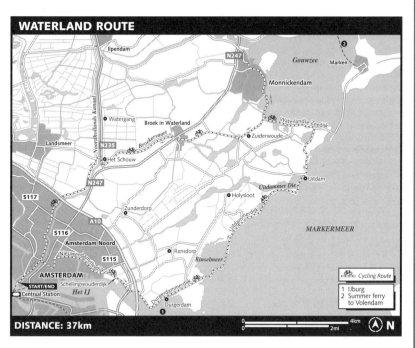

WATERLAND ROUTE

DISTANCE: 37km

Cycling Route

1 IJburg
2 Summer ferry to Volendam

spoonbills breed only in the Netherlands). Climb the dike at one of the viewing points for uninterrupted views to both sides.

The road – now called Uitdammerdijk – passes the town of Uitdam, after which you turn left (west) towards Monnickendam. Alternatively, you could turn right and proceed along the causeway to the former island of **Marken**. After visiting Marken, you could take the summer ferry to **Volendam** and backtrack along the sea dike to **Monnickendam**. Or you could return over the causeway from Marken and pick up our tour again towards Monnickendam. Mind you, these diversions to Marken and (especially) Volendam would add significantly to the length of your trip. For details of these three interesting towns, and the Marken-Volendam ferry, see IJsselmeer Towns in the Excursions chapter.

After visiting Monnickendam, return the way you came, but about 1.5km south of Monnickendam, turn right (south-west) towards Zuiderwoude. From there, continue to **Broek in Waterland**, a pretty town with old, wooden houses. Then cycle along the south bank of the Broekervaart canal towards Het Schouw on the Noordhollands Kanaal. Bird-watchers may want to cross the Noordhollands Kanaal (the bridge is slightly to the north) and head up the west bank towards **Watergang** and its bird-breeding areas. Otherwise, follow the west bank back down to Amsterdam North, straight cycling all the way to the ferry to Centraal Station.

VECHT ROUTE
65km, 6½-8 hours

The Vecht River south-east of Amsterdam was an important waterway to Utrecht before the completion of the Amsterdam-Rhine Canal but it's peaceful now. The scenery is not as starkly rural as along the Amstel River, though the small towns, woods and 17th- and 18th-century country mansions provide plenty of variety.

Getting from Amsterdam to the starting point of this trip is rather tedious, so it's best to take your bicycle on the train to **Weesp** (see Getting Around the Country in the Excursions chapter for details). Unfortunately you can't hire your bicycle at the Weesp train station because you won't be returning there.

Weesp itself is not very interesting, but **Muiden** and especially Muiden Castle to the north are, and it's only 3.5km along the pleasant, east bank of the Vecht. See the Excursions chapter for details about Muiden.

Weesp station is virtually on the Vecht River (turn left as you exit). Follow the west bank south for a few hundred metres and cross the bridge to the opposite bank. Turn left (north) to go to Muiden if you wish; otherwise head south for 4km as the road winds along the river, with farmland to your left. For the last kilometre or so the road heads inland a bit but returns to a bridge across the river (just bear right when you get to the N236 main road). Cross the bridge to the other (west) bank and continue south along the river.

One kilometre farther on you'll pass an old **fort**, part of a series of forts built before WWI to protect Amsterdam from invasion. The idea was to flood the land to deter approaching troops, but this tactic was already outdated by the start of the 20th century. The forts along this so-called 'inundation line' are now on the Unesco World Heritage List.

Continue along the Vecht and you'll arrive at the town of **Nigtevecht**. At the west end of town you cross the sluice to the Amsterdam-Rijn Kanaal (Amsterdam-Rhine Canal), with another fort across the choppy waters. However, stay on the west bank of the Vecht and continue south. This is a pretty stretch along the Hoekerpolder, which takes you 6.5km to Vreeland.

At Vreeland, say goodbye to the Vecht and head west – not along the N201 main road but along a road through farmland a little to the north – until you reach the Amsterdam-Rhine Canal again. Turn left (south) and cross the bridge over the canal. This takes you into the town of Loenersloot where you turn right (north) and follow the Angstel River to Baambrugge. Here you cross the Angstel to the other (west) side and continue north-west in the direction of Abcoude.

Don't go all the way to Abcoude though: after about 2.5km you should turn left at a T-junction. Proceed under the A2 motorway, past the settlements of Zeldenrust and Holendrecht, and eventually you'll end up at another T-junction at Stokkelaarsbrug. This is where the Winkel River (which you've been following for the past 3km or so), joins the Waver River.

At this point you hook up with the Amstel Route described earlier, except you'll be riding in the opposite direction. Turn right onto the east bank of the Waver, and after 1km, turn left onto the west bank of the Bullewijk River which takes you to pretty **Ouderkerk aan de Amstel**. Here you cross the second bridge over the Bullewijk, maybe pause for a refreshment at one of Ouderkerk's many riverside cafés, and head down the east bank of the Amstel River back to Amsterdam.

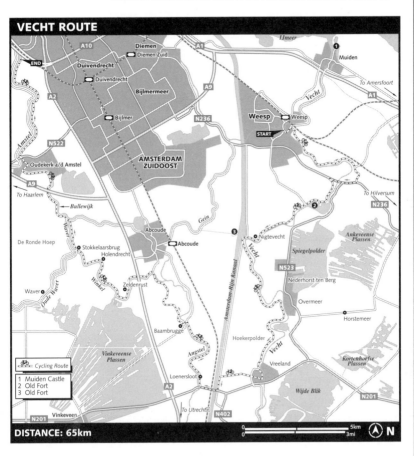

VECHT ROUTE

Cycling Route

1 Muiden Castle
2 Old Fort
3 Old Fort

DISTANCE: 65km

0 ___ 5km
0 ___ 3mi

N

Excursions

This is a small country, and you can visit many areas on day or overnight excursions from Amsterdam. All the major cities are less than 2½ hours away by train, even distant Maastricht (in the south-eastern province of Limburg) and Groningen (in the north-eastern province of Groningen). Many sights are concentrated in the west of the country, in the provinces of North and South Holland (Amsterdam itself is in the south of North Holland), and are less than an hour's drive or train ride away.

GETTING AROUND THE COUNTRY

See the earlier Getting There & Away and Getting Around chapters for general information about travelling by car or public transport. There's a dense network of freeways but in most cases the train is your best bet, or the bus in some regional areas.

Train

Dutch trains are fast and comfortable, especially the new double-decker ones with the horizontal blue stripes, but their famed efficiency has taken a dive with privatisation, cost-cutting and the ensuing organisational chaos. Many services have been cut back, presumably temporarily as the mess is sorted out.

Services along the major routes stop around midnight (often much earlier on minor routes), but there are night trains once an hour in both directions along the Utrecht-Amsterdam-Schiphol-Leiden-The Hague-Delft-Rotterdam route. Tickets for these cost the same as during the day or evening and can be bought at the counter (if it's open) or ticketing machines. If you don't buy a ticket beforehand, notify the conductor as you board the train, in which case you'll pay considerably more – 20% more on a long trip but up to 400% more on a short one!

Trains can be a *Stoptrein*, a faster *Sneltrein* (Fast Train, indicated with 'S'), or an even faster Intercity (IC). EuroCity (EC) or ICE International trains travel between Amsterdam and Cologne and only stop in Utrecht and Arnhem; they're quite fast (a 10-minute saving to Arnhem) but you pay a €2.04 supplement at the counter or ticket machine. From Amsterdam, the high-speed *Thalys* only stops at Schiphol (from The Hague it only stops in Rotterdam) and requires a special ticket, available at the international ticket office in Centraal Station.

There are frequent trains from Centraal Station to most corners of the country and it's unlikely you'll have to wait long, though whether they leave on time is another matter. Make a note of return trains listed on the timetable board at your destination.

The national train timetable book costs €4.99 from train-station counters and newsagencies, but don't bother unless you're planning numerous trips to small destinations only serviced by local stop-trains. It includes a brief user's guide in English, German and French on pages 16–21. If you're online, check Ⓦ www.ns.nl; click on 'Reisinfo' (Travel Info) in the top left-hand corner and choose the English-language option. If you prefer an expensive and not always helpful human touch, ring the national public-transport number, ☎ 0900-92 92 (€0.48 a minute), from 6am to midnight weekdays, from 7am weekends and public holidays.

All major train stations have luggage lockers and/or depots, and 100 stations throughout the country rent bicycles (with a discount in combination with a train ticket – see Bicycle Rental in the Getting Around chapter). Some of these rental places are privately run and not attached to the station, so check where you need to go.

You can bring your own bicycle on the train for an additional €5.67 regardless of the destination, so long as the train has a special bicycle section (many of them do, indicated with a sticker on the relevant wagon), but not on weekdays between 6.30am and 9am or 4.30pm and 6pm (no restrictions in July and August). There are no restrictions or

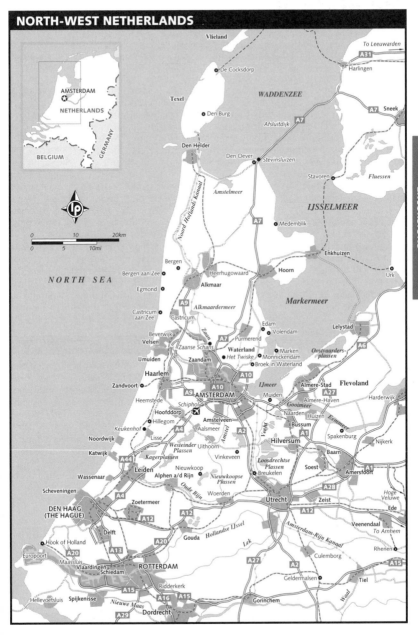

NORTH-WEST NETHERLANDS

fees for collapsible bikes so long as they can reasonably be considered as hand luggage.

Train Tickets With a valid ticket you can disembark anywhere along the direct route. In other words, with a ticket from Amsterdam to Rotterdam you can visit Haarlem, Leiden, The Hague and Delft along the way, but backtracking is not permitted. A return ticket is 10% to 15% cheaper than two one-ways but, like one-way tickets, is only valid on the same day. The only exception is a weekend-return *(weekend-retour)*, which costs the same as a normal return and is valid from 7pm Friday to 4am Monday.

Children aged under four travel free if they don't take up a seat; those aged between four and 11 pay a so-called *Railrunner* fare of €1.13 if accompanied by an adult (maximum of three kids, otherwise it's 40% discount on the normal fare) or they get a 40% discount on the normal fare if travelling alone. Pets in a bag or basket travel free; pets on a lead cost €3.06 regardless of the destination.

A *Dagkaart* (Day Card) for unlimited train travel throughout the country costs €35.62 (2nd class) or €55.25 (1st class), which is the same as you'll pay for a return ticket to any destination more than 233km away. Add €3.97 for an *OV-Dagkaart* (Public Transport Day Card) and you'll have use of trams, buses and metros as well.

If you plan to do a lot of travelling, consider investing €44.92 in a *Voordeel-Urenkaart* (Advantage Hours Card), valid for one year, which gives 40% discount on train travel on weekdays after 9am, as well as all weekend, on public holidays and throughout July and August. (For travel on weekdays before 9am, tell the counter attendant you have a Voordeel-Urenkaart and they'll provide a normal ticket to the first station where the train leaves after 9am, and a discount ticket thereafter.) The discount also applies to up to three people travelling with you on the same trip, and you can take one pet on a lead free of charge. As well, the card allows you to rent the cheapest Hertz car for €24.96 a day (normal price €35.85 – see Car Rental in the Getting Around

chapter). A similar version of this card for those aged 60 and over gives an additional seven days' free travel a year, plus 25% discount on travel to 18 European countries. The card is available at train-station counters (passport photo required, plus driving licence or passport for the 60-plus version).

In July and August you can buy a *Zomertoer* (Summer Tour) ticket that allows three days' unlimited train travel within the country during any 10-day period for €44.92 (only 2nd class); the version for two people travelling together costs €58.54. Stamp your ticket in the yellow machines at the stairways to the platforms. If you pay an extra €9.08 (€13.16 for two) the ticket becomes a *Zomertoer Plus* which is also valid for all trams, buses and metros during those three days.

A *Waddenbiljet* (Wadden Ticket) combines the train, ferry and bus tickets required for a visit to one of the Wadden Islands in the north of the country (Texel, Vlieland, Terschelling, Ameland or Schiermonnikoog), and so long as you don't take more than a day each way you can stay there for

---

Train Ticket Machines

More and more stations are relying on ticketing machines to cut personnel costs and queues at the few remaining counters, which is a bit of a problem for visitors because in most cases instructions are in Dutch only. Check where you want to go on the alphabetical list of destinations and enter the relevant code into the machine; then choose 1st/2nd class, *vol tarief/korting* (full fare/discount – eg, if you have a discount card, discussed in Train Tickets), *alleen vandaag geldig/zonder datum* (only valid today/without date – if you choose the latter you can travel some other time but you'll have to stamp the ticket in one of the yellow stamping machines near the platforms when you do), and finally choose *enkele reis/retour/5-retourkaart/weekend-retour* (one way/return/5-return ticket/weekend-return). The machine will then indicate how much it wants to be fed – coins only (change is given).

up to a year if you like. The ticket costs the same as two one-way train fares, and a 40% discount applies if you hold a *Voordeel-Urenkaart*, though pensioners may be better off buying all tickets separately because of ferry discounts.

Train Taxi More than 100 train stations offer an excellent train taxi *(treintaxi)* service that takes you to/from the station within a limited area. This costs €3.50 per ride if you buy your special taxi ticket at a train-station counter or ticketing machine; buy another one for the return ride or else it's €4.50 from the driver. Note that these prices are per person – each person needs a separate ticket. The service operates daily from 7am (from 8am Sunday and public holidays) till the last train, which varies from station to station.

These are special taxis (normal taxis don't take part in this scheme) and it's a shared service – the driver determines the route, which might take a bit longer than with a normal taxi, but it's usually much cheaper if there are only one or two of you. Ask the counter attendant or taxi driver for a pamphlet listing all participating stations. The taxi will probably be waiting at the special blue column outside the station (press the call button otherwise); for a trip back to the station, ring ☎ 0900-873 468 294 (€0.34 per minute) at least half an hour in advance.

Unfortunately some major stations (Amsterdam CS, The Hague CS or HS, Rotterdam CS) are excluded but Delft, Leiden Centraal and Utrecht CS are in the scheme – and the train taxis there operate all night because of night trains.

Bus
Regional buses are run by Connexxion and Interliner but they're the same company (call ☎ 0900-92 92 for timetables or ☎ 0900-266 63 99 for ticketing and other inquiries). Buy your ticket from the driver. It's worth knowing about the *Zomerzwerfkaart* (Summer Roving Ticket), available from the driver from June to August. This gives a day's worth of unlimited bus travel anywhere in the country for €7.50 – great value.

NORTH OF AMSTERDAM
The finger of land north of Amsterdam used to be known as West Friesland; today it's the northern tip of the province of North Holland, whose capital is Haarlem. Much of it is polder that has been claimed from the water in the past 400 years.

East of here lies the IJsselmeer (IJssel Lake), which used to be known as the Zuiderzee (Southern Sea) before it was cut off from the open sea in 1932 by a large dike, the 30km Afsluitdijk (Barrier Dike). This impressive dam (it's not really a dike because there's water on either side) connected the provinces of North Holland and Friesland, but more to the point, completely changed the economic outlook for the seafaring towns along the eastern coast of North Holland. Many reinvented themselves as tourist destinations.

Waterland
Just north of Amsterdam is the drained peat area of Waterland, a region of green farmland with dikes, ditches and some unique flora and fauna. It's an important bird-breeding area. The construction of the Noordhollands Kanaal in the 1820s cut the area in two. In the west near Landsmeer is the nature reserve and recreational area Het Twiske – see the introduction to Activities in the Things to See & Do chapter.

The eastern half of Waterland in particular is well worth exploring for its isolated farming communities that seem frozen in time. If you're looking for an interesting cycling trip on a pleasant summer's day, this is it – see the separate Cycling Tours section for details.

IJsselmeer Towns
Several towns along the IJsselmeer have proud maritime histories and are well worth visiting.

Hoorn The lively little port of Hoorn, which gave its name to Cape Horn at the southern tip of South America, was the capital of West Friesland and a mighty trading city (one of the six founding members of the United East India Company). Many of its 17th-century buildings are still intact, and its old harbour full of wooden fishing boats and barges is as picturesque as they come. Be sure to visit the impressive **Westfries Museum** *(☎ 0229-28 00 22, Rode Steen 1; admission free; open 11am-5pm Mon-Fri, 2pm-5pm Sat & Sun)* with a wide-ranging collection recalling Hoorn's past riches. The ANWB/VVV office (☎ 0229-21 83 43) is at Veemarkt 4.

Enkhuizen North-east of here, Enkhuizen was another founding member of the East India Company, and an important fishing and whaling port. There's some interesting architecture but the big attraction is the wonderful **Zuiderzee Museum** *(☎ 0228-35 11 11, Wierdijk 12-22; admission €9.08; open 10am-6pm daily)*, especially the outdoor section (open April to October) with a reconstructed village; the maritime exhibits in the former East India Company buildings in the indoor section are also worth a look. The VVV (☎ 0228-31 31 64) is at Tussen Twee Havens 1.

Medemblik North-west of Enkhuizen is Medemblik, one of the oldest towns along the IJsselmeer, with a history dating back to the early Middle Ages. Its Gothic **cathedral** is worth visiting, as is its medieval castle, **Kasteel Radboud** *(☎ 0227-54 19 60, Oude-vaartsgat 8; adult/child €2.27/1.14; open 11am-5pm Mon-Sat 1 May-15 Sept, 2pm-5pm Sun year-round)*. Also of interest is the **Stoommachinemuseum** *(Steam Engine Museum; ☎ 0227-54 47 32, Oosterdijk 4; adult/child €2.27/1.14; open 10am-5pm Tues-Sat Apr-Oct)*, which has some impressive machinery that's occasionally fired up for demonstrations, including a steam tram that runs to/from Hoorn (see the following Getting There & Away section). The VVV (☎ 0227-54 28 52) is at Dam 2.

Edam Closer to Amsterdam is Edam, a pretty town that was once a whaling port but is now known mainly for its cheeses. The **cheese market** *(Wed morning Jul & Aug)* is smaller than the one in Alkmaar (see later in this chapter) but just as touristy. The stained-glass windows in the 17th-century

Grote Kerk are stunning. The VVV (☎ 0299-31 51 25) is at Damplein 1 in the town centre.

Volendam South-east of Edam is Volendam, a former fishing port that reinvented itself as a tourist town when the Afsluitdijk killed the fishing industry. It's picturesque enough but be prepared for hordes of tourists – you'll encounter fewer of them when you explore some of the pretty streets behind the harbour. The VVV (☎ 0299-36 37 47) is at Zeestraat 37.

Monnickendam Monnickendam also attracts tourists and justifiably so: its meticulously restored 17th-century houses and old fishing cottages are picture-postcard material, and the whole setup is far less tacky than in Volendam. The tower of the former town hall has a beautiful carillon with mechanical knights that, sadly, only plays at 11am and noon on Saturday. The VVV (☎ 0299-65 19 98) is at Nieuwpoortslaan 15.

Marken Marken was an isolated fishing community on an island that was connected to the mainland by a causeway in the 1950s. Tourists flock here in summer to photograph people in costume. The location is impressive and you can easily imagine how harsh it must have been here with frequent Zuiderzee storms. Note the diagonal wooden beams in the water at the wharf, which provided protection against drift-ice. For more information, contact Monnickendam's VVV.

Getting There & Away Useful Connexxion buses leaving from the Open Havenfront in front of Centraal Station about every half-hour include No 111 to Marken, No 110 to Volendam and Edam (or No 112 only to Edam), and No 114 to Hoorn. An inexpensive day excursion would be to take a morning bus from Amsterdam to Marken, which has pleasant trails along the shore. Hike around the island in a couple of leisurely hours, then take the ferry from Marken to Volendam (€3.40 one way, leaves every 30 to 45 minutes from April to September only). Edam is only five minutes from Volendam by bus No 110. From

Volendam or Edam, catch a bus back to Amsterdam – with the possibility of a stop at Monnickendam if you take bus No 110.

If you use a strip ticket this would only cost six strips from Amsterdam to Marken and another seven from Volendam back to Amsterdam – slightly cheaper than with the *Zomerzwerfkaart* discussed earlier. In winter, or whenever the ferry isn't operating, you could backtrack from Marken to Monnickendam on bus No 111, then catch another bus up to Volendam from there. For the money, this is one of the best-value day trips in Europe.

Another, and very enjoyable, way to see some of the IJsselmeer towns farther north is via the so-called 'Historic Triangle', involving a train, narrow-gauge steam tram and boat. From Amsterdam, take the 9.49am train to Hoorn station (arrives 10.30am), cross the footbridge over the tracks to the steam-tram station, and buy a ticket for the tram that leaves for Medemblik at 11.05am (arrives 12.10pm). This costs €11.80 including a boat from Medemblik to Enkhuizen, which leaves Medemblik at 12.45pm from April to October and drops you off at the Zuiderzee Museum at 2pm (another boat leaves Medemblik at 4.30pm in July and August but skips the museum and goes straight to Enkhuizen station). After a look around the Zuiderzee Museum, take the ferry from the museum to Enkhuizen station and buy a one-way train ticket back to Hoorn (€2.95), assuming you have a return ticket Amsterdam-Hoorn to begin with. Unfortunately, the limited schedules of steam tram and boat mean that you won't be able to spend time in Hoorn and Medemblik (you could, of course, get a *very* early start and at least spend a couple of hours in Hoorn). For more information on tickets and schedules, call the steam-tram people on ☎ 0229-21 48 62.

NORTH-WEST & WEST OF AMSTERDAM
Alkmaar
☎ 072 • pop 93,000
This pleasant town with a picturesque old centre is famous for its **cheese market** *(10am-12.30pm Fri Apr-Sept)*, staged in the main market square (Waagplein). Arrive early if you want to get more than a fleeting glimpse of the famous round cheeses being whisked away on sledges carried by porters with brightly coloured straw hats (the colours denote which guild they belong to).

Other attractions include the **Waag** (Weigh House) with its **Hollands Kaasmuseum** *(Dutch Cheese Museum; ☎ 511 42 84, Waagplein 2; adult/concession €2.27/ 1.36; open 10am-4pm Mon-Thur & Sat, 9am-4pm Fri Apr-Oct).* Across the square is the interesting **Nationaal Biermuseum** *(☎ 511 38 01, Houttil 1; adult/concession €2.04/1.13; open 10am-4pm Tues-Fri, 1pm-4pm Sat, 1.30pm-4pm Sun Apr-Oct; 1pm-4pm Tues-Sun Nov-Mar).*

Nearby are the seaside resorts of **Bergen**, **Egmond** and **Castricum**, which require a bit of effort to reach but are far more pleasant than overdeveloped Zandvoort (see the later Zandvoort section). The VVV (☎ 511 42 84) in the Waag at Waagplein 3 provides information on the surrounding areas as well.

There are two trains an hour from Centraal Station (€5.33, 30 minutes) and at the other end it's a 15-minute walk south-east to Waagplein.

Zaanse Schans
Several authentic working **windmills** stand along the Zaan River at Zaanse Schans just north of Zaandam, a bustling city north-west of Amsterdam. There are a few small **museums** among the old houses of the Zaanse Schans 'tourist village' but it costs nothing to stroll around and several attractions are free, such as the cheesemaker's shop (free samples) and the wooden shoe factory with a contraption that copies clogs in a similar way to a locksmith's key machine. A tourist boat does 45-minute cruises on the Zaan several times a day (€4.10, children half-price) from April through September. For more about the area, check W www.zaanseschans.nl.

Zaanse Schans is a great picnic spot, so take a lunch and don't forget your camera! Also be sure to visit old **Zaandijk** situated directly east across the Zaan from Zaanse Schans. It's far less visited by tourists and provides a more authentic appreciation of 'old Holland'.

In **Zaandam** itself, you could pay a quick visit to the small wooden **cabin** (☎ 075-616 03 90, Krimp 23; adult/child €2/1; open 1pm-5pm Tues-Sun) where Tsar Peter the Great of Russia stayed incognito for five months in 1697. He worked as a shipwright's apprentice on the nearby wharves, where he learnt much about shipbuilding, drinking and swearing in Dutch. The Zaandam VVV (☎ 075-616 22 21 or ☎ 635 17 47) is at Gedempte Gracht 76.

Getting to Zaanse Schans by train takes about half an hour. From Centraal Station, take the Stoptrein towards Alkmaar and get off at Koog Zaandijk – it's an eight-minute, well-signposted walk to the Zaanse Schans open-air museum.

To continue to Zaandam, you could take the train but you could also cross the large bridge to the left of Zaanse Schans, take the first street on your right into Zaandijk and board the southbound bus No 89. Ask the driver to let you out at the large canal in the centre of town; Zaandam's pedestrian shopping mall is directly in front of the bus stop. All in all, in good weather it's a great afternoon out.

IJmuiden
☎ 0255 • pop 7000

The huge **North Sea locks** are one of the main attractions in this town at the mouth of the North Sea Canal – the largest is 400m long and 45m wide. Few people realise, however, that IJmuiden is also the largest fishing port in Western Europe, home to factory trawlers that stay out in the North Atlantic for weeks at a time. Several fish restaurants line the fishing harbour. The huge **beach** at low tide is a kite-flyer's delight, but the steel mills on the northern side of the locks are less attractive. The VVV (☎ 51 56 11) is at Zeeweg 189.

The easiest and most enjoyable way to get here by public transport is to take the hydrofoil (Amsterdam ☎ 639 22 47) from Pier 7 behind Centraal Station (hourly on the hour, half-hourly during peak times), which costs €6.81/3.98 return per adult/child. It skims

along the North Sea Canal and 25 minutes later deposits you in Velsen, 3km short of IJmuiden itself, from where you catch Connexxion bus No 82 or 83 into town. It's a good idea to take a bicycle (an extra €3.29 return) because things are a bit spread out. Cycle from Velsen along the dike towards the locks and go across the 'small' and 'middle' locks to the big lock on the far side; along the way you'll find an interesting information centre.

If you travel by road along the North Sea Canal, you'll have the surreal experience of passing huge, ocean-going ships that float well above road level.

Haarlem
☎ 023 • pop 150,000

The capital of the province of North Holland is a small but vibrant city with a beautiful centre similar to Amsterdam's. There are lots of pleasant places to eat, drink and shop, and a couple of great museums that can easily be covered in a day if you don't plan to visit the nearby Keukenhof gardens as well (see the following South of Amsterdam section). Be warned, though: in the evenings and on Sunday Haarlem is dead.

The VVV (☎ 0900-616 16 00) is at Stationsplein 1, just outside the impressive, semi-Art Nouveau **train station** (1908). From here it's a 10-minute walk southwards, straight down Kruisweg, to the city's pleasant central square at Grote Markt.

The **Frans Hals Museum** (☎ 511 57 75, Groot Heiligland 62; adult/child €4.53/free; open 11am-5pm Mon-Sat, noon-5pm Sun), another 10 minutes south of Grote Markt, features many of the master's group portraits and works by other great artists – a must-see if you're interested in Dutch painting. The **Teylers Museum** (☎ 531 90 10, Spaarne 16; adult/child €4.50/1; open 10am-5pm Tues-Sat, noon-5pm Sun), just east of Grote Markt, is the oldest museum in the country (1778), with a curious collection including drawings by Michelangelo and Raphael and lots of fun objects.

On Grote Markt, the impressive Gothic cathedral, the **St Bavo** (☎ 553 20 40; adult/child €1.50/0.90; open 10am-4pm Mon-Sat)

Vecht River at Vreeland

Visit a working windmill.

Ransdorp, in the Waterland region

The 13th-century Muiderslot (Muiden Castle)

Imposing Enkhuizen architecture

Coastal resort of Zandvoort

View from Utrecht's Dom Tower (465 steps)

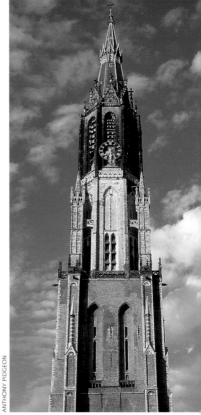

Delft's Gothic Oude Kerk, eight centuries old

Pond beside the Binnenhof government buildings, The Hague

– or Grote Kerk – is home to the stunning Müller organ. One of the most magnificent organs in the world, it was played by a 10-year-old Mozart and also by Haydn. You can hear it roar at 8.15pm Tuesday (May to October) and also at 3pm Thursday (July and August).

Intercity trains run every 15 minutes to/from Centraal Station (€2.95, 15 minutes) and Leiden (€4.42, 30 minutes).

Zandvoort

The seaside resort of Zandvoort is 10 minutes by train from Haarlem. In summer it seems as if half of Amsterdam deposits itself here, and the only reason you might want to do likewise is that it's easy to get to – trains leave every 30 minutes from Centraal Station and a return trip costs €6.81 (do not – repeat, not – try to get here by car on a sunny weekend day in summer). The famous Formula One road-racing track in the dunes still hosts motor-sports events, but lost its (and therefore the country's) round of the world championship in the 1970s when smug residents complained about noise.

A worthwhile day trip involves a return ticket to Zandvoort, stopping off in Haarlem en route. After lunch in Haarlem, continue to Zandvoort and stroll along the beach before returning to Amsterdam.

SOUTH OF AMSTERDAM

The compact Randstad ('rim-city') is the circular urban agglomeration formed by Amsterdam, The Hague, Rotterdam and Utrecht, and smaller towns such as Haarlem, Leiden and Delft. It's the Netherlands' most densely populated region, with a 'green heart' of farmland and lakes that begins immediately south of Amsterdam. The region's many sights are highlighted by the bulb fields, which explode in intoxicating colours between March and May.

Amstel & Vecht Rivers

A trip along the Amstel south of Amsterdam is a popular excursion for cyclists, taking in some unexpectedly rural scenery. Southeast of Amsterdam, the winding Vecht River is another cyclists' paradise, and a popular touring route to Utrecht. See the separate Cycling Tours section for further details.

Nieuwkoopse Plassen

The Nieuwkoop Lakes south of Amsterdam and west of the Vecht River are former peat lakes in an old polder area in the Randstad 'green heart'. You can go windsurfing, sailing, rowing or canoeing, but the lakes are also a nature reserve with the world's largest colony of purple herons. In the town of **Nieuwkoop**, Tijsterman (☎ 0172-57 17 86, Dorpsstraat 118) rents boats, and the similarly named restaurant next door has a pleasant terrace and good *dagschotels* (dishes of the day) from €12.

From Centraal Station, take bus No 170 along the Amstel to Uithoorn and change to bus No 147 (50 minutes). By car, take the A2 towards Utrecht, turn off at Vinkeveen and follow the signs to Mijdrecht, De Hoef and Nieuwveen to Nieuwkoop.

Aalsmeer

This town south-west of Amsterdam hosts the world's biggest **flower auction** *(☎ 0297-39 39 39, Legmeerdijk 313; adult/child under 11yrs €4/2; open 7.30am-11am Mon-Fri)* in Europe's largest commercial complex (over one million square metres, or 150 football fields). The experience will blow you away. Bidding starts early, so arrive between 7.30am and 9am to catch the action from the viewing gallery. Selling is by Dutch auction, with electronic lights showing the high starting price, dropping until someone takes up the offer. By the way, Thursday is very quiet and *not* a good day to visit. Take bus No 172 from Centraal Station, leaving every half-hour.

Keukenhof & Bulb Fields

The whole region between Hillegom and Katwijk (west of Leiden) is full of bulb fields – tulips, daffodils and hyacinths – that burst into bloom each spring and carpet the countryside in bright swathes of red, yellow or purple. See the boxed text 'Tulips – The Beloved Bulb' for more information.

The **Keukenhof** *(☎ 0252-46 55 55, Stationsweg 166, Lisse; adult/child €11/5.50;*

open 8am-7.30pm daily late March-late May, gates close 6pm) is the world's largest flower garden. Located between the towns of Hillegom and Lisse south of Haarlem, it attracts a staggering 800,000 people for a mere nine weeks every year. Nature's talents are combined with artificial precision to create a garden where seven million tulips and daffodils bloom, perfectly in place and exactly on time. Its opening dates vary slightly from year to year, so check with the Amsterdam VVV, the Keukenhof itself or W www.keukenhof.nl.

A huge **Flower Parade of the Bulb Fields** moves from Noordwijk (on the coast, west of Lisse) to Haarlem on the first Saturday after 19 April – again, check with the VVV or Keukenhof.

In Lisse, the **Museum de Zwarte Tulp** *(Black Tulip Museum; ☎ 0252-41 79 00, Grachtweg 2A, Lisse; adult/child €2.75/ 2.05; open 1pm-5pm Tues-Sun)* displays everything you want to know about bulbs, including why there is no such thing as a black tulip. The Lisse VVV (☎ 0252-41 42 62) is at Grachtweg 53A. To reach Lisse, take bus No 50 from Haarlem station. For the Keukenhof, change at Lisse to bus No 54.

Leiden
☎ 071 • pop 120,000

Leiden is a cheerful city with an aura of intellect generated by its 20,000-strong student population. The university, the oldest in the country, was a present from William the Silent for withstanding a long Spanish siege in 1574. A third of the residents starved before the Spaniards retreated on 3 October, still the date of Leiden's biggest festival.

Most sights lie within a confusing network of central canals, about a 10-minute walk south-east of the train station. The VVV (☎ 0900-222 23 33) is at Stationsweg 2D, five minutes' walk from the station on the way into town.

The **Rijksmuseum van Oudheden** *(National Museum of Antiquities; ☎ 516 31 63, Rapenburg 28; adult/child €6/5.50; open 10am-5pm Tues-Fri, noon-5pm Sat & Sun)* has a world-class collection and tops Leiden's

---

Tulips – the Beloved Bulb

Tulips have captured the fancy of the Dutch, and humans in general, for centuries. At times this love has been an absolute mania (see the boxed text 'Mad about Tulips' in the Things to See & Do chapter).

While it's easy for some to pooh-pooh such adoration of a simple flower, there's no denying the magnificence of their displays each year during tulip season. Thousands of people arrive from all over the world to see the bulbs in bloom. Postcards just don't do justice to the vast fields of colour.

The first stop on any tulip tour is the **Keukenhof**, a 32-hectare park that stretches on and on, with greenhouses full of more delicate varieties. Just wandering about can easily take half a day. There are several cafés for when you need a break from the blooms. From the edges of the gardens, you can see the stark beauty of the commercial bulb fields stretching in all directions.

Tulip lovers won't want to limit their time with the plants to just the Keukenhof. The 16,500 hectares of **bulb fields** around the Randstad are also ablaze with colour throughout the tulip-blooming period. The broad stripes of colour stretching as far as one can see are a spectacular feast for the eye. The bulbs are left to bloom fully so that they will gain full strength during the growing season, after which nearly half a billion euros' worth of bulbs are exported worldwide.

Different plants will be in bloom at different times, but most people home in on the tulip weeks which are *usually* around the middle of April.

To appreciate the blooms you have several transport options. By train, take one of the frequent local (meaning slow) trains between Haarlem and Leiden. These pass through the heart of the fields. By car, cover the same area on the N206 and N208, branching off down tiny side roads as you wish. But like so much of the Netherlands, perhaps the best way to see the bulb fields is by bicycle (smell the scents). You can set your course along the smallest roads and get lost in a sea of colour.

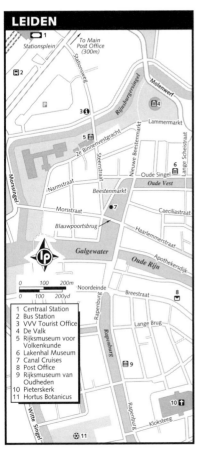

LEIDEN

To Main
Post Office
(300m)

Stationsplein

Stationsweg

Molenwerf

Rijnsburgersingel

Lammermarkt

2e Binnenvestgracht

Nieuwe Beestenmarkt

Lange Scheistraat

Oude Singel

Oude Vest

Narmstraat

Beestenmarkt

Morssingel

Morsstraat

Caeciliastraat

Blauwpoortsbrug

Haarlemmerstraat

Galgewater

Oude Rijn

Apothekersdijk

0   100   200m
0   100   200yd

Noordeinde

Breestraat

Rapenburg

Lange Brug

Rapenburg

Rapenburg

Witte Singel

Kloksteeg

1 Centraal Station
2 Bus Station
3 VVV Tourist Office
4 De Valk
5 Rijksmuseum voor Volkenkunde
6 Lakenhal Museum
7 Canal Cruises
8 Post Office
9 Rijksmuseum van Oudheden
10 Pieterskerk
11 Hortus Botanicus

list of 11 museums. Its striking entrance hall contains the Temple of Taffeh, a gift from Egypt for the Netherlands' help in saving ancient monuments from inundation when the Aswan High Dam was built.

Another worthwhile museum, near the station, is the **Rijksmuseum voor Volkenkunde** *(National Museum for Ethnology; ☎ 516 88 00, W www.rmv.nl, Steenstraat 1; adult/child €6/3.25; open 10am-5pm Tues-Sun, library 10am-12.30pm & 1.30pm-4.30pm Mon-Fri)* which focuses mainly on the former Dutch colonies and has a larger collection of Indonesian stuff than the

Tropenmuseum in Amsterdam. It also has lots of material from Oceania and Japan.

The **Hortus Botanicus** *(☎ 527 72 49, Rapenburg 73; adult/child €4/2; open 10am-6pm daily summer, 10am-4pm Sun-Fri winter)* is Europe's oldest botanical garden (begun in 1587). It's larger than the one in Amsterdam and also more pleasantly laid out. This is where Carolus Clusius from Vienna set up shop in 1592 when he was hired by the university to research medicinal plants; ask one of the attendants for directions to his herb garden outside the grounds. Besides the helpful herbs, he also planted some bulbs from Turkey called tulips – and the rest, as they say, is history.

The 17th-century **Lakenhal** *(Cloth Hall; ☎ 516 53 60, Oude Singel 28-32; adult/child €4.10/2.50; open 10am-5pm Mon-Fri, noon-5pm Sat & Sun)* houses an assortment of works by old masters, as well as period rooms and temporary exhibits.

De Valk *(The Falcon; ☎ 516 53 53, Tweede Binnenvestgracht 1; adult/child €2.50/1.50; open 10am-5pm Tues-Sat, 1pm-5pm Sun)*, Leiden's landmark windmill, is a museum that will blow away notions that windmills were a Dutch invention.

There are trains every 15 minutes to/from Amsterdam (€6.12, 35 minutes).

The Hague (Den Haag)
☎ 070 • pop 450,000

The Hague is the country's seat of government and residence of the royal family, though the capital city is Amsterdam. Officially it's known as 's-Gravenhage (the Count's Domain) because a count built a castle here in the 13th century, but the Dutch call it Den Haag. It's the third-largest city in the country and the capital of the province of South Holland.

It has a refined air, created by the many stately mansions and palatial embassies that line its green boulevards north and northwest of the city centre, though there's a far poorer side to all this finery south of the centre. Much of the centre itself has been transformed into a concrete jungle and architectural showcase in the last 25 years and the construction mania shows no signs

EXCURSIONS

of abating. There's a lot to see but it's all a bit scattered: prestigious art galleries, the biggest indoor jazz festival in the world in mid-July, and the miniature town of Madurodam.

Orientation & Information Trains stop at Station HS (Hollands Spoor), 20 minutes' walk south of the centre, or CS (Centraal Station), five minutes east of the centre (head straight up Herengracht). The main VVV office (☎ 0900-340 35 05, **W** www .denhaag.com) is at Koningin Julianaplein 30 in front of CS; the other is in the seaside suburb of Scheveningen (same phone number), at Gevers Deynootweg 1136.

Things to See & Do The **Mauritshuis** *(☎ 302 34 56, Korte Vijverberg 8; adult/child €7/free; open 10am-5pm Tues-Sat, 11am-5pm Sun)* is a small but grand museum. It houses the superb royal collection of Dutch and Flemish masterpieces (several famous

Vermeers, and a touch of the contemporary with Andy Warhol's *Queen Beatrix*) in an exquisite 17th-century mansion.

The parliamentary buildings around the adjoining **Binnenhof** (Inner Court) have long been the heart of Dutch politics, though parliament now meets in a new building just outside the Binnenhof. One-hour tours take in the 13th-century **Ridderzaal** (Knight's Hall) and leave from the visitor's centre (☎ 364 61 44) at Binnenhof 8A Monday to Saturday from 10am to 3.45pm (adult/child €5/4.30).

Outside the Binnenhof, the **Gevangenpoort** *(Prison Gate; ☎ 346 08 61, Buitenhof 33; admission & tour adult/child €3.65/2.70; open 11am-5pm Tues-Fri, noon-5pm Sat & Sun)* has tours on the hour (last tour 4pm) showing how justice was dispensed in early times. Nearby, the 1565 **old town hall** on Groenmarkt is a splendid example of Dutch-Renaissance architecture, but unfortunately you can only admire it from the outside.

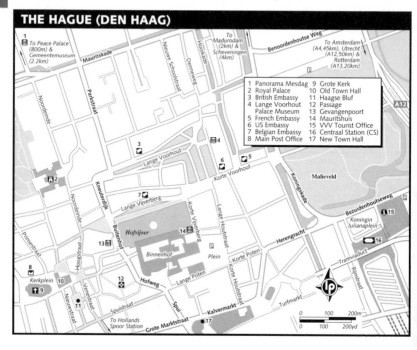

THE HAGUE (DEN HAAG)

1 Panorama Mesdag
2 Royal Palace
3 British Embassy
4 Lange Voorhout Palace Museum
5 French Embassy
6 US Embassy
7 Belgian Embassy
8 Main Post Office
9 Grote Kerk
10 Old Town Hall
11 Haagse Bluf
12 Passage
13 Gevangenpoort
14 Mauritshuis
15 VVV Tourist Office
16 Centraal Station (CS)
17 New Town Hall

The huge **new town hall** *(Cnr Grote Marktstraat & Spui)* is a much-criticised architects' delight. The same applies to two new government buildings that dominate the city-centre sky, commonly referred to as the tits and the penis. For completely bizarre architecture, visit the **Haagse Bluf** project ('Hague bluff' is a dessert consisting of beaten egg whites and jam – full of air but it tastes all right) south of the old town hall and west of Venestraat: a few (brand-new) Dutch Renaissance facades jump out of stark steel-and-glass panels, and the contrast is so extreme it's art.

Admirers of De Stijl, and in particular of Piet Mondriaan, won't want to miss The Hague's Berlage-designed **Gemeentemuseum** *(Municipal Museum; ☎ 338 11 11, Stadhouderslaan 41; adult/child €6.81/2.27; open 11am-5pm Tues-Sun)*. It houses a large collection of works by neo-plasticist and other artists from the late 19th century onwards (Picasso etc), as well as extensive exhibits of applied arts, costumes and musical instruments. Mondriaan's unfinished *Victory Boogie Woogie* takes pride of place (as well it should, since the central bank paid €38 million for it to commemorate the end of the guilder); stare at it for a couple of minutes and you'll be gripped by the vibrancy of his ode to the USA. To get here, take tram No 10 from HS or 17 from CS, or bus No 4 or 14.

The adjoining **Museon** *(☎ 338 13 38; open 11am-5pm Tues-Sun)* displays the world and its people for school kids, while next door is the **Omniversum** Imax theatre *(☎ 354 54 54)* showing the usual big-screen thrills (in Dutch).

Another worthwhile art museum is **Panorama Mesdag** *(☎ 364 45 44, Zeestraat 65; adult/child €3.40/1.80; open 10am-5pm Mon-Sat, noon-5pm Sun)* which, together with the nearby **Mesdag Museum** *(☎ 362 14 34, Laan van Meerdervoort 7F; adult/child €2.27/1.13; open noon-5pm Tues-Sun)*, displays works by the Hague School of artists who so influenced Mondriaan in his early years. The Panorama houses the impressive *Panorama Mesdag* (1881), a gigantic, 360-degree painting of Scheveningen viewed from a dune, painted by Hendrik Willem Mesdag (1831–1915).

The **Peace Palace** *(☎ 302 41 37, Carnegieplein 2; adult/child €3.40/2.27)* is home to the International Court of Justice. It can only be visited on guided tours at 10am, 11am, 2pm and 3pm Monday to Friday – inquire there or at the VVV. You can also attend public hearings but need to book seats in advance (naturally, security is strict with some of the issues under investigation). To get there, take tram No 17 or bus No 4 from CS, or tram No 8 from HS.

Towards Scheveningen is **Madurodam** *(☎ 355 39 00, George Maduroplein 1; adult/child €10/6.80; open 9am-8pm daily mid-Mar–June, 9am-10pm daily July & Aug, 9am-6pm daily Sept–mid-Mar)*, a miniature town containing everything that's quintessentially Netherlands. It's big with children and adults alike. Take tram No 1 from HS or CS, or Tram No 9 or bus No 22 from CS.

Scheveningen is an important fishing port and an overdeveloped seaside resort. There's plenty of beach, a funfair pier, a casino and the landmark Kurhaus hotel. It gets very crowded on summer weekends.

Saturday is a busy shopping day in The Hague as elsewhere in the country, especially in the morning, which is a good time to visit. The indoor general **market** south of Grote Marktstraat gets quite lively. The **Passage**, a glass-covered shopping arcade between Spuistraat, Buitenhof and Hofweg, is a stylish affair.

Getting There & Away Trains connecting The Hague with Amsterdam (€8.05, 45 minutes), Delft (€1.93, five minutes), Leiden (€2.50, 10 minutes) and Rotterdam (€3.40, 15 minutes) travel via Station HS. The line that takes in Schiphol airport (€6.13, 40 minutes) via Leiden on its way to/from Amsterdam uses CS. It's a bit confusing because some trains to Schiphol branch off to Amsterdam Zuid WTC and don't go to Amsterdam Centraal Station – check before you board and change in Leiden if that's the case (you'll seldom wait more than 15 minutes). Utrecht trains (€8.05, 45 minutes) all use CS.

Delft

☎ 015 • pop 95,000

Historic Delft is well worth visiting for its 17th-century buildings and distinctive blue-and-white pottery – the famous delftware that 17th-century artisans copied from Chinese porcelain. Delft is home to the country's largest technical university, which helps explain the high proportion of young males.

The train and neighbouring bus station are a 10-minute stroll south of the central Markt. The VVV (☎ 212 61 00) is at Markt 83–85.

Things to See & Do Most visitors come here to buy delftware, and there are three places where you can watch working artists. The most central and modest outfit is **Atelier de Candelaer** (☎ 213 18 48, Kerkstraat 13A-14; admission free; open 9am-5.30pm Mon-Fri, 9am-5pm Sat, 9am-4.30pm Sun; closed Sun in winter). It has five artists, a few of whom work most days.

The other two are really factories and are outside the town centre. **De Delftse Pauw** (☎ 212 49 20, Delftweg 133; admission free; open 8.30am-4.30pm daily summer, 8.30am-4.30pm Mon-Fri, 11am-1pm Sat & Sun winter) is the smaller, employing 30 painters

who work mainly from home (take tram No 1 to Pasgeld, walk up Broekmolenweg to the canal and turn left). It has daily tours but you won't see the painters on weekends. **De Porceleyne Fles** (☎ 251 20 30, Rotterdamseweg 196; admission €2.27; open 9am-5pm Mon-Sat, 9.30am-5pm Sun; closed Sun in winter) is the only original factory operating since the 1650s, and is slick and pricey. Bus Nos 63, 121 and 129 from the train station stop nearby, or it's a 25-minute walk from the town centre.

The 14th-century **Nieuwe Kerk** (☎ 212 30 25; adult/child €2.04/0.68 including entry to Oude Kerk; open 9am-6pm Mon-Sat summer, 11am-4pm Mon-Sat winter), next to the Markt, houses the crypt of the Dutch royal family and the mausoleum of William the Silent. The Gothic **Oude Kerk** (Heilige Geestkerkhof; adult/child €2.04/0.68 including entry to Nieuwe Kerk; open 9am-6pm Mon-Sat summer, 11am-4pm Mon-Sat winter) looks every one of its 800 years, with its tower leaning 2m from the vertical. Among the tombs inside is Vermeer's.

Opposite the Oude Kerk is the **Prinsenhof** (☎ 260 23 58, St Agathaplein 1; adult/child €3.50/3; open 10am-5pm Tues-Sat,

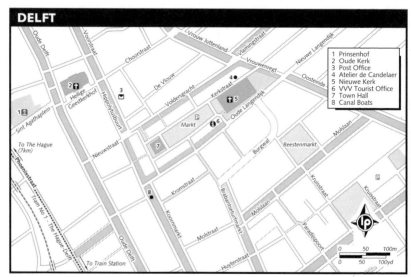

DELFT

1 Prinsenhof
2 Oude Kerk
3 Post Office
4 Atelier de Candelaer
5 Nieuwe Kerk
6 VVV Tourist Office
7 Town Hall
8 Canal Boats

1pm-5pm Sun), a collection of buildings where William the Silent held court until he was assassinated in 1584 – the bullet hole in the wall has been enlarged by visitors' fingers and is now covered by perspex. The buildings host displays of historical and contemporary art.

Getting There & Away Delft is 10 minutes by train to Rotterdam, less to The Hague. A pleasant alternative transport to/from The Hague is tram No 1, which leaves every 15 minutes from in front of Delft train station for the 30-minute trip.

Rotterdam
☎ 010 • pop 600,000

The catastrophic bombardment of the country's second-largest city on 14 May 1940 left it crippled then and somewhat soulless today. Its centre is modern, with mirror-window skyscrapers and some extraordinarily innovative buildings. The city prides itself on this experimental architecture as well as on its port, the largest by tonnage in the world.

It used to be said, rather flippantly, that they make money in Rotterdam, spend it in Amsterdam, and work out how in The Hague. Today Rotterdam has a definite energy that seems in part drawn from the 'anything goes' attitude for reconstruction. The nightlife is good, a large immigrant community adds life and there are some excellent museums. In 2001 it was designated one of the Cultural Capitals of Europe.

The Delta Works in the province of Zeeland south-west of the city, with massive causeways, bridges and mobile dams, were constructed after the disastrous floods of 1953; the works represent Dutch water-engineering at its most grandiose.

There is no real city 'centre'. The sights are scattered over a large area, accessible by determined foot-slogging, metro or tram. They lie within a region bordered by the old town of Delfshaven, the Meuse River (Maas in Dutch) and the Blaak district. The VVV (☎ 0900-403 40 65) is at Coolsingel 67.

Things to See & Do The city's major museum is the completely renovated **Boijmans**

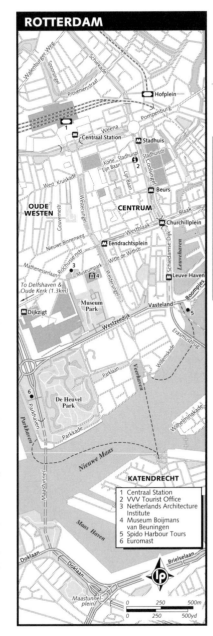

ROTTERDAM

1 Centraal Station
2 VVV Tourist Office
3 Netherlands Architecture Institute
4 Museum Boijmans van Beuningen
5 Spido Harbour Tours
6 Euromast

EXCURSIONS

van Beuningen (☎ 441 94 00, W www.boijm ans.rotterdam.nl, Museumpark 18-20; adult/concession/child under 18yrs €5.67/3.40/free; open 10am-5pm Tues-Sat, 11am-5pm Sun), a rich gallery of art from the 14th century to the present (Dutch, Flemish and Italian masters, Kandinsky, surrealists including Dalí etc). On one of Rotterdam's many grey days, this museum can easily fill a day.

The 185m-high **Euromast** (☎ 436 48 11, Parkhaven 20; tram: No 8; adult/child €7.03/4.54; open 10am-7pm daily) offers stunning views of the city and its harbour.

Architects and architecture fans will feel right at home in Rotterdam. The **Netherlands Architecture Institute** (☎ 440 12 00, Museumpark 25; adult/child €4/2; open 10am-9pm Tues, 10am-5pm Wed-Sat, 11am-5pm Sun), fittingly housed in an architecturally stunning building, stages a series of ambitious special exhibitions throughout the year in its cavernous public spaces. There's a good café and a large library. The Archicentre (☎ 436 99 09) in the same complex offers architecture tours of the city in association with the VVV. Take tram No 5, or the metro, to Eendrachtsplein.

One of the oldest surviving districts is **Delfshaven**, the former port for the city of Delft (now closed off), where the Pilgrim Fathers set off for the New World in the Speedwell. They joined the Mayflower in Southampton but had to return there several times for repairs; eventually they gave the Speedwell up as unsafe and crowded on to the Mayflower. Before leaving Delfshaven they worshipped in the Oude Kerk, Aelbrechtskolk 20 (metro: Delfshaven).

Spido (☎ 275 99 88, Leuvehoofd 1) runs daily 75-minute harbour cruises every 45 minutes (adult/child €7.50/4.55), day trips on Tuesday to the heart of the modern harbour at Europoort (€33 including a warm meal), or day trips on Wednesday through the northern part of the Delta Works (€35.50 including a warm meal), taking in the windmills at Kinderdijk and the historic fortified town of Willemstad.

Getting There & Away There are trains every 15 minutes to/from Amsterdam

(€10.89, one hour), Delft (€2.50, 10 minutes), The Hague (€3.40, 15 minutes) and Utrecht (€7.03, 40 minutes). Half-hourly services run to/from Middelburg, the capital of Zeeland (€15.66, 1½ hours), and Hook of Holland (€3.85, 30 minutes).

Utrecht
☎ 030 • pop 235,000

Utrecht is a historic city, the ecclesiastical centre of the Low Countries from the early Middle Ages. Today it's an antique frame surrounding an increasingly modern interior, lorded over by the tower of the Dom (Cathedral), the country's tallest church tower. The 14th-century canals, oncebustling wharves and cellars now brim with chic shops, restaurants and cafés. The student population (Utrecht is home to the country's largest university) adds spice to a once largely church-oriented community.

The most appealing quarter lies between Oudegracht and Nieuwegracht and the streets around the Dom. Note the canals, which are unique to Utrecht with their former warehouse facades below street level. None of this historic character is evident when arriving at the train station, which lies behind Hoog Catharijne, the Netherlands' largest indoor shopping centre and a modern-day monstrosity. The VVV (☎ 0900-128 87 32, €0.50 a minute) is at Vinkenburgstraat 19, between Neude and Oudegracht, about 10 minutes east of the station.

Things to See & Do There are excellent views from the **Dom Tower** (☎ 233 30 36, Domplein 9; adult/child €4.50/2.70; open 10am-5pm Mon-Fri, noon-5pm Sat & Sun) if you survive the 465 steps to the top.

There are 14 museums, most of them bizarre hideaways for paraphernalia – a sewer museum is one example. However, those around the Museum Quarter, about 1km south of the Domtoren, are reasonably serious. The excellent **Museum Catharijneconvent** (☎ 231 72 96, Nieuwegracht 63; adult/child €5.90/2.95; open 10am-5pm Tues-Fri, 11am-5pm Sat & Sun) winds through a 15th-century convent and has the country's largest collection of medieval

Dutch art. The **Centraal Museum** (☎ 236 23 62, Nicolaaskerkhof 10; adult/child €6.80/ 3.40; open 11am-5pm Tues-Sun) has a wide-ranging collection that always seems to be getting rearranged. There are applied arts dating back to the 17th century as well as paintings by some of the Utrecht School artists.

Of the smaller museums, the **Grocery Museum** (☎ 231 66 28, Hoogt 6; admission free; open 12.30pm-4.30pm Tues-Sat) is worth 10 minutes. The one-room collection sits above a sweet shop filled with the popular Dutch *drop* (salted or sweet liquorice). The **Nationaal Museum Van Speelklok tot Pierement** (National Museum from Musical Clock to Street Organ; ☎ 231 27 89, Buurkerkhof 10; adult/child €5.45/3.40; open 10am-5pm Tues-Sat, noon-5pm Sun) has a colourful collection of musical machines from the 18th century onwards, demonstrated with gusto on hourly tours.

Getting There & Away Utrecht is the national rail hub, and there are frequent trains to/from Amsterdam (€5.33, 30 minutes), Arnhem (€8.05, 40 minutes), Den Bosch (€6.13, 30 minutes), Maastricht (€19.74, two hours), Rotterdam (€7.03, 40 minutes) and The Hague (€8.05, 45 minutes).

EAST OF AMSTERDAM
Muiden
☎ 0294 • pop 6800
This historic town at the mouth of the Vecht River has a large yacht harbour, where you can rent sailing boats to tour the IJsselmeer (see Activities in the Things to See & Do chapter) or join an organised trip to the derelict fort on the island of Pampus which is on Unesco's World Heritage List. The VVV (☎ 26 13 89), Kazernestraat 10, has details.

The main attraction in the town itself is **Muiderslot** (Muiden Castle; ☎ 26 13 25, Herengracht 1; adult/child €5/3.50; open 10am-5pm Mon-Fri, 1pm-5pm Sat & Sun Apr-Oct; 1pm-4pm Sat & Sun Nov-Mar), a 13th-century castle where the popular count of Holland was murdered by jealous colleagues in 1296. In the 17th century the multitalented PC Hooft entertained his male and female friends here; these gatherings of

the century's greatest artists and scientists (including Vondel, Huygens, Grotius, Bredero and probably Descartes) became known as the *Muiderkring* (Muiden Circle). The period rooms dating from this time can be visited only on guided tours and are quite spectacular – it's the most visited castle in the country for good reason. Unfortunately there are no tours in English but it's still worth having a look.

To get to Muiden, take the twice-hourly Connexxion bus No 136 from the terminus at Weesperplein metro stop; it travels past Hotel Arena and Amstelstation.

Naarden
☎ 035 • pop 16,600
The fortifications and moat in the shape of a 12-pointed star around this little town were built in the late 17th century, partly in response to the Spaniards' total massacre of the inhabitants a century earlier. The perfectly preserved walls and bastions were still staffed by the army until the 1920s, and can be visited at the **Vestingmuseum** (Fortress Museum; ☎ 694 54 59, Westwalstraat 6; adult/child €5/3; open 10.30am-5pm Tues-Fri, noon-5pm Sat & Sun Apr-Sept; noon-5pm Sun Oct-Mar). The VVV (☎ 694 28 36) is at Adriaan Dortsmanplein 1B.

The town has become a bit of a tourist attraction and is well worth exploring for its quaint little houses and impressive **Grote Kerk** (☎ 694 98 73, St Annastraat 5; adult/child €2.04/1.14; open 1pm-4pm daily May-Sept, organ concerts 3.30pm-4pm Sat), with stunning vault paintings and famous *St Matthew Passion* performances over Easter. It's worth climbing the tower for a great view of Naarden's layout and the Vecht River (at 2pm and 3pm May to September, also at 4pm June to August) – book with the VVV.

Czechs will be interested to know that the 17th-century educational reformer Jan Amos Komensky (Comenius) is buried here in the Waalse Kapel (Walloon Chapel). His life and work are related next door at the **Comenius Museum** (☎ 694 30 45, Kloosterstraat 33; adult/child €2/1; open 10am-5pm Tues-Sat, noon-5pm Sun), which includes the chapel. Opening times were set to

EXCURSIONS

change at the time of writing – ring ahead to avoid disappointment.

There are two trains an hour from Centraal Station to the station at Naarden-Bussum (€2.95, 15 to 20 minutes), or more trains if you change at Weesp, but bus No 136 (see the earlier Muiden section) also brings you here.

Hoge Veluwe & Arnhem

The Hoge Veluwe (High Veluwe, pronounced VAY-loo-wer), about an hour's drive east of Amsterdam, is the country's largest national park and home to one of its best museums, the prestigious Kröller-Müller museum, with a vast collection of Van Goghs and sculptures.

The town of Arnhem is about 10km south of here, the site of fierce fighting in 1944 between the Germans and Allied airborne troops during the failed Operation Market Garden. Today it's a peaceful town, the closest base to the park if you're travelling by public transport. The Arnhem VVV (☎ 0900-202 40 75) is just east of the train station at Willemsplein 8, but is closed Sunday. Buses to the various sights leave from in front of the station, though huge reconstruction works at the station may change this.

Things to See & Do Arnhem is a pleasant town, worth a quick look. Its pedestrianised centre around the well-hidden Korenmarkt is a five-minute walk from the station – head down Utrechtsestraat, cross over Willemsplein and cut through Korenstraat.

The **Airborne Museum Hartenstein** (☎ 026-333 77 10, Utrechtseweg 232; trolleybus: No 1; adult/child €4/3; open 10am-5pm Mon-Sat, noon-5pm Sun) in the western suburb of Oosterbeek is housed in the villa where the Allies had their temporary headquarters. It has a great audiovisual show (also in English and German) explaining the battle.

The **Dutch Open-Air Museum** (☎ 026-357 61 11, Schelmseweg 89; bus: No 3; adult/child €10.55/7.05; open 10am-5pm daily 1 Apr-1 Nov) has a collection of rural buildings including farmhouses, workshops and windmills, and is more attractive than it sounds, though the 'HollandRama' multimedia hype-fest is a bit over the top.

The **Hoge Veluwe** park (visitors centre ☎ 0900-464 38 35 or ☎ 0318-59 16 27, Houtkampweg, Otterlo; adult/child/car €4.54/2.27/3.86; open 9am-sunset daily), covering nearly 5500 hectares, is a strange mix of forests and woods, shifting sands and heathery moors that provide a sense of isolation found nowhere else on the Dutch mainland. Red deer, wild boar and mouflon (a Mediterranean sheep) roam here. The area is most impressive from mid-August to mid-September when ablaze with heather, or during the red deer's rutting season in September, and is best seen on foot or cycle – 1500 bicycles are available free of charge from the visitors centre inside the park, including 150 at each entrance.

There are three entrances, but if you're using public transport the easiest route is on special bus No 12 that leaves from the station in Arnhem and goes to the visitors centre. It runs several times a day from early April to 31 October. Alternatively, catch bus No 107 from Arnhem bus station to Otterlo. From there, either follow the signs to the entrance 1km away and then walk the remaining 4km to the visitors centre, or wait for the hourly bus No 110 towards Hoenderloo and Apeldoorn, which travels through the park and drops you off at the visitors centre. If you're not visiting Arnhem, the easiest option is to take the train from Amsterdam to Ede-Wageningen, just west of Arnhem, and catch the same bus No 110 from there.

The **Kröller-Müller Museum** (☎ 0318-59 10 41, Houtkampweg 6, Otterlo; adult/child €4.54/2.27; open 10am-5pm Tues-Sun) is a 1km stroll from the Hoge Veluwe visitors centre. Its 278 Van Goghs are only a start: there are works by Picasso and Mondriaan, and out the back is Europe's largest sculpture garden (open till 4.30pm), with works by Dubuffet, Rodin, Moore, Hepworth and Giacometti, among others (allow at least an hour for the garden).

Getting There & Away Trains to/from Amsterdam (€11.80, 65 minutes) and Rotterdam (€14.41, 75 minutes) go via Utrecht (€8.05, 40 minutes).

Language

The Dutch revel in showing how well they speak English and they are arguably the best speakers of English as a second language in the world. All the same, any effort to learn even the basics will be greatly appreciated.

Dutch nouns come in one of three genders: masculine, feminine (both with *de* for 'the') and neuter (with *het*). Where English uses 'a' or 'an', Dutch uses *een*, regardless of gender.

There's also a polite and an informal version of the English 'you'. The polite is *u* (purse your lips and say 'ee'), the informal is *je*. As a general rule, people who are older than you should be addressed as *u*.

Pronunciation
Vowels

a	short, as the 'u' in 'cut'
a, aa	long, as the 'a' in 'father'
au, ou	pronounced somewhere between the 'ow' in 'how' and the 'ow' in 'glow'
e	short, as in 'bet', or as the 'er' in 'fern' (without pronouncing the 'r')
e, ee	long, as the 'ay' in 'day'
ei	as the 'ay' in 'day'
eu	a tricky one, similar to the 'eu' in French *couleur* – try saying 'eh' with rounded lips and the tongue forward, then slide the tongue back and down to make an 'oo' sound
i	short, as in 'it'
i, ie	long, as the 'ee' in 'meet'
ij	as the 'ey' in 'they'
o	short, as in 'pot'
o, oo	long, as the 'o' in 'note'
oe	as the 'oo' in 'zoo'
u	short, similar to the 'u' in 'urn'
u, uu	long, as the 'u' in 'flute'
ui	a very tricky one, similar to the 'eui' in French *fauteuil*, without the slide to the 'i'; pronounced somewhere between au/ou and eu

Consonants

ch, g	a strong guttural 'kh' sound as in Scottish *loch*
j	as the 'y' in 'yes'; sometimes as the 'j' in 'jam' or the 's' in 'pleasure'
r	trilled with the tip of the tongue
s	as in 'so' or as the 'z' in 'zoo'
v	similar to English 'v'
w	similar to English 'w'

Greetings & Civilities

Hello.	*Dag/Hallo.*
Goodbye.	*Dag.*
See you soon.	*Tot ziens.*
Yes.	*Ja.*
No.	*Nee.*
Please.	*Alstublieft/Alsjeblieft.*
Thank you.	*Dank u/je (wel)* or *Bedankt.*
You're welcome.	*Geen dank.*
Excuse me.	*Pardon.*
How are you?	*Hoe gaat het met u/jou?*
I'm fine, thanks.	*Goed, bedankt.*
What's your name?	*Hoe heet u/je?*
My name is ...	*Ik heet ...*
Where are you from?	*Waar komt u/kom je vandaan?*
I'm from ...	*Ik kom uit ...*

Language Difficulties

Do you speak English?	*Spreekt u/Spreek je Engels?*
I don't understand.	*Ik begrijp het niet.*
Please write it down.	*Schrijf het alstublieft/ alsjeblieft op.*

Getting Around

Where is the ... ?	*Waar is ... ?*
bus stop	*de bushalte*
metro station	*het metrostation*
train station	*het (trein)station*
tram stop	*de tramhalte*
What time does the ... leave?	*Hoe laat vertrekt de ...?*
What time does the ... arrive?	*Hoe laat komt de ... aan?*
bus	*bus*
train	*trein*
tram	*tram*

I'd like a one-way/ *Ik wil graag een enkele*
return ticket. *reis/een retour.*
I'd like to hire a *Ik wil graag een auto/*
car/bicycle. *fiets huren.*

Directions

What street/road *Welke straat/weg is*
is this? *dit?*
How do I get to ...? *Hoe kom ik bij ...?*
Can you show me *Kunt u het op de kaart*
on the map? *aanwijzen?*
(Go) straight ahead. *(Ga) rechtdoor.*
(Turn) left. *(Ga naar) links.*
(Turn) right. *(Ga naar) rechts.*
at the traffic lights *bij het stoplicht*
at the next corner *bij de volgende hoek*

Accommodation

camping ground *camping*
guesthouse *pension*
hotel *hotel*
youth hostel *jeugdherberg*

Do you have any *Heeft u kamers vrij?*
rooms available?
How much is it per *Hoeveel is het per*
night/per person? *nacht/per persoon?*
Is breakfast *Is het ontbijt*
included? *inbegrepen?*
May I see the *Mag ik de kamer zien?*
room?

Around Town

Where is (the) ...? *Waar is ...?*
bank *de bank*
city centre *het centrum*
embassy *de ambassade*
exchange office *het wisselkantoor*
post office *het postkantoor*
public toilet *het openbaar toilet*
telephone centre *het telefoonkantoor*
tourist office *de VVV*

What time does it *Hoe laat opent/sluit*
open/close? *het?*

Food

Could I see the *Mag ik de menukaart*
menu, please? *zien alstublieft?*
I'm a vegetarian. *Ik ben vegetariër.*

Signs

Ingang	Entrance
Uitgang	**Exit**
Vol	**Full/No Vacancies**
Informatie/	**Information**
Inlichtingen	
Open	**Open**
Gesloten	**Closed**
Politiebureau	**Police Station**
Verboden	**Prohibited**
Kamers Vrij	**Rooms Available**
WC/Toiletten	**Toilets**
Heren	**Men**
Dames	**Women**

breakfast *ontbijt*
lunch *lunch/middageten*
dinner *diner/avondeten*
restaurant *restaurant*

Shopping

How much is it? *Hoeveel is het?*
Can I look at it? *Kan ik het zien?*
It's too expensive *Het is mij te duur.*
for me.

bookshop *boekwinkel*
chemist/pharmacy *drogist/apotheek*
clothing store *kledingzaak*
laundry *wasserette*
(super)market *(super)markt*
newsagency *krantenwinkel*
stationers *kantoorboekhandel*

Health

I need a doctor. *Ik heb een dokter*
nodig.
Where is the *Waar is het*
hospital? *ziekenhuis?*
I need medication *Ik heb medicijnen*
for ... *nodig voor ...*

I'm ... *Ik ben ...*
asthmatic *astmatisch*
diabetic *suikerziek*
epileptic *epileptisch*

antiseptic *ontsmettingsmiddel*
aspirin *aspirine*
condoms *condooms*

Emergencies

Help!	*Help!*
Call a doctor!	*Haal een doktor!*
Call the police!	*Haal de politie!*
Call an ambulance!	*Haal een ziekenauto!*
Go away!	*Ga!*
I'm lost.	*Ik ben de weg kwijt.*

constipation	*verstopping*
diarrhoea	*diarree*
nausea	*misselijkheid*
sunblock cream	*zonnebrandolie*
tampons	*tampons*

Time & Dates

What time is it?	*Hoe laat is het?*
When?	*Wanneer?*
today	*vandaag*
tonight	*vanavond*
tomorrow	*morgen*
yesterday	*gisteren*

Monday	*maandag*
Tuesday	*dinsdag*
Wednesday	*woensdag*
Thursday	*donderdag*
Friday	*vrijdag*
Saturday	*zaterdag*
Sunday	*zondag*

Numbers

1	*één*
2	*twee*
3	*drie*
4	*vier*
5	*vijf*
6	*zes*
7	*zeven*
8	*acht*
9	*negen*
10	*tien*
20	*twintig*
100	*honderd*
1000	*duizend*
10,000	*tienduizend*

one million	*een miljoen*

1st	*eerste*
2nd	*tweede*
3rd	*derde*

What's in a Name?

Dutch, like German, strings words together, which can baffle a foreigner trying to decipher (let alone remember) street names. *Eerste Goudsbloemdwarsstraat* (First Marigold Transverse Street) is a good example! Chopping a seemingly endless name into its separate components might help a bit. The following terms appear frequently in street names and on signs:

baan – path, way
binnen – inside, inner
bloem – flower
brug – bridge
buiten – outside, outer
buurt – neighbourhood
dijk – dyke
dwars – transverse
eiland – island
gracht – canal (for drainage)
groot – great, large
haven – harbour
hoek – corner
hoofd – head, main
huis – house
kade – quay
kanaal – canal (for transport)
kapel – chapel
kerk – church
klein – minor, small
laan – avenue
markt – market
molen – (wind)mill
nieuw – new
noord – north
oost – east
oud – old
plein – square
poort – city gate
sloot – ditch
sluis – sluice, lock
steeg – alley
straat – street
toren – tower
tuin – garden
veld – field
(burg)wal – (fortified) embankment
weg – road
west – west
wijk – district, city quarter
zuid – south

Glossary

(See also the Language chapter for a list of terms commonly encountered in street names and sights.)

bruin café – brown café; traditional drinking establishment

café – pub, bar; also known as *kroeg*
coffeeshop – place to buy and consume marihuana products (as distinct from a *koffiehuis* or a tearoom)
CS – Centraal Station

dagschotel – dish of the day in restaurant
drop – salted or sweet liquorice

eetcafé – café serving meals

gasthuis – hospital or hospice
gemeente – municipality
genever – Dutch gin
GG&GD – Municipal Medical & Health Service
GVB – Gemeentevervoerbedrijf; the Municipal Transport Company
GWK – Grenswisselkantoren; official money exchange offices

hof – courtyard
hofje – almshouse

koffiehuis – espresso bar (as distinct from a *coffeeshop*)

koffieshop – see *coffeeshop*
koninklijk – royal
krakers – squatters

meer – lake

NAP – Normaal Amsterdams Peil; zero reference (sea level) for measuring elevation
NS – Nederlandse Spoorwegen; national railway company

polder – land reclaimed from the sea or lakes by building dykes and pumping the water out

Randstad – 'rim-city'; the circular urban agglomeration formed by Amsterdam, The Hague, Rotterdam and Utrecht, and smaller towns such as Haarlem, Leiden and Delft, surrounding a green 'heart'
Rijk – the State

spoor – train station platform
strippenkaart – strip ticket used on public transport

veer – ferry
Vlaams – Flemish
VVV – Vereniging voor Vreemdelingenverkeer; tourist office

winkel – shop

zee – sea

238

Thanks

Many thanks to the readers who used the last edition of this book and wrote to us with useful information and suggestions:

Amie Albrecht, Trygve Anderson, Steve Bailey, Michael Ballard, Broz Bart, Wes Beard, Rogier Beekman, Maria & Tony Benfield, Gavin Berkerey, Andre Bookelman, Helen Bradley, Eric Brouwer, Aaron Caramanis, Maurice Carboeux, Tim Christie, Crystal Chua, Paul Conway, Brenda Cooke, Ana Clara Costamagna, Ricardo Cuan, Anna Day-Lewis, Shane Demalmanche, Erwin & Diana van Engelen, Owen Fairclough, Amanda Feeney, Tyler Flood, Peter Franzese, Periklis Georgiadis, Bart Giepmans, Emma Gladwinfield, Phyllis Grant, Beth Gray, John Griffith, Thomas Von Hahn, Andrea Hargitay, Mrs Harper, Linda Hendry, Lisa Herb, Amy & Birger Horst, Damon Johnson, Miles Johnston, Sarah Jowsey, Vaibhav Kamble, Aatol Kim, Jacqueline van Klaveren, Minette Korterink, Nicole Kroon, Art Leon, Michael Lin, Barbara Lopes-Cardozo, Nick Lux, Thomas Madden, Rebecca Manvell, Erna Mastenbroek, Aileen McGunnahan, Brian McNamara, Lucas Meijknecht, Constance Messer, Ming Ming Teh, Rebekah Moore, John Morcombe, Marlies van den Nieuwendijk, Ricardo Olaeta, Aaron Osterby, J Padget, Stephen Park, Christina Philippou, Tim Pollock, Francesco Randisi, Paul Roos, Randi Rosenbluth, Moran Ruzga, Steve Sheldon, GaebeleAngela Shen, Jeff Skinner, Shonah Smith, K Smith-Jones, Nathalie van Spaendonck, Stacey & Brett, Lyn Steele, Jaime Stein, Rudy Suminto, Jenny Tap, Anouchka-Virginie Thouvenot, Brenda Toocaram, R Vos, Theo Wallace, Paul Willems, Rebecca Wood, Maryam Yahyavi

LONELY PLANET

You already know that Lonely Planet produces more than this one guidebook, but you might not be aware of the other products we have on this region. Here is a selection of titles that you may want to check out as well:

Netherlands
ISBN 0 86442 705 0
US$17.99 • UK£11.99

Europe phrasebook
ISBN 1 86450 224 X
US$8.99 • UK£4.99

Europe on a shoestring
ISBN 1 86450 150 2
US$24.99 • UK£14.99

Western Europe
ISBN 1 86450 163 4
US$27.99 • UK£15.99

Amsterdam City Map
ISBN 1 86450 081 6
US$5.95 • UK£3.99

Read This First: Europe
ISBN 1 86450 136 7
US$14.99 • UK£8.99

Amsterdam Condensed
ISBN 1 86450 133 2
US$9.99 • UK£5.99

Amsterdam CitySync
ISBN 1 86450 228 2
US$49.99 • UK£29.99

Available wherever books are sold

Index

Text

Bold indicates maps.

Boxed Text

Places to Stay

Places to Eat

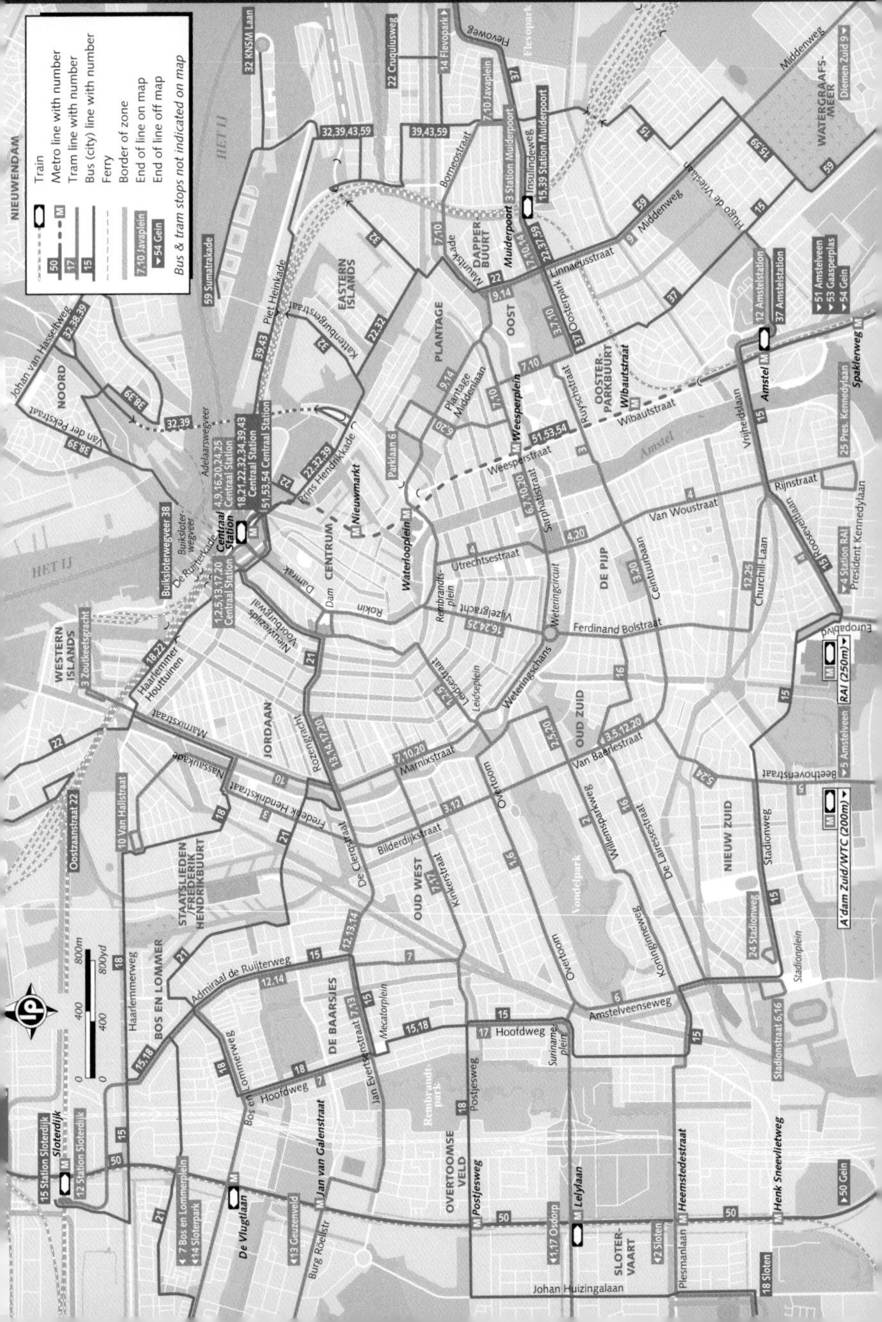
Train
Metro line with number
Tram line with number
Bus (city) line with number
Ferry
Border of zone
End of line on map
End of line off map
Bus & tram stops not indicated on map
NIEUWENDAM
NOORD
HET IJ
WESTERN ISLANDS
EASTERN ISLANDS
CENTRUM
JORDAAN
PLANTAGE
DAPPER BUURT
OOST
OOSTER-PARKBUURT
DE PIJP
OUD ZUID
OUD WEST
STAATSLIEDEN /FREDERIK HENDRIKBUURT
BOS EN LOMMER
DE BAARSJES
OVERTOOMSE VELD
SLOTER-VAART
NIEUW ZUID
WATERGRAAFS-MEER
Centraal Station
Nieuwmarkt
Waterlooplein
Weesperplein
Wibautstraat
Muiderpoort
Amstel
Spaklerweg
RAI (250m)
A'dam Zuid/WTC (200m)
Henk Sneevlietweg
Heemstedestraat
Lelylaan
Postjesweg
Jan van Galenstraat
De Vlugtlaan
Sloterdijk
Vondelpark
Amstel
Flevopark
Rembrandt-park

MAP 1 - GREATER AMSTERDAM

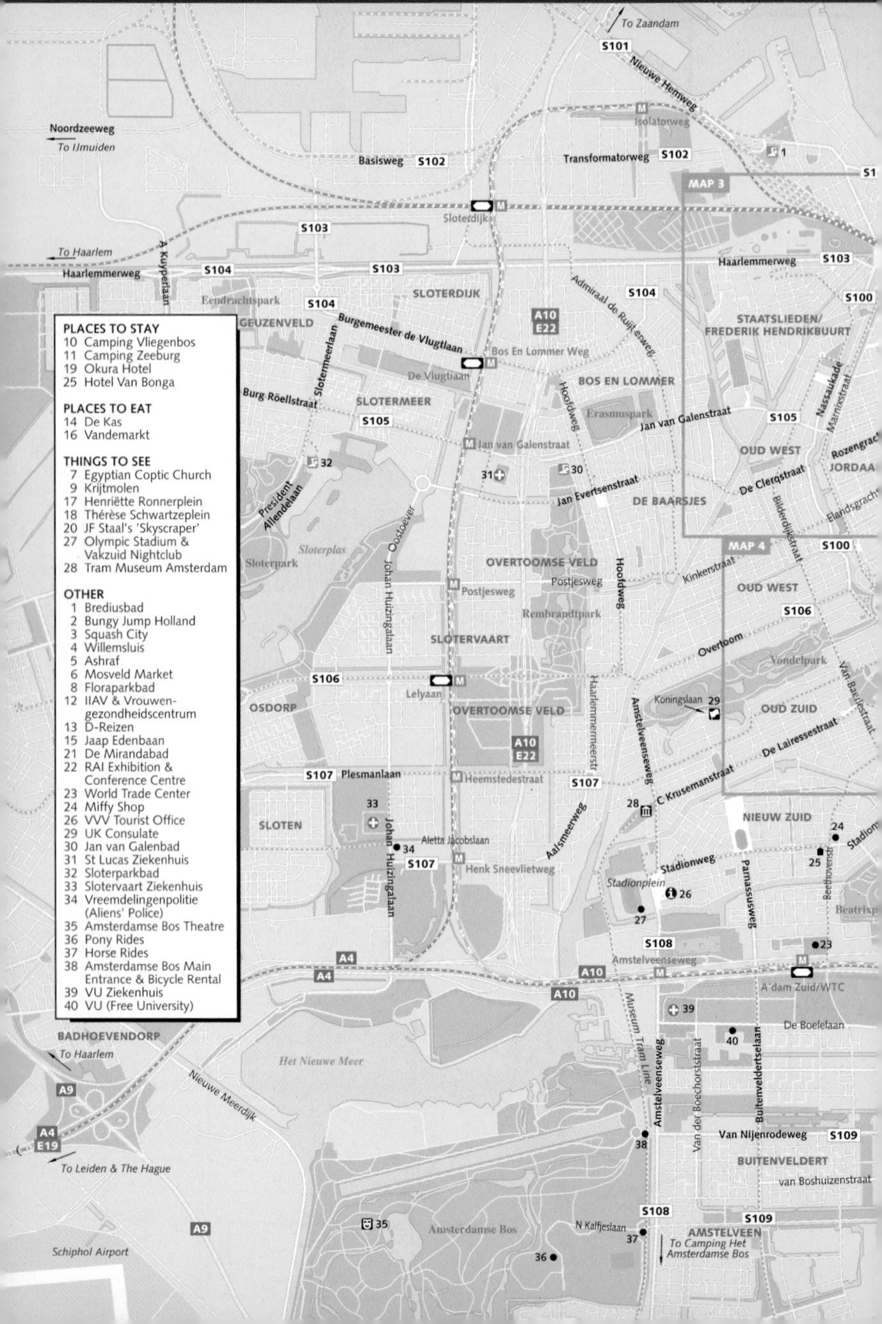

To Zaandam
S101
Nieuwe Hemweg
Noordzeeweg
To IJmuiden
Isolatorweg
Transformatorweg S102
S1
Basisweg S102
MAP 3
S1
To Haarlem
Haarlemmerweg
Sloterdijk
Haarlemmerweg S103
S103
S104
S103
S104
S100
SLOTERDIJK
STAATSLIEDEN/
FREDERIK HENDRIKBUURT
Eendrachtspark
GEUZENVELD
Burgemeester de Vlugtlaan
Admiraal de Ruijtsweg
S104
De Vlugtlaan
Bos En Lommer Weg
A10
E22
S105
BOS EN LOMMER
Burg Röellstraat
SLOTERMEER
Erasmuspark
OUD WEST
JORDAA
Rozengra
S105
Jan van Galenstraat
De Clerqstraat
Elandsgrac
President
Allendelaan
32
Jan van Galenstraat
MAP 4
31
30
Jan Evertsenstraat
Sloterplas
DE BAARSJES
S100
Sloterpark
OVERTOOMSE VELD
Kinkerstraat
OUD WEST
Postjesweg
S106
Postjesweg
Rembrandtpark
Overtoom
Vondelpark
SLOTERVAART
Koningslaan 29
OUD ZUID
S106
Lelylaan
De Lairessestraat
OSDORP
OVERTOOMSE VELD
A10
E22
28
C. Krusemanstraat
NIEUW ZUID
24
S107
Plesmanlaan
S107
Heemstedestraat
33
Stadionweg
25
SLOTEN
34
Aletta Jacobslaan
Stadionplein
S107
Henk Sneevlietweg
27
26
23
S108
A4
39
A4
A dam Zuid/WTC
De Boelelaan
40
BADHOEVEDORP
To Haarlem
A9
Het Nieuwe Meer
VU Ziekenhuis
A4
E19
S109
To Leiden & The Hague
Van Nijenrodeweg
38
BUITENVELDERT
A9
van Boshuizenstraat
S108
S109
35
37
AMSTELVEEN
To Camping Het
Amsterdamse Bos
Schiphol Airport
Amsterdamse Bos
36

PLACES TO STAY
10 Camping Vliegenbos
11 Camping Zeeburg
19 Okura Hotel
25 Hotel Van Bonga

PLACES TO EAT
14 De Kas
16 Vandemarkt

THINGS TO SEE
7 Egyptian Coptic Church
9 Krijtmolen
17 Henriëtte Ronnerplein
18 Thérèse Schwartzplein
20 JF Staal's 'Skyscraper'
27 Olympic Stadium &
   Vakzuid Nightclub
28 Tram Museum Amsterdam

OTHER
1 Brediusbad
2 Bungy Jump Holland
3 Squash City
4 Willemsluis
5 Ashraf
6 Mosveld Market
8 Floraparkbad
12 IIAV & Vrouwen-
   gezondheidscentrum
13 D-Reizen
15 Jaap Edenbaan
21 De Mirandabad
22 RAI Exhibition &
   Conference Centre
23 World Trade Center
24 Miffy Shop
26 VVV Tourist Office
29 UK Consulate
30 Jan van Galenbad
31 St Lucas Ziekenhuis
32 Sloterparkbad
33 Slotervaart Ziekenhuis
34 Vreemdelingenpolitie
   (Aliens' Police)
35 Amsterdamse Bos Theatre
36 Pony Rides
37 Horse Rides
38 Amsterdamse Bos Main
   Entrance & Bicycle Rental
39 VU Ziekenhuis
40 VU (Free University)

MAP 2

MAP 6

VVV Walking Tours
Red route
Blue route
Green route
Grey route
Purple route
Brown route

150m
150yd
75
75
0
0

Het IJ

Bijlmerweg
Buiksloterweg
Melaineweg
Buiksloterwegveer

De Ruijterkade
De Ruijterkade

Centraal Station
Stationsplein
Stationsplein
Centraal Station

Open Havenfront

Oosterdok
Oosterdokskade
Het Waal
Prins Hendrikkade
Prins Hendrikkade
Geldersekade
Oudezijds Kolk
Zeedijk
Vredenburg
Nieuwe Brug
Nieuwe Brugsteeg
Oudezijds Armsteeg
Damrak
Wijngaardstraat
Warmoesstraat

Prins Hendrikkade
Droogbak
Westerdoksdijk
Nieuwe Westerdokstraat
Binnen Wieringerstraat
Binnen Vissersstraat
Brouwersgracht
Singel
Panama
Singel

Haarlemmer Houttuinen
Buiten Brouwersstraat
Binnen Brouwersstraat
Haarlemmerstraat
Heremarkt
Herengracht
Keizersgracht
Prinsengracht
Korte Prinsengracht
Haarlemmerdijk
Vinkenstraat
Korte Prinsengracht

Nieuwezijds Voorburgwal
Martelaarsgracht
Nieuwendijk
Zoutsteeg
Gravenstraat
Smaksteeg
Engelsesteeg
Stromarkt
Kattengat
Korsjespoortsteeg
Teerketelsteeg
Herengracht
Raamsteeg
Roomolenstraat
Lange Niezel
Oudezijds Voorburgwal
Nieuwezijds Kolk
St Jacobsstraat
Kerkemelkst
Kolksteeg
Korte Kolksteeg
Korte Niezel
Sint Olofspoort
Nieuwebrugsteeg
Nieuwe Nieuwstraat
D van Hasseltst
Oude Nieuwstraat
Nieuwmarkt
Handboogstraat
Onze Lieve
Suikerbakkerssteeg
Lijnbaanssteeg
Spuistraat
Nieuwendijk
Zeedijk
Haringpakkerssteeg
Oudezijds Voorburgwal
Blauwburgwal
Lange straat
Herenstraat
Keizersgracht
Brouwersgracht
Prinsengracht
Regulierst

Haringpakkerssteeg

MAP 2

MAP 6

MAP 5

JD Meijerplein

Mr Visserplein

Waterlooplein

MAP 4

Amstel

Binnen Amstel

MAP 3

CENTRUM

NIEUWMARKT

Prins Hendrikkade

Geldersekade

Waalseg

Binnen Bantammerstraat

Nieuwe Jonkerstr

Nieuwe Ridderstr

Binnenkant

Oude Schans

Waalseilandsgracht

Oude Schans

Rechtboomssloot

Montelbaansgr

Kromme Waal

Monnikenstraat

Koningsstraat

Korte Koningsstr

Nieuwmarkt

Keizerstraat

Kleersloot

Dijkstraat

Korte Dijkstr

St Antoniesbreestraat

Snoekjessteeg

Snoekjesgracht

Nieuwmarkt

Nieuwe Hoogstraat

Jodenbreestraat

Koningslaan

Hoogkadijk

Houtkopersburgwal

Houtkopersdwarsstraat

Zwanenburgwal

Zwanenburgwal

Zandstr

Zandstr

Zanddwarsstr

Waterlooplein

Houthaven

Verversstraat

Staalkade

Rusland

Kloveniersburgwal

Rapenburg

's Gravelandse Veer

Raamgracht

Nieuwe Uilenburgerstraat

Jonas Daniël Meijerplein

Muiderstraat

Oudeschans

Korte Niezel

Zeedijk

Geldersekade

Zeedijk

Korte Niezel

Molensteeg

Oudezijds Voorburgwal

Oudekerksplein

Oudekennissteeg

Wijde Kerksteeg

St Annenstraat

Ledeldksteeg

St Janssteeg

Warmoesstraat

Oudezijds Achterburgwal

Bloedstraat

Bethaniënstraat

Koestraat

Bloedstraat

Barndesteeg

Oude Hoogstraat

Spinhuissteeg

Rusland

Slijkstraat

Kloveniersburgwal

Groenburgwal

Stadhuis

Staalstraat

Amstel

Oudezijds Voorburgwal

Oude Doelenstr

Pijlsteeg

St Agnietenstr

St Agnietenstraat

Spinhuissteeg

Rusland

Oudezijds Achterburgwal

Oudezijds Kolk

Oude Turfmarkt

Binnen Gasthuisstr

Binnen Gasthuispad

Grimburgwal

Turfdraagsterpad

Kloveniersburgwal

Nieuwe Doelenstraat

Muntplein

Amstel

Oude Turfmarkt

P. Noorderstr

St Annenstraat

Oudekerksplein

Pieter Jacobsz

Damstraat

Warmoesstraat

Nieuwebrugsteeg

Zoutsteeg

Dam

Dam

Rokin

Rokin

Singel

Kalverstraat

Spui

Nieuwezijds Voorburgwal

Paleisstraat

Gasthuismolensteeg

Raadhuisstraat

Singel

Berenstraat

Singel

Singel

Koningsplein

Heisteeg

Handboogstraat

Voetboogstraat

Kalverstraat

Begijnensteeg

Begijnhof

Nieuwezijds Voorburgwal

Rozenboomsteeg

Spui

Spuistraat

Nieuwe Doelenstraat

Langebrugsteeg

Grimburgwal

Nes

Pieter Jacobsz

Taksteeg

Duifjessteeg

Enge Kapelsteeg

Wijde Kapelsteeg

Wijde Lombardsteeg

Enge Lombardsteeg

St Pieter Poortst

St Pieterspoortsteeg

Nadorst

St Barberenstr

Kuipersstraat

Beursplein

Beurspassage

Nieuwendijk

Kalverstraat

Spuistraat

St Luciënsteeg

Wijde Steeg

Voetboogstraat

Heiligeweg

Sint Jansstraat

Enge Kerksteeg

Leliegracht

Torensteeg

Torensluis

Singel

Leliegracht

Lijnbaanssteeg

Singel

Romeinsarmsteeg

Oude Nieuwstraat

Dirk van Hasseltssteeg

Nieuwezijds Kolk

Gravenstraat

Zeedijk

Mozes en Aäronstr

Eggertstr

Blauw Erf

Mandenmakerssteeg

Martelaarsgracht

Nieuwendijk

Dam

Damrak

Damrak

Oudebrugsteeg

Papenbroekssteeg

Jonge Roelensteeg

Gravenstraat

Molsteeg

Spuistraat

Gasthuismolensteeg

Herengracht

Berenstraat

Huidenstraat

Wijde Heisteeg

Gasthuissteeg

Dirkvanhasselts

MAP 2

PLACES TO STAY
19 Hotel BA
23 Hotel Groenendael
25 Liberty Hotel
33 Hotel Brian
38 Anna Youth Hostel
42 Flying Pig Downtown Hostel
45 Golden Tulip Barbizon Palace
48 Black Tulip Hotel
55 Hotel The Crown
58 Stablemaster Hotel
63 Frisco Inn
64 Hotel Beursstraat
73 Hotel Continental
76 Bob's Youth Hostel
94 Hotel Winston; Winston
   Nightclub
110 Christian Youth Hostel 'The
    Shelter City'
115 Zosa Hotel & Soupkitchen
123 Grand Hotel Krasnapolsky
158 The Grand Westin Demeure
175 Stadsdoelen Youth Hostel
188 Hotel Hoksbergen
216 Waterfront Hotel
218 Hotel Agora
228 Hotel de l'Europe

PLACES TO EAT
5 Lof
6 New Deli
8 De Belhamel
11 Pier 10
24 Village Bagels
39 Keuken van 1870
40 Dorrius
59 Si-Chuan Kitchen
82 Foodism
84 Villa Zeezicht
85 La Strada
87 Werkendam
99 New King
100 Hoi Tin
101 Hemelse Modder
104 Café Bern
108 Blauw Aan De Wal
112 Ristorante Gusto
119 Oriental City
120 Sukasari
126 De Roode Leeuw
137 Supper Club
142 Stereo Sushi
154 Pannenkoekenhuis Upstairs;
    3-D Hologrammen
176 Atrium
183 De Visscher
189 Grekas
192 Caprese
195 Haesje Claes
196 d'Vijff Vlieghen Restaurant
197 Kantjil en de Tijger

206 Caffe Esprit
213 Vlaams Friteshuis
232 Puccini
233 Tom Yam

CAFÉS/PUBS
2 Dulac
20 Magic Minds
21 The Blarney Stone
31 't Arendsnest
35 In de Wildeman
49 Molly Malone's
50 Queens Head
57 Last Waterhole
62 Himalaya
65 Getto
80 Café ter Kuile
88 De Drie Fleschjes
95 Durty Nelly's
97 Lime
111 Lokaal 't Loosje
113 Maximiliaan
122 Proeflokaal Wijnand Fockinck
134 Seymour Likely
135 Diep
136 Bar Bep
138 Absinthe
139 NL Lounge
152 Blincker
153 Café-Restaurant Kapitein
    Zeppo's
184 Pilsener Club (Engelse Reet)
191 Gollem
199 Café Dante
200 Hoppe
201 Luxembourg
212 De Schutter
230 Café De Jaren
234 Café-Restaurant Dantzig

ENTERTAINMENT
3 Barney's
9 Rokerij
34 Akhnaton
36 Cuckoo's Nest
41 The Web
51 Casablanca
69 Argos
70 Cockring
81 Grey Area
86 Homegrown Fantasy
105 Cotton Club
109 Bethaniënklooster
118 Greenhouse
140 Abraxas
151 Frascati Theatre
168 Bimhuis
185 Kadinsky
211 Meander
214 Dansen bij Jansen
217 Odeon
229 Universiteitstheater

THINGS TO SEE
7 Westindisch Huis & John
  Adams Institute
18 Victoria Hotel
26 Ronde Lutherse Kerk
28 Multatuli Museum
29 Greenland Warehouses
44 Seksmuseum Amsterdam (de
   Venustempel)
46 St Nicolaaskerk
47 Schreierstoren ('Wailing
   Tower')
53 Scheepvaarthuis
56 Museum Amstelkring
66 Geels & Co
67 Prostitution Information
   Centre
68 Oude Kerk
72 Beurs van Berlage
92 Effectenbeurs
96 Erotic Museum
98 Guan Yin Shrine
102 Montelbaanstoren
106 Waag & Cafe
116 Hash & Marihuana Museum
124 Nationaal Monument
127 Nieuwe Kerk
128 Royal Palace
129 Magna Plaza
144 Madame Tussaud Scenerama
156 Huis aan de Drie Grachten
    (House on the Three Canals)
157 Universiteitsmuseum De
    Agnietenkapel
160 Oostindisch Huis
164 Trippenhuis
166 Zuiderkerk
169 Gassan Diamond Factory
170 Museum Het Rembrandthuis
172 Pintohuis
173 Pentagon Housing Estate
174 Former Leeuwenberg
    Sewing-Machine Factory
177 Allard Pierson Museum
179 Miracle Column
181 Amsterdams Historisch
    Museum
182 Civic Guard Gallery
193 Presbyterian Church
194 'Clandestine' Church
204 Lutheran Church
205 Maagdenhuis
215 University Library
223 Rasphuis Gateway
235 Stopera; Muziektheater
238 Holland Experience
241 Mozes en Aäronkerk
243 Joods Historisch Museum
244 Portuguese-Israelite
    Synagogue
245 Dockworker Statue

MAP 2

Christophe's chefs dine al fresco before the dinner rush.

NIKKI HALL

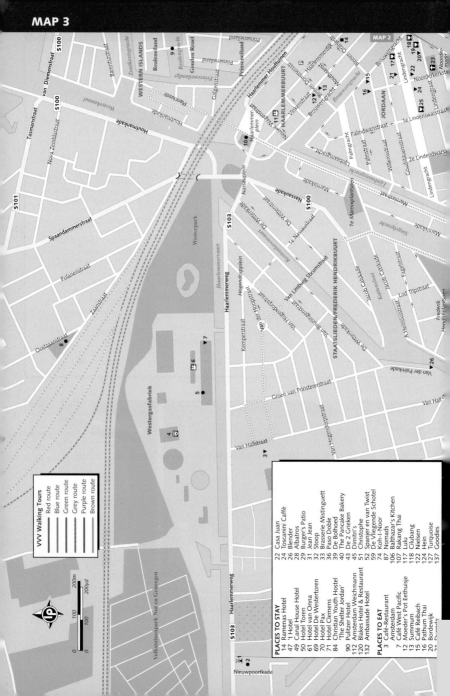

MAP 3

VVV Walking Tours
- —— Red route
- —— Blue route
- —— Green route
- —— Grey route
- —— Purple route
- —— Brown route

PLACES TO STAY
14 Ramenas Hotel
47 't Hotel
49 Canal House Hotel
50 Hotel Toren
61 Hotel van Onna
69 Hotel De Westertoren
71 Hotel Pax
77 Hotel Clemens
84 Christian Youth Hostel
    'The Shelter Jordan'
90 Pulitzer Hotel
112 Amsterdam Weichmann
120 Blakes Hotel & Restaurant
132 Ambassade Hotel

PLACES TO EAT
3 Café-Restaurant
    Amsterdam
7 Café West Pacific
12 Moeder's Pot Eethuisje
13 Summum
15 Café Reibach
16 Pathum Thai
20 Bordewijk

22 Casa Juan
24 Toscanini Caffé
26 Blender
28 Albatros
29 Burger's Patio
31 Jean Jean
32 Stoop
36 Brasserie Mistinguett
38 Puo Doble
39 De Bolhoed
40 The Pancake Bakery
43 De 2 Grieken
45 Dimitri's
51 Christophe
52 Spanjer en van Twist
59 De Vliegende Schotel
74 Koh-I-Noor
87 Nomads
106 Balthazar's Kitchen
107 Rakang Thai
117 Lulu
118 Cilubang
122 Nielsen
124 Hein
127 Turquoise
137 Goodies

MAP 3

Map labels (geographic): MAP 2, MAP 4, S100, S105, JORDAAN, OUD WEST, STAATSLIEDEN/FREDERIK HENDRIKBUURT, Nassaukade, Nassauplein, Van Oldenbarneveldtplein, Van Oldenbarneveldtstraat, Frederik Hendrikstraat, 2e Hugo de Grootstraat, Hugo de Grootgracht, Hugo de Grootkade, De Clercqstraat, Bilderdijkstraat, Bilderdijkgracht, Da Costagracht, Singelgracht, Marnixstraat, Marnixkade, De Marnixplantsoen, Westerkade, Lijnbaansgracht, Passeerdersgracht, Prinsengracht, Keizersgracht, Herengracht, Singel, Leliegracht, Raadhuisstraat, Rozengracht, Lauriergracht, Elandsgracht, Bloemgracht, Egelantiersgracht, Westermarkt, Kostverlorenvaart, Kwakersstraat, Kwakersplein

CAFES/PUBS
- 17 Café Thijssen
- 18 Het Papeneiland
- 19 Finch
- 25 Vandenberg
- 30 De Tuin
- 34 Café 't Monumentje
- 35 Café Nol
- 41 De II Prinsen
- 42 Café De Vergulde Gaper
- 53 Café De Smalle
- 54 De 2 Zwaantjes
- 56 De Prins
- 58 De Reiger
- 97 Van Puffelen
- 99 Saarein II
- 119 De Doffer
- 128 Wolvenstraat 23
- 133 Pompadour

ENTERTAINMENT
- 4 Westergasfabriek Theater
- 5 Club De Ville
- 6 Het Ketelhuis
- 11 The Movies
- 83 Mazzo
- 89 COC Amsterdam
- 100 Korsakoff
- 101 Maloe Melo
- 103 De Trut
- 118 La Tertulia
- 121 Felix Meritis Building

THINGS TO SEE
- 1 Windmill
- 8 Het Schip Housing Estate
- 46 House with the Heads
- 63 Anne Frankhuis
- 64 Greenpeace
- 65 René Descartes' Residence
- 67 White House & Theatermuseum
- 68 Bartolotti House
- 76 Homomonument
- 77 Westerkerk
- 91 Groote Keyser
- 110 Houseboat Museum
- 138 Bijbels Museum
- 139 Krijtberg

SHOPPING
- 38 Mechanisch Speelgoed
- 44 Santa Jet
- 48 Architectura & Natura Bookshop
- 55 Paul Andriesse Gallery
- 57 Exota Kids
- 60 De Belly
- 66 Art Kitchen
- 72 Vrouwen in Druk
- 78 Josine Bokhoven
- 79 Galleria d'Arte Rinascimento
- 80 Simon Levelt
- 81 Kitsch Kitchen
- 82 Christodoulou & Lamé
- 84 Kitsch Kitchen Kids
- 92 Analik
- 93 Exota
- 94 Art Works
- 95 Lady Day
- 96 Montevideo
- 98 The English Bookshop
- 102 Aschenbach & Hofland Galleries
- 105 De Looier Antiques Market
- 108 De Speelmuis
- 109 Kramer & United
- 113 Bakkerij Paul Année Entrees
- 114 De Kaaskamer
- 115 De Witte Tanden Winkel
- 116 Local Service
- 123 Kunsthaar
- 125 Boekie Woekie
- 126 Wijnkoperij Otterman
- 129 Razzmatazz
- 130 Laura Dols
- 131 Lieverlee Literaire Reisboekhandel
- 134 Van Ravenstein
- 136 Frozen Fountain

OTHER
- 2 Internationaal Homo/ Lesbisch Informatiecentrum & Archief
- 9 Drieharingenbrug
- 10 Haarlemmerpoort
- 23 Noorderkerk
- 37 Marnixbad
- 62 Albert Heijn Supermarket
- 73 Bike City
- 75 Pink Point of Presence (PPP)
- 86 Albert Heijn Supermarket
- 88 Wasserette Rozengracht
- 104 Moped Rental Service
- 135 Police Headquarters Centrale Bibliotheek (Main Public Library)

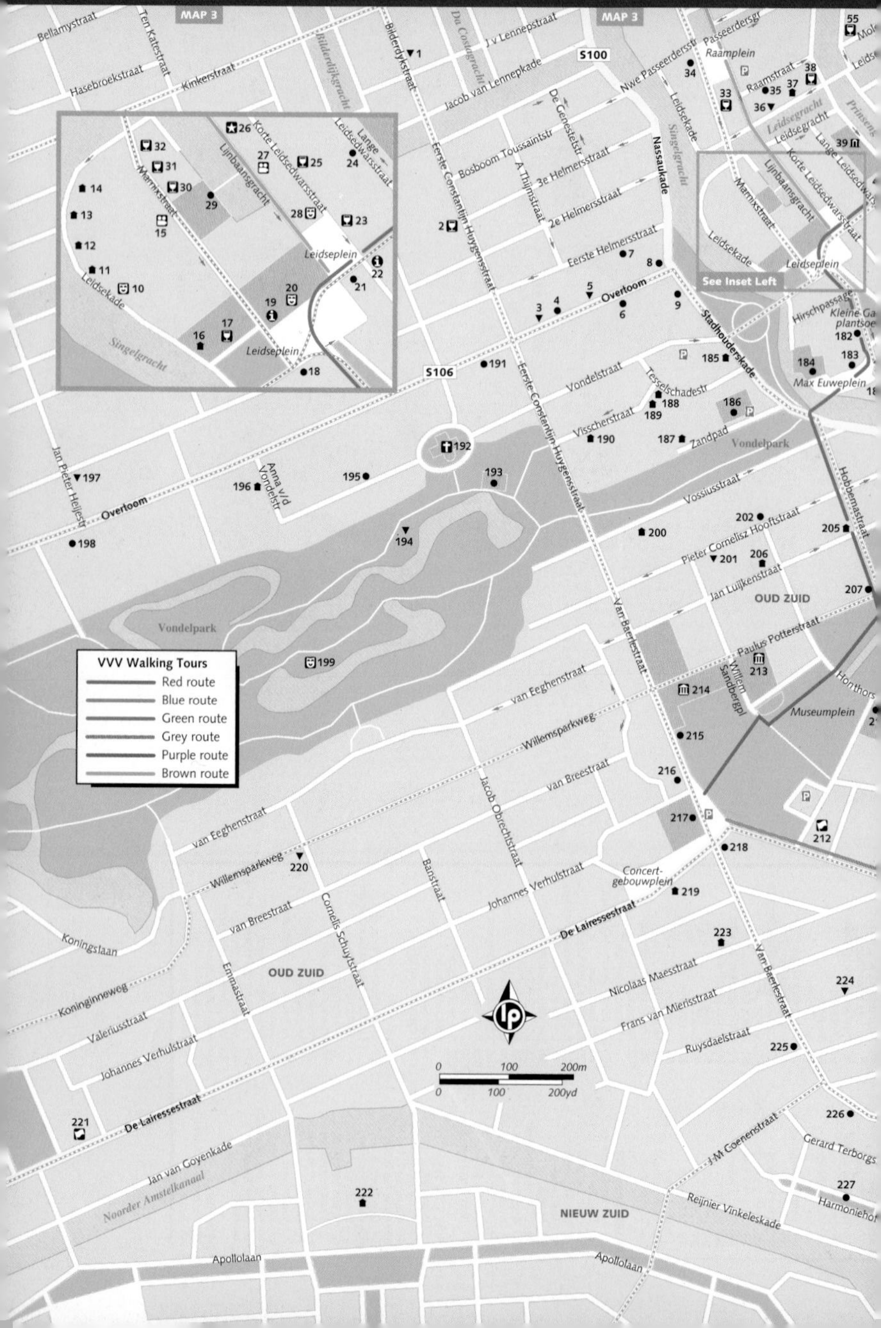

MAP 4

MAP 3

MAP 3

Bellamystraat
Ten Kattestraat
Haasebroekstraat
Kinkerstraat
Bilderdijkstraat
Bilderdijkstraat
Da Costagracht
J v Lennepstraat
Jacob van Lennepkade
Nwe Passeerdersgr
Passeerdersgr
Raamplein
Raamstraat
S100
55
Mole
34
Raamplein
33
35 37 38
36
Leidsegracht
Korte Leidsedwarsstraat
Lange Leidsedw
39

26 Korte Leidsedwarsstraat
Lange Leidsestraat
Leidsekruisstraat
27
25
24
Lijnbaansgracht
Marnixstraat
De Genestetstr
Bodboom Toussaintstr
A Thijmstraat
3e Helmersstraat
2e Helmersstraat
Nassaukade
Leidsegracht
Lijnbaansgracht
Marnixstraat
Leidsekade

32
31
30
29
28
23

14
13
15
12
11
10
Leidsekade
Singelgracht

16 17
18

Leidseplein

19
20
21
22

Leidseplein

See Inset Left

Leidseplein

Eerste Helmersstraat
7
8
Eerste Constantijn Huijgensstraat

2
3 4 5 Overtoom
6
9

191

S106

Vondelstraat
185
Eerste Constantijn Huijgensstraat
Stadhouderskade
Hirschpassage
Kleine Ga
plantsoe
182
184
183
Max Euweplein

192
Terselschadestr
188
189
186
Visscherstraat
190
187 Zandpad
Vondelpark

195
193
Vossiusstraat
Hobbemastraat

197
196
Anna v/d Vondelstr
Overtoom
194

198

Jan Pieter Heijestr

Vondelpark

202 Roemer Visscherstraat
200
201 Pieter Corneliszoon Hooftstraat
206
205

Jan Luijkenstraat
OUD ZUID
207

Paulus Potterstraat
213
Sandberg
Honthors
Museumplein

214

199

VVV Walking Tours
Red route
Blue route
Green route
Grey route
Purple route
Brown route

van Eeghenstraat
Willemsparkweg
van Breestraat
Jacob Obrechtstraat
215
216
217
212
218
219
Concert-
gebouwplein
Van Baerlestraat

Willemsparkweg
220
van Breestraat
Cornelis Schuytstraat
Banstraat
Johannes Verhulststraat
De Lairessestraat
223
224
225

van Eeghenstraat
Koningslaan
OUD ZUID
Emmastraat
Nicolaas Maesstraat
Frans van Mierisstraat
Ruysdaelstraat
Van Baerlestraat

Koninginneweg
Valeriusstraat
Johannes Verhulststraat
226
Gerard Terborgs
227
Harmoniehof
J M Coenenstraat
Reijnier Vinkeleskade

221
De Lairessestraat
Jan van Goyenkade
Noorder Amstelkanaal
222
NIEUW ZUID

Apollolaan
Apollolaan

0 100 200m
0 100 200yd

MAP 4

MAP 4

PLACES TO STAY

11 Hotel Quentin
12 Hotel King
13 Hotel Kooyk
14 Hotel Impala
16 American Hotel
37 International Budget Hotel
45 Hotel Orfeo
49 Seven One Seven
53 Amistad Hotel
66 Hotel Aero
101 Hotel Hans Brinker
127 Hotel De Admiraal
130 Golden Tulip Schiller Hotel
132 City Hotel; Lellebel
138 Hotel Fantasia
140 Seven Bridges
149 Hotel Orlando
152 Hotel de Munck
153 Hemp Hotel
155 Hotel Prinsenhof
164 Hotel Nicolaas Witsen
166 Hotel Kap
171 Euphemia Hotel
185 Marriott Hotel
187 City Hostel Vondelpark
188 Owl Hotel
189 Hestia Hotel
190 Hotel Parkzicht
196 Hotel de Filosoof
200 Flying Pig Palace Hostel
205 Hotel Museumzicht
206 Jan Luyken Hotel
219 Hotel Bema
222 Hilton Amsterdam
223 Hotel Peters

PLACES TO EAT

1 Riaz
3 Toomeloos
5 Dwinger
36 NOA
42 Bojo
44 De Blauwe Hollander
47 Piccolino
56 Pastini
62 Thai Corner
69 Café Walem
70 Café Morlang
74 Gauchos
76 Gary's Muffins
78 Sichuan Food
80 Zet Isie
82 Saturnino
85 Dynasty
86 Le Pêcheur
88 Rose's Cantina
93 Pygma-lion
95 Pasta e Basta
110 Memories of India
120 Szmulewicz

139 Sluizer
142 Moko
144 Tujuh Maret
145 Tempo Doeloe
146 Take Thai
148 Coffee & Jazz
150 Zuidlande
154 De Huyschkaemer
157 Pata Negra
158 Golden Temple
163 Yoichi
165 De Vrolijke Abrikoos
167 Carrousel
176 Deshima Proeflokaal
181 Wagamama
194 Round Blue Teahouse
197 Lalibela
201 Enorm
208 Cobra Café-Restaurant
220 Spring
224 Le Garage
231 Albert Cuyp; Albina
232 Más Tapas
233 De Ondeugd
238 Madam Jeanette
239 De Soepwinkel
241 Eufraat
242 District V

CAFÉS/PUBS

2 De Ruimte
17 Café Americain
23 Reynders
25 Eylders
30 Lux
31 Kamer 401
32 Weber
33 De Koe
38 De Pieper
55 Café Het Molenpad
77 April
79 Downtown
118 Café Rouge
119 Mulligans
123 Vivelavie
124 Mediacafé De Kroon
129 Café Schiller
131 Old Bell
159 Oosterling
229 The Dubliner
234 O'Donnell's

ENTERTAINMENT

10 Theater Bellevue & De
    Smoeshaan Café
15 Bellevue/Calypso Cinema
20 Stadsschouwburg
21 The Bulldog
24 Brasil Music Bar
27 Cinecenter
28 Boom Chicago

29 Melkweg
41 De Uitkijk
43 Jazz Café Alto
46 Bourbon Street Jazz & Blues
    Club
54 De Spijker
65 Global Chillage
81 Havana
83 Other Side
84 Ministry
87 Soho
89 Exit
111 De Duivel
114 Tuschinskitheater
115 Club Showtime
116 Montmartre
117 De Kleine Komedie
121 You II
125 Escape
128 Heeren van Aemstel
135 iT
136 Back Door
179 Paradiso
182 De Balie
193 Filmmuseum
199 Vondelpark Theatre
217 Concertgebouw

THINGS TO SEE

39 Paleis van Justitie
48 Milk Factory
57 PC Hooft Store
68 Metz Department Store &
    Café
75 Bloemenmarkt (Flower
    Market)
90 Kattenkabinet
91 Goethe Institut
96 Keizersgrachtkerk
107 Museum Van Loon
108 ABN-AMRO Bank Building
109 Geelvinck Hinlopen Huis
113 Munttoren
133 Museum Willet-Holthuysen
137 Amstelhof
141 Amstelkerk
160 De Duif
186 Byzantium Complex
192 Vondelkerk
195 Hollandse Manege
204 Rijksmuseum
213 Van Gogh Museum
214 Stedelijk Museum
227 Harmoniehof
236 Heineken Experience
243 Cooperatiehof

SHOPPING

8 Perry Sport
9 Bever Zwerfsport
34 Demmenie

MAP 5

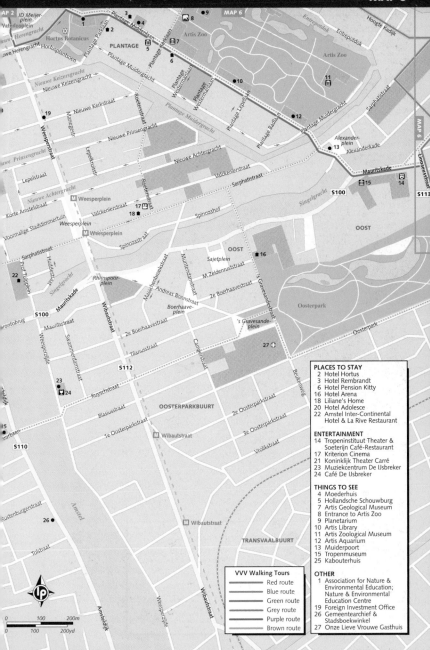

VVV Walking Tours
— Red route
— Blue route
— Green route
— Grey route
— Purple route
— Brown route

MAP 6

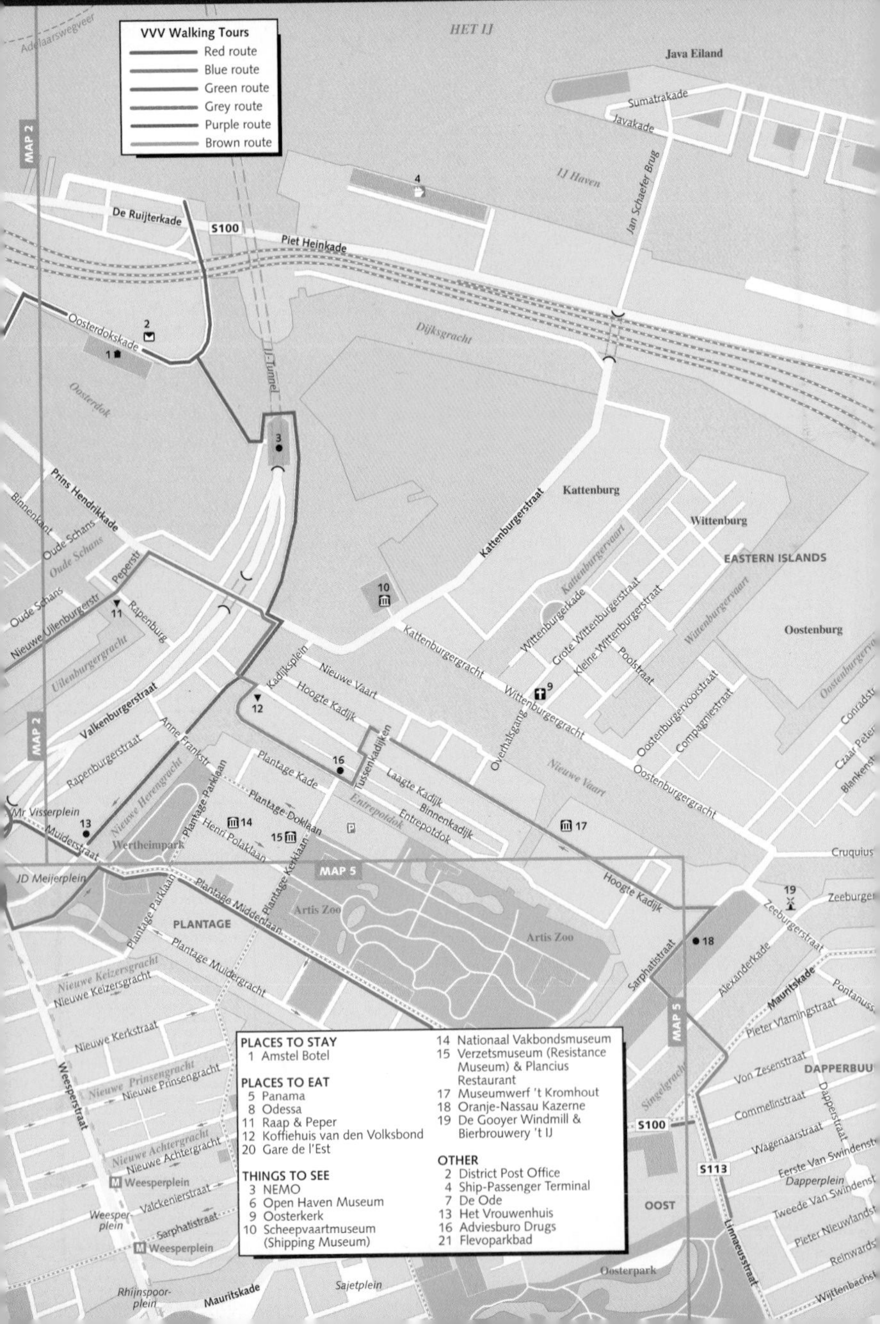

HET IJ

Java Eiland

Sumatrakade

Javakade

IJ Haven

Jan Schaefer Brug

De Ruijterkade

S100

Piet Heinkade

Oosterdokskade

Dijksgracht

IJ-Tunnel

Oosterdok

Prins Hendrikkade

Kattenburg

Wittenburg

Kattenburgerstraat

EASTERN ISLANDS

Binnenkoit

Oude Schans

Peperstraat

Oostenburg

Oude Schans

Rapenburg

Kattenburgergracht

Nieuwe Uilenburgerstr.

Rapenburg

Kattenburgerkade

Grote Wittenburgerstraat

Kleine Wittenburgerstraat

Poolstraat

Oostenburgervoorstraat

Compagniestraat

Uilenburgergracht

Nieuwe Vaart

Kadijksplein

Hoogte Kadijk

Wittenburgergracht

Oostenburgergracht

Conradst

Valkenburgerstraat

Overhaalsgang

Nieuwe Vaart

Czaar Peter

Anne Frankstr.

Rapenburgerstraat

Plantage Kade

Laagte Kadijk

Oostenburgergracht

Blankenstr

Nieuwe Herengracht

Plantage Parklaan

Plantage Doklaan

Lutnerskade

Entrepotdok

Binnenkadijk

Entrepotdok

Cruquius

Mr Visserplein

Henri Polaklaan

Plantage Kerklaan

Muiderstraat

Wertheimpark

Hoogte Kadijk

Zeeburgerst

Zeeburg

JD Meijerplein

Plantage Parklaan

MAP 5

Artis Zoo

Artis Zoo

Sarphatistraat

Alexanderkade

Mauritskade

Plantage Middenlaan

PLANTAGE

Plantage Muidergracht

Pieter Vlamingstraat

Nieuwe Keizersgracht

Von Zesenstraat

DAPPERBUU

Nieuwe Keizersgracht

Singelgracht

Commelinstraat

Nieuwe Kerkstraat

Wagenaarstraat

S100

Dapperst

Nieuwe Prinsengracht

Eerste Van Swindenstraat

Nieuwe Prinsengracht

Dapperplein

S113

Tweede Van Swindenst

Nieuwe Achtergracht

OOST

Nieuwe Achtergracht

Pieter Nieuwlandst

Weesperplein

Weesperstraat

Valckenierstraat

Reinwards

Sarphatistraat

Weesperplein

Wijttenbachs

Rhijnspoor-plein

Mauritskade

Sajetplein

Oosterpark

Oosterpark

MAP 2
MAP 5

VVV Walking Tours
Red route
Blue route
Green route
Grey route
Purple route
Brown route